BOOKS BY JAMES DUGAN

The Great Iron Ship

Man Under the Sea

Undersea Explorer:
  Story of Captain Jacques-Yves Cousteau

Captain Cousteau's Underwater Treasury
  (WITH JACQUES-YVES COUSTEAU)

Ploesti: The Great Ground-Air Battle of 1 August 1943
  (WITH CARROLL STEWART)

American Viking

The Living Sea (WITH JACQUES-YVES COUSTEAU)

World Without Sun (WITH JACQUES-YVES COUSTEAU)

The Great Mutiny

BOOKS BY LAURENCE LAFORE

Modern Europe (WITH PAUL BEIK)

Learner's Permit

The Devil's Chapel

The Long Fuse:
  An Interpretation of the Origins of World War I

Philadelphia: The Unexpected City
  (WITH SARAH LEE LIPPINCOTT)

Stephen's Bridge

The End of Glory:
  An Interpretation of the Origins of World War II

Nine Seven Juliet

DAYS OF EMPEROR AND CLOWN

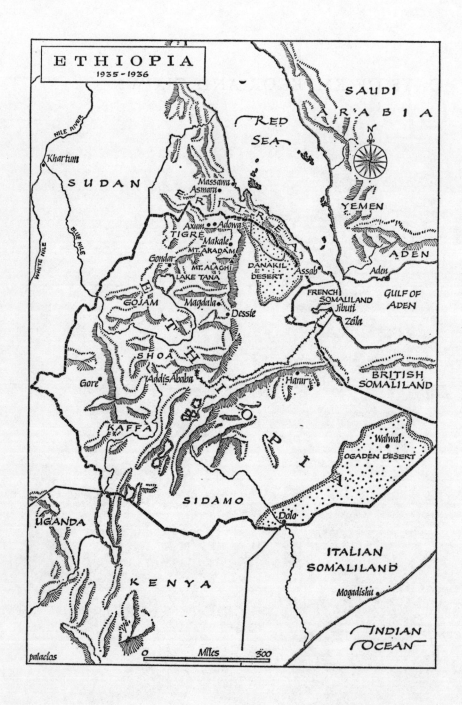

ETHIOPIA
1935-1936

SUDAN

SAUDI ARABIA

RED SEA

Khartum

NILE RIVER

WHITE NILE

BLUE NILE

Massawa

Asmara

ERITREA

YEMEN

Axum Adowa

TIGRE

Makale

MT. ARADAM

Gondar

MT. ALAGHI

LAKE TANA

DANAKIL DESERT

Assab

ADEN

Aden

GOJAM

Magdala

Dessie

FRENCH SOMALILAND

Jibuti

Zeila

GULF OF ADEN

SHOA

Gore

Addis Ababa

Harar

BRITISH SOMALILAND

KAFFA

Walwal

OGADEN DESERT

ETHIOPIA

UGANDA

SIDAMO

Dolo

ITALIAN SOMALILAND

Mogadishu

KENYA

palacios

0   Miles   300

INDIAN OCEAN

Days of Emperor and Clown

THE ITALO-ETHIOPIAN WAR 1935-1936

by James Dugan and Laurence Lafore

1973
DOUBLEDAY & COMPANY, INC.
GARDEN CITY, NEW YORK

The caption on page 233 from the drawing by Helen E. Hokinson first appeared in the September 28, 1935, issue of *The New Yorker* copyright 1935 by F-R Publishing Corporation.

Crossroads of World History Series

ISBN: 0-385-04608-1
LIBRARY OF CONGRESS CATALOG CARD NUMBER 72-95714
COPYRIGHT © 1973 LAURENCE LAFORE AND RUTH DUGAN, EXECUTRIX
    OF THE ESTATE OF JAMES DUGAN

To *Katharine and Frederick Opper*
Beloved friends of James Dugan
and of L.L. and R.L.D.

FOREWORD

This book was begun by James Dugan, who died in May 1967. He had been working on it for several years, and in the course of his preparation had collected an imposing library of works on the Italo-Ethiopian war. He had read extensively about its background, had consulted an immense volume of periodical and archival sources, had interviewed a number of surviving participants, and had visited Ethiopia. Upon his death he left a great body of material—notes, transcripts of interviews, bibliographical data, and a number of passages, mostly scattered and brief but adding up to a considerable manuscript, which he intended, at least tentatively, to incorporate in the book. He did not leave, however, any outline or other scheme of organization. It was possible to tell from his notes and from the passages he had marked in books and periodicals what some of his special interests were and where some of his emphases would have fallen, but it was not possible to reconstruct any general plan of the book as he envisioned it.

I was asked by his widow, Ruth Dugan, and by the publisher, Doubleday & Company, Inc., to complete the unfinished work. My own training and writing as a historian has been mainly in European diplomatic history, and I had long before come to believe that the Italo-Ethiopian war of 1935–36 was not only of great interest in itself but played a most significant role in shaping opinion and events that lay behind World War II. When I began to work on the subject, I saw other important implications. The war was a major and illuminating event in that chain of historical processes, once almost entirely disregarded and now seen as among the most important of the twentieth century, that shaped the relations between European and African peoples and in general between the institutions and attitudes and power of the great industrial societies and those other societies that had long been subjugated by them. Any student of any event is likely to see inordinately significant and decisive implications in his subject. It may be argued that all historical events *are*, in a way, both significant and decisive, determinants in some measure of everything that happened later; still the focus of a specialist is likely to be narrow and the weight he gives to his subject exaggerated. I have tried, in writing this book, to assess justly the special importance its subject seems to me to have for the destiny of the world. Still, as it approached completion, my belief deepened that what happened in Ethiopia in the 1930s was of larger significance than has been generally thought.

I think that Jim Dugan had reached some of the same conclusions, and I think he would have agreed with most of the larger interpretations that I have been led to set forth. But the book is certainly not the book that he would have written. His training and techniques were different from mine in many respects and so, in some, was his view of the world.

He was a professional writer of very great talent and distinction, extraordinarily versatile in varied fields. He was especially well equipped to undertake this book: he had written, with enormous thoroughness and sophistication, on military and naval history in *Ploesti* and *The Great Mutiny*, both based on monumental research and presented with the brilliance of style and insight that marked all his writings. He was a superb reporter. He was widely traveled and incredibly widely read. He had one of the most perceptive and wide-ranging minds of anyone I have ever known. My own training and experience have been quite different; they include considerable travel and residence abroad, experience in the Foreign Service, and intimate acquaintance with journalists and publicists, but my career has been mainly academic. Jim Dugan was inclined to impatience with the fraternity of academic historians; I would agree with some of his criticisms and misgivings, but my way of looking at things has, nonetheless, been shaped chiefly by academic traditions and standards. On the other hand, my own historical writing has been aimed at a wider public and a larger understanding than that of many professional historians, and in writing this book I have tried to adopt the broad view and broad appeal of the professional writer rather than the scholarly and monographic practices of the professional historian.

I have used almost all the passages Jim Dugan had written, embedding them (I hope without conspicuous breaks in style) in my own prose. Still, they represent a small percentage of the whole, and in any event the organization of the material, and its development, have been entirely mine. If there are errors and omissions, which there certainly must be, they are my responsibility.

It is fair to add, I think, a word about my own view of history. It seems to me very decidedly that the study of history is the study of contexts, of causes and effects arising from particular events interweaving themselves in particular ways with particular settings. History does not repeat itself; the interest of any event in the past arises precisely from uniqueness, just as the interest of an individual, similarly formed by the interaction of individuality and setting, arises from uniqueness. Parallels that may seem to exist between past and present are always misleading. The past cannot in any specific way "explain" or "prove" anything about the present or the future. The past is illuminating, but what is illuminated is the enormous intricacy and particularity, and hence the unpredictability, of historical development. Past events may seem to have a superficial similarity to those of the present; their settings never do. But past events make present settings, and the past is always alive in ourselves and our world.

Throughout the preparation of this book Ruth Dugan has been an unfailing companion and collaborator. Her special skills and understanding have been indispensable to its completion and so have her very great generosity and sympathy.

L.L.
Iowa City, 1972

CONTENTS

LIST OF ILLUSTRATIONS

The voice I hear this passing night was heard
In ancient days by emperor and clown . . .

KEATS
Ode to a Nightingale

DAYS OF EMPEROR AND CLOWN

PROLOGUE

Avanti!

The rainy season in the Ethiopian highlands ends in September. On September 29, 1935, Benito Mussolini, the dictator of Italy, sent a telegram to the commander of the Italian forces in the East African colony of Eritrea: "Avanti! I order you to begin the advance."

Three days later a proclamation was issued to the troops:

> The day has come. . . . You will have to endure fatigue and sacrifices and confront a strong and warlike enemy. The greater will be the merit of the victory for which we are striving, the clean victory of the new Fascist Italy.

The church bells of Asmara, Eritrea's highland capital, rang out. Italian soldiers in the streets sang the Fascist anthem, *Youth.* Italian planes set out to bomb the Ethiopian town of Adowa.

The war that now began brought together, on battlefields in unexplored mountains, two continents, two creeds of good and evil, two visions of civilization. Unforeseeably, it was a war that would shape the minds of men and women in far places and would finally determine the policies of great and distant governments, in London, Berlin, Washington, and Tokyo. It would decide the time and the terms of the vast conflict called World War II. It would help to cause the revolution in the thinking of Americans that would lead them years later to Yalta, Tokyo, and Saigon. But it was also a duel between two men, the leaders of two nations, armed in panoply and resolution, two men as remarkable, as magistral, as complex as any men of the twentieth century. They stood for great historical forces, but they were also individuals, and if they had been different individuals perhaps there would have been no war and no enormous aftermath.

Benito Mussolini was unleashing potent forces, of a magnitude he did not imagine. For he presented his cause, to Italy and to the world, in ways that discredited it (along with Fascism, which he had invented) and helped to discredit western civilization as well. The war shook westerners' confidence in their own enlightenment, in their peculiar capacity for progress, in the idea of progress itself. To people everywhere Fascism came to seem a negation of virtue, to appear as a symptom of all that was wrong with civilization. And this was in part anyway the result of Mussolini's personality. He was imaginatively innovative and deeply destructive. What he created, he also killed. He came to seem, in retrospect, like a caricature of the internal contradictions of the Christian, capitalist, national culture that produced him. He was at once a genius and a fool, fascinating and repulsive, eloquent and empty, idealistic and cruel.

His nemesis was a black African prince named Tafari, known to the world as the Emperor Haile Selassie I. He was a dynastic autocrat who, it was believed, ruled quite literally by the grace of God and was directly descended from King Solomon. He was master of a people that was, by every western standard, very backward indeed. He commanded an army that was arrayed in war paint and armed with spears. He was a ferocious national and tribal leader, and in western minds his political past contained mysteries that hinted tribal superstitions and tortures. But after Mussolini began the attack upon his empire, Haile Selassie came to represent not barbarism but principle, not savagery but civilization. He spoke in gentle tones the language of western idealists, of peace, brotherhood, and the rights of the poor and the weak and the oppressed. He was the prophet of hope. For enlightened people in Europe and America, he was everything that Mussolini was not.

In some ways, though, the two leaders were oddly alike. They were both small of stature, and they both acted, and looked, like giants—a fact easily explicable in psychological terms. They were both audacious, resolute, and fierce, but both were deeply devoted to their wives and children and excessively fond of animals. (It was a neat and symbolic irony that in the time of their friendship Mussolini had presented Haile Selassie with two lion cubs.) Both inspired fervid esteem and loyalty, but both inspired passionate enmities as well. They had risen over enormous obstacles to become masters of their nations. They talked in terms of crusades and visions. They were moody, incalculable, obstinate. They were both brilliant orators. But their characters and their destinies were as different as white and black, as the white and black worlds they represented and sought to glorify.

The bells of Asmara tolled for both worlds and for all future generations. But the bombs that fell on Adowa were tokens not of the future but of the past, and they were the product of another odd relationship between the protagonists. For the history of Italian involvement in Ethiopia was old, and the bombs were the token of revenge for an old Italian defeat.

In 1896 the Italians had fought and lost at Adowa. At the height of Europe's grandeur and imperial sway, they had been humiliated in their attempt to build a great empire in East Africa. In 1935 they proposed to erase that humiliation and to resume the old course of imperial conquests. But the times were running in other courses, and the dream of a new, Fascist empire was obsolete before it was born. Ethiopia had survived the first Italian attack, and in the end it would survive the second, but Fascist Italy would not. The age of colonial empires was ending, and the age when Europe ruled the world was over. The Ethiopian triumph in 1896 that had left fourteen thousand of a European army dead or prisoners had been the first success in a long campaign to break the planetary sovereignty of Europeans; the black emperor of a big and empty land lost in the high mountains, encircled by a confusion of deserts, jungles, and undrawn frontiers, sounded reveille for a sleeping world.

In 1935 Italy made the last effort that any European country would make to build a territorial empire overseas. At the time it looked like the fulfillment of the long process whereby Europeans had won their world power, but it was in fact an incident of its epilogue.

When the Italians crossed the frontier on October 3, 1935, they were unknowingly enacting the climax of the old story of Europe's national states. But it was the climax of another, and much older story as well. Mussolini liked to talk of the rebirth of Italian national greatness; but he also liked to talk of the rebirth of the Roman empire. The eagles of his legions were the eagles of Augustus. And he faced an enemy whose polity was older than Rome's. Again there was an ironic resemblance: Ethiopia and Italy were—along with Japan, whose history is oddly similar—at once the youngest and the oldest of the world's states. Both had rebuilt themselves in the nineteenth century from the chaos of division and partition. The rebuilding had, in both cases, been inspired and made possible by memories of an antique greatness. Italy existed because Rome had once been the capital of the European world. Ethiopia existed because, alone of all the countries of Africa, its unbroken continuity from the dim eras of the Old Testament gave a coherence that other African peoples had lacked. The war that began in September 1935 brought face to face two societies unimaginably different, but with something in common: the pride and uncertainty of societies that are aware alike of past power and present peril. Italy was the least and latest of the European great powers. Ethiopia was the only surviving independent state of Africa,* threatened with extinction like the rest.

In 1935 Caesar set out for the realm of the queen of Sheba. It proved a strange journey to a strange kingdom.

* The republic of Liberia, small and much under the control of Americans, was an insignificant and slightly unreal exception.

1

The Sons of Solomon

The battle of Adowa had been fought and won in 1896 by a kinsman, predecessor, and protector of Haile Selassie, the Emperor Menelek II. He was, like many of Ethiopia's recent rulers, a man of extraordinary talents and character, a fit destroyer for the sordid ambitions of royal Italy.

Menelek II had come to the throne in 1889, to rule a chaotic country whose governors and princes were in chronic rebellion and secession, whose citizens suffered with a standard of life as poor as anywhere in the world, whose frontiers were undefined and shifting, which was threatened by the arrogance of European ambition and the might of European arms and wealth. He was possessed of peculiar powers, and like many such men he was peculiar in other ways as well. A British emissary (to whom the emperor sent, as escort, a company of the imperial guard, a band of flautists, and a mule caparisoned in silk and gold, so he might make his entry into the imperial presence in suitable style) found Menelek both amiable and imposing, with a "powerful, dark, small-pox pitted face."[1] He was decidedly a presence—six feet tall, stout, with striking eyes. His head was wrapped in a kerchief under a wide-brimmed hat, and he wore a black silk cloak embroidered in gold. He entertained his many European visitors lavishly, with imported wines and native dishes. Some of them might find Ethiopian customs, and the highly spiced traditional foods, disturbing. But all of them found the emperor intelligent, alert, and in full command of all situations. Many of them felt that they were in the presence of a great man, a molder of destinies.

A man of high intellect although little education, he surrounded himself with ample displays of pomp and acted unfailingly as a true autocrat. And in some ways he undoubtedly saw himself as a western statesman, a competitor of other western statesmen, and acted like one. To a surprising extent he was successful. The first and most portentous of Menelek's achievements was the crucial victory at Adowa. It was the end product of a small coincidence.

It arose initially from the circumstances of his succession. There was—and is—no clear provision in Ethiopia for selecting a successor when a ruler dies. He had to be a member of the imperial family, but winning the contest for the throne seems to have been regarded as a test of fitness; the claimant whose strength and craft brought him to power was more likely to be an able ruler than one elevated by the accident of being first born. Menelek, in his fight to become emperor, had invoked outside aid, notably that of the Italian government, which had colonies and military strength on Ethiopia's borders. After his coronation he had signed a treaty of friendship with the Italians, called the Treaty of Uccialli, by which Italy recognized him as emperor.

Menelek II believed that in the treaty he had defined and thereby arrested the spread of Italian influence. In 1885 the Italians had occupied the old Turkish port of Massawa, Ethiopia's chief outlet to the Red Sea. Four years later their rule was extended from Massawa to the highlands, a region geographically part of Ethiopia and inhabited by peoples who spoke an Ethiopian language. The treaty recognized Italian sovereignty over this region, where the Italians established their capital in the town of Asmara. It was being organized as a colony called Eritrea, a name derived, as Ethiopia was, from ancient Greek geography.

But the situation between Menelek and the Italians was unstable, and there was anxiety and ambition on both sides. The anxiety was heightened by an oddity: the treaty had been written in both Amharic and Italian versions; but Menelek had prudently signed only the version he could read; and it, therefore, was binding. The Amharic version varied from the Italian in one important phrase: it read, in an English approximation, that the Ethiopian government *might* communicate with the European powers through the king of Italy; the Italian version had the sense that the Ethiopian government *must* communicate with other governments through the king of Italy.

The latter reading meant that Ethiopian foreign relations would be conducted by Italy and that Ethiopia became, in its entirety, an Italian protectorate. Such was the interpretation the Italians chose to put on it, and they so informed the powers.

So both sides, wary now, prepared for conflict. The Italians, hungry for territory and prestige and the putative profits of a great empire, envisioned the now-familiar process where foreign states were reduced first to vassalage and then to colonies. The Ethiopians had their own ambitions, beyond the safeguarding of their state and these, it was feared in Rome, included the conquest of Eritrea. A climax approached, and when it was reached it was both stunning and absurd. A great battle, one of the decisive battles of history, was to be fought and to be won and lost as the consequence of a mistake about the name of a mountain. Behind Mussolini and Haile Selassie lay this story, half Homeric tragedy and half low farce.

What happened was characteristic of the worlds and ways of Ethiopia and Italy. It was also characteristic of the grand and terrible comedy of imperialism, the uneven combat between Europe and the rest of the planet. But now at last the combat was not so uneven; the vulnerability of the Europeans would be revealed.

The Italian governor of Eritrea in 1896 was a bold and ambitious general named Oreste Baratieri. His position was difficult; he thought that Ethiopia must be defeated, but in Rome there was no support, or at least divided support, for an energetic military policy. The situation was typical of the process of colonial expansion: a government at home hesitant, divided, and economical, demanding victories without being willing to pay for them, and a man on the scene more convinced than his superiors of the virtues and the necessities of a spirited and expensive policy and desperately demanding the men and money necessary to execute it. His representations at Rome began to have effect after the Ethiopians won some skirmishes. At last supplies and men were sent. The decision to make a colony had been taken, and on January 18, 1896, the Italians demanded the annexation to Eritrea of a large part of northeastern Ethiopia, control over the government in the rest of the empire, and the right of Italian subjects to purchase land at will. Baratieri was ordered to advance. Menelek II moved his army toward the border, into the town of Adowa.

The defense of Ethiopia was to be made on the rocky, jagged mountains just east of Adowa. It was a market town, a place of some local importance on an important road—or track. It looks today, and it must have looked in 1896, a sleepy and squalid village, straggling up a green hillside above a brook and pleasant fields. It is overshadowed by two knolls, each crowned with a church walled by ancient ramparts. The houses are of stone but, to western eyes, mean and dirty. The streets are indeterminate patches of grass and rocks. There is a little market place by the brook, with one-story shops, and a population of a few thousand, very poor. The valley is fertile, and the town, seen from a distance with its green fields and its trees and its churches, is pretty but insignificant, lost in the mountains and plains around it, infinitely unconscious of its destiny. But destiny abides there, for there an African state salvaged its independence and its civilization; and there, perhaps, the decline of the west began.

The Italians' situation was unfavorable from the beginning. They were, even with the new forces that had arrived at Massawa, hugely outnumbered. Their supply lines, over empty miles of incredibly rough country with no roads, were precarious. Their transport was mainly mule teams, and these had been decimated by epizootic disease. They were faced with a determined advancing army. Either immediate and decisive victory must be won or a perilous and humiliating retreat undertaken. Baratieri decided to attack at once.

His decision has been endlessly discussed and passionately criticized in Italy ever since, as has every other aspect of his conduct of affairs. Observers outside of Italy have been inclined to defend him and to lay the blame for the catastrophe that followed not on him but on fate. All battles are decided by the balance of incompetence; but the single incredible blunder that one of his generals made had a meaning that transcended the customary ineptitude of generals.

Still, there are grounds enough for judging the whole Italian venture rash. Baratieri was not aware of either the numbers or the able generalship of the Ethiopians. He did not know that assembled at Adowa with the emperor were Menelek's best general, Prince Makonnen; his most experienced and ferociously patriotic general, Prince Alula; the able Minister of War; and the Empress Taitu, a woman of high intelligence and passionate xenophobia. Nor did Baratieri know

that the Italian forces were surrounded by, and in fact included, men
devoted to the Ethiopian cause. He did not know the Ethiopians
were equipped with French arms. He did not know that he had
been deceived by false intelligence that led him to think that the
Ethiopian army would take the first of March, an Ethiopian religious
feast, as a holiday and would depart on a traditional pilgrimage to the
shrines of nearby Axum. He made plans for his attack accordingly.
Furthermore, the Ethiopians were not only greatly superior in numbers;
they were much better informed and much more skillful at using information. And this was because they were fighting on their own terms
in their own land. Under certain conditions, a balance of incompetence might work against a European army.

Baratieri had four detachments, the fourth to be held in reserve.
He planned a three-pronged advance to high ground, the series of
high and rugged hills that commanded Adowa to the east, mountains
that rise steeply several thousand feet above the plateau. They are
very grand to see and, like everything else in this country, very
strange—bare rocky peaks and crags of grotesque profile; a huge, un-
earthly, formidable bastion around the green vale of Adowa. So formidable are they, so vast and desolate, so utterly wild and trackless, so
unpromising for the invader and so favorable to the defender, that
a traveler today must still wonder at the ineffable audacity of Baratieri and his generals. And it was the wildness of the country that
ruined the Italians. It had never been mapped, of course, by the
Ethiopians, and the Italian maps were both incomplete and inaccurate.
Modern armies are almost as dependent on maps as on firearms, and
a primitive army is at an advantage in unmapped country.

The Italian attack began early in the morning of March 1, 1896.
The advance on the southernmost of three objectives, a height named
Chidane Meret, was commanded by General Albertone. His march
went faster than did those of the two generals to his north, and
Albertone reached the hill he thought was Chidane Meret by day-
break. But once there he found no sign of General Arimonde's force,
which should have been on his right. He was informed by native
runners that his map was wrong, that the real Chidane Meret was
some miles further on. Perhaps his map *was* wrong; perhaps the runners were deliberately deceiving him. Either way, it was the strength

of an elemental culture in uncharted lands that undid him. For he decided to continue his advance and did so into the arms of the waiting Ethiopians.

His force, now widely separated from the rest of the Italian army, was surrounded and defeated, and the other two detachments found themselves outflanked and outfought. A retreat was ordered, but it was too late. Of the Italian force, probably more than half were killed (including all three of the generals commanding the three columns) and most of the rest were taken prisoner.* Perhaps twelve hundred survived; they were taken to Addis Ababa and put to work on the construction of the cathedral of Saint George. They were eventually sent back to Eritrea when the cathedral was finished; it stands today a strange monument to the prisoners, an impeccable imitation of Italian Renaissance architecture.

The Italian government said later that all of them had been mutilated and most of them castrated, but careful examination of the records has indicated that most of the survivors were in good health, and only thirty of the Europeans had been mutilated. The native Eritrean soldiers fared worse; many of them had had a hand and a foot cut off since they were regarded as traitors rather than enemies. Mutilation had been a traditional treatment for Ethiopians' prisoners of war—in contrast to the treatment adopted by the British under Kitchener when, two years later, he reoccupied the Sudan and allowed his prisoners to starve to death. Menelek and his generals, however, had issued stringent orders to abandon the practice of mutilation, and most of the captors had obeyed.

When the news of the battle reached Rome, the government of Prime Minister Francesco Crispi resigned at once.

Adowa may have been the most important battle—next to Sedan where Prussia defeated France in 1870 and was able to make the German empire—in which any European army took part in the nineteenth century. It not merely ensured the survival of Menelek's country; it is not unreasonable, in the 1970s, to see it as the beginning of the end of the rule of Europeans over the world and to see in the

---

* Estimates of both the size of the force and the losses vary hugely, from 14,000 to 25,000 in the case of the former, from 4,500 to 12,000 in the case of the latter. In any event, the disaster was exceedingly costly.

nation that brought about this end and this beginning a chosen
instrument of destiny.

The bar of the Addis Ababa Hilton hotel, built in 1969, is lighted
by a stained-glass window. It is a fine work of art by a contemporary
Ethiopian artist which tells, in neoprimitive panels that would do
credit to Chartres, the story of the queen of Sheba. The black queen
and her attendants visit Jerusalem; they are received by King Solomon.
They return to their homeland. The queen gives birth to a son, who
is the ancestor of the present ruler of Ethiopia.

For the emperors are of the House of David. The fact is written
into the Constitution of 1955: "The imperial dignity shall remain
perpetually attached . . . to the line which descends without interruption from . . . the Queen of Sheba and King Solomon of Jerusalem."
It is very much a living force in Ethiopian life. In a culture where
art counts heavily, where painters abound, it is a favorite theme. The
artist of the Hilton's stained glass worked in traditional forms, but
much of Ethiopian painting today is extremely advanced. Abstract
Expressionists, whose technique certainly owes nothing to tradition,
are quite as attracted by the Sheba story as the painters of liturgical
icons. And much inner logic is thus revealed; for Ethiopia is an Old
Testament land, were the Song of Songs and the Ten Command-
ments are a living lyric and a living law and where the sons of
Solomon are kings and prophets still. This is the key to all that has
happened there for the last two thousand years. Ethiopia is Canaan in
the age of transistors. Its sovereign is the Conquering Lion of Judah.

The genealogy is inscrutable and, from the literal-minded standpoint of western scholars, legendary. But as myths frequently are,
it is important; it not only has a visible immediacy in Ethiopian life,
but it also stands for two undoubted realities. Ethiopia is a land of
Judaic origins—its present language and liturgy palpably reveal them.
And while skeptical strangers may doubt that David is literally among
his ancestors, Haile Selassie is the son of a dynasty that can be traced
back for fifteen hundred years with at least as much confidence as
Elizabeth II's ancestry can be traced to Edward the Confessor in the
eleventh century.

Ethiopia's civilization is the only one from the era of the Roman
empire that survived into modern times with unbroken political con-

tinuity or with substantial resemblance to its classical state. It survived owing to an isolation almost as complete as Japan's. The society that Menelek II, in the late nineteenth century hurriedly organized into the likeness of a European state was, and is, as surprising a relic of the ancient world as would be a Peru or a Mexico whose language, sovereignty, religion, and national consciousness were still in all important respects Incan or Aztec, untouched by alien rule.

The old civilization subsists in the mountains, the home of the dominant peoples of modern, as of ancient, Ethiopia. The modern territory, reaching a thousand miles from the Red Sea in the north to Kenya in the south, and a like distance from its border with the upper Sudan in the west almost to the Indian Ocean in the east, includes (but in no way coincides with) the much smaller heartland. The political frontiers were made in living memory. In ancient times, the bounds of Ethiopian rule were fluctuating and uncertain. Our knowledge of them comes from the accounts of travelers, and the place names they give are often unidentifiable. At times, the rule of the Lions of Judah reached much farther than that of their modern successor; at the other times it was confined to a province or two in the northern and central parts of the modern empire. When Ethiopia re-entered the European world a century ago, its vague limits enclosed an area less than a third of the present state.

The modern empire of Ethiopia is a very complex tapestry of races, languages, religions, and cultures. The official religion is Christian and the official language is Amharic, but probably fewer than half the people practice the one or speak the other. There are millions of Gallas and Somalis—peoples of related ethnic origins, some of them Christian but more often Moslem, and some of them pagan. There are Arabs in the east, and in the west Negroes, both Moslem although ethnically entirely different from one another. And each of the main groups is infinitely subdivided and mixed. No census has ever been taken; an ethnic census, let alone an ethnic history, of the peoples of the Ethiopian empire would be not only intricate but impossible; statistics do not figure largely in Ethiopian ways of doing things. There was no adequate map of Ethiopia until the air age, and even now the business of map making is not complete. But in the highlands the living past, the ancient continuity, the long Amharic tradition, is palpable. The tourist can see it everywhere—in the churches as in the Hilton bar.

Topography explains it. The terrain is as strange as any in the world. The physical facts can be read on a relief map: a vast highland running north and south, more than five hundred miles long and about half as wide, rising up to fourteen thousand feet, surrounded by low-lying deserts, on the Red Sea and Indian Ocean to the north and east and in the valley of the White Nile to the west. But no map can give the slightest indication of the reality. In the north the plateau rises in a few miles from sea level to eight thousand feet. And when the summit is reached, wonder at the change from desert to cool forests and rolling fields is lost in greater wonder at the huge peaks and valleys. The highland represents the most gigantic piece of erosion in the world, cut by innumerable gorges and valleys, many of them on the scale of the Grand Canyon. On spurs and mesas that rise from the canyons, even when their sides are vertical and their surfaces a few acres, there are fields and sometimes villages and churches. The landscape is sometimes lunar and sometimes infernal, but it is never merely earthly.

Topography has imposed, and still imposes, isolation and with it timelessness. There are some roads now, and Ethiopian Airlines efficiently connects the centers of population. But there are still many Ethiopians who live beyond the reach of any communication with the outside world except by foot or donkey, and their village life has changed in no detail from that of a thousand years ago. Until the last century, when the first continuous contacts with Europe began, what is now true of much of the country was true of all of it. The process of "opening up" the Ethiopian highlands has been uneven, as it has been incomplete; it is said that the first wheels that many Ethiopian countrymen ever saw were on airplanes, and while this may not be literally true, it accurately suggests the unsettling juxtaposition of the neolithic and jet ages that the huge scale of the jagged land has bequeathed to Haile Selassie's empire.

There are other peculiarities of Ethiopian territory that have determined its past and baffle those who would shape its future. It is, at least in many places throughout the plateau, fertile and rich in natural pasturage. The society that developed there and subsisted in remarkably static form for several thousand years was pastoral and, until recently, partly nomadic. In the early seventeenth century a Portuguese Jesuit traveler noted that in the province of Gojam, in the highlands, cows meant wealth; they were driven from one pasture to another, their tribal owners practicing no agriculture and having no fixed home.[2]

The tendency to *use* the land, rather than cultivate it beyond the point absolutely necessary for survival, persists, and with a growing population of people and animals, particularly the omniverous goats, a rich country, by reason of its very richness, has been turned into a poor one. And it is poor in other ways important in the twentieth century: apparently Ethiopia is almost devoid of mineral resources. Except for a little potash and a little gold, the sorts of raw materials that have attracted conquerors and supported modern economies are, so far as anyone yet knows, almost wholly absent. So far, nobody has found any oil.

But if today poverty preoccupies the baffled experts in economic development, it is elevation, and the isolation associated with it, that has been the most dramatic force in Ethiopian history. It has set the inhabitants of the highlands off from their neighbors in the rest of Africa and in Arabia. It saved them from successful invasion for thousands of years, until the Italians came with their road builders and their airplanes. Alan Moorehead has observed the ecological fact that became the decisive strategic fact in Ethiopian history: Moslem invaders from the lowland deserts found, when they tried to assault the infidel stronghold in the mountains, that their camels, the militarily indispensable means of transport, staggered and died on the high, cool plateau. There were many expeditions indeed, and many of them were partly successful, but there always remained some part of the plateau that was inviolate. Christianity and with it the Ethiopian state survived, surrounded by the Moslem world.

Ethiopia not only was the one place in Africa and western Asia where the ancient Christian church survived unconquered by the Moslems; it was also the place where Judaism survived. Visitors today are taken to see Jewish villages in the highlands, their physical and human aspects indistinguishable from the surrounding Christian villages except that there is a synagogue instead of a church and the pottery is decorated with the Star of David. These are the *falashas*, who have tranquilly practiced their Jewish faith for several thousand years, unconquered by Moslems, undisturbed by Christians. They are the only

Jews in the world whose ancestors were not touched by the Diaspora. There is no more startling testimony to the powerful conservative effect that the mountain ramparts have provided.

The highlands, sensational in their scenery, are highly salubrious. The ills of the desert and the jungle do not beset the inhabitants of the plateau. These are the people known as Amharas, or, in European usage, Abyssinians, entirely different from the other peoples of Africa and from their fellow citizens who surround them on the deserts and lowlands and the escarpment of the plateau. They are, for a people largely unserved by modern medicine, healthy and long-lived, and handsome, tough, and vigorous. They form a very distinct group, usually readily distinguishable by appearance from the multitudinous types of other Africans: they tend to be very tall and very slender, with wiry bodies and thin but muscular limbs. Their faces are rectangular, with narrow, thin noses and straight mouths, looking often like classical statues or wall drawings from ancient Egypt. Geography has divided them among themselves, as it has separated them from their neighbors: communications are so difficult that frequently provincial divisions have almost, although not quite, destroyed the central government and reduced the empire to a chaos of warring chieftains. But the unifying force of the plateau has been stronger than the divisive forces of the gorges and mountains. The Amharas became, and long remained, the only nation aware of itself as a nation, in the western sense, in black Africa. They are by origin very mixed. Long before the Christian era one of the Hamitic groups, living in the high country west of the Red Sea, was conquered by Semites from Asia across the straits. At the time of conquest or soon after these Semites had been converted to Judaism and brought Jewish religion and culture with them to Africa. The prophets of the Old Testament came, and they stayed.

The mixture of Hamite and Semite produced the language called Geez, and a flourishing civilization and empire whose seat was at Axum, a town in the modern province of Tigre in northern Ethiopia, whose splendor and sophistication rivaled ancient Rome's.

Axum *is* the Rome of Ethiopia, and Geez's linguistic place has striking similarity to that of Latin in modern Europe. The languages of modern Ethiopia include two major ones, Amharic and Tigrine, along with many dialects, all descended from Geez in much the way that French and Italian are descended from Latin. Geez is the language of the Church. Like Rome, Axum had in the first millennium of the Chris-

tian era a wide empire which bequeathed to the twentieth century not
only language but law and a strong cultural tradition. It was converted
to Christianity in the same century, the fourth, that saw Constantine's
conversion, and Constantine himself proclaimed the legal equality of
the citizens of Axum with those of Rome. Like Rome, the empire began to decline and fell on evil days in the second half of the millennium, beset by similar internal troubles and by the same vigorous and
hostile competitor, Islam. The Roman empire, governed then from
Byzantium, maintained a brilliant though gradually fading existence
for a thousand years after the old capital in Italy had fallen to barbarian
hands, but it finally collapsed in division and decay and disappeared
in 1453. Ethiopia, similarly isolated in its mountains, underwent a comparable devolution, but its core survived.

Compared to Rome, little is known of Axum in its days of greatness or of the later empire in its days of decadence and isolation, but
there are artifacts to indicate the milestones. Coins record the conversion as the cross appears on them in Ezana's reign and shows that he
bore, like Haile Selassie, the title of King of Kings. In the remains of
great palaces, on huge stones in the deep, dark cellars, Christian crosses
are carved, stunning evidence of an uninterrupted continuity with
churches built fifteen hundred years afterward. The most famous and
conspicuous monuments of Axum are the steles, startling monoliths.
The largest of them is sixty feet tall and is carved to resemble a tower,
with outlines of doors and windows cut into it. There are many others;
a little distance from the village, there is a field of them, slender,
white, upright stones ten or twenty feet high, rising among the corn
tilled by modern farmers. It is one of the most striking sights in Ethiopia.

Not much is known about the cult the steles represented, but the
remains have exerted a strong fascination for the Ethiopians. They
identify them with the civilization of ancient Sheba. Axum is today
their Holy City. The imperial regalia are kept there, and the emperors
are crowned on an ancient, crude stone seat in the shadow of the tall-
est stele. It is the most tangible of the numerous tokens of a very long-
lived continuity.

The isolation of Ethiopia, singularly complete, was the result of
two historical forces that complemented geography and lasted in all im-

portant ways until the second half of the nineteenth century, with one curious interruption. The two forces were Christian heresy and the might of Islam.

Early Christianity was both flexible and factious. Its doctrines were inchoate; only gradually were the definitions of orthodoxy achieved and accepted. One of the great issues of Christian doctrine was, as it still is, the conflict about the Trinity. It is a difficult doctrine, which conceives a single God in three Persons, one of whom shares the attributes of humanity while remaining divine. Some modern western Christians, like the Unitarians, simply refuse to accept the complexities of the Trinity and insist that Christ was wholly human. Fifteen hundred years ago the same difficulties led to an opposite belief: that Christ was wholly divine. This view was rejected by the Council of Christianity at Chalcedon in 451, but some of the most important Christian provinces persisted in the heresy. They included Egypt and the provinces bordering it, including Ethiopia. The dissenting church came to be called, by westerners, Coptic, a word some scholars say is a European corruption of the word "Egyptic."* The obstacles to contact with the rest of Christendom, never quite total, were enormous.

Islam was to be an even more formidable barrier isolating Ethiopia. Moslem power extended over most of Arabia; it engulfed and destroyed the Jewish and Christian civilization there and crossed the Red Sea into territories near Ethiopia. In the year 642 Egypt fell to the Moslem conquerors, and Ethiopia was divided from the rest of Christendom, confined, without access to the sea, by its highland ramparts.

It was the Portuguese who, in early modern times, first broke through the barrier, by then some nine hundred years old. Portuguese explorers entered Ethiopia and reached the court. They were held there for the rest of their lives, apparently as interesting museum pieces. But they did not resent their enforced stay. A second embassy arrived thirty years later, in 1520. Among its members was Father Francisco Alvarez, the embassy's chaplain and chronicler, and he met and talked to the surviving leader of the earlier mission, by then an old man. He had settled down, married an Ethiopian lady, and taken full part in local life. He supplied Father Alvarez with enormous amounts of information, as he was, in Alvarez' words, "a man who knows all the

* The name is not used, and is indeed disliked, in Ethiopia. The proper name is the Ethiopian Orthodox Church.

languages that can be spoken . . . and who knows all the things for which he was sent."

The second embassy remained six years. Permission to leave was withheld, as it had been from its predecessor, but Moslem attacks made the Ethiopian government anxious for Portuguese aid, and the Europeans (who had been treated most affably through their stay) were eventually released and returned to Portugal to arrange an alliance. And Alvarez gave Europe its first account of Ethiopia in modern times. His detailed and circumstantial report was friendly, even enthusiastic. He had found a civilization which, while exotic, was not inferior. Europe's own state of development had not yet reached the point of sophistication where non-European cultures could be disdained. Alvarez indeed had much respect for the Ethiopian government and the military and diplomatic skill with which it handled the numerous alien and heterodox peoples within its territory. The legal and religious systems seemed, to the Latin priest, impressive.

Before the Reformation, religious divergences among Christians were less serious and deplorable than they were to become later in the century, and Alvarez noted with tolerant respect and scientific interest the variations in doctrine and liturgy of Ethiopian Christianity. On the Ethiopian side, there was an equally genial display of ecumenicalism. When, a year after the embassy had left for Rome and Lisbon, the Ottoman Turks defeated an Ethiopian army, captured the ancient and important port of Massawa, and desecrated and looted churches in the center of the old Axumite civilization, the King of Kings asked for, and in due time received, a Portuguese expeditionary force. Together, Portuguese and Ethiopians fought and eventually beat the massive and enterprising armies of a great Moslem general, Ahmed Gran, and by 1527 the safety of the King of Kings, Claudius, and his realm was assured.

But the Reformation instilled in the Roman Catholic world new rigidity and militancy, and presently Jesuits began to try to convert Ethiopia to Latin orthodoxy. The priesthood and populations resisted. Resentments mounted against the spirited agents of Rome, and failing mutual tolerance turned to enmity. Not all of it can be taken as the impatience, on the Latin side, among representatives of a more sophisticated culture with a more primitive one: one of the things the Jesuits complained about most was the refusal of Ethiopian clergy and laymen to take the threat of witchcraft seriously. In the seventeenth century, the emperor, fearing for the stability of the state, expelled the Jesuits. Thereafter, for two hundred years, isolation recurred, interrupted by the more and more frequent visits of European travelers, armed now not with papal bulls but with notebooks, scientific interests, and an immense appetite for knowledge.

The interlude of the Portuguese and Jesuit presence in Ethiopia is a historical curiosity, but it is an illuminating one. The next two centuries of Ethiopian isolation (starting about the time New York and Boston were being founded) ended with the coming of a British army in 1867. In those two hundred years the rest of the world changed much more than Ethiopia did. Europe was progressing fast, in population, wealth, learning, enterprise, fire power, and, most of all, administrative efficiency. Ethiopia was changing, too, but in an opposite direction, perhaps because the threat of Islam was no longer strong enough to hold the empire together. The eighteenth and early nineteenth centuries saw the power of the princes grow. The emperors and their court at Gondar counted for less and less. Ethiopia became, and long remained, an inland kingdom composed of warring principalities.

The Islamic enemy, in the form of the Ottoman empire, was also beginning to weaken. The entire region the Turks had controlled in northeastern Africa was disintegrating into petty principalities of clashing tribes and religions.

Surprisingly, however, the process of disintegration was reversed in Ethiopia. Its history oddly recapitulated that of the Europe of earlier centuries. The decay of Roman institutions had seen the emergence of local principalities whose feudal leaders bore striking resemblances to the princes and provincial kings of Ethiopia. The long work of building a central government had at length been undertaken by the kings whose suzerainty the European princes acknowledged; the prestige of the kings had allowed them to create an administrative structure through which to govern. Ethiopia produced their counterparts, and by the middle of the nineteenth century the institutions of Ethiopia had reached the stage that western Europe had reached in the fifteenth.

The first stage of revival was in the familiar pattern, one that was to be repeated later in Persia and Turkey: a talented and forceful usurper seized power and restored central control. The usurper in this case was a tribal leader named Kassa, who claimed Solomonic descent.

He conquered the provinces of Amhara and Tigre and in 1853 took the title of King of Kings and the name of Theodore III.*

Theodore was a remarkable man. He understood that the salvation of his empire was primarily a military matter; the restoration of internal unity, the extension of his jurisdiction over the undefined regions on the borders of the Abyssinian heartland, and its defense against assailants from outside all required military power, which he most efficiently provided. He was a great soldier. But he was also a good diplomat and politician. By a combination of war and politics he restored the authority of the monarchy and by the 1860s a working Ethiopian state again existed. But the Emperor Theodore had the defects of his qualities. Omnipotence, as it has sometimes done before and since in usurpers of genius, unseated a reason already sufficiently unstable. His autocracy was increasingly and unbearably cruel in a society not at all unused to cruelty. He depended heavily upon two men, John Bell and Walter Plowden, agents of London and representatives of that remarkable race of English adventurers who periodically fared forth, like T. E. Lawrence, to espouse the cause and culture of distant lands. When, in 1860, Bell and Plowden both died fighting for Theodore during an uprising in the province of Tigre, the emperor massacred fifteen hundred citizens to avenge their loss. Thereafter his conduct became increasingly pathological.

His madness had important effects of a bizarre and illuminating sort, and had the Ethiopian state depended entirely on circumstance and charismatic leadership it would not have survived. He became a religious fanatic and attempted to convert the Galla Moslems by force. If Ethiopia were to exist as anything more than a mountain principality, it would have to be as a multinational and religiously diverse empire, and the efforts toward religious unity were not only ill-advised but might have been disastrous.

What *was* disastrous, for Theodore and temporarily for his country, was an incident that reflected his paranoid improvidence and illustrated the curious quality of British imperial power and the way it was exercised. Plowden's successor as British representative, a man named Cameron, arrived at the new capital at Magdala, which Theodore had built for himself on the eastern edge of the highlands, southeast of

* Ethiopian rulers, like those of China or Japan, and like the popes of Rome, assume new names on ascending the throne.

Gondar. Cameron brought a letter of greeting from Queen Victoria to her fellow ruler. Theodore, very pro-English, was much pleased and in answer wrote a long letter to Victoria proposing the establishment of embassies at London and Magdala. The letter was apparently misfiled by the Foreign Office in London; in any event, it was never answered. Theodore was outraged. Cameron and all the other Englishmen in the country, along with assorted other Europeans, were seized and put in dungeons in chains. The representatives who were sent out to secure the release of the prisoners were likewise imprisoned. After consideration, the British government sent a large military expedition to free them.

The force was commanded by a very distinguished soldier, Sir Robert Napier, who later became a field marshal, a baron, and commander in chief of the Indian army. He conducted his march, under most difficult conditions, with great skill and audacity; twelve thousand men with forty-five elephants—the elephants have entered Ethiopian folklore and become legendary—required more than three months to cover the rugged three hundred miles from the Red Sea coast to Magdala. They met no opposition until, in April 1868, they fought a decisive battle before the capital; two of the British force were killed and seven hundred of Theodore's. The distracted emperor offered Sir Robert an Easter gift of a thousand cows; this generous gesture proving of no avail, Theodore shot himself. The British occupied the capital and sacked the library that Theodore had established and took home some four hundred manuscripts, along with the imperial crown, to enrich the British Museum and the Bodleian. In the House of Commons Disraeli announced with the characteristic bravura that was to transform colonial expansion into a romantic vision that the "standard of St. George had been hoisted on the mountain of Rasselas." It is a characteristic irony that St. George is also a patron saint of Ethiopia, and his standard needed no hoisting; it had always been there.

The expeditionary force then withdrew and left the country to civil war.

The success of Napier's venture owed more to Theodore's madness than to the imaginative deployment of elephants. His megalomania had shaken the local chieftains, and it was their support for Napier that allowed the elephants to complete their peculiar task. The effort to build a strong central government had failed, with the not unusual aftermath of a European conquest. If the British had wished to remain, it is quite possible that they could have established permanent dominion in Ethiopia. But in 1868 they had as yet no motive for doing so. The last phase of colonial expansion had not yet begun, and the British control over the Suez Canal and occupation of Egypt, the installation of British power in the upper Nile, and the establishment of the British in the eastern Mediterranean were still a few years off. The purpose of the expedition had been to show the flag and free the prisoners and punish a mad emperor, not to annex his empire. A new Solomonic heir, John IV, succeeded in establishing himself as Theodore's successor, and the process of regeneration resumed.

The first real threat arising from foreigners' ambition to make an empire came not from a European power but from another African one. Egypt since the days of its ancient greatness had been subject to even more vicissitudes than Ethiopia, but it had preceded it in entering the European world. Ismail Pasha, the viceroy (khedive) of Egypt, was nominally a provincial governor for the sultan at Constantinople. He had asserted virtual independence, and he was seeking to create a great power on the European model. His state's frontiers, like Ethiopia's, were undefined, and his ambitions were exorbitant. At home he bankrupted himself with expensive programs of modernization, which proved the undoing of his efforts to save Egypt's independence from the grasp of the Europeans. On his borders he undertook a large extension of territory or, more precisely, undertook to create conditions that would enable him to draw frontiers on the European model, where none existed, around an area imperially wide. He took over Massawa, the Red Sea outlet of Ethiopia, from his overlord of Turkey and advanced inland to take over the sultanates that lay in uncertain relationship to Ethiopia on its eastern edges. Then he moved on the central realms of Theodore's successor, John IV. But major Egyptian expeditions were disastrously defeated in 1875 and 1876. A frontier was in fact drawn, but to Ethiopia's advantage.

The Egyptian failure had large effects. The self-confidence of John IV was momentarily increased and that of the Ethiopians permanently so. Expansion into the ruins of Ismail's empire began. There was a successful campaign that left Ethiopia in control of the Galla country and the region around Harar, southeast of the heartland and an island of Amharic Christian Abyssinia in Moslem regions. Ethiopia, like Egypt but with more lasting success, was beginning its career of behaving like a European state. The outward drive from the heartland toward the oceans had begun.

Other factors, intricately interlocking, emerged. A nativist reaction developed in the regions that the Egyptians, governed now under British protection, had conquered in the old Nubian lands, what is today Sudan. There, at the confluence of the two Niles, in the town of Khartum, in 1884, the ferocious rebels surrounded an Anglo-Egyptian garrison under the command of the wayward, legendary General Gordon and, after ten months' siege, exterminated it. It was the final blow to the Egyptian treasury and the Egyptian dreams of empire. On the urgent advice of their British advisers, the Egyptians pulled out of the territories they had annexed along the Red Sea and inland toward the Ethiopian highlands. As the Egyptians withdrew, European powers began to replace them on the coast.

An Italian trading company had leased from a local sultan a Red Sea port, the small town of Assab, near the southern end of the sea, where its waters join those of the Gulf of Aden and the Indian Ocean's through a narrow strait. In 1882 the Italian government took over Assab and began to interest itself systematically in the affairs of East Africa. In 1888 the Italians established a protectorate over some dim regions on the Indian Ocean coast south of Ethiopia in what is now Somalia. The French and the British had established control over territories evacuated by the Egyptians, after the revolt of the dervishes, further north on the Somali coast, around the horn of Africa. The Moslem country along the whole coastline that lay to the east and south of Ethiopia, for the most part excessively forbidding deserts called the "Hell Hole of Creation," was falling into the hands of competing European colonial powers.

There was a competitive effort, dilatory at first but gradually more determined, to extend the influence of the Europeans within Ethiopia. Nationals of the countries that had established colonies on the borders and of more remote ones—Russians and even Japanese—began to appear; government agents arrived with promises and demands at the Ethiopian court. For the foreigners there was the hope, largely illusory, of commercial or economic advantage; there was the reality of political and strategic advantage; there was the competition itself, which fed a belief on the part of people like the Russians that they musn't be left out. There was a frontier for Europeans here, perhaps a safety valve. John IV observed of the Italians that they "are coming here for ambition and aggrandizement; because there are too many of them [in Italy] and they are not rich."[3]

Then came Menelek II and Adowa. The Ethiopian triumph had drastic effects everywhere, first felt in the realm of European diplomacy. The nineties were a decade when the tentacles of Europe, projecting into alien lands and tangling in strange places, transmitted impulses to the capitals of the powers that affected and sometimes determined policies and politics. In the mid-eighties, the cornerstone of European politics was the Triple Alliance of Germany, Austria-Hungary, and Italy—Italy had been driven into it in 1882 by the frustration of an earlier unsuccessful venture in empire building, in Tunisia, which lay across the Mediterranean from Sicily and was a center of Italian commerce and of some Italian settlement. The Italians hoped to annex it as a colony, but in 1881 the French had occupied it. Franco-Italian relations became hostile, and a sort of cold war broke out. Since Italy and Germany thus had a common potential enemy, Italy joined the Triple Alliance. It was a pattern that was to be repeated, with more sensational results, a half century later.

While this was going on in Europe, intricate steps were leading into deeper and deeper involvement of all the great powers, except Austria, in African affairs. It is neither possible nor relevant here to examine the causes of the scramble for Africa: whether it was occasioned, as Lenin believed, by the evolution of monopoly capitalism into a final stage of competition; or by the projection of an ebullient nationalism that had reached a peak of success and power in Europe. Or whether it was the result of a series of interacting historical accidents—the spread of missionary zeal; the widening gaps between the Europeans' technical capacity for easy conquests and the non-Europeans' ability to defend themselves; the peculiar form of sublimation in adventure and derring-do for men who, like Kitchener and Gordon, were raised in a culture where virtually all human urges were systematically repressed by a prevailing ethic of institutionalized priggery; and the important medical fact that quinine had made possible the control of malaria and with it the survival of Europeans in tropical Africa. Whatever the deep causes of late nineteenth-century imperialism, it became first a fashion and then a mania, and it is certain that one element in it was strategic and pre-emptive: the safety of one colony required the acquisition of neighboring territories to protect it from menacing European rivals or from forays by bordering natives.

The most critical competition in the 1890s centered around control of the Nile Valley. Since the British occupation of Egypt in 1882 and the establishment of British power at the headwaters of the Nile in Uganda, over fifteen hundred miles south of Alexandria, there had been a recurrent impulse in London to try to link the two positions. The motives were intricate, revolving mainly around the fact that the British feared that the prosperity, in fact the existence, of their Egyptian protégé could be threatened by any hostile power in control of any stretch of the upper Nile, either the Blue Nile in Ethiopia or the White Nile in the barely explored Nubian lands that today form the Sudan Republic. The principal threat came from the French, who had established themselves both to the west and in the Somali country on the east coast, in what is now Jibuti. The French were Britain's principal colonial rivals. They were bold, intelligent, and almost incredibly energetic and determined in their remarkable expansion of territorial control through thousands of miles of Central Africa. And they were much interested in establishing themselves on the Nile and, perhaps, establishing a French empire that would extend all the way across Africa from the Atlantic to the Indian Ocean.

Ethiopia lay precisely athwart the avenue to such a venture in empire building, and it was as a consequence of their interest in the area that the French had been active and affable at the court of Menelek and had armed him for his victory at Adowa. The French were determined in their efforts to win his friendship—to assist him in frustrating Italian ambitions that were almost as unwelcome to the French as to the Ethiopian—by supplying him with ample arms to defend himself.

One of the many by-products of the British occupation of Egypt had been a degree of British diplomatic dependence on Germany. The French, who had important legal rights in Egypt and who had, before 1882, been moving toward establishing some kind of control of their own, were violently hostile to the British. German support was necessary, and this forced Britain into a measure of co-operation with the Triple Alliance. In this devious fashion, Ethiopia had become an important pawn in the German effort to build and maintain an anti-French front in Europe.

The effects of Adowa on this intricate situation were explosive. The Italians, deeply distraught, were persuaded that their allies were proving worthless. Germany and Austria had given them no kind of support or assistance; they saw their own defeat as a French rather than an Ethiopian victory, and the very purpose that the Triple Alliance had been supposed to serve, the Italian cause in their cold war with France, had been lost. The Crispi government in Italy had been warmly pro-Austrian and pro-German. Its overthrow, and the intense disillusionment and shock that gripped Italy, brought to office a government by the Marquess Antonio di Rudini. Rudini was a liberal, an anti-imperialist; he commented on the European belief that colonies were status symbols, with ruthless realism: Italian ventures in Africa, he said, had been undertaken out of a spirit of pure snobbery.[4] Italy's position had become so precarious, the alliance had been proved so nearly valueless, that the endemic hostility to France had to be eliminated. Rudini set about the task. As support for the Triple Alliance waned, Franco-Italian relations improved, and in the end an amicable settlement of colonial rivalries was reached in 1904, by which the Italians agreed to French occupation of Morocco in return for a free hand for Italian conquest of Libya. These were the last two major areas of Africa, outside of Ethiopia, not yet under European control.

The French had been obliged to abandon their ambitions in East Africa by stern British resistance in the Sudan, and thereafter, as the Triple Alliance disintegrated, the shape of the Franco-British-Italian coalition that was to fight and defeat Germany and Austria in World War I took shape. By defeating the Italians in 1896, Ethiopia had become the touchstone of a great realignment of world affairs in the 1900s. Rarely in human history have such vast changes turned on the destiny of a small people struggling to salvage its freedom. The King of Kings, Menelek II, heir of Solomon, had worked greater wonders than he dreamed of when he ordered his troops to advance on General Albertone's column at Chidane Meret, the hill mismarked on an Italian war map.

There were, however, still greater wonders that needed to be worked in Ethiopia before the promise of Adowa could be fulfilled in a workable state and society, able to exist in the modern world. Menelek II, having proved the savior of his country, could now set about becoming its father. The victory at Adowa had given him a chance. Victories no less hard won followed.

Menelek was peculiarly fitted for the job. As might have been expected of a genius of his land and era, he was a strange mixture of what seemed to contemporary Europeans barbarism and civilization. No one after Adowa questioned his genius. No one doubted that the big, black, jovial potentate, while he might look to westerners like a figure from a musical comedy, was a shrewd statesman. Foreign governments respected him, and some even took him seriously. With his displays of pomp, his gorgeously caparisoned mules, and the more than oriental splendor of his court, with his hugely hospitable welcome to Europeans, he was an impressive sovereign whom foreign rulers treated as an equal. He was the only person for whom Victoria of Britain ever deigned to make a recording: she sent him a record of her spoken greeting, along with the instruction to destroy it as soon as he had played it. (He courteously did so, and the only chance that posterity would ever have to hear the queen's voice was lost.)

Africans were, and are, sometimes less admiring of Menelek than were contemporary Europeans. He is denounced now by African ideologues as a ruthless imperialist and even as a racist. He is said to have observed to a Haitian who was trying to secure his sponsorship for an international fund to improve the lot of the Negro, "In coming to me . . . you are knocking at the wrong door . . . You know, I am not a Negro at all; I am a Caucasian."[5] Whether or not the report is true, and it may well be since the Amharas tended to differentiate themselves sharply from other black Africans, he was entirely an Ethiopian; Ethiopia's enemies, whether African or European, were equally enemies, and he contrived with brilliant success to defeat them all by wit, guile, and guns.

His accomplishments were gigantic, but they were of necessity fragmentary, since his aim was to remake his country, in important ways, into the image of a European power. Regarded from the 1970s, his ambition may seem gravely misplaced as well as imperialistic—and illusory. Regarded by contemporaries, it seemed commendable if hopeless. And there were indeed elements of farce and sometimes, westerners thought, childishness, which they judged predictable in an intelligent man trying to civilize the primitive society that had produced him. It may be argued now—Menelek thought so at the time—that

there was an element of psychological projection in this; the westerners saw what they expected to see and wanted to see. It was comforting
for them to dwell in their minds on the barbaric splendors of his court,
on his despotism and his preoccupation with western gadgets, on his
head kerchief and broad-brimmed hat, on his fondness for honoring
guests with endless deafening tattoos of drums and regiments of soldiers
shouting eerie war cries. It was typical of an impetuous tyrant that he
noticed with fascination an Australian eucalyptus growing in the British
legation gardens—the minister was an amateur botanist—and ordered
his subjects throughout the empire to plant eucalyptus trees in large
numbers. But it was not the work of a fool. The eucalyptus flourishes
in the climate of the highlands. It is quick-growing and commercially
valuable and has the peculiar quality of immediately growing up from
its roots when it is cut down. Today the empire is blanketed with
eucalyptus trees; their elegant verdure has become the most characteristic feature of the landscape.

Some of Menelek's other accomplishments as a statesman similarly
seemed like the rather childish amusements of a primitive chieftain
beguiled by western technology. He installed electricity in his palace, developed a palace guard on European lines, established in 1902 a weekly
news magazine (called *Intelligence*) published in four copies, each of
which was hand-written. (There was no printing press in the country.) At the new capital at Addis Ababa, which he had founded in 1889,
he hoped to build a European city that would be, like Peter the
Great's St. Petersburg, a showpiece and focus of westernization. But like
many another new capital, from Petersburg to Brasilia, it remained for
many seasons raw and inconvenient, and to the British mission that
went to negotiate a treaty in 1897 it seemed still nothing more than a
military camp surrounded by hovels, an imagined rather than a real
city, whose principal sight was the den where the imperial lions were
kept. He was fascinated by automobiles (never having seen one) and
in 1907 at fantastic risk and expense one was delivered to him, driven
across the roadless country by an intrepid young Englishman. It proved
entertaining to the emperor, although of little use even in Addis
Ababa, where there were no paved roads.

He professed profound interest in education, but not until the end
of his reign, in 1908, were any public schools established (there were
some missionary schools earlier), and then only a lyceum (where

education was provided in European languages) in Addis Ababa and a primary school in Harar. Like the legendary chieftains of the jungle, he was said to be pleased by the trinkets that European representatives showered on him.

But judgments of childish futility proved to be very superficial. Even his apparent fondness for trinkets owed something to policy: when an English emissary arrived in 1897, bringing with him ceremonial presents including silver candelabra and rifles, the emperor observed, in thanking him, that "Other nations have treated me as a baby and given me musical boxes, magic lanterns, and mechanical toys."[6] If telephones, automobiles, and electricity were toys for him, the telegraph was not. Telegraphy was a very important accessory to modern government. And vaccination, which he also introduced, represented a much-resisted, drastic reform.

His other reforms were often insubstantial, and it may be questioned whether modernization by decree was, or ever is, salutary. Certainly many of its consequences have been dismal. But salutary or not, it was formative. For one thing, Menelek gave his people the habit of empire. Later generations of Ethiopians were to inherit revealing conflicts with their neighbors. In 1962 the prime minister of Somalia was to speak of "Euro-Abyssinian colonialism," for a substantial proportion of the Somalian peoples still lived in the Ethiopian empire. It is due to Menelek's legacy that Ethiopia is a multinational state and that many of its minorities are bitter and rebellious.

He created, moreover, a new elite not less oppressive, and more destructive of the ancient folkways, than the old. As had happened before, the servants of the state who extended its rule and governed its new provinces were rewarded with both power and land; they became a class of combined aristocrats and speculators. A nation-wide land-owning privileged class came into existence side by side with the ancient institutions of land tenure that had in many places been communal and conditional. But while the new society that Menelek was building was, by later standards, old-fashioned, oppressive, and vulgar, it was in a great tradition. It was the way in which powerful governments had been created in the past in agrarian and military societies in Europe and everywhere else; it had worked elsewhere to create a potent polity capable of self-defense, and it worked in Ethiopia too.

Menelek's work was dangerous as well as difficult, especially when it involved dealings with the predatory Europeans.

One urgent need, or so he judged, was capital. Foreign governments and businessmen were solicited. A stream of eminent visitors, with maps or with investments in their baggage, began to arrive. The Europeans sent emissaries they deemed suitable. Incongruously, Prince Henry of Orléans, whose family had lost the French throne in the Revolution of 1848, arrived to represent the French republic; he came with a Sèvres dinner service. The French were interested mainly in negotiating rights to build a railway from Addis Ababa to Jibuti, the French-held post on the Somali coast. A concession was made to a French-organized company to construct a line. Menelek thought that railways symbolized modernity and hoped to stimulate an Ethiopian export trade in coffee and skins. He knew it was a tricky matter, that there were dangers in concessions. He faced a dilemma later familiar in all underdeveloped areas, of weighing the need for economic development against political hazard. Need transcended hazard. The railway was begun. After numerous financial collapses and ultimate bankruptcy, the company was taken over by the French state. Work continued slowly; trains finally ran from coast to capital twenty-five years after it had begun. The Russians, who had been active in Ethiopia since the late eighties (and who had supplied some of the arms that had prevailed at Adowa), sought and secured concessions, mainly for mineral and agricultural exploitation.

Frontiers were no less urgent a need. Political borders were vague and sometimes meaningless in Africa, where the European idea of sovereignty was strange and where huge spaces, empty and unmapped, separated nomads and tribal centers. The idea of a frontier, of a sort of watertight state that could be shown in a separate color on a map, was not very old in Europe itself, and Europe's innumerable frontier problems were an inheritance from the recent past when it had not mattered whether a province was the fief of a French or of a German ruler. But now frontiers were essential in Europe, and if Ethiopia were to survive as a modern state surrounded by European colonies, it too must have them. The legalistic and often meaningless task of defining the borders was undertaken through interminable negotiations with the governments that controlled neighboring territories—Britain, France, Italy,

Egypt. Lines of a sort were drawn, but many of them were unsurveyed and the territories they ran through unexplored.

In 1897 Menelek made a treaty with the British defining the border with British Somaliland. In 1902 another treaty with Britain settled the whole of the western frontier south from the Red Sea and bordering Sudan. The principal British interest was the defense of Egypt, and in the next stage of negotiations, the British secured two promises: that the flow of the Blue Nile, essential to the Egyptian agricultural economy, would never be diverted (a purely hypothetical danger, since no power of man *could* divert it); and the right to build a flood-control dam on Ethiopian territory (subject for years afterward to complicated diplomacy, the dam was never built).

The maps thus arbitrarily, sometimes even imaginatively, drawn gave rise to complications. Years later, in 1934, one of the new frontier lines precipitated the war in which Italy tried to avenge Adowa and make Ethiopia a colony.

A fanatical Somali Moslem leader, known to his enemies as the "Mad Mullah," was disrupting the European Somalian colonies and the adjacent province of Ethiopia after 1900. His campaign, in the name of Islam and the Somalian people, was eventually contained by joint action of British, French, and Ethiopians in the vast desert of Ogaden between Harar and the Italian settlements on the Somali coast. The border between Italian territory and Ethiopian was then defined, in 1908. Menelek was obliged to forgo an ancient claim to Mogadishu, which now became the capital of Italian Somaliland. The desert, uninhabitable except for occasional oases, was divided along an unsurveyed and rather speculative line. This frontier, casually sketched in on maps without any knowledge of the geography involved or exact definition of its whereabouts in relation to known features, seemed unimportant at the time. Nobody wanted or could use the Ogaden. But there events of a later generation gave Italy the notion and pretext for its second assault on Ethiopian independence.

The international standing of Ethiopia remained speculative. Foreign governments might send princely emissaries, they might seek concessions and sign treaties, but the Europeans continued to regard Ethiopia as potential booty. Only their own rivalries prevented an attempt on its independence. Sometimes they tried to settle its fate among themselves. In 1906 the French, British, and Italians had agreed among themselves, without consulting Menelek, to recognize one another's right (in the event of "changed conditions" in Ethiopia) to protect their own interests and national ambitions in each of three geographical spheres that they vaguely sketched out: for the British, in the valley of the Blue Nile and its headwaters at Lake Tana; for the Italians, in a wide band of territory between Eritrea and Italian Somaliland, cutting crescentlike through Ethiopia west of Addis Ababa; for the French, in an avenue along the half-built rail line between Jibuti and the capital. This looked remarkably like a plan for ultimate partition; when Menelek was informed of it, he so regarded it. He protested vigorously and told the three powers that whatever they might decide in such matters would have no effect on the full exercise of Ethiopian sovereignty in the territories concerned.

By then he was near the end of his effective rule. He was in declining health, paralyzed by strokes. Most of the country's problems were unsolved. Poverty, feudal warfare, an inchoate central government, the threat of foreign conquest, all remained little changed. Now that the French, British, and Italians were in good relations with one another, danger seemed to threaten Ethiopian independence, and even greater dangers were threatened by the approaching inevitable struggle for the throne. Ethiopia required a second man of destiny. It got one.

2
The Lion of Judah

The Emperor Haile Selassie I, King of Kings and Conquering Lion of Judah, is a world statesman. His impact has been enormous; his name is know everywhere. Middle-aged Americans recall that the lead soldiers of their youth were shaped and uniformed in the likeness of his army. Everyone who watched the funeral procession of John Kennedy will remember his solemn appearance as the most moving, and in some ways the most reassuring, moment of that tragic time. He presides at intervals over congresses of African states that seek to bring unity to the peoples of the continent. By his policies and position, but especially by his character, he helped powerfully to shape the conditions and new attitudes that have brought a score of black delegates to the United Nations and begun the long work of emancipating black Americans. He is the most powerful black man of modern times.

Like his country and his continent, he has come a long way. When he was born there was nothing in Ethiopia, nothing in the place of Africans in the world, nothing even in the position and policies of his kinsmen and predecessor Menelek II that could have prophesied expectations of fame or influence on such a scale. His path to eminence was a long and dangerous one. The story of his rise is complex and often obscure; it reflects the complexities and obscurities of Ethiopia as Menelek left it.

The very date of Menelek's death is uncertain. It has since been officially stated to have occurred in December 1913, but is usually said to have taken place in 1911. At the time, however, no public announcement was made, and it seems that for some time anyway after he was dead he was being impersonated (an imperial impersonator had long been a recognized official) in an effort to assure the installation of the successor the court desired. Public interest was discouraged; concerned citizens who gathered in front of the imperial palace to learn news of his illness were forcibly dispersed.

This was indicative of the nature of Ethiopia, where prudence has not the same moral borders as in the western world. There was no clear law of inheritance. The modern European notion that the eldest son automatically succeeds, the doctrine that the throne is never empty— "the king is dead, long live the king"—was quite alien. There was, as there had often been before, a long and mysterious struggle for the throne, one that contemporary Ethiopian writers do not discuss. But it is clear that what happened was something like what happened in England in the fifteenth century, during the Wars of the Roses and the usurpation (if it *was* usurpation) of Richard III. The fate of Menelek, and the even more indefinite fate of his appointed heir, Prince Joshua, remain as dark as the fate of the Yorkist princes in the Tower of London. There was the same long and violent struggle among claimants, and it ended, as England's feudal age had ended, with the appearance for the first time of the apparatus of a modern state forged out of chaos by a powerful autocrat. The order and nationalism of the Tudors were not very unlike those of the reign of Haile Selassie I.

In Ethiopia, as was partly true in medieval England, succession was at least partly determined by nomination of one of the members of the reigning family. The nearest and clearest heir to Menelek was his daughter Judith, but in 1908 or 1909 he named as successor the son of another daughter (whose legitimacy was questioned), Prince Yassu, or Joshua, who was proclaimed emperor, as the heirs of medieval French kings had been proclaimed in their fathers' lifetimes. Joshua, however, like Edward V, had powerful enemies: many leaders of the Church (despite his name, his father, Prince Michael, had been born a Moslem); the powerful Dowager Empress Taitu; the Princess Judith; and young Prince Tafari, the son of Menelek's ablest and most enlightened lieutenant, Makonnen, who was also of the Solomonic line.

Joshua is a dim figure in Ethiopian history. His ancestry, his life, and his death are all veiled in uncertainty and mystery. But his personality, in the early years at least, emerges fairly clearly. He was an impulsive, hedonistic, and immoral youth. In religious matters he was flexible to the point certainly of cynicism, perhaps of pathology. His sympathies apparently lay with his Moslem forebears, and he was suspected of having ceased to be a Christian. He abandoned his Christian wife and practiced polygamy. He gave a Turkish representative an Ethiopian flag decorated with a crescent and the inscription "There is no God but Allah." In a society where no stigma is attached to drunkenness, he was renowned for the consistency with which he maintained a state of advanced inebriation. In a society where sexual morality is not particularly strict, he was regarded as libertine to the point of debauchery. He was extravagant with other people's money: he gave his father, as a present, the entire imperial treasury. His assiduity in attending to affairs of state was not notable: he often spent the entire day in bed with, as the British chargé d'affaires delicately put it, "his too numerous concubines," while chieftains and statesmen waited.

He was, in short, a youth clearly unfit to rule, especially to rule an empire dominated by a Christian church and people. But he was supported by his determined father, who was a powerful man, and by some of the Moslem peoples. And he was not without a tactical sense that led him to try to exploit these assets. He failed; the real power remained in the hands of the Dowager Empress Taitu and her supporters. But there was a period of peril and civil strife, enormously complicated by World War I which began only eight months after the official death of Menelek. It determined the course and outcome of the fight for the throne of the King of Kings. It also assured Ethiopia's survival by dividing the predators who had designed to destroy it.

The story of the war as a force in Ethiopian history is almost unbelievably intricate, and is still very obscure, but in effect it boiled down to something like this: the Moslems and Joshua put their money on the Germans and their allies, the Moslem Turks; the Christians, the dowager empress, and her daughter Judith, and their supporter Prince Tafari, put their money on the British, French, and Italians. When the Germans and the Turks lost, Joshua had been deposed, and Judith reigned as empress with Tafari as her regent.

The defeat of the Germans and Turks had vast effects on all of Islam. The crescent and the star were very much in the decline; most of the Islamic world was under the rule of France and Britain, who ended World War I in occupation of most of the Turkish empire. For a generation Islam was to be a colony and pawn of Europeans. Within Ethiopia the rule of the Christian Amharas was now unchallenged, and the regent Tafari shortly emerged as the most important man in a state in which his religion was supreme.

Prince Tafari, who was to reign as Haile Selassie I, was born at the beginning of the last decade of the nineteenth century, officially in 1892. There is some vagueness, matched by the disagreement about some other details of his family background (some say he was one of ten, others of twenty-two, children; and there is equal confusion about his own first marriage and its issue). The vagueness, like that attending Menelek's death, is important; it tells something about the background of a man who was to become one of the great figures of the twentieth century. The intense reticence practiced by the imperial family reflects the opacity of a society where vital statistics were unknown and, by the Church, disapproved of.

His mother was of Solomonic descent, kin to Menelek. His father, Makonnen, was governor of Harar and there had set up a court and helped to make it a cosmopolitan town where visiting Europeans were received in state and went home to report a degree of urbanity and enlightment unknown elsewhere in Ethiopia. There Tafari was born and raised in the beautiful, fertile farmland beyond the walls of the ancient city, and he was educated in the belief that he might one day be called to Menelek's throne.

Prince Makonnen, a man of charm as well as power, had traveled in Europe, beginning with a diplomatic mission in 1889, and his government in Harar, in a time when the provinces were still largely self-governing if their princes were strong and had the confidence of the emperor, was a laboratory of modernization. Makonnen judiciously combined European notions with Ethiopian traditions, and in the defense of a modern judicial system he invoked the oldest and strongest of those traditions: "The great Solomon was a just king. Justice is the most important rule of life. God will judge us as we have judged."[1] It was a pattern that, for his son, became a vision and a cause. In accordance with this pattern, Tafari was educated in a way typical both of Ethiopia's rather casual ecumenicalism and of Makonnen's western sympathies, by a Frenchman, Father Samuel. He was trained in boyhood as a hunter and soldier, but also as a ruler. He had a very keen sense of his destiny, it is said, even in childhood. He did not stand near the throne genealogically, but he was qualified by his Solomonic descent as a candidate for it, and his father's power and fame gave grounds for his boyhood belief in an imperial future. Leonard Mosley says that he began to prepare himself seriously for emperorship when he was seven years old, voraciously reading in Ethiopian history and learning the legends, heroic and hagiographical, that far more than fact gave it meaning and life. Father Samuel was a good tutor for a future statesman; he encouraged the sense of destiny and disciplined his pupil's able mind and bearing. At eleven Tafari was a handsome figure, princely, proud, and confident.

He was a good linguist. Under the French priest's guidance he became bilingual in French—which he habitually spoke in later life. And it seems to have been this accomplishment, brought by his father to the attention of Menelek, which characteristically appealed to the old emperor. When Tafari was still in his teens he was taken to the court at Addis Ababa and became a protégé of the King of Kings. He was approaching destiny fast.[2]

Tafari remained, and he remains today, an elusive personality. His record, indeed, suggests several incompatible personalities; it includes evidence of vaulting ambition; devotion to the ancient legends; relentless and sometimes savage treatment of his enemies; an almost excessive skill at intrigue and manipulation; the countenancing of brutality; dedication to pomps and displays of barbaric ostentation; peculiarities like his fascination with lions, the symbol of his state, his throne, and his person. All of these seem to westerners the qualities of a primitive chieftain. In an opposite way, his dedication to the forms of western culture —to technology, bureaucracy, public and rather regimented education along lines artificially, even abjectly, imitative of Europe; preoccupation with airlines and power plants—these seem to some advanced people in the west as symptoms of a crass and unperceptive readiness to import all that is worst in industrial societies into a world where they can only prove disruptive and can lead only to exploitation. Gentleness; deep affection for his family (and for animals); immense personal dignity; kindness and friendliness; a passionate if paternalistic dedication to the welfare of his people; most of all, a solemn and incontrovertible sincerity in devotion to international peace and order—these must seem to almost everyone the fine expression of universal human values.

Throughout his long career he has made very contradictory impressions upon foreigners, suggesting not only a multifaceted personality, the product of a strange and alien civilization, but more directly an impulse on the part of those whom he meets to find in him what they want, and expect, to find. In the early years, before the crisis with Italy, he was expectably regarded as an oddity, as Menelek had often been. Interviewers were prepared to find, and often did find, a picturesque savage. During his European trip in 1924, the London *Times* discovered with some surprise that he was a man "of considerable enlightenment," who made a "very favorable impression" on statesmen and others who met him. But not all appraisals were this favorable. Minott Saunders, the Paris correspondent of the Ottawa *Evening Citizen*, reported second-hand on his strange ways. "He made it quite plain that he might be expected to do unexpected things." Canadian readers were told that "western ideas were just too much for him," that he could not understand why a French Cabinet should resign instead of calling out the army to keep them in power. He is quoted as asking, "What good is an Army to a head of State unless he can use it to fight for him?"[3] The methods whereby he had achieved power were judged both barbaric and brutal. At his coronation, which was the first occasion on which he, or Ethiopia, made headlines throughout the world, he was regarded by some foreigners as a foolish and slightly sinister clown.

But such appraisals were drastically revised after 1934. Approaching martyrdom and the conduct of Ethiopia's affairs before the League of Nations transformed him from an exotic native ruler into a statesman of dignity and importance. Much more friendly and certainly more serious efforts were made to characterize him. Will Barber of the Chicago *Tribune* wrote in 1935, "War is the last thing you would associate with this quiet man. . . . Nevertheless . . . if war comes he will lead his armies into the field with an Ark of the Covenant borne . . . at his side." And Barber went on to present him as the reverse of a barbaric tyrant who could not hope to understand western ideas of constitutional government; rather he appeared as an apostle of civil liberty. "Censorship," the emperor told him, "is necessary in a country which has something to hide. Ethiopia lives in the full light of the sun, and has nothing to hide."[4] In the same year a correspondent of the *Journal de Genève* interviewed him and wrote a serious and perceptive profile: he had a "surprising capacity for work and indomitable energy," "He gives the impression that in knowing how to dominate others he knows first of all how to dominate himself." He was presented as a man of contrasts,

gentle but keen, sentimental and affectionate but resolute, a traditionalist and a modernist, "distant but familiar, mysterious but simple."[5]
It was a fair estimate, but it could hardly have been presented five years
earlier to readers who expected "native" rulers to be absurd. By the
mere act of threatening him, Mussolini had made him a personage, and
people tended for a while to see him as the embodiment of western
ideals. The notion of clownish natives began to die in 1935.

Seen from the vantage point of a world that has since changed
much more, Haile Selassie looks now less mysterious and elusive than
he seemed to friendly journalists in the 1930s. He was, above all, an
Ethiopian. Ethiopia is a peculiar society by European standards, but the
exotic is less often disdained in the 1970s than it was in the 1920s. The
lions, the autocracy, the seeming savagery, these are things that are
Ethiopian. Personal kindness, family loyalties, a total absence of vindictiveness, and fewer inhibitions about violence, ferocious devotion to
his people, even, it may be said, an innocent credulity in the triumph
of God, these all form an Ethiopian harmony. But the key is older and
simpler than that. Ethiopia is, pre-eminently, a society whose morality
was shaped by Scripture. The Old Testament is the foundation of the
Amharic tradition. The emperor speaks like, and is like, a biblical figure—sometimes an Isaiah, sometimes a Jeremiah, always an Ezekiel.
The elusiveness of his personality, the apparently incompatible purposes
and the fiery resolution with which he pursues them, the autocracy and
the solemn prophetic utterances, all seem harmonious and explicable
when the Emperor Haile Selassie I is viewed as a patriarch, an Israelite,
a prophet. He is also—perhaps most dramatically—a David; later he was
to kill Goliath. In youth he was a graceful and gallant king to whom
power came in adolescence. In 1906, when still in his teens, he was
made a provincial governor. He had visibly inherited his father's talents
and westernizing aims, and his strength of character as well. He was already famous for patience, resolution, bravery, and resource. He had to
be, to survive the court intrigues and civil strife, medieval brawls that
one English writer has compared to the situation in *Macbeth*.

When Menelek's reign ended, Tafari's position was very strong;
he had supporters in many quarters. He was himself partly of Galla
blood, which helped in dealing with the Galla regions. He had, as a governor, a strong base of power. In 1913 he had married Princess Menen,
a great-granddaughter of Menelek (and also a niece of Joshua). He was

close to his cousin Judith, who became empress when he became regent. Some of his men were very able westernizers. One of them, a German-educated chief named Gabré-Hiwat Baykedagn, summarized the philosophy of the new regime that was taking shape: "When, O people of Ethiopia, will you wake from your sleep? When will you open your eyes and see what things are being done in the world?"[6] Prince Tafari was clearly a true successor to Menelek, and in his years as regent he continued Menelek's work.

The major part of this work was to bring the country under control of the monarchy and so secure internal peace and a chance to impose reforms. The diversity of the provinces and the differing degrees of autonomy they enjoyed under governors, princes, sultans, and kings (the title of king was conferred at will by the King of Kings) not only made war and disunity endemic; it also made rapid change difficult. The conversion of provincial governments from fiefs into bureaucracies proceeded slowly, but it proceeded. A revolution, more gradual but not less portentous than the one that had transformed Japan half a century before, was taking place.

But as in Menelek's day, the disunity of the empire was matched in hazard by the projects of European predators. In the aftermath of World War I, when colonial empires in Africa still looked secure, the gap between Ethiopia's paper sovereignty and its domestic weakness was just as great a source of danger as it had ever been. The tripartite Treaty of 1906 had shown how precarious was the respect paid Ethiopian independence by the great powers; to safeguard it, internal modernization was essential, but internal modernization depended, reciprocally, upon international safety. Success in dealing with this puzzle was Regent Tafari's accomplishment in the 1920s. It was a game of chess played with ivory chessmen against machine guns, but stalemate, at least, was temporarily achieved.

The most important legal safeguard of independence that could be secured was membership in the League of Nations. This meant, automatically, acceptance of full sovereignty by all the member states, which was practically all the states in the world except the United States, Germany, and the Soviet Union. It also involved a *guarantee* that each would protect the sovereignty and integrity of the other members. The guarantee was flimsy, in all truth; the League had not yet showed, and never was to show, either the disposition or the capacity to defend its members against one another. It was, after all, nothing more than a world-wide gesture of good will, invented and accepted because Woodrow Wilson's massive susceptibility to illusion made others hesitate to question it. The League, for all political purposes, consisted of representatives of independent states, bound by their own constitutions and loyalties to follow what appeared to be their national interests. Nonetheless, League membership did count for something in a negative way; it meant that in international law, and in the view of the world opinion, those who held it should be immune from invasion or colonization. It put the label of legal majority upon a state. It was clearly the choice of wisdom to confirm Ethiopia's full sovereignty by securing membership in the League. Membership was formally applied for in 1923. To achieve it, it was necessary to demonstrate that Ethiopia was indeed a mature and civilized state. Given the standards of maturity and civilization among the people who ran the League, that was a formidable task. The negotiations that led up to Ethiopia's admission to the League were difficult for other reasons, too, reasons that showed that maturity and civilization might mean different things to different people. They clearly demonstrated that the appetite of the great powers, despite their battering in World War I, were not diminished. If anything, the battering had intensified colonial ambitions.

The chief sponsorship of the admission of Ethiopia to the League came from Italy and France; the chief opposition came from Britain.

The sponsorship now looks ironic and the opposition captious. The British position was based, ostensibly, on the idea that the requirements for membership in the comity of nations were European standards of a civilized state: full control over its own territory and legal and judicial arrangements embodying decent—that is, European—standards, including abstention from the more blatant forms of savagery, such as slavery and torture. None of these requirements were met by Ethiopia, and there was some reason, although not much imagination, in the argument that Ethiopia could not be regarded as a plausible member of the family. The fact was that the test for membership could be met only by a state with a fairly advanced economy in the European definition. Ethiopia, almost totally illiterate, whose people still lived by a very elementary subsistence agriculture practiced in a very archaic village culture, had little in the way of a market economy. Ethiopians had no sense of agriculture—or indeed any other economic activity—as a profession.

What was grown was what was necessary to maintain life. Currency, profits, commercial distribution, all were alien to most Ethiopians. Wealth was measured largely in cattle, and cattle were kept partly because they represented wealth and not simply as a source of meat or milk. Everything in Ethiopian life reflected the imposition of a somewhat crude facsimile of European statehood upon an entirely alien society. The opposition to Ethiopian membership was strongly advanced not only by the imperial power, Britain, but also by the most civilized and advanced and least-colonial minded countries like Norway. Their governments, not open to accusations of sordid motives, believed that a world order could not emerge if full equality were given to primitive cultures. It is interesting now to note that the strongest hostility came from socialists in all countries.

Primitivism is not a self-defining term. Anthropologically speaking, Ethiopia was a very advanced culture indeed. Its communal village societies were enormously complex. In some respects, such as the position of women (for whom equality in marriage, property rights, and social position generally was far more nearly approached than in France or Italy), Ethiopia could be said to be much more advanced than Europe. Its arts and crafts and its ecclesiology were ancient, intricate, and ripened by long practice. It was largely in their incapacity to produce goods, their attitude toward production, their illiteracy, and their closely related attitudes toward the sanctity of human life and liberty that the Ethiopians seemed barbarous to Europeans. Slavery was largely a matter of economics, as were the abject poverty, ineffable indolence, and tribal stratification that so disturbed European observers.

It was slavery that became the principal touchstone and measurement for Ethiopia's unsuitability for membership in the family of nations. For many conscientious people the issue was very real, and hostility to Ethiopia was for a while strong among British idealists. The notion of Ethiopian membership in the League produced in the 1920s a large, galvanic shudder. Ten years later a similar campaign, conducted by similar people, produced an even greater shudder of pity and horror when Ethiopia's rights as a League member were assaulted by its former sponsor Italy. Nowhere in the whole story of ironies that is the history of the Ethiopian War is there any more remarkable irony than this sudden shift in the objects of concern of conscientious Englishmen.

There were undoubtedly reasons for revulsion against Ethiopia's peculiar institution, given the background of British humanitarians. The deposed Joshua had been a slave owner and, what was a good deal more striking, an enthusiastic slave raider and trader. He had undertaken a number of slaving expeditions and sold the captives to Moslem Danakils and Somalis for eighty dollars a head, treating them in the meanwhile with what was described as abominable cruelty.[7] At the end, his reign had been drowned in blood baths; the troops that drove him out of Harar in October 1916 slaughtered his Moslem supporters and celebrated in the capital by sacrificing men and animals, with whose blood the victorious warriors covered their faces. The chief minister, Prince Hapta George, owned thousands of slaves. It was not entirely surprising that some people thought Ethiopian membership might pollute the atmosphere of Geneva.

The more deplorable facts were called to the attention of the British public by the Anti-Slavery and Aborigines Protection Society. Among other things, it was pointed out that the Ethiopian butler of the British legation was a large slave holder, and although the minister, Claude Russell, defended him (by saying that his slaves represented his life savings), the revelation affected the attitude of the British government, particularly solicitous for its public image, toward League membership.[8] The opposition to Ethiopia's admission to the League was in part determined by domestic politics.

High-mindedness was mixed, as it so often is, with arrogance. The London *Times* leader on the eventual admission of Ethiopia argued that "Though Christian Abyssinia has been admitted, with some heart-searching and hesitation, to membership in the League of Nations, she is a byword for disorder and barbarity: the disorder of feudal and tribal anarchy and the barbarity of the slave trade. In fact, the spectacle presented by the one indigenous African state that has succeeded in retaining its complete independence is perhaps the best justification that can be found for the partition of the rest of Africa among European powers."[9] No doubt some of British opinion was affected by fear of an unsettling effect on the rest of Africa. But the high-minded kind of opposition to Ethiopia was more interesting, and in some circles it had a lasting effect. In 1929 the wife of the Liberal party leader, Sir John Simon, who was shortly to become foreign minister in the government that faced Italian ambitions in Ethiopia, wrote a book called *Slavery*. (Her husband wrote a preface.) It was single-minded in its determination to point out the evils and the persisting prevalence of this cancerous institution, and it focused sharply on Ethiopia. "Ras Tafari," Kathleen Simon wrote, "the mouthpiece for the great Rasses of Abyssinia, has frankly admitted . . . that slavery exists everywhere in the country; indeed it is openly asserted that the whole economic structure of the country reposes on slave-ownership." She did recognize that Tafari himself was acutely aware of the evil and was explaining why it was difficult to extirpate it. But the book brought Ethiopian slavery to the attention of some good people who may well have been led thereby to sympathize with Italy's professed intention of bringing civilization. "It is known that the Italian government is in possession of a great deal of information bearing on the condition of slavery in and around Abyssinian territories. Italian consuls are active in the endeavors to secure liberty of any captive slaves passing through territories under the influence of the Italian government." While most of Britain's high-mindedness was on Ethiopia's side in the war, some remained on the side of Italy.

The preoccupation with slavery was sometimes generous in its motives, but it sometimes disregarded a fact that the early English evangelical opponents of slavery had carefully pointed out: that the condition of workers in Europe was often almost as unfree as that of African slaves. A twentieth-century equivalent of this fact shortly emerged, but was often disregarded: the condition of the Italian people under Mussolini was similarly unfree and was becoming progressively more so, while the government of Ethiopia, catapulted into the European age, was evidently trying to liberate its peoples.

In the British government, policy was largely detached from any real concern for Ethiopian slaves, except insofar as domestic political considerations dictated solicitude for them. The motives of the French and Italians were similarly interested. The French had sponsored Ethiopia's application to the League in the first place; Mussolini's first reaction had been the logical one of opposing it, since membership would legally subtract Ethiopia from the few remaining colonizable parts of the world. But advisors pointed out that opposition would probably be unavailing, while support would open doors to the extension of Italian influence.[10] The support of both France and Italy for the application was decisive. After lengthy debates, Ethiopia was admitted in September 1923 as a member, with conditions.

The Regent Tafari accepted the conditions. They concerned control of the arms traffic and the elimination of slavery with all deliberate speed and with League assistance. He was now able to force the obstinate empress and her extremely conservative friends into action. A beginning was made in 1924, when it was decreed that henceforth all children of slaves would be born free and all slaves should be automatically emancipated on the death of their owner. The decree was not generally obeyed, but it marked a significant step in modernizing the society, as distinct from the superficial modernization of the state. The regent's international policy thus served his domestic purposes.

League membership also furnished the means for parrying the next attempt of European powers to meddle. In 1925, in connection with negotiations to settle their outstanding colonial disputes, in particular the drawing of the border between Eritrea and the Sudan, the British and Italian governments reached an agreement upon the allocation of certain opportunities for economic development in Ethiopia, strongly reminiscent of the three-power agreement of 1906. The Italians recognized Britain's right to build the dam, often contemplated, on the Blue Nile, at Lake Tana and a road leading to it from Sudan. The British recognized Italy's right to build a railroad from Eritrea to Italian Somaliland. Both public works would be, of course, on Ethiopian territory, but the Ethiopian government was not notified of these negotiations until it was presented with the agreement.

Regent Tafari's response was ingenious and characteristic. He exploited to the fullest the Covenant of the League and his membership in it. He protested to the Italians and the British, and to the Assembly of the League he presented a message that was a skillful and prophetic piece of public relations. It ran in part:

> TO THE STATE MEMBERS OF THE LEAGUE OF NATIONS
> We have been profoundly moved by the conclusion of this agreement arrived at without our being consulted or informed, and by the action of the two Governments in sending us a joint notification. In the first place, on our admission to the League of Nations we were told that all nations were to be on a footing of equality within the League, and that their independence was to be universally respected, since the purpose of the League is to establish and maintain peace among men in accordance with the will of God.
> We were not told that certain members of the League might

make a separate agreement to impose their views on another member even if the latter considered those views incompatible with its national interests. . . .

Throughout their history, they have seldom met with foreigners who did not desire to possess themselves of Abyssinian territory and to destroy their independence. With God's help, and thanks to the courage of our soldiers, we have always, come what might, stood proud and free on our native mountains.

The world of black peoples and of colonial empires was, in the 1920s, in a state of curious balance. Reflexive convictions had formed in the west in recent times that characteristics called racial included not merely physiological traits but intellectual and moral capacities; and these convictions had as yet been barely shaken. An enormous body of erroneous anthropological data had been amassed to support them. The first serious scientific attacks on them, by Americans like Willis Weatherford and Melville Herskovits, had not yet touched more than a narrow circle of opinion. It was assumed by most whites, as a matter of revealed truth, that blacks, and particularly African blacks, were innately inferior—were, in fact, as Kipling had remarked, "half devil and half child"—and must necessarily remain in indefinite tutelage.

But in other spheres changes in opinion were taking place in the west that prepared a favorable reception for Tafari's message. If European belief in white superiority was largely intact, a countervailing belief in the sanctity and independence of small nations had grown prodigiously. It had always been part of the public law and public conscience of Europe. In 1914 World War I had been fought by the Allies on the pretext, and partly with the purpose, of protecting Serbia and Belgium against predatory assault by powerful neighbors. The mythology developing around war aims had converted a tenet of expediency into one of morality. The peace settlement and the Covenant of the League both reflected this: peace and principle alike demanded the safety and sovereignty of small powers. Aggression against them was at once the chief wickedness of international conduct and the chief threat to international security.

It will be observed that the notion was essentially a conservative one. The small states (like all the states that were to be protected from attack) were those that already existed. The sanctity of statehood implied the freezing of all existing frontiers in perpetuity, not to mention the institution of the sovereign state itself. It was a notion fully consonant with the interests and traditions of the victors, in particular France, Britain, and the United States.

It was also a principle that could be exploited by the regent of Ethiopia in the 1920s and 1930s. Its anomalies offered him opportunities, although they also offered threats and uncertainties. Italian ambitions had assured his League membership, but they also threatened dangers. The British were devoted to the cause of existing frontiers; but they were also (by necessity, as it were) devoted to the principle of civilizing backward areas, and they were alert to the danger of contagion that an independent African state, fully accredited in the society of nations, might spread among colonial peoples. The position of the French was somewhat different. No less concerned about contagion than the British and even more convinced of Europe's civilizing mission, they were a good deal less attached to the moral and practical principle of the sanctity of small states as an ecumenical necessity. They were much more practical in their outlook; what mattered in Paris was not dim ecumenical principles but the security of France. Their attention was much more centered upon Europe, where, they conceived, all threats to France were likely to arise. There was consistently displayed in France a much greater flexibility about non-European change than was evident in Britain, both in public opinion and in high policy. If the ambitions of Italy overseas could be gratified, then Italy-in-Europe might be a more willing and reliable buttress of French safety.

These complications were shortly demonstrated. In 1928 the Italians signed a treaty of friendship and arbitration with the regent, including an important clause for stimulation of trade between the two countries. It was consistent with Italy's program of peaceful penetration, somewhat haphazardly pursued since 1923; it may have been precipitated by Ethiopia's concession to an American firm to build the dam on the Blue Nile, which nullified the Italian agreement with Britain and thereby ended the possibility for mutual support in Rome and London for a policy of something more active than peaceful penetration. From the Ethiopian standpoint, the 1928 treaty looked like another diplomatic success, since it not only added another legal bulwark against Italian depredations but secured, on paper, some important advantages for Addis Ababa, including port privileges in Eritrea. But there were disadvantages as well. For one thing, the more colonial-minded officials in Rome regretted the generosity of the Italian negotiator, Giuliano Cora, the minister in Addis Ababa, who was sympathetic to Ethiopia. Some of his opponents are even said to have suggested that the treaty be used, if Ethiopia failed to live up to it, as a basis for military action.[11] In any case, the opportunities it presumably opened came to nothing.

There were also complications resulting from Tafari's policies within Ethiopia. There was fear among the provincial chieftains that the further consolidation of Ethiopia's international position would weaken theirs. The growing centralization and Tafari's impulses toward modernization were strongly opposed not only by the chieftains but also by the Church, the aristocracy, and apparently much of the population. Opposition to change arose as the opportunity for it increased. One powerful obstacle had just been removed with the death of Archbishop Matthew, a passionate reactionary; in the same year, 1926, another reactionary, Hapta George, the most important man in the empire and the close adviser of the empress, also died. But strong opponents remained, and their reactionary needs took a familiar form: military operations by a provincial governor to impose his will on the central government. This time it was dealt with in an unfamiliar way, characteristic of the novel methods of Tafari.

The rebel was old Governor Balka of the province of Sidamo, in the Rift Valley several hundred miles south of the capital. Balka, a eunuch and a former protégé of Menelek, had the views and practices of most of the old-fashioned chieftains. He was a large slave holder and trader—it was said that he habitually cut out his slaves' tongues to prevent them from gossiping—and he declined to transmit taxes to Addis Ababa or permit its agents to enter his province. The issue, familiar in medieval Europe, was clearly a struggle between the old order and the new one of the sovereign state.

When the regent, in 1927, summoned the chieftains to pay homage to him, Balka at first refused to come and then, after a long delay, appeared, with an army of ten thousand men. He was received at a banquet of barbaric splendor given by the regent. While their leader was feasting, his men, encamped on the edge of the town, were approached by an imperial army, threatened, lavishly bribed, and sent home. When Balka returned to his camp he found that his forces had disappeared. He took refuge in a church and tried to invoke the protection of the hierarchy. Tafari surrounded the church with troops and after a short siege Balka surrendered. He was forcibly retired to a monastery.

The incident illustrated the recalcitrance of conservative forces as they grew more and more aware of the threat not merely to their position but to their medieval universe. The method of dealing with it, particularly the monastery, if not medieval was by European standards very early modern.

The Italian treaty precipitated the climactic episode in conservative resistance, the most serious action against the power of the regent in the 1920s. The elder statesmen of the empire attempted to dispossess Tafari in a palace coup in October 1928. They secured the support of the Empress Judith, herself intensely conservative and apparently resentful of the man who had deprived her of power and was threatening to deprive her country of its archaic purity. The regent was summoned to the imperial presence, and the imperial bodyguard surrounded the palace, evidently intending to arrest him. His wife, however, called out loyal troops. They entered the palace and disarmed the bodyguard. The elder statesmen immediately accepted the situation. The regent was given the title of king. In earlier reigns it had been freely conferred on local potentates; it had represented the constitutional fact that the empire was a collection of kingdoms and that the King of Kings was no more than their chosen overlord. By making himself a king, the regent, who was also heir to the throne, emphasized the supremacy of the dynasty and the sovereignty of its government. In a society where symbolism was intensely important, it had more than a titular significance.

Prince Gugsa of Gondar, the husband of Judith, himself a Solomonic prince and an enterprising provincial governor, in 1930 organized another march on the capital, again in collusion with the empress. King Tafari's victory at Ankim, north of Addis, in March 1930, in which Gugsa was killed, was largely the product of intelligence about the rebel troop dispositions, supplemented by leaflets informing rebels that Tafari had the support of the Church, which were the work of the Ethiopian air force. Tafari had created it a few months earlier, and its personnel consisted of two French pilots. Like Menelek's newspaper, handwritten in four copies, the air force was a token, but it was also a strategic fact. And the same anachronistic intertwinings of the air age and feudal warfare was remarkably illustrated by the death of the Empress Judith on the day after that of her husband—she died, it was officially announced, of a broken heart. The usual impenetrable mystery attending the personal history of members of the imperial family prevailed; rumor attributed the death not to a broken heart but variously to diabetes, typhoid fever, poisoning, and strangling. Her fate remains, like so many of her relatives', shadowy. She was buried within six hours; the next morning the primate proclaimed Tafari King of Kings, and he moved into the imperial palace. The government immediately undertook negotiations to purchase the imperial carriage of the Hohenzollerns from the government of the German republic, as a coronation coach for the new sovereign.

The House of Hohenzollern had been grandiose, glittering, and gilded in its displays of the might of the German empire. It has also presented itself as the bulwark of civilization against the barbaric hordes of Slavdom. The coach, imported into a sprawling, half-built African capital with unpaved streets, took on a curious rightness in the minds of the Europeans who attended the ceremonies that were intended to mark not only the installation of another scion of Solomon on the ancient throne but the debut of a modern Power.

The coronation was what today might moderately be called "a spectacular." It misfired as an occasion for acclaiming Ethiopia's modernity. Nonetheless, it was important. It certainly succeeded in attracting more attention from foreign publics than the country had ever before. Not all of it—not most of it, even—was favorable, but it put Ethiopia on the map, as it was intended to do. And in a very real sense, it marked the beginning of Haile Selassie's reign and his revelation of himself as a major figure on the world scene. After the coronation, no one could disregard him; and the extraordinary display, the large-scale advertising it represented, added in a way to his power. It impressed, if perhaps sometimes grudgingly, both foreigners and Ethiopians. It permitted him to begin a period of drastic, almost revolutionary, change, for which his previous career had been a preparation. One of the great events of the time, the festivity, like so many Ethiopian events, combined pageantry, dignity, and absurdity. It was a show and, most visitors thought, a circus. To many it showed not that Ethiopia had reached adulthood as a nation but that it was incapable of ever doing so. Its real meaning was, however, different and unperceived.

The street that connected Saint George's cathedral (built after Adowa by Italian prisoners of war) with the imperial palace was renamed Haile Selassie I Avenue and hastily macadamized. (The surface lasted through the ceremonies but went to pieces soon afterward.) The policemen were given uniforms, although they refused to wear shoes. Leonard Mosley reports that some twenty thousand prostitutes received instant "cures" for venereal disease along with instruction in useful phrases in English, French, and Italian.[12] Lepers were obliged to leave town. Hotels and pavilions equipped with modern plumbing were run up to accommodate distinguished visitors.

The distinguished visitors arrived in force, a crowd of somewhat cynical journalists and not less cynical official representatives and tourists. One especially cynical English journalist said that the Ethiopians thought the foreigners—a marshal of France, sons of the kings of Great Britain and Greece, the special representative of President Hoover, and many others—had come as vassals to render homage to the King of Kings.* They were treated to regalements and entertainments that oddly combined the native with phony western elements in the New Ethiopia that was being announced. There was a solemn assemblage of the princes of the empire, wearing European-style coronets—and lions' manes. Rigid European court etiquette (borrowed from Sweden) had just been decreed; the emperor provided the citizenry with free banquets of raw meat. To the Englishman Waugh it seemed a mockery of civilization; but his definition of civilization was perhaps sufficiently demonstrated when he wrote, "it is absurd to pretend that Ethiopia is a civilised nation . . . a few miles outside of Addis Ababa there is not a single motor road."

The coronation was not less a mockery to other foreigners. One tourist, an American named Ellen La Motte, was similarly struck by the superficiality, the inappropriateness, of the European trappings. It was all, she thought, a travesty and an absurdity. She was obliged

---

* Evelyn Waugh, Waugh in Abyssinia, p. 7. The story is to be regarded with caution; Waugh was neither an impartial nor a reliable witness. He was violently hostile to Ethiopia and, when war came, strongly pro-Italian. But the story at least illuminates the way in which many Europeans reacted to the coronation, and is not entirely implausible.

to stay in a cow shed, hastily converted by a local hotelier into guest rooms, and to fight armies of huge ants. The porters at the station carried her baggage on their heads. It looked to her a squalid, festering, inefficient society—"In Abyssinia," she wrote, "nothing ever gets finished," and the coronation was but a symbol of the unfinished state of efforts to civilize the country. She saw no architecture, no crafts, no art, worth noticing. Most of the inhabitants lived in thatched mud huts once in a while "capped with an empty Perrier bottle," the only efforts at embellishment she saw. The ceremonies were not only farcical but wickedly extravagant in a country where poverty was everywhere. The new imperial crown had cost, she heard, twenty-five thousand dollars. In the palace the chairs for foreign guests were covered in gold leaf, with enormous carved lions'-paw legs. The coronation took place in a sort of vast circus tent. Attendance was limited to foreigners and the court and ministry; "no Abyssinian of humble rank" attended. She heard that there were popular grumbling and xenophobic demonstrations in one of which fifteen people were shot down by the authorities. The food was not merely unpalatable but dangerous; one foreign visitor died of food poisoning. A graft-ridden, backward, repellent society of childish savages, she concluded. She was relieved to escape alive and in good health.[13]

But Haile Selassie I, as he styled himself now that he was emperor, was a patriarch and a prophet. For his people, steeped in Old Testament ways, the coronation was a sacred and important rite. It was only half its purpose to call westerners to witness Ethiopia's coming of age; the other half was to dazzle Ethiopians with the knowledge that their ruler was a real emperor who could, at whim, pave roads and raise triumphal arches. If some people thought that marshals of France and British princes were swearing fealty to an overlord, so much the better for the prospects of forcing the country into the paths of righteousness that Haile Selassie conceived.

The next five years were very active ones for the pursuit of righteousness. There was a long list of achievements. Many were superficial, and none were more than beginnings that scarcely touched the fabric of the village life. They were nonetheless important, for they began the work of creating a new leadership and a practicable framework for further change. Internal peace was more nearly secure than it had ever been in modern times; the various forms of rebellious localism were ending. The only major disturbance revolved, significantly, around the person of the dethroned and imprisoned Emperor Joshua. In 1932 his escape was contrived as part of an effort by one of the provincial chieftains, Prince Hailu of Gojam, to thwart Haile Selassie's ventures. But the rising was suppressed after only three days and the traitors were imprisoned.[14]

Aside from this strange incident, the trend of the times was now tidally in an opposite direction. In 1931 a constitution was promulgated by the emperor. It has frequently been remarked that since the constitution left the autocracy of the crown unaffected and created a parliament without real power, it was meaningless. Such assertions are statements of anachronism: what was attempted was not conservatively to preserve autocracy but radically to create it. Its purpose and importance was to wipe out the traditional and legal fact that the central government was merely an overlordship of provincial chieftains. It established the idea of sovereignty to replace the old order and converted the inhabitants of the country from chattels of their princes into citizens and subjects of the emperor. Ethiopia, in its constitutional structure, was transferred abruptly from the condition of European governments in about the twelfth century to the condition in which they existed in the eighteenth. It was the power of the central government to *act* that had accounted for the shape of western change in modern times; it was not the limitations placed upon the government by parliamentary regimes. The power to act Haile Selassie now, in law, achieved.

Given the aim of converting an "archaic" society to a "modern" one, the crucial preface was building a civil service and an educated class of Ethiopians to staff it. Since the educated class was almost entirely lacking, foreign experts played an important role. They were selected from countries sufficiently remote or disinterested so that their governments were not likely to involve the experts in bids for influence—Sweden, Switzerland, and the United States.

The American expert, Everett Colson, was a fascinating figure who, in a long and remarkable career, had had important positions in the Philippines, China, and Haiti and was to have a much more important one in Ethiopia. He was indeed to be one of the great figures in the drama whose overture was now commencing. He had a taste for obscurity, as he had for public service in distant places, and his name was unknown to his compatriots. In Ethiopia he is famous, and one of the chief streets of the capital is named for him. He was admired, even adored, by many Ethiopians and westerners in Addis Ababa, but he remains elusive. As one of the Ethiopian statesmen of the time put it later, "he was a dedicated man. When one has said that, one has said everything."[15]

This strange, imposing person was a native of Portland, Maine, and an employee of the United States Treasury. He was sent to Addis Ababa in answer to the emperor's request for a financial expert, and he became from the first a close adviser of the court. A highly efficient, patient, skeptical expert on finance, he was largely responsible for the measure that laid the foundations for a national economy. A major cause, and most striking outward sign, of Ethiopia's pre-medieval condition was the fact that it had no currency; or, more precisely, it had a variety of currencies, none of them official. The principal media of exchange were Maria Theresa dollars, coins minted on a private enterprise basis at various points in the Near and Middle East. Each coin bore the date 1780 and the effigy of the Holy Roman empress (believed by some Ethiopians to be the effigy of the Virgin Mary). In the eighteenth century the original Maria Theresa *thaler* had been, because of its excellence, something like an international monetary standard— the American dollar, named for it, was one of its offspring. These brand-new ones maintained the old standard of excellence and commanded general confidence, but the Ethiopian state had no control over them. There was a Bank of Abyssinia, a branch of the British-controlled Egyptian Bank, established under charter by Menelek, which produced bank notes, but the paper currency—also outside the control of the government—was not highly regarded. In 1931 a state bank was founded, with the usual powers of a central bank to lend money to individuals and the government and to issue Ethiopian dollars. The fiscal history of the bank was as unstable as its lending policies: interest on its equities varied from 100 per cent per year to 0 per cent thereafter. But the necessary structure for a national economy and a national financial policy, as well as the financial independence of the state, now had rudimentary beginnings.

Education, no less than currency, was necessary to provide a functioning bureaucracy of the modern sort, and in the first five years of

Haile Selassie's reign ten new schools were started. Young Ethiopians were encouraged to study abroad, and they formed, by 1935, a very small but important nucleus of a westernized and educated elite. The successors to Menelek's class of loyal landowners were to form an intelligentsia trained for the age of technology and bureaucracy, and in the early 1930s considerable progress was made toward its creation. A few of the provincial governments, under active modernizers, were provided with the outlines of modern administrative services, and provincial lines were redrawn to create several altogether new "model provinces," which had new governments and, in one case, a new city founded as its capital. New printing presses were introduced and several weekly newspapers appeared. With the advice of Belgian experts, a modern army was being built up out of the old Imperial Guard, designed to replace the old feudal levies, and a war college was set up. Progress was very small, but it was a significant token.

An effort was also made to improve health conditions. It, too, was of necessity rudimentary. A British medical missionary named John Melly, young, ardent, and hopeful, who reached the country in 1934 with the ambition of setting up a medical school and inculcating Christian ideals at the same time, was appalled by conditions, both hygienic and social. He wrote that in Addis Ababa, "which outstrips the rest of the country by five hundred years," there were no sewers, "water supply, or electric light." For a population comparable to that of Canada's, "there are about 400 hospital beds—practically all Missionary Hospitals and practically all in this town. And the whole country is positively ridden with disease . . . Infantile paralysis, T.B., and leprosy . . . typhus, smallpox, and venereal disease (about 90 per cent of the population) are rife." In the hotel where he was entertained by a provincial governor, he was obliged to put two basins of water on the floor with a lighted candle in each—"to trap the more adventuresome fleas." Robbers were hanged by the wayside "—and left hanging for three days." But he found the country "indescribably lovely" and some of the people charming, and he was struck by evidence of improvement, by progress in medicine and education, "the outward and visible signs of the organization and progress which have been taking place in Ethiopia in the last decade. The work of the law courts, the abolition of punishments like amputation of the hand for robbery, the emperor's gift of premises for a hospital for sick animals, his tireless fight against slavery, and the building of much-needed roads, are all examples of less spectacular but vitally needed reforms. And this progress is spreading in an ever-increasing circle from the seat of government at Addis Ababa."[16]

In the first four years of his reign, Haile Selassie had defined his prophecy and was pursuing its fulfillment with vigor. He was the prophet of a new society made in the image of the humane ideals of Judaism and Christianity, one that would combine the sources of western strength—national unity and freedom, education, economic development to assure reasonable living standards, administrative efficiency, modern medicine—with Ethiopian tradition and culture.

No one yet understood the awful chasms and disruptions that such aims might produce in alien soil, any more than anyone understood that industrial affluence could produce its own disasters. No man of good will in the early 1930s could have watched his efforts without applause. The issue then was between people like John Melly, preeminently a man of good will, who lamented in anguish the tardiness and insufficiency of the progress, and those who supposed people like the Ethiopians incapable of making it. Many of the latter were affronted, and contemptuous in the face of the Ethiopian efforts.

When progress was abruptly cut short in 1935, attitudes toward the Italian invasion reflected, at least roughly, the two points of view. Ethiopia was brought sensationally to the center of world attention, and each viewpoint appeared as a final, unchangeable pole in the planet from which men viewed the universe.

For those who espoused the Ethiopian cause, the country presented itself as a small, courageous state bravely fighting for its independence and for a chance to progress against a brutal aggressor. For those who favored the Italian cause, as many did throughout the world, Ethiopia was a barbarous, formless amalgam of slaveries and savageries quite unentitled to independence or to the name of state. Both views contained some truth and both conveyed an impression absurdly wrong. Ethiopia was an empire constructed by peoples of ancient and highly particular culture, a sort of frozen version of the ancestral culture of the west with an unbroken political continuity older than that of any European country. It was not at all, as its more naïve defenders in Europe and America tended to suggest, a sort of potential African Sweden. Slavery indeed existed and the oppression of conquered peoples by the Amharic masters. Conditions of life and thought were incredibly elementary. The government, by the modern European standard, was inchoate. It was exceedingly doubtful if it ever could (or should) become a replica of European civilization.

Ethiopia was, in short, unique; nothing like it existed, or ever had existed before, or would ever exist again. If it was absurd to see it as a sort of nascent Sweden, it was more absurd, and brutally stupid as well, to regard it as did the foreign visitors described by Evelyn Waugh. In 1936 he wrote, "Only an infinitesimal number [of Europeans] have suffered the indignities of travelling in Abyssinia. Those that have are inclined to be intemperate about it.

"The essence of the offense was that the Abyssinians, in spite of being by any possible standard an inferior race, persisted in behaving as superiors; it was not that they were hostile, but contemptuous. The white man, accustomed to other parts of Africa, was disgusted to find first-class carriages usurped by local dignitaries; he found himself subject to officials and villainous-looking men at arms whose language he did not know, who showed him no sort of preference on account of his colour, and had not the smallest reluctance to using force on him if he became truculent. There were, of course, large tracts of Ethiopia where any stranger, white or Abyssinian, was liable to be murdered on sight."

Waugh disdained such provinciality, but he shared it, too. He was, like his more generous and percipient countryman John Melly, a symbol and a symptom of the provinciality of Europeans confronted with a world that belied all their values and their assumptions. Almost at once, those European values and assumptions were given a last inglorious chance to prove themselves and failed.

3

The Son of Romulus

The emperor of Ethiopia was in truth a prophet, a patriarch, and a son of Solomon, but in the 1930s he came to stand for all the things that idealistic, forward-looking people in the industrial west accepted as self-evident truths and commendable goals. The dictator of Italy, a working-class socialist, a true son of Europe's age of industry and conflict, became the hero of reactionaries. To progressive people he was brutally turning back clocks; he became for them a wrecker and a devil.

The paradoxical things that each of the two men, as they were seen by humanitarians and men of good will in western Europe and North America, seemed to represent were things that Europe had developed and exported, two faces of a European civilization that was full of inner tensions and contradictions. On the one hand, the humane vision of a world of individuals engaged in fulfilling their own personalities while living tranquilly in society—a vision of peace, prosperity, and progress. On the other hand, the belief that individuals by nature were, and should be, combative and competitive; that only through strife could personal fulfillment be attained; that prosperity and progress could be achieved only if the individuals diverted their instincts into serving a society which should, as a whole, be itself combative and competitive. "Strife," Mussolini said in 1920, "is the origin of all things."[1]

Such a simple view, a naïve and very European opposition of good and evil, determined the course of events because western Europe and North America were running the world. But Haile Selassie I and Mussolini were much more—and much less—than the embodiment of such ideas. They were rulers, who like all rulers faced problems for which principles and visions offered no clear guidance. They were, of necessity, empiricists, manipulators, and opportunists. All men in power are. But men in power also have their principles. And so did Haile Selassie and Mussolini. The war between them was a war of principles as well as a war of continents and cultures and nations.

For the African, it was overtly, almost ostentatiously so; he talked always in terms of his vision of righteousness. The Italian, wildly inconsistent and volatile, praised inconsistency; what mattered, he believed, were visceral reactions, not ideas—but this, too, is a sort of vision of righteousness and a principle. In Mussolini's career emerged one transcendent principle, deep and flamboyant, the identification of national with personal success. It was not entirely absent from Haile Selassie's.

In all outward respects, the contrast between the two men seems total. Benito Mussolini was a bright boy and a very poor boy, born in 1883 in a mountain village near Bologna, of grievously disadvantaged parents who were, however, not without intellectual pretensions. His mother was a school teacher, his father an unsuccessful blacksmith and a passionately revolutionary ideologue. The son was named by his father for the Mexican liberator Benito Juárez, and he was raised in a fervid atmosphere where poverty and injustice were viewed as remediable by violent action. He learned from his father that all religion was fraud, all tradition oppression, all past and present societies corrupt. It is hard to imagine a total contrast with the boyhood of Haile Selassie—or a more painful boyhood for a gifted child in a society where such views were unacceptable. He was, in terms of bourgeois morality, a bully, a quitter, a troublemaker, a failure. His schoolmates threw stones at him out of mere prejudice against an outsider; he patronized a witch who sold love philters; he stabbed another boy; he talked politics incessantly. He was, by personality as well as principle, an anarchist.

Mussolini was produced by a set of circumstances peculiar to the Europe of the late nineteenth century. Like so many other young men of promise, he was deformed by the contradictions and inadequacies of European society. It was the great age of nations, when sovereignties were seen as both beneficent and ultimate and people spoke confidently of traits of national character, not doubting that they were genetic facts. The poverty and oppression of a very large part of the

Italian population, the retrograde social and economic order, the hazards of periodic depression, were reflected during Mussolini's youth in a distressing appearance of inefficiency and corruption in the Italian state. This appearance was seen not only as a cause of hardship and injustice; it was also deemed by patriots responsible for the inability of Italy—which was at once a nation, a state, a principle, a tradition, and an ideal—to assert itself, its greatness, glory, and destiny. For a revolutionary, such considerations might be judged unimportant, but they touched the personalities of many Italian rebels. The nation was a vast, ubiquitous fact, part of the essential furniture of every mind. It was significant that Mussolini, while he might excoriate the Italian state as a tool of social oppressors, was fanatically devoted to the land, and to his village and the culture he grew up in. They were, in psychological terms, the only security and the only identity he had.

Mussolini certainly thought that he was a product of what his nation was, although in the end the proposition became for him reversed; he began to believe that what he was, the nation was. His was a curiously chaotic personality, and he frequently failed to draw distinctions between himself and outside entities.

The story of Mussolini's rise and power is the study of the conflicts in the nation and in himself. When bad times came to Italy in the early 1930s and the unfulfilled promises of his rule became manifest, he found in the long and embarrassing story of Italy's unresolved ambitions in East Africa a chance for glory, reassurance, and revenge.

Prime Minister Rudini had described the adventure of 1896 as an expression of pure snobbery. This view was at the time shared by many Italians. It was not shared by all, and as years passed Adowa came to be called, more and more often, a humiliation requiring vengeance. Gabriele D'Annunzio, the most hysterical of the avengers, referred to it as a "shameful scar" and never forgot it. Benito Mussolini, thirteen at the time, was to write that he was forever obsessed by the memory of "ten thousand dead and seventy-two cannon lost."[2] It may be doubted whether this sentiment was more than retrospective, but certainly many, many Italians felt personally humiliated by the national defeat.

There were deeper reasons for the sense of humiliation. The creation of Italy in the 1860s had required a considerable act of faith and of will on the part of those who were determined to achieve it;

it had been necessary to believe that "Italy" would transfigure its citizens and lead them to fulfillment. No less compelling a vision could have justified, or generated, the necessary energies. But "Italy," once achieved, fulfilled nothing. Most Italians were not visibly changed by the enormous epiphany in their national life. They continued to eat rice and pasta, to sleep in the sun, to dwell in poverty, poetry, and music, to produce—and export—enormous families, to take and receive bribes. The government of the renascent nation seemed, like the governments of the principalities that preceded it, corrupt, repressive, and unedifying. It showed little taste for glory and no capacity for achieving it. The vision unfulfilled was transmitted to a generation whose appetite for grandeur had not even the palliation of comparing present unity with lively memories of the divided nation. Thus, in the age when the self-respect of individuals was frequently associated with the greatness of their nations, a good deal of individual neurosis expressed itself in dreams of national glory. Adowa inflamed the emotions produced by a sense of national inadequacy.

There were wide forces that inflamed emotions further. Toward the end of the nineteenth century a certain restlessness of spirit—incipient revolt against reasonableness, compromise, and slow material progress within the existing institutions—was spreading all over Europe. It was evident in the growth of both anarchism and chauvinism, in Nietzsche's pathological defiance of Christianity, law, and order, in the surging hatred of democracy among the anti-Dreyfusards in France, in the long series of assassinations of heads of state. In Italy the malaise was especially noticeable.

Its most conspicuous exponent was D'Annunzio. He had read Nietzsche and quite frankly viewed himself as a superman. He insisted that great men, in particular great artists, could not be bound by conventions—or laws. He was elected to the Chamber of Deputies in 1897 and announced that he was not to be regarded as the representative of his constituents but rather as the "deputy of beauty." He took his seat first on the extreme Right and then, announcing "I go toward life," moved to the extreme Left. In one play, *The Dead City*, he glorified murder, incest, and patriotism. In another, called *Glory*, he applauded the exploits of Francesco Crispi, the prime minister who had presided over Adowa and been discredited by it (the play was booed by the Roman audience; D'Annunzio had as yet found no mass public for his peculiar notions). He addressed Victor Emmanuel III, on his accession in 1900, with a fiery poem which threatened him with nemesis "if thou wilt not give greatness and glory to the Italian nation."[3] His poetry, which commanded a wider audience and more enthusiastic approbation as the twentieth century unfolded, glorified the beauty of fire, murder, war, aggression, and sexual promiscuity. So did his private life.

A moral nihilist who saw no present but mediocrity and corruption and no future but in violent and rebellious self-expression, D'Annunzio believed himself to be a hero and recommended his brand of heroism as a way of life and a test for virtue. "Sail toward the world," he commanded his audience. Like a great many other people in Europe, D'Annunzio confusedly borrowed terms from Darwin and called war "the awakener of the weak" and "the hygiene of the world."[4]

Enrico Corradini, another brilliant writer, was converted to the creed of chauvinism by the "shame of Adowa." He demanded an end to the old arguments about Italian foreign policy, whether to align with democratic, anti-clerical Latin France or with Catholic, conservative Austria. He called for a foreign policy stridently assertive and entirely Italian. He was horrified by the emigration that was draining from overpopulated Italy the best of its youth, leading them to assimilation in foreign countries. He spoke of "the slave mentality" of the Italians, their submissiveness and acquiescence in national mediocrity. He demanded conquest in Africa where new Italian nations could be built by the people now abandoning their nationality and their nation in foreign parts. There clearly appeared, in Corradini's writings, a less familiar element, of left-wing nationalism. Most recent chauvinisms, in Italy and elsewhere, had been built on rightist and patrician assumptions. Corradini envisaged the future of Italian greatness as a product of common people, a proletarian imperialism. He was as impatient of the ruling classes, capitalists, aristocrats, monarchists, and priests as he was of liberalism and international submissiveness. His jargon was that of a leftist revolutionary. And this conjunction of proletariat revolution with idolatry of the nation and a metaphysic of salutary conflict blazed the trail for the political evolution of the young Mussolini, who was by then achieving a reputation for himself as a revolutionary newspaper man. He was to transform these notions by the force of his peculiar personality and a favorable constellation of circumstances into a rhetoric that gave to him a sensational career and to the world a shattering ideology. It is possible, in retrospect, to see as logical the route that led him from anarchism to his, and the world's, apocalypse in distant Ethiopia.

After 1900 more and more Italians, even moderate and respectable ones, were renewing their interest in Africa. Every colonial power claimed peculiar qualifications for the task of bringing civilization to benighted indigenes: the British, for example, their administrative talents and concern for sanitation; the French, their universalist principles of liberty, quality, and fraternity, and the dramas of Racine and Corneille. The *causes* for empire-building were of course not these; but millions of Europeans, including businessmen who calculated profit margins on colonial exploitation, were beguiled to the point of frenzy by their own noble aims. And in the age when empire building was a test of character, the Italians, too, claimed special qualifications. Some of these were tangible enough. They were accustomed to hot climates and knew how to cope with them better than the British or French or the Dutch or Germans. And Italians did not suffer, as the British or Germans or Dutch suffered, from any strain of racial bigotry or national insularity mixed with their jingoistic fervor; Italy was a cosmopolitan country, and the eclecticism of its origins was seen, even by Mussolini, as the great source of its cultural glories. Like other Mediterranean peoples, Italians were able to mingle in hot climates with exotic folk of strange complexion, without patronage and without self-consciousness.

While it is difficult now to realize it, there was a powerful idealism, especially noticeable among young people, behind the expansion of Europe. Some Italian doctors, for example, believed that they had a mission to bring their skills to the alleviation of the ills that afflict people in places like East Africa. Italians were experts in tropical medicine, and the doctors' undoubted sacrifices inspired respect among fellow citizens who saw in their work vindication for the work of civilizing the natives. Another special qualification was thought to arise from the heritage of imperial Rome. Some subjects of the dull Victor Emmanuel III identified themselves with forebears who had been ruled by Augustus. The ancient Romans had been engineers and soldiers of the first order. Early twentieth-century Italians were also, at least, excellent engineers—the roads and railroads they built in their own formidable mountains showed it. Road building had a peculiar significance in what followed. It symbolized the peculiar genius of Italy. Highways came to seem an abstraction of civilization as well as its material foundation; they were avenues of strategy. Nowhere in the world, not even in the United States, has highway engineering figured so largely in the self-image of a culture.

Tropical medicine and highway building were the most substantial expressions of the sense of colonial destiny that powerfully grew in the early twentieth century in Italy. The problem was to find a place where they could be suitably practiced.

Libya, known at the time to many Europeans as Tripoli, the Turkish desert province across the Mediterranean, was the nearest and most inviting possibility. In 1910 a congress of nationalists, a bewilderingly diverse assemblage of leftists, like Corradini, and old-fashioned rightists, called for national dedication to preparation for war and greatness and deplored the limpness of the unadventurous government of Prime Minister Giovanni Giolitti. In 1911 Corradini founded a magazine called *The National Idea* to disseminate the call to glory. One journalist wrote, "Tripoli must be ours or we will suffocate."[5] The statement was purely rhetorical. Aside from some small, bedraggled ports and a few thousand fierce, nomadic tribesmen, Libya consisted of a desert wholly unlikely to divert Italian emigrants from the well-beaten trails to the promised lands of the western hemisphere or to offer opportunities for Italian banks to invest their capital under the protection of the Italian flag.

Prime Minister Giolitti, as much a realist as Rudini before him when faced with an opposite reflex in public opinion, ordered an attack on Libya in the fall of 1911, and the annexation of Libya to the Italian crown was soon proclaimed and applauded, although the fighting dragged on in the new colony until it was submerged in much larger international crises.

The campaign in the desert split the Italian Socialist party. Like most European socialist parties, it was already implicitly divided between those inclined to accept the existence of the bourgeois state and to try to squeeze social reforms from it and those who believed in the purity of revolutionary ideals. The former supported the annexation of Libya; the latter passionately opposed it.

Among the latter was Benito Mussolini. By 1911 he had achieved a certain standing and influence in Socialist circles. He was fulfilling the promise of the recalcitrant and pugnacious boy who stabbed his schoolmate, who, in the words of a classmate, regarded education not as an opportunity but a punishment. He had spent most of the first decade of the century, in his late teens and early twenties, in restless movement—first as a workman in Switzerland, France, and Germany, where he met a mixed crowd of international revolutionaries and contributed articles to socialist papers; then doing military service, back in Italy; then as a local party worker in his home region and as an organizer in Austria's Italian-speaking province of Trentino, just north of the border; later, as secretary of the Italian Socialist party in Forlì, near his birthplace, and editor of the local paper, *The Class Struggle*. He was a violent young man, publicly applauding the work of a Socialist who had set off a bomb in a crowded theater in Buenos Aires. His associates in revolutionary socialism thought he was moved by ambition, hostility, and a deep sense of personal frustration. The eminent Russian anarchist thinker Angelica Balabanoff, who knew him in Switzerland, wrote of him long afterward, "his hatred of oppression was not that impersonal hatred of a system shared by all revolutionaries. It sprang from his own sense of indignity and frustration, his passion to assert his own ego and from a determination for personal revenge."[6] In *The Class Struggle* he incited readers to assassination, rebellion, and armed resistance against the state.

Mussolini's opposition to the Libyan war brought him a wide reputation. He denounced Italy's imperialism, its "violation of the homeland of others in order to extend to it her own pauperism,"[7] in such persuasive and intemperate terms that he was sentenced briefly to jail. He became a national figure and a martyr, and his spirited assault on colonialism won him the reverence of Socialists throughout the country. At a banquet given to celebrate his release from prison, a veteran party leader said, "From today you Benito are not only the representative of the Romagna Socialists but the *duce* (leader) of all revolutionary Socialists in Italy."[8]

The Italian Socialist party being split, Mussolini became an important man in the anti-war faction, which was the larger. He was preaching violent revolution, abolition of monarchy, aristocracy, church, and private property, scrupulous avoidance of all collaboration with the state, undying opposition to colonialism and war. In recognition of his passion, his martyrdom, and his persuasive oratory, he was made editor of the party's national paper, *Avanti* (*Forward*).

Neither the party nor the paper was large enough to have much effect on the nation as a whole or on the policies of the government. But a new and potent leader of the Left had appeared, at precisely the moment when nationalists were growing in numbers and were undertaking more systematic attacks on the liberalism represented by the government of Giolitti. Two extremisms were now in vigorous existence. The events of the next few years were to bring them together in the synthesis foreshadowed by Enrico Corradini.

Italy had been, since the early 1880s, the ally of Austria and Germany, but since the disappointing attitude of its allies at the time of Adowa, enthusiasm for the alliance had progressively dwindled. When, in 1914, European war broke out, with Austria and Germany aligned against Britain, France, and Russia, Italy proclaimed its neutrality, abandoning (without violating the letter of the alliance) its allies.

Neutrality was, however, embarrassing and delicate. In an age when many people equated military action with proof of national vigor and dignity, inaction was judged by many to be humiliating. More cogently, the defeat of one set of allies in the war would provide booty to be distributed among the other. Since the booty that Italy wanted was possessed by Austria, since it looked as if Italian participation might be enough to weigh the balance decisively, and since respectable Italian opinion sided instinctively with the defenders of democracy and international respectability against retrograde empires in central Europe, there was strong pressure from certain segments of the Italian nation to join the French and British. The pressures came also from outside. There was a flurry of bribery, and France, pursuing a policy it had followed for centuries, devoted its effort to sedulous cultivation of the extremely venal Italian press.

In the meantime Mussolini had begun to lose some of his influence. The Left had been overbold after Libya. Indeed, the government had faced and defeated something approaching a revolution, incited chiefly by Mussolini. Outbreaks leading to several deaths and the calling of a general strike were sponsored by his extremist group. It was partly because the revolutionaries were alarmed by the tendency of moderate

Socialists to participate in politics and to see hope for peaceful change in the granting of a democratic franchise, which Giolitti had achieved three years earlier. Political democracy, the revolutionaries thought, was a danger and a delusion. "Italian democracy can never be sufficiently combated," Mussolini said.[9] But the general strike was short-lived, and Mussolini found himself further separated from the mass of moderate Socialists. He was still editor of *Avanti* and his standing was still high with the extremists, but his position was relatively isolated after the spring of 1914. If he were to become a *duce* of anything except a rebellious faction, he must place himself at the head of a more popular cause. The war gave him his chance.

During the fall of 1914 the debate on Italian policy toward the war obscured almost all domestic issues. Pro-French opinion was developing rapidly, especially on the moderate Left. But the extreme Right was also in favor of intervention, for quite opposite motives: their admiration for fighting as a matter of principle and their lust for the "unredeemed" provinces, areas of neighboring Austria-Hungary inhabited by people of Italian language and culture. As one historian of modern Italy has written, "What they—the nationalists—wanted was war, on whose side mattered little: war not for ideals or sentiments but 'in order to be great.'"[10]

In November of 1914 Mussolini came out for intervention, after initially adopting a passionate opposition to it. It meant a break with the revolutionaries he had effectively led—he was obliged to resign his editorship of *Avanti*. He was expelled from the Socialist party. But he did not retreat from revolutionary and proletariat socialism. He saw revolution and socialism and the prosperity of the common man as the very function of fighting. "He who has steel, has bread," he wrote, and, "Revolution is an idea that has found bayonets."[11] He immediately launched a new paper, *Il Popolo d'Italia* (*The People of Italy*). He began to organize a prowar revolutionary socialist group and then united it with an existing syndicalist group, the Fasci di Azione Rivoluzionaria (Unions of Revolutionary Action). The synthesis of Corradini was approaching completion.

It was widely believed at the time and later that Mussolini's conversion was due to French bribes, provided by the government of Paris through the intermediary of patriotic French socialists. There is strong evidence to support the theory, at least to the extent that the financial backing for *Il Popolo d'Italia* came from France.[12] In any case, the conversion from resolute pacificism to passionate interventionism is entirely consistent both with the turbulent character of the Italian revolutionary spirit, whether on left or right, and with the no less turbulent character of Mussolini himself. He loathed inaction and thirsted for leadership. He had never been in the least troubled by inconsistency; people who knew him said that he often reversed his views completely in the course of a single sentence. Now his own temperament and his great journalistic and oratorical skill blended with opportunity—the European war, the fashion for glory, the insecurity of Italian national pride, the strong revolutionary tradition, the hatred of privilege, the highly publicized shabbiness of Italian liberal institutions, the Nietzschean lusts of D'Annunzio, the habituation to strong-man rule, the opportunities offered by French bribes—to give him a future.

In May of 1915—"the radiant May," as the interventionists called it—Italy declared war on its ally Austria-Hungary and shortly afterward Mussolini took leave from his editorship to become a non-commissioned officer. He remained in the army two years and was released from it, after recovering from serious war injuries, in August 1917, when he returned to *Il Popolo d'Italia*. By then, military and national catastrophe was approaching.

The Italians had entered the war under serious handicaps. The army was large, but it was poorly equipped and on the whole badly officered. The frontier with Austria provided overwhelming advantages to the enemy; it ran through the high Alps and hills near the sea, whose crests were controlled by Austria. Both for offense and defense, the Italians were very unfavorably placed. Their economy and finances, never particularly strong, were incompletely mobilized for war. Worst of all, their population and even their government had been deeply divided, and the neutralists—heterogeneous elements including some Catholics, Socialists, and Liberals who opposed the war—were almost certainly in a majority. But the government thought that if it waited too long Italy would be cheated of the spoils that both sides were bribing it with. Like most people, the ministers expected the war to be over soon. But it was not, and two and a half years after Italy entered it and failed in all efforts to break the Austrian lines, the Austrians with German help launched an offensive that led to a catastrophic Italian defeat, called Caporetto, in October 1917. The enemy poured down the

Alps and across the plains of Venetia. Italy held out at the Piave, though barely, until the collapse of its enemies permitted it a final token victory over Austria-Hungary in October 1918, as that empire was sinking into disorder and disintegration.

It might be supposed that the supreme tragedy and humiliation of Caporetto and its aftermath would have served to discredit interventionists like Mussolini who had brayed that participation in the war would test Italy's nationhood and bring its warriors to glory and its boundaries to imperial greatness. In fact, the national disaster had the opposite effect. Defeat steeled Italian national consciousness as victory would not have done, and it greatly aggravated the essential and elementary problem that Mussolini embodied in so pronounced a fashion: the need to identify national with personal success converted Caporetto, for a large part of the nation, as it had converted distant Adowa for a small part of it, into a personal insult to be avenged.

All this was further aggravated by the peace settlement. The attempts to lure Italy into war by promising it other peoples' territory had whetted Italian appetites, and in the period between the "radiant May" and Caporetto the appetite had grown larger still. There had been extensive negotiations with the Allies, Britain and France, and while the arrangements arrived at remained secret, something was known, more suspected, and much more hoped about the prospective fruits of victory. The more voracious Italians hoped to receive, in Europe, the unredeemed provinces in Austria and a protectorate over Albania. In Asia they expected large slices of Turkish territory, including the town of Smyrna, the principal seaport of Asia Minor and largely inhabited by Greeks; and in Africa, substantial portions of former German colonial territory as well as some French and British holdings (notably French Somaliland, which lay between Eritrea and Italian Somaliland) and a free hand in Ethiopia.

These were enormous demands, exceeding even what the Allies had agreed to in the period when they were still hoping that Italian military efforts might prove helpful in defeating Austria and Germany. Italy's disaster had the natural effect of making the Allies less generous and Italy's competitors, like Serbia and Greece, less acquiescent in the sacrifice of territory—like Dalmatia or Smyrna—which they also wanted. But it made some Italians hungrier than ever. The very cost of defeat— amounting to something over half a million dead and another half million disabled—gave Italy, in the eyes of some Italians, the rights of a martyr. What had seemed before an empire to be gloriously won was now regarded as a consolation prize.

The most important personage at the Peace Conference was the President of the United States, whose forces had in the end turned the stalemate into German and Austrian defeat. And Woodrow Wilson, not bound by the secret concessions earlier made to Italy, intensely disliked them. He fought the Italian claims all the way, and while Italy in the end got a part of the Austrian territory it wanted and a rather speculative claim on parts of Turkish territory, it received nothing else. The demand for Ethiopia and other African territories was disregarded. Insult was added to injury, and a sense of national outrage spread. It spread most widely in two groups, the old exuberant nationalists like D'Annunzio and the young veterans, especially the heroic daredevils who had staffed the elite units, the *arditi* in the army, and the submarine-chasers and air force pilots.

Ardor and outrage did not characterize by any means the entire Italian population. Larger parts of it reacted in other ways: with melancholy and despair; with alarm about the future, particularly the economic future; with angry rejection of the whole war effort and the national idea; with demands for social justice and an end to private property. There had been, even before Caporetto, a wide seam of defeatism, and many defeatists tended to reject the whole existing order that had led them into the horrible, bloody mess, and with it the new capitalism that had flourished with wartime industrial expansion. The war had produced inflation, which had lowered real wages, brought grief to the peasantry, and shaken the position of the bourgeoisie. There was, in short, an ample supply of combustible materials, and an important part of the population was in revolt against the social order.

Mussolini and the capable followers who began to assemble around him as the war ended succeeded, in subtle and complicated ways, in exploiting both international humiliation and domestic misery. His expulsion from the Socialist party in 1914 had been accompanied by much bitterness and strong language. Mussolini continued to call himself a Socialist, but his rancor against his former colleagues was ardently aroused. It was fortified by the Socialist association with defeatism, the Socialists' encouragement of harassing strikes, disaffection in the army, and calls for negotiated peace, and, most particularly, by the support of many Socialists for the Russian Bolshevik Revolution, which had very nearly wrecked the whole Allied war effort and had strengthened the Germans and Austrians in their war against Italy by freeing forces that had been tied up on the eastern front. The Mussolini of 1919 was still rantingly leftist, but he was even more rantingly anti-Bolshevik and hostile to the Italian Socialist party. In March 1919 he reactivated his old Unions of Revolutionary Action under a new name, the Unions for Combat (Fasci di Combattimenti), consisting mainly of veterans. At first, the only coherent program was for *action* of an undefined sort and for larger benefits for veterans and their families. A program was not drawn up until June. It was conventionally, violently leftist. The demands were specific and along the lines of most advanced socialist demands in Europe at the time—abolition of the aristocratic Senate, woman suffrage, workers' participation in the direction of industry, wider welfare measures, confiscation of war profits, confiscation of the property of religious orders, a peaceful and constructive foreign policy.

The program might have belonged to the Socialists, but the language of the movement was flamingly nationalistic and anti-socialist. It lacked coherence, to the point where nobody could have any clear view of what the Fascisti wanted. And this condition reflected what was already amply clear and was to become much clearer—the extreme flexibility of the movement's most effective publicist. It came as little surprise to anyone when, in the parliamentary elections held in November 1919, Fasci di Combattimenti failed to win a single seat, while the Socialists did well.

But events conspired to alter this situation. The outlines of a more persuasive program, suitably novel and imaginative, were provided to the Fascisti; and the times began to run in courses where ambiguity and incoherence were positively advantageous.

The program, or at least the general atmosphere of a program, was provided by D'Annunzio. In August 1919, at the head of a force of freebooters, he seized the city of Fiume, which lay east of Trieste, in former Austrian territory. It was largely inhabited by South Slavs and claimed by the new state of Yugoslavia and was at the moment being administered by an international expeditionary force. D'Annunzio set up, for more than a year, a regime that foreshadowed, in its paraphernalia and its methods, Mussolini's Fascist Italy. D'Annunzio coupled terrorism and a police state with an enormous and picturesque panoply of black velvet uniforms, black fezzes, and public ceremonials. He borrowed nineteenth-century Catholic ideas of society organized on the basis of corporations, embodying group interests and responsibilities and thus eliminating the struggle between proletariat and bourgeoisie. The corporations were to represent the principal occupations and professions. He appealed in grandiose terms to the spirit of youth.

D'Annunzio was eventually driven out by the Italian navy, and Fiume was set up as a free city. Mussolini, although he had ardently backed the adventure in the beginning, disavowed it when its futility became progressively more evident, and he said—what must have embarrassed him later—that the Italians were in no mood for wild nationalistic adventures. Some of the more ardent *fascisti* urged a national insurrection to support D'Annunzio but Mussolini, reasonably enough, said that such a venture would be unrealistic. But despite this tempering the wind to the shorn lamb, Fiume had given him something like a model. Terrorism, panoply, corporations, appeals to youth, freebooting, and extreme chauvinism were to be the essential nature of Mussolini's operation thereafter.

The events of 1920 and 1921 justified the ambiguity of the Fascists. They appeared sometimes revolutionary but invariably anti-socialist, and they were organized into paramilitary squadrons which were in a position to fight the Socialists. At the same time the Socialists were being seized with ever greater revolutionary ardor. Strikes proliferated, factories were seized, mass demonstrations became endemic as a postwar depression worsened the disillusionment and despair produced by the war itself. The government became more unstable than ever; in the face of crises, ministries were short-lived and ministers more and more mediocre.

The *squadristi*, the military arm of what was now being called *fascismo*, engaged in counterdemonstrations, and under the leadership of the extremely able Italo Balbo they began a series of municipal coups d'état, in which city governments were seized and anti-socialist measures enacted; the cities were then returned to their impotent legal rulers. Something approaching chaos was developing. At this point, with the road to power opening, Mussolini prudently began to retrench, to exploit the desperate alarm of the authorities and the privileged classes. Progressively he abandoned republicanism (the royal House of Savoy was publicly conceded to symbolize the nation), anti-clericalism (the Church was said to represent the Italian cultural tradition and to be the heir of the imperial ideals of ancient Rome), and opposition to capitalism ("the true history of capitalism," he said, "is just beginning"). In the parliamentary elections of May 1921 he made quiet political deals with the government parties, which precisely violated the nihilist and revolutionary bombast of the *fascisti* but enabled him to secure seats in the Chamber for himself and thirty-four Fascist colleagues. He welcomed into the movement and the *squadristi* great numbers of peasants and lower middle-class people who saw in Fascism a defense, which the government could not offer, against socialism and who drowned the old core of ex-syndicalist leftists. By the summer of 1922 Fascism had several million adherents; it had won elections; it had the name and organization of a national political party; it possessed a powerful private army; lavish contributions to its treasury were flowing in from bankers and industrialists; and it now commanded the uneasy tolerance of some distraught politicians and army officers, some hierarchs of the Church, and of many of the privileged classes. Of its early character nothing much was left except a rejection of legal methods and a fiery dedication to the idea of national greatness.

The seizure of power had already begun. The authority of the state was crumbling. A long cabinet crisis in July had demonstrated the inability of the democratic parties to collaborate in an anti-Fascist front, and the Socialists, torn now by division between moderates and Communists, were disintegrating. More towns were being occupied and held by Fascists, who seized the government offices, burned Socialist and labor union headquarters, and established what amounted in many places to a rival government. In October the Fascist Party Congress met at Naples, and plans were formulated for a "March on Rome," an insurrection in the nation along lines already practiced in the provincial towns. The March began on October 26, 1922, with the mobilization of local parties and the departure of large numbers of party members for Rome, mostly by ordinary trains.

The foundering government of democratic Italy was at the moment in the hands of an honest, able, modest, desperate politician named Luigi Facta. Having tried repeatedly both to resign and to organize some strong parliamentary coalition, having negotiated vainly with everybody including the Fascists themselves, he made ready to proclaim a stage of siege and belatedly to outlaw the movement which was both a political party and an army. The first stages of this policy were indeed undertaken, and with unflawed success. Everywhere, the armed forces proved loyal, contrary to Facta's apprehensions, and in many places the Fascists abandoned their control of towns without resistance. But on October 28 the king of Italy, Victor Emmanuel III, refused his prime minister's request for his signature on the orders for the state of siege and Facta resigned. That afternoon, the king invited Mussolini to form a government.

The king had evidently been moved by fears of civil war, by doubts about the reliability of his own army, by fear of a coup by his ambitious and pro-Fascist cousin, the duke of Aosta, and perhaps most of all by his cautious, timid temperament. He was a man of very limited ability and even more limited horizons who disliked responsibility and craved serenity. He was, however, neither unprincipled nor compliant, and he was not sympathetic to Mussolini and the Fascists personally. He seems to have regarded them as crude and dangerous vulgarians, but he believed that they represented so large and vigorous a section of Italian opinion that it was possible neither to disregard nor to dissolve them. He appointed Mussolini prime minister as the least of evils, in the belief that placing him in a position of responsibility by legal means might disarm the more violent and threatening manifestations of the Fascist movement.

Victor Emmanuel was not alone. The terrors of the age and the outward weakness of liberal democracy blinded many to the emptiness of Mussolini's erratic promises. George Bernard Shaw, the most imaginative of British socialists, spoke for a world of confusion when he wrote, "Signor Mussolini, banking on his belief that the people, out of all patience with the delays, obstructions, evasions, and hypocrisies of endless talking, *fainéant* parliaments, wanted not liberty (which he described as a putrefying corpse) but hard work, hard discipline, and positive and rapid state activity; in short real government threw constitutionalism to the winds and became at once an acknowledged and irrepressible dictator."[13]

The opposition was hounded and persecuted until gradually most of the non-Fascist politicians, whether they had openly opposed the regime or grudgingly accepted it, were driven into silence or exile. By the end of the year 1924 the opposition press had been shut down, subversive groups and individuals were being imprisoned and murdered, non-Fascist local governments were being forcibly ousted, and the Chamber of Deputies had become a convention of Fascists. In the course of the next years, all political parties except the Fascist were outlawed, all labor unions except the Fascist syndicates dissolved, and strict censorship and a secret police established. The Fascist party was given official status, and its membership permeated the state service. Fascism began to penetrate and control the courts and the educational system. The monarchy was reduced to nullity, the Senate abolished, and an elaborate blueprint, inspired by D'Annunzio's Fiume model, for the organization of society into corporations representing occupations had been drawn up. The control of the nation by the party, and of the party by its Duce, had been achieved.

The regime was, to a remarkable extent, the reflection of Mussolini and his personality. He was, in some respects, unique. But he was also an example of a gifted but peculiar personality moved by powerful drives over which he evidently had no control, whose very intensity enabled him to communicate an inspiring sense of urgency and passion to his listeners and readers. And he was also in part a symbol of his times, a working-class person led to unconscionable ambition by the evils of a class-ridden society, badly educated, thrown up by the powerful, elemental engines of a democracy whose power surpassed its maturity. It was a literate public that made his career possible: his forum was the press. He was not the first demagogue to become a tyrant, but he was the first journalist to become an autocrat. Luigi Barzini, a newspaperman who later became the author of a brilliant book on Italy, wrote, "The very qualities that made him an excellent rabble-rousing editor made him a disastrous statesman."[14]

The "man on horseback" might be more truly described as an "editor on a throne." He spoke the language of the workers, but his driving motive seems to have been to differentiate himself from them; for he was also a psychopath on a throne. He displayed all the classic symptoms, which grew more noticeable as he aged. He was impulsive, bigoted, ill-informed. He liked to dress up in costume. He liked to have his own way, to insult the proud and the mighty. He liked pageantry and loathed detail. He was almost childishly incapable of rational analysis, or of dealing with figures, or of accepting unwelcome facts. He postured and blustered and acted out assorted roles for which he was ill-suited, from farm worker to world statesman. It was interesting and important that the people who most consistently despised him and penetrated his sham were foreign correspondents. They understood him as a cheap polemicist translated to power.

Power he possessed, and in much more than a formal political sense. He had overpowering magnetism. Nothing else could explain the spell he cast or the fact that his very numerous and devoted admirers could put up with him. But he was never content with any power or accomplishment he attained, as he could never tolerate the attainments of others. Still, the power of his unfulfillable personal needs translated itself into the power to please, to awe, to impress. He commanded the respect of the most improbable victims and the adoration of many.

He charmed and fooled people as worldly and experienced as Austen Chamberlain, the British foreign secretary, who judged him a patriot and "the simplest and most sincere of men . . . I trust his word when given."[15] One of his least restrained admirers was the American ambassador at Rome, Richard Washburn Child, an old-line Progressive who ardently supported both Roosevelts. A journalist of some eminence, he had been a speech-writer for President Harding, who sent him to Rome. After his return in 1924 he became a chief apologist in the United States for Italian Fascism. He preached that it was a new and inspiring form of democracy and so instructed the readers of such magazines as *The Saturday Evening Post*. In 1928 he wrote, "The Duce is now the greatest figure of this sphere and time. No man will exhibit dimensions of greatness equal to those of Mussolini."* Other American Progressives, Lincoln Steffens and Herbert Croly, editor of *The New Republic*, publicly applauded the Fascist regime. The radical, Stark Young, said Mussolini had "saved Italy."[16] Most of the other American leftist periodicals, like *New Masses*, *The Communist*, and *The Liberator*, simply disregarded Fascism most of the time, and few were critical of it in the 1920s.

Winston Churchill said in 1927 that he "could not help being charmed by Mussolini's gentle and simple bearing," and he had observed to him that "if I had been an Italian I am sure I would have been wholeheartedly with you. . . . Your movement has rendered a

* Child, Foreword to Mussolini's *Autobiography*, p. 10. It is thought that Child may have written, or rewritten, a good deal of this work himself. It never appeared in Italy.

1. *The steles of Axum, strange and vast monoliths, are the chief surviving monuments of an ancient and brilliant civilization. They mark the imposing continuity, partly historical and partly legendary, of the Ethiopian state. Here the queen of Sheba is believed to have reigned, and here the rulers of Ethiopia, including Haile Selassie, have been crowned.*

2. *The Emperor Theodore, whose powerful rule consolidated the decaying Ethiopian empire in the middle of the nineteenth century and whose subsequent madness almost destroyed it. Here he threatens a British missionary, Henry Stern. Stern was not in fact shot, but he was flogged and imprisoned for impertinence. Such incontinent behavior by Theodore alienated his own people, led to invasion by a British army, and ended in the emperor's suicide.*

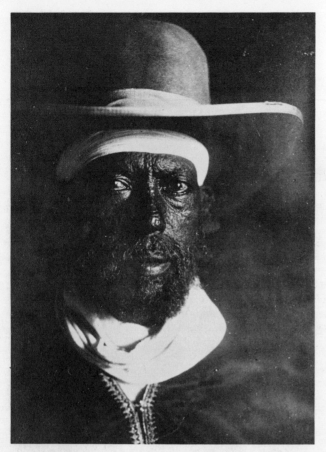

3. Menelek II came to the throne in 1889. He was a man of stupendous powers: he vastly expanded Ethiopia's boundaries, he defeated the Italians, he began the huge task of building a modern state. His intelligence and character, universally recognized by contemporaries, are discernible in the photograph. So are his habits of dress which, to Europeans, evidenced a grotesque mixture of modern methods with barbaric traditions and habits.

4. Menelek II began to build a modern state, but its trappings were traditional and impressed Europeans as barbaric. It was an odd reaction for Englishmen, familiar with Beefeaters and the ermine of English peers. Here is the prime minister, in the last years of Menelek's reign, in the early 1900s, with his gorgeous suite.

5. Harar was, in 1935, the second city of Ethiopia. It had been for centuries the seat of a Moslem sultanate, more or less independent, which was annexed to Ethiopia in the later nineteenth century. Its aspect and culture are Arab rather than African. Its city walls, its mosques and gardens have a charm that recalls Asia and reflects the extraordinary diversity of modern Ethiopia.

6. Haile Selassie I, like his predecessor Menelek, combined a powerful determination to impress the world with Ethiopia's modernity and western forms and reforms with a fervent dedication to traditional Ethiopian culture. Here, in a coronation portrait, he wears the crown made for him, which represents the splendor and antiquity of his empire's past.

7. The western aspirations, or façade, of Haile Selassie's ceremonials as illustrated in his coronation coach. The coach was built for the German emperors in the nineteenth century and purchased in 1930 from the government of the German republic.

8. Four years after Haile Selassie's coronation, Hitler and Mussolini met for the first time in Venice. They got on indifferently. Hitler disliked the Italians, and Mussolini disliked Hitler. But there was an outward show of solidarity that foreshadowed the ultimate alliance of two nations as deeply divided by historical memories, cultural values, interests, and temperaments as any in Europe and united uneasily by a vague ideological affinity, by common enmities and mutual dependence.

service to the whole world . . . provided the necessary antidote to the Russian poison." The remark, not uncharacteristic of Churchill's rather wholesale grandiloquence, was an important illustration of Fascism's most potent source of appeal; it was taken to represent a wholesomely anti-Communist alternative to foundering constitutional government. But the success of its anti-communism included what Churchill may have seen as a convenient ornament and did not understand as a basic dynamic: an intense mystique of aggressive nationalism.

Mussolini made a favorable impression on King George V of Great Britain, who after a state visit in the early days of Fascism, spoke of Italy as being "under the wise guidance of a strong statesman."[17] Intellectuals were impressed. More conventional men than Bernard Shaw admired him. Nicholas Murray Butler, the pontifical president of Columbia University, did, and so, to the point of treason, did Ezra Pound. Emil Ludwig, the liberal German writer, was convinced he was a great man. He had, generally speaking, a good press abroad; newspaper proprietors tended to admire him; some, like Lord Beaverbrook of Britain and Adolph Ochs of the *New York Times*, extravagantly. Sir Philip Gibbs, the eminent author, informed readers of the *New York Times* about Mussolini's "acute, subtle and far-seeing mind."[18]

His success in hypnotizing so many people was the product of role-acting and play-producing; his skill as actor and director complemented the ranting intensity that accounted for his success with parts of the Italian public. He could appear on occasion as a simple but forceful man, on others as a judicious statesman, sometimes as a demigod. In all roles he made a strong impression, often favorable and much heightened by his skill at stage setting. He was expert at photographic effects. Like many short men with strong wills to dominate, he was adept at giving an impression of height and power. Photographers became stooped through gratifying his wish to be pictured from below, in poses that exaggerated his height, dramatized his outthrust chin, and put his small body into proportion with his large head. He was eminently good newsreel material in an era when movies were preceded by newsreels. He appeared in them, over two decades, more often than any other public figure of his time—orating from the balcony of the Palazzo Venezia, where he stood on a concealed pedestal, strutting past a military review, dedicating a monu-

ment, fondling infants, gorgeously costumed, potently purveying whatever trait of personality became the occasion.

He could disgust and repel as well as charm and persuade. Among
journalists, the reactions of Ernest Hemingway were indicative of both
Mussolini's flexible capacity to please and the percipience of his fellow
professionals. Hemingway, a working journalist as well as a rising
writer of fiction, first interviewed him in Milan in 1922 and, like so
many English-speaking visitors, found him a simple and sincere man,
not at all the arrogant monster his enemies had pictured him. But
two years later, at Lausanne, Hemingway saw him not in a personal
interview but as a public figure in an international conference and
immediately revised his view; the dictator was a swaggering ruffian,
unsure of himself and blustering to conceal his uncertainty; his black
shirt and white spats were unholy sartorial symbols of impossibly
combined poses of revolutionary Strong Man and inept traditional
diplomat.[19] Austen Chamberlain found the dictator the simplest and
most sincere of men, but Lord Curzon, Chamberlain's patrician predecessor, seems to have thought him a petty buccaneer. Prime Minister
Bonar Law thought, after meeting him, that he was a lunatic. One of
his closest collaborators, a most important contributor to Fascist success,
Cesare Rossi, whom Mussolini quite unjustly charged with responsibility for the murder of the respected Socialist leader Giacomo Matteotti,
wrote him, "Your cynicism, of which you have already given appalling
proofs, is now aggravated by your complete loss of self-control."[20]
Shaw's fellow Fabian H. G. Wells was not deceived by the trappings
of the regime that fooled so many of his compatriots; he saw that
Fascism was wrecking thought and education in Italy and all serious
and independent thinkers. A. L. Rowse, the somewhat snobbish scholar
of All Souls, shrewdly described him as "a short, stocky butcher, with a
heavy ill-shaven jowl."[21] But to most of his interviewers he seemed a
quiet man, a good listener, flatteringly well-informed (like an experienced American politician) about the stranger's background and
interests. His magnetism was granted by friend and enemy alike, and
many an enemy was sent away from an interview converted to friendship. When Walter Starkie, the Irish troubadour, was given an audience
with him, Mussolini's first words to him were, "I have heard the news
about the death of Kevin O'Higgins. I admired him." O'Higgins
was an Irish patriot who had been murdered the day before, and

whether or not Mussolini had ever heard of him before he consulted his cue cards, the effect on Starkie was overpowering. He proclaimed, "Mussolini's first words nearly made me jump, for it was as if he had been able to read my inmost thoughts. Where is the lofty Caesarism? Indeed, I met a man who not only treats me with courteous familiarity but shows a genuine interest in the affairs of my country."[22]

Mussolini's essays in foreign policy in the early years seemed to display the characteristic kaleidoscopic alternation of roles. He seemed at times to be constructively negotiating to achieve peace and international order, but he also announced that Italy must regard itself as in a state of "permanent war." In 1923 he ordered, on a small pretext, the shelling and occupation of the Greek island of Corfu and then defied in extravagant terms the efforts of the League of Nations to procure a settlement. During the tortuous negotiations that led to the Locarno Treaty, whereby an illusory but encouraging effort was made to solve the outstanding issue of European politics by an international guarantee of France's German frontier, he impertinently and irrelevantly inserted the demand that a similar guarantee be provided for Italy's Austrian frontier, only to back down in humiliation when he found that the other powers would not listen to him. At the Locarno conference he swaggered and boasted like a boy and was incontinently outraged when the foreign correspondents, appalled by the murder of Matteotti, refused to attend one of his theatrical press conferences.

There have been, as a result, deep differences of opinion among historians who have studied Italian diplomacy as well as among contemporary notables who met him. Some have seen his policies as based entirely on whim. Others have thought he was honestly trying to establish a reputation as a responsible statesman. A recent and thorough writer sees him as moved by a consistent hostility to France and by the aim of colonial expansion.[23]

In general the years of the late 1920s were an age of stability and optimism in Europe, and the opportunities, and need, for an adventurous foreign policy were minimal. The waters were sufficiently untroubled to discourage megalomaniac fishermen. In domestic affairs the first five years of the dictatorship seemed on the surface similarly encouraging. Starting a little before the middle of the decade, when Mussolini was consolidating his position, a period of economic revival leading to an international boom had begun. Mussolini was able to

boast that he had saved the lira, ended inflation, reduced unemployment, and brought economic and social stability to a society dramatically riven by hardship and conflict. In fact, all of Europe experienced
the same remission from hardship and disaster. Mussolini merely profited from an upturn in the cycle. Surprisingly, little basic change
took place; an old machine merely began to work again as international prosperity provided the necessary lubrication. In fact, the growth
of the Italian economy and Italy's gross national product proceeded
at a slower pace than those of other countries and at a pace very much
slower than that of Italy before or after Fascism. Moreover, real wages
fell. At its best, the vaunted revolution of Fascism amounted, in
economic terms, to stagnation, the product of a dictatorship that had
destroyed trade unions and frozen the control of a frightened and un-
enterprising class of conservative businessmen who sought safety, not
change. There was talk, and some performance, of spectacular public
works, of making Italy—almost wholly without known natural resources
—economically "self-sufficient." But these were emotional, not economic, accomplishments, and apart from the breaking of the power of
labor, there was no change in the economic structure.

The underlying immobility and rigidity of the Italian economy
under Fascism was to prove a matter of first-rate importance for the
world. For international depression deprived Fascism of its only real
claim to material success: as the world began to go under after 1929,
the fraudulence of Mussolini's claims to have found the secret of
prosperity were stunningly revealed, and the security of the regime
was accordingly endangered.

The Depression struck Italy with particular force because of the
very lack of resilience of its economic institutions. An elaborate façade
of innovations, the corporate state, the Fascist labor organization, and
a system of welfare benefits had been built in front of the ramshackle
edifice. Already, before the Depression, unemployment had been
mounting—from 180,000 in 1927 to 642,000 in 1930. Programs of
public works had been established to deal with it, the most important
of them being "the battle of wheat," which was essentially a large-
scale effort at land reclamation designed simultaneously to soak up
unemployment and to reduce dependence on food imports, thereby
alleviating increasingly serious trouble with Italy's international balance of payments. But public works, while in many respects useful,

cost money, and the government (whose account was already in deficit) was devoted for reasons both of doctrine and prestige to balanced budgets and a stable currency. When world depression deepened, the pressure on exports and on the currency grew stronger. Exports fell by two thirds, and emigrants' remittances and tourist spendings, both important in the balance of payments, declined comparably. There were flights of gold from the Bank of Italy. A second battle, "the battle of the lira," was launched as a sort of national crusade. It was essentially a reduction of wages designed to reduce the price of exports, to curb imports, and to eliminate the danger of inflation. The deflationary policy was in important respects successful; the value of the lira was maintained, despite expanded public works in the form now, mainly, of a navy building program. But currency values were saved at the cost of much increased taxes borne mainly by the poor (almost one half of Italian revenues came from indirect and regressive taxes, and the proportion was increasing) and by correspondingly increased bureaucratic control over the economy. By 1934 real wages were at the very least 10 per cent below the level of the bad years before Fascism.* Unemployment continued to mount as wages fell. Official figures showed that over a million people—one worker in seven—were out of work. Moreover, despite the façade of welfare benefits, unemployment relief payments were in fact very small— about forty cents a day. Eligibility was tightly restricted—no one was eligible unless he had previously contributed to unemployment insurance for eleven months, which ruled out all young people who reached working age in the Depression and all conscripts released from military service. Red tape involved in drawing benefits was formidable. Fewer than a quarter of the unemployed drew any relief at all, and those who did could not subsist on it.[24] The unemployed and their families therefore suffered greater hardship than the victims of the Depression in Britain or even Germany. It was estimated that the total relief payments in Italy were considerably less, annually, than in New York City. And the official statistics on unemployment were suspect; reliable foreign estimates placed the figure as high as two million, or more than 28 per cent of the labor force.

The inner inconsistencies of the regime were illustrated by the

* They were probably lower than in any western European country including Spain. Farm wages fell by more than 50 per cent in the early thirties.

government's response to the economic crisis. Its deflationary policies were, if harsh, theoretically defensible in terms of prevailing economic orthodoxy. But they were supplemented by another policy, much advertised, which illustrated the confusions produced by a program that was essentially a dictatorial application of old-fashioned liberal economics by a regime that was flamboyantly anti-liberal in its outward shows. Mussolini's greatest concerns were the small size of the Italian population—40,000,000—in relation to that of other great powers and a birthrate that was beginning to slow down. Deflation involved, in effect, a labor surplus; but at the same time that it practiced deflation the regime encouraged an expansion of the birthrate by strenuous propaganda and institutional measures such as a high tax on bachelors and generous benefits for large families. Mussolini himself, setting an example, produced two children of his middle years, the elder ten years younger than the youngest of his three older children. He bestowed medals on mothers of numerous families and sent telegrams to mayors and prefects urging them to do their best, both as public authorities and as individuals, to encourage procreativeness. The effect was negligible—indeed negative; the birthrate continued to slow down. But the makeshift illogic of Fascist economics was amply demonstrated.

These were in appearance the years of Mussolini's greatest political success; no overt threat as yet jeopardized the dictatorship. He had achieved a remarkable political coup in 1929 with the Lateran Treaties, which ended the long conflict between the Church and the Italian State and brought the hierarchy temporarily into active collaboration with the Fascist regime. Still, politically as well as economically, the early thirties saw ominous cracks opening in the Fascist position. Relations with France were bad, as they generally had been. Relations with Germany were bad. In 1934 Adolf Hitler visited Mussolini at Venice, and despite a certain ideological affinity and the enthusiastic public affirmations of solidarity, the two dictators got on indifferently. Mussolini regarded the Germans with deep dislike and contempt; he, who had once boasted that he was himself a barbarian, accused Hitler of barbarism.

Very little of this was known or understood abroad. Censorship propaganda, and a general admiration for the efficiency of the dictatorship persuaded foreigners that the Italian situation was much better than it was. The British Labour party newspaper, reflecting a tendency evident in some Labour circles, wrote, "The Fascist Government and the Fascist Party have a record in social legislation of which any democratic government might be proud. Even their bitterest critics and bitterest enemies admit that here Mussolini and his Ministers have done a good piece of work." In 1934 the *New York Times*, which also was inclined to admire Fascist Italy, quoted Mussolini approvingly when he declared to its correspondent, "Despite the striking increase in our population, Italian industry is absorbing its unemployed without appreciable lowering of wages as measured by their purchasing power." In every respect this statement was untrue, but the readers of the *New York Times*, many of whom notoriously regard it as authoritative, were left with the belief that Fascism had solved the economic problems that democracies were so dramatically failing to solve. The *Times* story was, indeed, positively ecstatic about the generous sacrifices made by the privileged classes of Italy to benefit the poor: "The hard times will be felt chiefly by the wealthy and middle classes, as the Fascist Party has redoubled its efforts this year to give the poorer classes a good time during the [Christmas] season."[25]

The fact was that in all essentials the standard of living in Italy was lower in 1932 than it had been in 1922; in Milan, the most economically advanced city, the consumption of meat per capita had fallen in those ten years from 38.9 kilograms to 27.[26] The Boston *Evening Transcript* on September 24, 1932, reported the reverse: "The statistics . . . show that the population . . . has more to eat than it ever had before."[27]

By 1934, then, the Fascist State was faced in all spheres, except that of party control over the instruments of domestic political power, with the threat of failure. The security of the regime was not yet compromised nor was its standing abroad, but its reputation at home was. Success—more than success, a dramatic display of achievement —was urgently needed.

Indeed, it was not only needed but expected. Mussolini had talked constantly of the virtues, and sometimes of the inevitability, of war. He had devoted much attention to the armed services. He had said that Italy "must expand or explode."[28]

The needs of Fascist Italy were to be met by political, not by economic, prescriptions. This fact may be seen as a personal response, not one demanded by public opinion or by influential supporters of Fascism. Expansion was not a policy that met with support from either economists or businessmen. Italian business, which had ardently supported Mussolini by a large majority, was not at all in favor of adventures; it wanted the comfortable stagnation that Fascism had provided in earlier days. There was no attraction for businessmen in bellicosity and certainly not in war. There is no evidence whatever to suggest, and there is much to belie, any notion that colonial expansion or international glory commended itself to Italian capitalists. They did not object to the Ethiopian adventure in its earlier phases, but they certainly did not push it; and later many of them came to dislike very much the dangers and the unsettling economic consequences that developed from it and from Mussolini's later adventures. They feared and disliked the disruption of trade patterns and of the balance of payments, and they were deeply alarmed by the budgetary deficits that international adventures involved.[29]

As Roland Sarti, a student of Fascist relations with industrialists, points out, "The industrialists were slow to grasp that in Mussolini's scale of values politics always came before economics."[30] Nor was there, before the event, any evidence of enthusiasm for adventures, colonial or otherwise, in any considerable section of Italian opinion. It is doubtful whether many ordinary people in Italy liked in advance the idea of war or were very warmly in favor of expansion. But the regime had committed itself in advance to the theory that Italian problems could be solved by a show of national greatness. Action appeared not only enticing but indispensable.

4

Incident

On the afternoon of December 5, 1934, a shot was fired—no one knows by whom—on the edge of Walwal. Walwal is not a town but rather a large green spot, watered by hundreds of springs (the name means "wells"), in the middle of the Ogaden plateau. It is surrounded by scrub-covered desert, where temperatures are usually over 100 degrees at midday and annual rainfall is rarely more than six inches. The desert is almost uninhabitable; Walwal, a few dozen acres pleasantly wooded, is emphatically an oasis in both the literal and figurative senses. It is frequented by a changing population of nomadic Somalis who roam with their cattle through the Ogaden, which stretches some eight hundred miles from the Gulf of Aden into Kenya. Walwal is about half way between the Ethiopian city of Harar to the northwest and the nearest point on the Indian Ocean, some two hundred and fifty miles from the oasis in what was in 1934 Italian Somaliland. It was the seat of a garrison, with an Italian captain in command of a hundred and fifty well-armed Somali troops. Encamped outside were about fifteen hundred Ethiopians, much less well equipped. When the shot was fired, the two forces plunged into battle. The first casualty was the ranking Ethiopian officer. The encounter lasted for twenty-four hours and cost the Ethiopians over a hundred dead, the Italian-Somali forces thirty. At the end, the Ethiopians withdrew.

It was the first blood shed in the new Italian-Ethiopian conflict; looked at from a certain viewpoint, it was the first bloodshed of World War II. From December 1934 the atmosphere of crisis in the world mounted fast and the guns were rarely silent. With Mussolini's ad-

venture in personal and national assertion began a process that re-
arranged alliances and changed minds and called forth prophets and
prophecies until peoples of places as remote as Chile and New Zealand
found themselves at war.

The initiative was Ethiopian; the Ethiopian forces had been dispatched to dislodge the Italians installed there. The oasis had its own
history and its own importance, whose interweaving with the monstrous consequences of the little battle are instructive. The petty
intricacies of nineteenth-century empire building, the habits of mind
it engendered met, head on, the age of ideology and total war.

The presence of the Italian garrison at Walwal in the autumn of
1934 was the result of the extreme sloppiness of diplomats in an
earlier age. Earlier Italo-Ethiopian agreements had defined a boundary
between Italian Somaliland and the Ethiopian empire as following a
line "one hundred and eighty miles inland from the Indian Ocean."
The territory involved an unexplored—and, it seemed, almost unex-
plorable—desert. It had never been surveyed or even looked at by
agents from either Rome or Addis Ababa. The coast line was sinuous,
which made drawing of the frontier difficult, and no one troubled to
mention whether the miles were statute or nautical miles (a nautical
mile being more usual in international intercourse and about a sixth
longer than a statute mile), but in view of the nature of the terrain
this did not seem to matter much. What mattered more was an inconsistent clause in another agreement that provided, even more
vaguely, that Italy should have a protectorate over the lands used by
the nomadic tribesmen of a number of listed sultanates far to the
southwest of Walwal.

The frontier remained unsurveyed, and only occasional, unsuccessful efforts were made to survey it. Since the speculative line was
constantly crossed and recrossed by the population, there was for practical purposes no frontier at all, a fact that emphasized the very partial
resemblance of Ethiopia to the European states that were the model
for its developing central government. On some maps, however, including all Italian maps, there appeared a clear demarcation—a perfectly straight line in the region in question—corresponding approximately to the 180-mile conception. This line passed about seventy-five
statute miles south of Walwal, leaving it well within Ethiopian terri-

tory. Even by the measure of nautical miles, Walwal was far inside. The Italians later said that Walwal's walls were habitually used by subjects of the sultan of Obadia, one of the listed sultans in the 1908 agreement; the assertion was extremely dubious, for the sultan's seat lay far to the west, but since the other criteria worked for Ethiopia, this hazier one had to be invoked.

The importance of Walwal lay entirely in its water. During the dry season, some of the Somali nomads—the only residents of the desert—depended on the wells. He who controlled the wells controlled the population, and he who controlled the population controlled the region. Anyone who was fool enough to want the southeastern Ogaden could control it by acquiring Walwal.

The reasons anyone did were complex. The Italian administrators of Somaliland wanted it mostly out of appetite for land, partly for defensive reasons, to prevent tribal invasions from the north, and partly because they seem to have hoped ultimately to bring all the Somali-inhabited regions—a vast territory—under their control. (Their successors, the Somalian government at Mogadishu, still does and periodically provokes Ethiopia for much the same reasons and in the same ways as did Italy.) The Ethiopians were concerned about the security of their empire, but for more complicated reasons as well. The country was landlocked and dependent for outlets to the sea upon the co-operation of the French (via the railway from Addis Ababa to Jibuti, in French Somaliland) and the Italians (via the trails to the Red Sea coast in Eritrea). The Ethiopians wanted very much to secure a port, and the only possible place they could hope to get it in the early 1930s was in British Somaliland, which lay between the French and Italian colonies, facing north on the horn of Africa. They hoped that it might be possible to make a deal with the British to trade a huge portion of the Ogaden south of British Somaliland for a corridor to the sea in the western part of the colony. Since the terrain was, to put it mildly, uninviting and had no population except for the nomads, this looked like a feasible project. Relations between Addis Ababa and London were at the time amicable. It had been agreed in 1931 to demarcate the frontier between Ethiopia and British Somaliland, vaguely sketched out in 1897. A joint commission had been appointed and by 1934, after slow and difficult explorations of the desert, the line had been finally drawn. The commissioners then proceeded to try to solve another problem, raised by the mere fact of establishing a frontier in regions whose peoples had no idea of what one was supposed to mean. The grazing and watering places of the nomads lay on both sides of it, and the distant rulers at London and Addis Ababa had agreed to protect the interests of the inhabitants. The commissions set out to do so and found that the principal watering place for the nomads from British Somaliland was Walwal.

It was the prospect of an attractive bargain to secure a seaport that led the Ethiopians at this point to concern themselves with Walwal; unless their dominion over the region was clearly established, they could not give it away. The importance of Walwal to British subjects in Somaliland gave the British government an interest in it.

But the Italians had stolen a march. In 1926, when the Ethiopian government had little interest in what went on in its wild and distant borderlands, the governor of Italian Somaliland had quietly begun to send *dubats* into the Ogaden. *Dubats* were Somali tribesmen, more or less armed by the Italians and more or less acting as their agents. They were operating in their native territory; they took no cognizance of frontiers, demarcated or otherwise. When they encamped in an oasis, it could not be construed as being under Italian occupation. But in 1930 a *dubat* military post, small but permanent, was established at Walwal, and a few Italian soldiers were sent there. The Ethiopians responded at first only half-heartedly to these sporadic incursions. An expeditionary force from Harar, the nearest seat of Ethiopian power, two hundred and fifty miles away, forced the *dubats* from a few watering spots and cleared some tracks. It approached Walwal but withdrew, apparently because of the rigors of the terrain and the effects of disease. There was no official discussion of the matter, which was left almost entirely to local leaders at Harar, and no Ethiopian protests were made to Rome. The whole Italian incursion was subclinical.

But it gradually hardened into annexation. In 1932 the governor at Mogadishu announced that no one would be allowed to use the Walwal wells without Italian permission. There was some small build-up of Italian-commanded forces at the wells and in neighboring places. The Ethiopians, increasingly alarmed and also interested in the possible deal with the British, now determined to assert their sovereignty in territory which, with every reason, they regarded as legally theirs. An Ethiopian force started south from Harar. On November 20, 1934, at Ado, twenty miles north of Walwal, it met the British-Ethiopian Boundary and Grazing Commission, the British members of which were two officers named Clifford and Curle, engaged in investigating the habits and paths of migrant Somali tribes. The whole party proceeded on toward Walwal.

The situation—with its intricate formalities, its concern with jurisdictions and boundaries and rights under international law—takes on an air of dreamlike unreality as the little bands of agents of far-away governments proceed through the desert: the irresistible power of Europe's tradition extending itself into a universe where none of it connected with external reality.

One of the British officers, A. T. Curle, has left a detailed account of the incident that illuminates these points and many others: the stoical disinterestedness of the British servants of empire, with their high regard for fact and impartial reporting, qualities that had built and preserved that empire; the strange collaboration of Ethiopian and British; the character of the Ethiopian armed forces; the impoliteness of the Italians; the formality with which the participants approached this otherworldly encounter. As a revelation of what happened at Walwal, of what had been happening for centuries when Europeans ventured in strange lands, and of the seemingly trivial episode that eventually shook the world, Colonel Curle's narrative is a remarkable document. "The emperor," he wrote,

> was very anxious that the Commission should be a success. The country had just joined the League of Nations and was starting to feel its feet. He thought that if he could get the boundary with British Somaliland fixed with the British and demarcated and the grazing rights question settled it would not only look well to the world but augur well for the settlement of his other frontiers, especially that of Somalia which was so vaguely defined and involved tribal problems.
>
> The seemingly large escort which accompanied the Commission to the Ogaden was partly for the reasons mentioned above but also for prestige reasons. Since early in 1930 Italian propaganda had been very active not only amongst Ethiopian subject tribes living in the region of the frontier but also with the Ogaden well in Ethiopia. Chiefs and influential men were given clothes and rifles and entertained to visits to Mogadishu and shown the military might of an Italian Colony of that epoch. It was hoped that an Ethiopian display of force might have an effect of counteracting

the strong Italian propaganda. I saw much of this propaganda as I travelled in the Ogaden in 1930 and was on good terms with many of the local chiefs.

The escort amounted to some 600 men—these were not made up of soldiers in the European sense but of mixed elements. They were supplied with a rifle usually a Fusil Gras but had to provide their own ammunition which often did not fit the rifle and was sometimes without a charge of powder. They were not in uniform and many had paid substitutes to do duty for them. In some cases the quota had been filled with the unruly youths who caused trouble in their villages. Donkeys and a motley crowd of servants and small boys came with them. There was nothing to carry water in and no arrangements for food beyond meat on the hoof. No motor transport, no medical service at all.

The British Section of the Commission started out with their motor lorries by narrow bush tracks on November 8th, 1934, (and) joined the Ethiopian Section at Gurati on 17th November. The Commission went to Walwal on 23rd November and found the Escort camped on the West of the track just within site of the Italian Post but on the edge of the Well area. The Ethiopian Section wanted to camp near some of the wells just East of the track and accordingly chased the Italian Banda who were about, three hundred yards into the bush and so secured two wells. I watched the show from the top of a lorry. Only the immediate escort of the Ethiopian Section took part—some twenty or thirty men but the area seemed full of armed men chasing each other—no one let off a shot but the Banda seemed surprised and took to their heels. The Ethiopian escort placed armed men in a line around the well area they had secured and towards evening Italian Banda took up a position opposite them. The British camped by one of the wells between two Ethiopian groups and at the request of the Ethiopians hoisted their flag.

The next morning Captain Cimmaruta arrived at the British Commission camp and at his suggestion to avoid any incidents it was agreed that the lines of troops should remain where they were. The Commission with Cimmaruta then walked round the lines. Some of the men had already dug in. In places the lines were about 20 yards apart. A warm discussion started and Cimmaruta wished to control all the wells—while we were arguing about this on the ground two light Italian aircraft appeared from the direction of Mogadishu and dived low on the Commission and one of the machines with the gunner training his automatic weapon on the Commission. Another flew round the British part of the camp and then made a dive towards the flag.

The Senior British Commissioner, Lt.-Col. Clifford, was very angry at what was clearly a deliberate provocation by the Italian authorities and at once told Capitano Cimmaruta that in order to reduce the tension and lessen the chances of further provocation and as a protest against the hostile demonstration by Italian aircraft he would withdraw the British Section Camp. The Ethiopian Section followed his example and the Commission moved to Ado on 25th November. The Ethiopian escort remained at Walwal . . . Their reason for staying was stated to be that a withdrawal in the face of provocation would have a most unsettling effect on the Ethiopian prestige with the local Somalis and might even lead to an uprising.

The lines of soldiery remained in position and dug in further.

The Ethiopians were firmly convinced that Walwal was theirs and would accept no favours and could only ask Cimmaruta what he was doing on Ethiopian territory. He maintained that Walwal was Italian and that he was condescending in allowing the Ethiopians to be there at all.

He created a very bad impression by his rudeness to the Ethiopians, referring to the soldiers as "shifta" and addressing letters to high Officials and using the word "voi." He refused to address letters to the Commission even when it was pointed out that we were there as a Commission not as individual nationalities. He tried to laugh off the aerial display as mere joie-de-vivre but that effort to describe such a very provocative action failed and he walked off in a rage having made of himself, to use an Italian expression, a bruta figura.

I was present the whole time during the discussions and Cimmaruta's rudeness and final withdrawal in a towering rage left a very bad impression. The Ethiopians were very correct and dignified.

The Commission remained at Ado collecting evidence of the frequentation of the area by British Protected Tribes.

I had just gone to sleep in my tent at about 11 pm . . . 5th December, when I was woken up by Ato Lorenzo Taezaz who told me that at 3 pm that afternoon fighting had broken out at Walwal. I spent all that night in the tent of the Ethiopian Commissioner listening to reports as they came in. The next day the Commission withdrew to Gurati and gave what help it could to the retreating Ethiopian forces.

The Ethiopian casualties were 107 killed and 45 wounded while the Banda lost 30 killed.

From the British and Ethiopian view point there is one outstanding factor which has never been explained. Did the Italian authorities at this juncture wish to have a show down with the

Ethiopians over Walwal in the light of their plans for the invasion
of Ethiopia later which must have been formulated by then?

My own personal opinion is that the whole incident, the ob-
struction by the Banda, the fighting which I did not see, were deliberate actions by the Italian authorities. No official wished to be
responsible and the constant passing backwards and forwards of
requests for instructions resulted in the unfortunate officer on the
spot having to create the incident and very clumsily it was too. I
heard a story in Italy after the war from an Italian friend I was staying with who told me that Marshal Graziani said of the authorities
in Somalia that "They could not even create an incident properly."[1]

It seems doubtful that Colonel Curle was right. The Italians were
presumably not averse to incidents, but the time was not yet ripe for
an incident to set off the war. Walwal may well have been the product
of a climate of opinion, not of a plan. The whole business, seen almost
forty years later, was dusty and archaic, a chapter from a nineteenth-
century romance of empire building and on the face of it an inconclusive one. It was a symptom of fluidity in a region whose inhabitants
had no real allegiance to a state, where politics was still almost indistinguishable from exploration, and where distant governments, with
much larger problems on their hands, had no policies or instructions
for their remote agents. But once it had happened, the incident became a large rock dropped in the pond of twentieth-century world
affairs.

The Italian government had been planning action against Ethiopia, for reasons that had nothing whatever to do with the garrison at
Walwal. But now an incident too suitable to be disregarded had been
presented, and it was to be used as a pretext. Pietro Badoglio, the
Italian chief of staff, although at the time opposed to the whole venture, tried afterward to justify the war on the grounds of Walwal. For
some reason, it has always seemed more respectable to go to war in
response to a minor insult than because of deep national motives, and
Badoglio wrote later that Walwal was decisive in transferring "the
problem . . . from the diplomatic to the military field. It was understood that the only possible means of solution must be a resort,
sooner or later, to arms."[2] But this was retrospective persiflage; the
decision had almost certainly been taken earlier, and Walwal was a

good excuse, if slightly inconvenient in its timing. Since the Italians were already there and had in fact won the battle, there was no reason whatever for the battle to have transferred the problem from one field to another.

The deep reason why the East African adventure had been judged desirable in the first place must certainly have arisen from the internal problems of Fascist Italy. The fact that Ethiopia seemed to Mussolini to offer a suitable solution to those problems indicates the inward obsolescence of Fascism. Colony building was a pastime that had lost its practicality, its profit, and much of its appeal for other European countries by 1934. But Mussolini, for all that his verbiage was stuffed with notions of novelty and revolution, for all that the official anthem of his regime was "Youth" ("*Giovanezza*"), thought of glory in very dated terms. There were plenty of reasons why glory might seem desirable and at the moment feasible, but none of these reasons were publicly advanced.

There was, it must be emphasized, no practical or material cause or motive for the annexation of Ethiopia in terms of national needs as measured by the standards of the 1930s. Ethiopia did not threaten any Italian interest and no substantial Italian interest would be served by its annexation. None of the conditions within Ethiopia, later advanced as pretexts or justifications for its destruction, directly affected Italy: it was to be said that Ethiopia, predatory and ruthless, was in a position to threaten the Italian positions in Eritrea and Somaliland; that Italy required "space"—a land under the Italian flag suitable for emigrants' settlement, suitable to receive Italian capital surplus (of which there was virtually none) for investment, and to provide needed raw materials (of which none except coffee were available in Ethiopia); and that the barbarism and slavery and oppression suffered by the victims of Ethiopian misrule required correction by a civilized power. These were all illusory or irrelevant. What *was* important was that Ethiopia was the last habitable portion of the world's surface that was still available for colonial expansion, that it adjoined existing Italian colonies, and that the humiliation of Adowa, the most embarrassing (or anyway, the most expungeable) incident of a long history of national embarrassments, invited vengeance. And, Fascism needed to justify itself.

It is difficult to know exactly how far Mussolini was personally moved by the desire for vengeance. It probably affected him in youth; in his memoirs, published posthumously, he claimed to have felt a deep and personal sense of outrage when, as a schoolboy, he had heard the news of Adowa. It was later reported, on the eve of the adventure, that his desk always bore books about the 1896 campaign.[3] (His 1928 *Autobiography*, on the other hand, while remarkably frank in some respects—it was never permitted to be published in Italy in his lifetime—is silent on Adowa.) But Ethiopia had been recurrently in Italian minds and Italian policy since 1896. In the colonial ministry this preoccupation was chronic; in places where high policy was made it was merely spasmodic.

Concern had been not only intermittent but also ambiguous. The exact aims were not defined, and the nature of the ambitions shifted. It was, in the years before 1914, conventional for governments to express an "interest" in certain territories; this committed them to nothing much beyond a pre-emptive position. It was this sort of thing that the Italians had from time to time proclaimed, and sought to safeguard, in Ethiopia after 1896.

The most important manifestations of the Italian "interest" had been: the agreement with France and Britain in 1906; the aspirations, unachieved and not seriously pursued, set forth at intervals from 1915 to 1918 as part of Italian war aims; and the agreement with Britain in 1925. In 1906 the Italians had been allotted a sphere of influence extending out from Eritrea and southward across the empire to the hinterland of Italian Somaliland, including a wide corridor to the west of Addis Ababa. The agreement represented for the European powers a staking out of claims and a means of averting disputes in the event of the dissolution of Ethiopia, prudent examples of international cooperation. To some Italians it appeared as a charter of liberties—"a 'magna carta' for Italian aspirations."[4]

Much more overt and far-reaching demands were voiced during World War I. The most extreme statement of Italian war aims, a manifesto signed by 3,000 prominent citizens in April 1917, demanded that the Italian war effort be rewarded with such extensive prizes as the cession—by France—of Jibuti and a protectorate over Ethiopia. The Italian position in the postwar years was so difficult internationally, as nationally, to make it impossible for the government to consider such ambitions. Even Mussolini, when he came to power, sought at first to win favors for Italy in Ethiopia. The most tangible expression of this policy was Italian sponsorship of Ethiopian membership in the League, which was one of Mussolini's bright ideas opposed by advisers. In the end, their insistency and Mussolini's inconsistency prevailed; then another shift in policy took place, and in 1925 Mussolini revived the policy of what might be called "subclinical partition."

The occasion was a sort of honeymoon in Anglo-Italian relations that arose, in part anyway, from Austen Chamberlain's esteem for Mussolini. British willingness to assuage Italians' African appetites had been demonstrated the year before when Britain had agreed to cede Jubaland, a part of British East Africa, which lay at the southern coastal border of Italian Somaliland and had been promised to Italy during the war. Now Chamberlain visited Rome; there were expressions of mutual esteem, and Italian and British diplomats collaborated on further agreements. The one about Ethiopia was secured on the initiative of the British, who were not at all averse to seeing the Italian influence, which they regarded as harmless and amicable, extended in East Africa. When the agreement was protested by the regent of Ethiopia, Rome and London retreated from inchoate schemes of partition, and Mussolini reverted again to the policy of extending influence through ingratiation.

This was the policy urged by many in the foreign ministry (in contrast to the ministry of colonies), in particular by Giuliano Cora, the astute minister in Addis Ababa who believed that a strong and independent Ethiopia would be a useful friend to Italy. Partly at his urging in 1928, Mussolini had invited the regent, the future Haile Selassie, to pay a state visit to Rome, and during the course of it negotiated a treaty of friendship. Circumstances of the utmost cordiality were contrived; Mussolini was photographed playing with the lion cubs he was giving as presents to his guest.[5] But the treaty remained in most of its substantial aspects unfulfilled; its failure to produce the benefits that Mussolini had expected filled him with irritation and inspired vague threats; Cora was recalled, and the cordiality to the regent ended abruptly. Still, there is no evidence that Mussolini seriously, much less systematically, contemplated invasion until 1932. Later he was to say that he had first begun, in 1925, to consider the best means for "our pacific expansion in that vast world, still enclosed in its prehistoric system and yet capable of great progress."[6]

What did begin to happen, however, was an increase of attention in lower levels of the Italian government. Raffaele Guariglia, the chief of Near Eastern and African affairs in the foreign ministry, was convinced of the utility of annexing Ethiopia and of preparing the way by careful negotiations with Britain and France. He feared that pusillanimity might one day invite the reinvigorated Ethiopia of Haile Selassie to attempt the conquest of Eritrea and Somaliland. He thought, in short, of traditional diplomatic methods, of the traditional system of competing and expanding states, of traditional fallacies. It was all very old-fashioned.

Guariglia left office in 1932, but his ideas, or some of them, now began to find favor in high places. They were supplemented (apparently on the initiative of civil servants) by more up-to-date methods of *internal* subversion in Ethiopia, of a sort perfected by the Communists and shortly to be widely practiced by the German Nazis and, later, by everyone else. A deliberate attempt to use Italian consular agents for purposes of political disruption was rather inefficiently undertaken. New consulates were established, and the consuls tried to make deals with dissident chieftains. But there were as yet no coherent plans. There was no military build-up in the colonies, and Mussolini had made no decision. He seems to have patronized the activities of the bureaucracy with general but aimless approval.

Several elements coincided to congeal aimlessness into plans to invade Ethiopia. The most surprising, if not the most urgent, was fear and jealousy of Germany. No final decisions seem to have been taken until after German-Italian relations became acutely bad. This is the supreme irony of the whole adventure: the possibility that the event that created the alliance of Hitler and Mussolini may have originated as as expression of enmity and defiance of Hitler by Mussolini. The alliance was made possible by the war, but the war was originally conceived as part of a large program to "stop Hitler."

For Mussolini's fear and jealousy of Hitler there were abounding causes. In Germany, in June of 1934, on the heels of Hitler's unsuccessful visit to Venice, a bloody purge of dissidents, many of whom were Hitler's oldest and closest comrades, had taken place at a cost of several hundred lives. Hitler not only accepted but boasted of responsibility, and Mussolini and his press were vehement in their comments: the Germans were excoriated as a nation of traitors, pederasts, and barbarians. In July the diabolic promise of the purge was borne out: a Nazi coup in Austria took place. It involved the assassination of Mussolini's protégé Engelbert Dollfuss, the Austrian chancellor.

Austria lay on Italy's sensitive Alpine frontier and was one of the satellite states from which Mussolini had been trying to construct a pro-Italian bloc in Central Europe. The murder seemed (although, as we know now, misleadingly) timed to appear almost as a deliberate Nazi insult to Mussolini, since at the moment it took place Frau Dollfuss was actually Mussolini's houseguest. Mussolini was enraged at this gory and overt invasion of what he considered his private preserve, and he ordered military measures. Four divisions—40,000 men—were ordered to the Brenner Pass. "Now let them come," he said. "We'll show these gentlemen [the Nazis] they cannot trifle with Italy."[7] The Germans hastily backed down, and the Austrian regime, quasi-fascist, highly conservative, dictatorial, anti-Nazi and pro-Italian, was salvaged. But the Italian government was left with the worst possible impression of German aims and motives—and, it may be judged, with an intense irritation and resentment at a German regime that was stealing marches on, and thunder from, the regime of youth, vigor, destiny, and salutary revolution, now rather ingloriously aging on the banks of the Tiber. One Italian writer, considering the Ethiopian adventure a generation later, has said that the attempted coup in Austria was what determined Mussolini to decide on the conquest of Ethiopia. He is said to have been so depressed by Germany's power and initiative that he reacted not merely with a compulsive need for Italian feats of arms but also with the conviction that glory and influence must be sought outside Europe.[8]*

A member of the Italian foreign office who was in close touch with Mussolini—then acting as his own foreign minister—later wrote, "The Italian venture in Africa was . . . born when Italian divisions were sent, after the assassination [of Dollfuss] to the Brenner to stem the flood of German expansion."[9]

It is possible that the specter of Hitler made the Ethiopian venture seem not only attractive but also urgent and feasible. But certainly

* Perhaps naturally, Italian writers since 1944 have tended to place great emphasis on the view that the enterprise originated in fear and dislike of Hitler. The interpretation can scarcely be regarded as an adequate *excuse* by non-Italians, but the obvious attraction it holds for Italian writers does not necessarily invalidate it.

neither the deteriorating European "situation," as diplomats called it, nor the overbearing and menacing deportment of Hitler, were the sole determinants of the East African enterprise. Another, similarly bizarre and conjectural, may have been that Mussolini was influenced by an old friend who wanted to end his rather unsuccessful military career in glory as commander in a safe but splendid little war. The notion is whimsical, but Fascism was in itself a gigantic whimsy.

Emilio De Bono had been one of Mussolini's earliest associates, one of the quadrumvirs of the March on Rome. He was sixty-seven years old in 1933, and his career had been a singularly frustrating one. He had been a general in World War I, but he had won no glory or acclaim—which may have accounted for his joining the Fascists in the first place. After the March on Rome he had been made first commander of the *squadristi* and then chief of the police. He was involved in the murder of the Socialist leader Matteotti, the most public of Fascism's early outrages, and was so generally incriminated as one of its architects that he was obliged to resign. He had been tried and acquitted by a rigged court and then appointed governor of Libya. From there he was transferred to head the ministry of colonies. In all his offices his record was indifferent, and he was regarded with embarrassment and disdain by most of his colleagues.

The colonial ministry, in the way of ministries, was always of the belief that its political chiefs were neglecting its sphere of interest, and it had always contained the most assertive and obstinate of the people who believed that Italy must, for reasons of strategy and prestige, contemplate a strong policy in Ethiopia. In the School for High Studies of Political Science, an elite training college in Naples with close connections with the government, lectures and publications were pointing out the indispensability of seizing Ethiopia.[10] De Bono was perhaps influenced by ministry officials and the intelligentsia. Early in 1932 he had discussed Ethiopia with Mussolini, and after an official visit to Eritrea that spring, he urged the strengthening of military bases in the colony. In July 1933 he organized a committee of the ministry to study ways and means and continued to urge action on the dictator.

It is his own, much-quoted, account of one interview that forms the basis for the supposition that it was to oblige an old friend that Mussolini agreed to plan for war.[11] Obviously the account cannot be trusted; De Bono was a vain and foolish man with a taste for romantic grandiloquence even more pronounced than that of most Fascists, and when he wrote he was also a frustrated and embarrassed man trying to salvage his self-importance. Still, his story harmonizes with the flavor of Fascist politics, that of a light opera conducted in hell, and the relevant passage of his memoirs is worth remembering, if with skepticism.

> It had been my proudest dream to end my public career as a soldier on active service. Of course, it was not yet possible to say in 1933—the year in which we began to consider what practical measures must be taken in the event of war with Ethiopia—whether there would or would not be war with that country; but I made up my mind to lose no time, and one day I said to the Duce: "Listen: if there is war down there—and if you think me worthy of it, and capable—you ought to grant me the honour of conducting the campaign." The Duce looked at me hard, and at once he replied: "Surely." "You don't think me too old?" I asked. "No," he replied, "because we mustn't lose time."
> *From this moment the Duce was definitely of the opinion that the matter would have to be settled no later than 1936, and* he told me as much.[12]

In any event, military planning did begin shortly thereafter; in the spring of 1934, when relations between Germany and Italy were beginning to get very bad, proposals for military build-up in Eritrea, looking toward eventual action against Ethiopia, were discussed and adopted by Mussolini, the heads of the colonial and foreign ministries, and the services. In July, at the time of the abortive Nazi coup in Vienna, the chief of staff, Badoglio, was sent to Eritrea to look over the ground. In the fall of 1934 Mussolini told the new Austrian chancellor, Kurt von Schuschnigg, that he expected war with Ethiopia in the near future.[13] The project, which had been entirely secret until May, was beginning to be widely talked about, and the American military attaché in Rome reported it as settled.[14] The American minister in Addis Ababa, when queried by the State Department, agreed. He was sure that the Italians had already drawn up a plan of conquest and occupation.[15] From Rome that summer, correspondents began to report military preparations in the Italian colonies; most of them quoted Italian authorities who said it was a preparation for defense against a bellicose Ethiopia (bellicosity was entirely the fiction of Italian officials; there was no indication of it in Addis Ababa). The American ambassador in Rome had no doubts about Italy's aggressive intentions. He accurately predicted in September 1934 that the Italians might contrive or invent an incident to justify a punitive expedition that would gradually develop as a war of conquest; or might, by encouraging insurrection in Ethiopia, secure a successor to Haile Selassie who would place his country under an Italian protectorate.[16]

There were open hints in the Italian press. As early as April 11, 1934, when Victor Emmanuel III visited Somaliland, *Tribuna* observed that the king was "consecrating the expansive mission of the Italian nation."

At some point between the fall of 1933 and the fall of 1934, then, the necessary element of policy, Mussolini's own decision, seems to have been made. It was consonant with all that is known of Mussolini's character that he should conceive a solution to Italy's needs in terms of a war against Ethiopia. Glory as a diet for the hungry was an old prescription; glory may have seemed a political necessity for Fascism because it was a psychological one for the dictator; glory would bulwark the East African colonies; glory would shadow Hitler's rising star; glory would safeguard Austria and would impress Italy's allies. Glory would solve all problems if it were quickly and cheaply won in Ethiopia where, during almost forty years, Italy's military pride lay bleeding.

But before Walwal the program of action was evidently still not definite, and there were strong forces urging its delay or abandonment. Badoglio, a cautious and clear-headed soldier, was well aware of the extreme difficulties of supply and the inadequacy of the installations in East Africa. He returned from his inspection in the colonies with a discouraging report on the almost total deficiency of forces in Eritrea and Somaliland. He was concerned, too, about the European situation and the prospect of uncovering the Alpine frontier at a time when Germany was apparently contemplating the destruction of Austria and possibly larger adventures. Badoglio, moreover, disliked and distrusted De Bono and his judgment on military matters (as, indeed, did everyone except Mussolini). He himself erred in the opposite direction in his efforts to deter the dictator; he told him that the conquest of Ethiopia would take seven years. Mussolini was, it is said, shaken but not dissuaded. The king of Italy, similarly cautious (as he always was) and clear-headed (as he sometimes was), was also hostile to Mussolini's plans, for similar reasons. He pointed out to Mussolini that any East African military enterprise would put Italy at the mercy of Great Britain (a country much admired and respected by the king) since it controlled the Suez Canal, the only practicable approach to the Italian colonies and to Ethiopia. He warned that it was illusory to hope, as Mussolini did, that the Ethiopian peoples and princes would dissolve in civil war when attacked; the same hope had been held and belied in 1896.[17]

All such difficulties, Mussolini believed, could be overcome in time, and he thought he had plenty of it. He seems to have been planning on commencing operations in the autumn of 1936, at the end of the rainy season in the Ethiopian highlands. Measures were being undertaken to build up an army for the invasion, but they were not, apparently, regarded as urgent. Agreement had to be reached with the British and French. In public, Mussolini (in contrast to everyone else in Italy) was still professing that no military action was planned and reassuring the Ethiopians about his friendly intentions. In September 1934 the 1928 treaty of friendship was specifically reaffirmed by a joint Italo-Ethiopian communiqué.

Then Walwal. The Italians had been rather desultorily comtemplating the arrangement of an "incident" as the occasion for a war, when they were ready for one. Probably an incident engineered by the Italian legation at Addis Ababa would, they thought, be most convenient. But now an incident was thrust upon them, one they could hardly disregard.

The Italian and Ethiopian governments immediately presented strong protests to one another. On December 9 Ethiopia appealed to Italy to agree to arbitration of the dispute, under the terms of the treaty of friendship of 1928. In answer, the Italians demanded redress for the wrong done them. They required apologies, a salute by an Ethiopian delegation to the Italian flag at Walwal (a recognition of Italian sovereignty), and $100,000 in damages. Even if a wrong *had* been done to them, these demands would have been so excessive as to constitute deliberate provocation. Then, on December 14, 1934, nine days after the encounter, the Ethiopians presented the matter to the League of Nations in Geneva as one "which threatens to disturb international peace." Prophecy was never more accurate: the wells of Walwal, for thirty-five years the object of a totally obscure and dilatory chess game, now suddenly appeared in the chief forum of world affairs and on the front pages of newspapers in the great capitals. The shape of a huge struggle, between moralities rather than diplomats and soldiers, suddenly appeared. For now commenced the drama in which injured Ethiopia would present itself as the embodiment of all that was most appealing and enlightened in the western system of values, a drama in which the leading actor, Ethiopia's emperor, made his appearance as the voice of the world's conscience. His character as prophet began to achieve planetary publicity and importance.

His policy was a logical sequel to his coronation, where the Ethiopian government had tried to present a façade of political maturity and European sophistication. It had failed then because elements of what westerners thought of as backward were too evident, the contrast between these elements and displays of pomp was too strong. The reality of what was being attempted and accomplished in Ethiopia escaped skeptical visitors in 1930; the peculiar moralism of the emperor was not then appreciated. But with the threat from Italy, potent emotions could be unleashed by a moral posture.

It was said later by one of the most thorough historians of Ethiopia, "However moral the Emperor's trust in the League, it was a political mistake and there were many Ethiopians who frankly told Haile Selassie so at the time."[18] It is also said that the appeal was foolish because it focused attention on the unimportant question of Walwal instead of on the real problem of Italian intentions.

The point is arguable. Perhaps the only hope for salvation lay in the long run and in the world's conscience. It may be, though, that there really were, in Addis Ababa, illusions about the effectiveness of League action. Sir Sidney Barton, the British minister, received instructions (which he acted on reluctantly) to try implicitly to discourage Ethiopia from appealing to Geneva and to say that the British government desired to have "no connection with the affair,"—sufficient indication that the most influential power in the League was not going to allow it to disrupt British relations with Italy.[19] But in Addis Ababa the League seemed (as it had when Ethiopia first sought membership) a tribunal through which moral indignation could be mobilized. It was virtually the only force in the world that Ethiopia could bring to its defense, and whatever the element of tactic there was in this, it also suited admirably the temperament of the emperor and his role as a biblical prophet who could speak not merely the language of European morality but also that of the world's conscience. To deal with just such outrages against international virtue was the purpose and function of the League of Nations; it might not be able to perform those functions, but the purpose was one that would appeal to people everywhere. Conceivably a different response in December 1934 might have been more effective in deterring Mussolini, but it would not have defeated his armies and it would have sacrificed the long-run advantage of virtue.

There were certainly no illusions about what the Italian armies were going to do. One Ethiopian is said to have observed after Walwal, "It is 1914 over again, and we are Serbia."[20] The sinister parallel was strengthened by everything that happened. The Ethiopians continued to urge Italians to negotiate and met with cast-iron rejections. Early in January 1935 General De Bono was named high commissioner for East Africa and departed to assume his duties; it was known that he was under instructions to prepare a base for military operations in Eritrea and Somaliland. The Italian press spoke openly of Italy's civilizing mission in Ethiopia.

There were all sorts of subleties and obstacles to pursuing the policy that had been decided on in Addis Ababa. Even if nothing more could be hoped for from the League than to provide a forum for presenting Ethiopia's case, that still required the co-operation of the British and the French. Tecle Hawariate, the Ethiopian minister at Paris who represented Ethiopia at the League, was an adroit diplomat. He was thoroughly westernized, one of Haile Selassie's new intellectual elite. He spoke French perfectly, and he was suave, dignified, and persuasive. His task demanded all of his considerable skills. He had to proceed not merely with correctness but with subtlety, tact, sometimes guile. By watching for his chances, by carefully manipulating the League Covenant and machinery, and the diplomats who habitually made decisions for the world in the League corridors, the Ethiopian succeeded in circulating his government's complaint and in getting it scheduled for discussion by the League Council. Frightened by the prospect of involvement, the British pressured the Italian government; hours before the Council meeting, Italy agreed to submit the Walwal incident to arbitration. The Council discussion was postponed.

It was, given their purposes, a clever move by the British and a frustrating one for the Ethiopians. No amount of arbitration could avert an Italian invasion if Mussolini decided to go ahead with one. But

Ethiopia—and morality—were at least on the agenda and in the headlines.

What determined the policies of the European governments was
something wholly remote from Ethiopia: the behavior of Adolf Hitler.
Hitler had nothing whatever to do with the desert wells of Ogaden, or
the hopes of Haile Selassie for an outlet to the sea, or the rudeness of
Roberto Cimmaruta, or even the problems and ambitions of Mussolini.
But it was the behavior of Hitler that sealed the fate of Ethiopia and at
the same time made it a decisive force in world history.

Everyone in Europe was watching Nazi Germany with trepidation;
everyone had heard Hitler talk about Germany's great destiny. In France
there was desperate alarm about a German attack. What the French
wanted was an anti-German coalition to contain Germany, maintain
peace, and save France. And this was what, early in 1934 when the German menace was becoming more obvious, they had set out to get. Despite the innumerable conflicts, rivalries, and suspicions that divided
Germany's putative victims, they were willing to listen to the French.
The Soviet Union was found ready to negotiate an alliance. Except
for Poland, the "succession states" of eastern Europe, those that had
won independence or territory in 1919, were ready to renew their collaboration with France. The British, reluctant to become involved in
continental politics or commitments to France, were formally benevolent. And Italy was very receptive. Louis Barthou, the French foreign
minister, planned a visit to Rome in the hopes of settling outstanding
sources of friction between France and Italy. For the French government, the only aspect of Mussolini's policies, domestic or foreign, that
mattered was his policy toward Germany.

There were several conflicts, some old and all arising from Italian
ambitions and frustrations. The basic one was Mussolini's persistent ani-
mosity to France, which was symptomatic of a very old Italian—mostly
a conservative and nationalist—state of mind. More specifically, the
Italians had been promised frontier rectifications in their favor, at
French expense, in the secret treaties negotiated to bring them into
World War I on the French side; the obligation was still outstanding.
Another problem was Tunisia, which the French had taken over as a
protectorate in the 1880s and which had always had a large number of
Italian residents. Mussolini had been much put out by the treatment of

Italian nationals as aliens in a country they regarded as an extension of their homeland.

These difficulties were large but not insoluble, given Mussolini's distrust of Hitler. With generosity, tact, and shared terror, they could be overcome and the Fascist State converted into an active ally against resurgent Germany.

There were, however, other obstacles, often unperceived in 1934. The biggest was the ideological one. The Versailles system and the League of Nations both had a deep foundation in the then current notions of democracy, and they embodied ideas of international conduct and morality peculiarly associated with liberal constitutional government. They had been made, indeed, to protect it, on the assumption that only free men in free nations could hope to live in peace. This assumption, in those times, seemed to many people in the west tenable, indeed self-evident. Mussolini himself had by his conduct in Corfu and elsewhere given plausibility to the view that dictatorships were by nature unassimilable and bellicose. His references to imperial Rome, his incessant allusions to the extreme merit of war as a molder of character, both individual and national, strengthened it. The French leaders might not believe that peace and freedom were inseparable; they might believe that peace consisted entirely of preventing Germany from getting out of hand, that the association of the Soviet Union and Italy in this venture was a matter of national need and could not be regarded as endangering international morality. But many people thought otherwise, some in France itself, many more in other countries. They saw peace not as a matter of restraining Germany but as a world-wide proposition, a matter not of needs but of morality, indivisible and ecumenical. Measurably increasing numbers of British voters, in particular, thought this way. Since Great Britain was the power whose support was far and away the most indispensable to France, and since its government was dependent on the good will of the electorate, this feeling of so many British voters was an important obstacle to the working of the coalition that the French were trying to build. It was also a force, the most important force, that Haile Selassie could call on in defense of his nation and his throne.

In 1934, however, the formal and tangible obstacles to agreement with Italy loomed much larger in Paris than philosophical ones—and were negotiable. The French foreign minister at the time of Walwal was Pierre Laval, a man not likely to concern himself with questions of abstract principle; he was much more likely to believe that by solving formal and tangible problems he would solve all problems that mattered. He believed that subtlety, negotiation, and compromise could procure anything. He even believed, unlike most Frenchmen, in the possibility of a negotiated friendship with Germany. He simply did not credit the fact that abstractions like democracy, or the indivisibility of peace, or the wickedness of aggression, could turn into political problems. Later, he was to demonstrate with stunning effect the consistency of his beliefs by attempting to mitigate—indeed, to eliminate—the incompatibility of French and German interests, after the defeat and occupation of France in 1940, by similar methods of painstaking negotiation about details. His view of world affairs, of emotional forces and of moral principles, was that of a pawnbroker negotiating a loan on a used watch. It was a quality of mind that, as history overtook him, gave Pierre Laval a world reputation for infamous villainy; but his defect was, perhaps, more nearly a simple lack of imagination.

During the weeks before Walwal, inconclusive conversations were taking place between the foreign offices in Paris and Rome, and their tenor was illuminating. It was made clear—in tactful diplomatic terms —that the Italians wanted quite a lot of things from France in return for hard promises to oppose Germany, including enormous territories in Central Africa and the whole of French Somaliland except for the port of Jibuti. These were flatly unacceptable, and it is possible that Laval's sinuous determination to reach agreement would have been confounded had it not been for Walwal. For Italy Walwal meant that the "solution of the Ethiopian problem"—i.e., the destruction of Ethiopia—was to be undertaken in haste and not in leisure, and this made it immensely important for Italy to secure the consent of France. Walwal, in short, removed the tangible obstacles to Franco-Italian understanding. Laval, without consulting the French foreign office, departed unexpectedly for Rome on January 3, 1935.

What happened when he got there has been a subject for debate ever since. Inferences have been drawn, denials issued, and contradictory recollections published. Many of the details remain uncertain. But the main features of the Laval-Mussolini agreement, reached on the night of January 6, 1935, are tolerably clear.

The public results were striking and, to people at the moment, perplexing. The Italians appeared to have given the French everything they wanted and to have received very little in return. But although this was not at all the sort of transaction that usually gratified Mussolini, he was exuberantly affable when he announced the formation of an un-shakable friendship between France and Italy. Published declarations stated that France and Italy would consult if Austrian independence were threatened or if any country (meaning Germany) attempted to modify treaty restrictions on the level of its armaments. The two countries would operate within the framework of the League and in co-operation with "interested states" (which meant France's allies, like Yugoslavia). The status of Italians in Tunisia was not to be improved.

Italy received, so far as public announcements went, nothing but an infinitesimal slice of French Somaliland, to be transferred to Eritrea, and a large but uninhabited portion of the Sahara (it was calculated that it contained sixty-eight residents), to be transferred to Libya. The Italians were also to be given a small share in the stock of the railroad from Jibuti to Addis Ababa.

In short, Italy had apparently entered the French system and abandoned its own demands. It rapidly became clear, however, that Mussolini had been provided with more private gratifications. Their exact nature is controversial, but their subject is certain. It was, of course, Ethiopia. Laval later said that what he had done was merely to renounce the three-power agreement of 1906. This meant, in effect, that France would not insist on *its* rights in Ethiopia in the face of any-thing the Italians chose to do there. But Laval knew that Mussolini was contemplating major operations. In a letter written to Laval in December (and published in 1955[21]) Mussolini had explained in detail that what he expected from the French was "sympathy" for the project of establishing Italian control over Ethiopia. Laval always in-sisted that he had no idea that Mussolini was planning a war, but he must certainly have suspected that the use of force was likely. He may have expected, and hoped, that Mussolini was planning a protectorate, secured by threats that would not unduly perturb world opinion.

There was vagueness—of a decidedly duplicitous character—on *both* sides. Mussolini certainly did not reveal that plans for war were decided upon and indeed rapidly developing. On the day the Laval-Mussolini agreements (such of them as were public) were announced,

De Bono had sailed for Eritrea to take supreme command of what proved to be the invasion forces. Both deceivers were deceived.

The effects of deception were delayed. Italian-French relations for a time remained extravagantly cordial. Mussolini spoke of the beginning of a new era, and arrangements were made to negotiate allocating European spheres of military responsibility between the new allies. He had, in short, the impression, furnished by Laval's guile, that he could count on unlimited French support. Later in the month, he had his ambassador at London sound out the British, although in terms even more general, and he received a similarly encouraging impression. At least, what he received was an encouraging absence of response. Sir John Simon, the foreign secretary, a man obsessively dedicated to the twin policies of letting sleeping dogs lie and of not interfering in dog-fights if the dogs woke up, found it prudent to abstain from comment on the vague statement that Italy had renewed its interest in Ethiopia.

Simon's policy, or lack of it, provided a commitment and a precedent for all later British action, or lack of it. The deep reasons are to be found partly in Britain's—and the world's—situation and partly in the foreign secretary's personality.

He was a statesman with an exceptionally long and distinguished career. He was a handsome, dynamic man with a commanding presence and a charming manner. (It was his pleasant custom to write notes of congratulation to new MPs, even those who were against him politically, on their maiden speeches.) Personal and intellectual power had brought him to office as a minister in Asquith's Liberal government in 1910; he ended his active life as a viscount and as lord chancellor in Churchill's wartime government from 1940 to 1945, thus achieving the most stately peak among Britain's high offices of state. He was, with brief interruption, a member of the House of Commons from 1906 until his elevation to the House of Lords in 1940, and he was very much one of the inner group of ranking statesmen whose collaboration, and often membership in governments, was deemed important or even indispensable by prime ministers. He was often described as the most brilliant lawyer of his day, and to many he seemed a man of the highest principles. He was admired by some for resigning his cabinet post of home secretary in 1916, to protest against the introduction of compulsory military service. He had, in short, a large reputation and considerable political clout.

Like many great lawyers who achieved the highest rank, he was of humble origins: he was of rigidly evangelical Welsh peasant background. His father was a Congregationalist minister in Manchester. In Britain's class system as it existed in the nineteenth and early twentieth centuries, the law was the best, often the only, path by which a talented man of simple background could attain high office and comradeship with the great men of the patrician club that ran the country. But ambitious men of humble birth who followed the legal path to social acceptance and political power were likely to be trimmers; many of them acquired reputations for being possessed of more tactic than integrity, and some of them were judged as very unscrupulous indeed. Lawyers are trained to be operators. And ascendant politicians in a tight class society were obliged to be both ingenious and discreet to the point of deviousness and ambitious to the point of unscrupulousness.

Simon has frequently been accused of all three defects of character. But purely political facts are more measurable and possibly more important. He was a Liberal in the age when the Liberal party was going to pieces, and his political future required that he abandon his former colleagues and beliefs. This he successfully did. He aligned himself against most Liberals during the General Strike of 1926, in which he made himself acceptable to Conservatives by adopting a position passionately hostile to Labour. In 1931 he abandoned the most fundamental of Liberal doctrines, free trade, to take up the Conservative program of tariff protection. This led to the second crucial political fact of his career. When the National Government was formed in late 1931 and presented itself as a coalition of all factions, although it was in fact dominated by the Conservatives and opposed by most Labour and Liberal MPs, a leading Liberal was urgently needed to lend verisimilitude. Simon was available, and he was given the foreign office. For this eminent post his political qualifications were suitable, although his training was not. He had never before been professionally concerned with European politics. The appointment was in a certain sense appropriate, and may have been intentional, for the National Government was determined to serve the national and imperial interests of a Britain torn by depression and dissent. The function of a secretary of foreign affairs in the years after 1931 was, from the standpoint of his colleagues, to keep them foreign. Non-involvement was not so much the policy as the imperative of the British government.

In his memoirs, Simon's justification for the negative stance in international affairs that he supported before 1931 and practiced afterward during his own term of office was characteristic and perhaps revealing of his personality. He argued that the real question in foreign policy is not what might be desirable but whether desirable aims should be sought if public opinion does not embrace them. He put it this way: "the real question is whether the people of this country and of the Commonwealth could at an earlier time have been swept unitedly . . . into a preventive war." (He was discussing an incident in the Near Eastern difficulties of the early 1920s, but he explicitly extended the argument to include all crises.[22]) It has widely been asked of Simon's conduct of affairs if the real question was not whether acts of leadership could not have prevented war altogether and if his concern for not moving ahead of opinion did not indicate an excess of political discretion rather than a nice appraisal of moral probabilities. In the opinion of one careful historian of the destruction of the Liberal party, he was a tactician pure and simple, and a tactician, if unconsciously, in his own interests and not those of his party or his nation.[23]

Tactic, unaccompanied by much attention to strategy, was the key to what began to happen in the winter of 1935. Simon, like Laval, had no interest whatever in Ethiopia, and neither did most of his cabinet colleagues. They were, with a few exceptions, unconcerned with what was happening in faraway countries of which they knew little. But the Italians interpreted Simon's indeterminate noises as indicating a countenancing of Italy's projects. Mussolini thought, at the end of January, that he was in possession of two blank checks.

This interpretation was based on a plausible appraisal of the record, which showed that Britain had generally been sympathetic to Italian colonial aspirations. It had had confirmation in British conduct at Geneva, where the Ethiopians were trying to get the Walwal incident taken up by the Council and were deflected by British influence.

The British were deeply alarmed at the possibility that Ethiopia, by contriving to invoke the League, would cause trouble between Britain and Italy. They did everything to keep things quiet, but aside from that they had no policy. In an effort to discover one, the cabinet privately arranged for an investigation by a committee, called the

Maffey Commission, to look into the situation and find out what Britain ought to do about it. The commission performed its task in a manner unconscionably thorough and leisured. Its report was not made until June. Pending it, the British government still had no policy, aside from the foreign secretary's particular reactions to each situation as it came up; and Sir John Simon moved, with stately, measured pace, along the path of least resistance. His refusal to take positions was, like Laval's, the signature on the blank check.

A decided unreality thus cloaked and perverted the League of Nations' treatment of the Ethiopian case from the beginning. The League was presumably considering a small skirmish in a distant desert and the proper location of a frontier that nobody had previously thought sufficiently important to define. What was really at stake was the existence of a member state. The judges were all parties to the case, particularly so since the executive heads of the League peace machinery, the secretary-general and assistant secretary-general, were respectively a Frenchman—Joseph Avenol—and an Italian—Massimo Pilotti—who were in close touch with, and, in a way, under orders from their own foreign offices. The League had, in a political sense, no existence at all as an independent agency. And the policies of the three leading powers were not at all what they seemed to be: their pious public pronouncements about the importance of maintaining peace and international law cloaked, in the Italian case, energetic preparations for a war of aggression and strenuous efforts to deflect the League from considering the case at all; in the French and British cases they cloaked an inner impulse to try to salvage good relations with Italy in the interests of encircling renascent Germany. It was this situation that was misunderstood by that part of the public that wanted to support the League as an agency for peacemaking. Such people misconceived "the League" as an independent, policy-making authority, a moral and administrative entity with a mind and destiny of its own. Actually it was merely a forum where the representatives of member governments stated (or concealed) their national intentions.

Ample confirmation of the inutility of the League was forthcoming. Despite Ethiopian prodding, no progress was made toward arranging arbitration of the Walwal incident. The Italians wanted to keep their hands absolutely free, and they simply refused to answer the frequent

Ethiopian notes and inquiries. On March 17, 1935, therefore, Tecle Hawariate returned to Geneva and told the League that Italy was threatening Ethiopia and the Covenant of the League must now come into operation. Unfortunately, the day before Hitler had publicly announced the rearmament of Germany and denounced the armament clauses of the Treaty of Versailles. The contingency foreseen in the Laval-Mussolini agreement thus brusquely materialized, and the French and British were given renewed grounds for seeking Italian friendship and support. They hastened to do so.

On April 11, 1935, they met at the resort town of Stresa, in Italy, to consider the German misdeed. Foreign Secretary Simon was the principal representative of Britain. (Prime Minister Ramsay MacDonald, was also present, but he was far advanced in senility and was carefully prevented from appearing in public; his presence was designed merely to lend weight to the proceedings.) Mussolini and the French Premier Pierre Flandin and Foreign Minister Laval all attended. The purpose was to present a united front in the face of law-breaking Germany, and in a limited and ineffective way this was achieved. Nothing was, or could be, done to stop German rearmament, and Simon declined to engage in any joint commitment to guarantee Austrian independence, which the Italians had urgently hoped for—Austria was, correctly, expected to be the next item on Hitler's agenda of outrages against law, good manners, and the existing order of things. But the three powers publicly asserted their united opposition to unilateral repudiation of treaties "which may endanger the peace of Europe." The words "of Europe" were added at the suggestion of Mussolini.

Peace in Africa was thereby implicitly excluded from the concerns of the powers. It had been expected that Ethiopia would also be discussed at Stresa, at least privately, but it was not. The British elaborately avoided mentioning it, although it was on everyone's mind to the point where the Opposition in the Commons' subsequent debate on Stresa asked persistent questions about a possible secret deal with Italy à la Laval. Clement Attlee, the future leader of the Labour party, one day to become prime minister, presciently observed that if the ministers had in fact, as they said, refrained from mentioning Ethiopia at all, their silence must be construed as condoning the Italian aggression which everyone knew was in the making.

His diagnosis of the ministers' policy was right; what he did not know was that the condoning was a product of a lack of a policy, not of a sinister one. When Mussolini proposed adding the fatal words "in Europe" to the communiqué, the British raised no objection and so gave a renewed impression of consent.

Simon seems to have had no real opinion about Ethiopia, either in the sense of a personal conviction about what could or should be done or in the sense of clear instructions from the cabinet. His chief colleague, Stanley Baldwin, had a similar aversion to taking action; and differences or indifference characterized the rest of the ministers. What Simon was doing may be called both evasive and duplicitous. (While Stresa was in course, he was already designing to sabotage the anti-German front by a naval treaty, permitting the Germans a measure of naval rearmament, with Hitler.) The tactician was deeply opposed to making commitments. The cabinet evidently approved this non-committal position. "Be tactful," MacDonald told the Italian ambassador, "and we shall have no objection."[24] The expert advice expected from the Maffey Commission, which was still considering what should be done, was an excuse for doing nothing. It is worth noting that in his memoirs, *Retrospect*, published in 1952, Lord Simon made no reference *whatever* to Ethiopia in recalling his experiences as foreign secretary.

In the month that followed Stresa, Italian intentions solidified, the military build-up was rushed, and the decision, taken months before, became for practical purposes almost irreversible. Troops, construction battalions, and matériel were flowing copiously through the Suez Canal on their way to Eritrea, and the most prominent of Fascist generals, Rodolfo Graziani, had already gone to Italian Somaliland to take command of the Italian forces there. This was public information, and no one supposed that the build-up was defensive in purpose. Mussolini at the end of the conference had triumphantly told his clever and skeptical ambassador at London, Dino Grandi, that it was clear that the British had said "Yes" to the Ethiopian venture. Grandi was unconvinced. A few days later when Simon told the League Council that it ought to require evidence of progress toward arbitration or else take up the Italo-Ethiopian dispute itself, which was exactly what the Italians did not want, it looked as if Grandi's doubts were justified. But then Simon, in private conversation with him, indicated that he was prepared to accept Italy's policy in East Africa but hoped that Mussolini would handle it in ways that would not embarrass the British government before its own public. Then it seemed that Mussolini had been right in supposing that silence meant consent.

It looks now as if a firm position clearly taken and set forth by Britain at any time before the end of the Stresa conference might have dissuaded the Italians from their destruction of Ethiopia or, at the very least, delayed it, averted war, preserved the League of Nations, and avoided the irreconcilable alienation of Italy and the wrecking of Franco-British relations. It was the decent, gentlemanly Simon, quite as much as the ruthless despot Mussolini, who ruined the empire of Ethiopia and with it the hope for a coalition to restrain Hitler's Germany.

5

The Politics of Evasion

In 1935 the governments of France and Britain thought peace was more important than Ethiopia and that peace could best be assured by buying off Mussolini and averting their glances and their policy from East Africa. The only hope, from the Ethiopian standpoint, lay in changing this belief, and this was what the emperor and his advisers set out to do. The world had to be made to believe that peace was indivisible, that aggression must be prevented or punished, that men of good will must unite against the brutality of Fascist ambitions. Responsible statesmen could not evade the problem, as Sir John Simon tried to do; they had to face it and solve it. The emperor of Ethiopia had to become, as he has since been called, the conscience of the world.

It was an ambitious and, it might seem, a hopeless aim; but to a remarkable extent, the press and public of other countries *were* involved. In the year following Walwal, a gigantic conflict began to develop in public opinion in the western world, and the Ethiopian cause gained support. It was a conflict that on one side found manipulators like Laval, evaders like Simon, and isolationists like many Americans. On the other side were internationalists, those who thought of men as equal, of good and evil as ecumenical. In the middle, to be converted, were the vast groups that disliked trouble, including foreign entanglements and dangers, but also were vaguely attracted by principles of morality.

To convert this last group, it was necessary for Ethiopians to be—or appear—both "correct" and forbearing and to abide strictly by the letter of international law. Throughout all that followed, they succeeded with imposing consistency. Simon himself spoke of the "very conciliatory and constructive attitude" of the Ethiopian government. Some foreigners in Addis Ababa might ascribe the correctness to cynical self-interest, but they could not deny its impressiveness. And when the long waiting period was over, no one could deny that the tide of western opinion was changing, or that Haile Selassie was becoming the first black African to be a world statesman.

He was well served. Many of his advisers were learned and able men, representatives of the new intelligentsia that could, both literally and figuratively, speak in western tongues. Foreign Minister Hirouy was a distinguished scholar and humanist. Tecle Hawariate, notably *salonfähig*, was an eloquent diplomat in the most orthodox European tradition. Like the emperor, these men knew how to frame and phrase a policy that would persuade an alien public.

There were the foreign advisers as well. The American Everett Colson, while he might with excessive modesty disavow the importance of the role, was the key man among them. He was also an extremely interesting person who embodied, with incredible exactitude, the stereotype of the Yankee. Shrewd, forthright, honest, ingenious, he was also monumentally loyal. He fascinated the Europeans and Ethiopians, as the revelation of brilliance and subtlety behind a blunt and slightly crude American exterior often does. George Steer of the London *Times* wrote of him, with admiring surprise, that there was nothing unusual in Colson's house except his "stamp collection and his mind."[1] His taste was banal, his appearance—he was a heavy, commonplace-looking person—undistinguished. He did his conversing and conferring while reclining on a couch, smoking his pipe, detached, calm, laconic. He was very old-fashioned in his economics; in politics he was a Wilsonian liberal who detested colonialism and, good Yankee that he was, distrusted the subtleties and refinements of Europeans. The emperor liked him and relied on him, and with his colleagues, the Swedish General Erik Virgin, the Swiss jurist Raymonde Auberson, and T. E. Konovaloff (a White Russian who was minister of works and became the emperor's chief military aide), Colson was a co-architect of Ethiopian policy. A logical destiny thus made him, inadvertently, a builder of the American-dominated world that was to replace the foundering dominion of imperial Europe.

Much of Ethiopia's diplomatic correspondence and many of the public pronouncements of its leaders were jointly drafted by Haile

Selassie, Colson, and Auberson. It is said that Colson provided the ideas and Auberson the translation into refined French (in which, the second language of the emperor as well as the language of diplomacy, they ultimately appeared). The emperor drafted some of the documents himself and revised the others. It was a curious but logical collaboration of three continents and three cultures that set forth the precepts of the world's conscience.

The line taken was both highly moral and deeply moving. It made enemies look like gangsters and whilom friends like traitors. It rebuked power politics and ennobled law and morality. It presented the picture of an innocent victim, defenseless against mighty and evil malefactors. It was cast in precisely the terms that would catch the imagination and call to action all men of good will who conceived of peace and salvation in the only form that anybody, including the Soviet Union and world communism, understood in those times: the League of Nations and its formulas and procedures for international settlement of disputes and international action to restrain and punish war makers.

"The procedures of the League," the Ethiopian government said at Geneva,

> must not be the occasion of fresh delays . . . These delays must not be utilized for the continuation of military preparations and of dispatches of troops and war munitions . . . Otherwise, once these preparations had been completed, nothing would be easier than to create incidents and, with the help of a Press campaign, to find pretexts for aggression. Ethiopia possesses no military force comparable with that of her powerful neighbor. She has no newspapers, no means of propaganda to influence public opinion and present all the circumstances, whatever they may be, in a light favorable to herself. To defend her rights, her only remedy is appeal to the League of Nations.[2]

And later, Tecle Hawariate wrote to the secretary-general of the League, after the British had imposed an arms embargo,

> Will the Council remain unmoved in the face of this situation, which is growing steadily worse? Will it allow this unequal combat to continue between two Members of the League of Nations, one of which, all powerful, is in a position to employ, and declares that it is employing, all its resources in preparing for aggression, while the other, weak and pacific, and mindful of its international undertakings, is deprived of the means of organizing the defence of

its territory and of its very existence, both of which are threatened? Will the Council assume responsibility, in the eyes of the world, for allowing preparations to continue unchecked for the massacre of a people which constitutes a meanace to none?[3]

It was all extremely skillful; it was also incontrovertibly true. By such messages to the League and the world, Ethiopia succeeded in putting its case before an enormous and impressionable audience. It also succeeded, in the long run, in converting anti-fascism into a force that united the most disparate and implausible partners in a great world struggle.

It is difficult, now, long after World War II, to realize how speculative a prospect that was. At the beginning of 1935 there was very little in the way of coherent opposition to fascism as a dangerous international force. Nazi Germany, however people felt about it, had so far committed depredations only against Germans. It was widely supposed that Italy and Germany were almost irreconcilably hostile to one another. The notion of fascism as monolithic, inescapably predatory, directed toward ideological world dominion in the same way that Communism was, had not yet been invented. It first began to take shape when the outrageous behavior of Mussolini in East Africa was brought, dramatically, to the forum of the League of Nations.

The seismic effects of the crisis were not entirely due, of course, to the propriety of the Ethiopian position or the sympathy it evoked. That sympathy corresponded to deep ideals, illusions, hopes, and frustrations everywhere. And it owed something, too, to some coincidental and extraneous circumstances. Three circumstances in particular helped to convert Ethiopia into a martyr, a symbol, and in some ways a world power.

The first was climate. Walwal, coming at a time when Italy was still far from prepared for battle, took place six months before the beginning of the rainy season that would make battle unfeasible for another four. Ten months must intervene before Italy could get its war under way, ten months in which the Ethiopians could try to parry nemesis and the yeast of internationalism could work in western opinion.

The second was the state of world press and radio news. Reporting had by now become big business. A *need* for news had developed, economic (for the proprietors of papers and broadcasting companies) and psychological (for readers and listeners). Lavish financing in the collection or even—in a certain sense—the creation of news was a very good investment. Newsmen began to assemble in Addis Ababa, and so provided the Ethiopians with a public.

Third, the British were going to hold an election. It had, by law, to take place before September 1936, but the government could choose any date it pleased before that. Compelling political considerations made it desirable to hold one sooner. The date eventually chosen coincided, within weeks, with the ending of the rainy season and the beginning of the war.

In some ways the news coverage of the Ethiopian War and the events that led up to it was much more than simply an illustration of the ascendant influence of the mass media. It was also a vindication of freedom of the press. The Ethiopians welcomed correspondents and made only inadequate efforts to control what they wrote. For a journalist in Ethiopia that year, freedom of the press was a reality, and the results were benefits for the government that, a little uncertainly, permitted it. In Italy, on the other hand, where the press was strictly controlled, the government thought of public relations in terms of handouts and verbatim reporting of public speeches. The consequence was stultification of news sources, and in the long run it worked against Italy.

Addis Ababa, by the summer of 1935, was becoming one of the world's major news capitals. That fact, if it did nothing else, brought Ethiopia to the forefront of consciousness in the western world, to a degree that no other part of Africa had been brought to its consciousness in a generation. It gave a reality and an immediacy to the war which, quite aside from anything else, lifted it from the category of an obscure peripheral conflict. Ironically, it was the journalists' presence and the fact that they had to write something, rather than any sympathy for the Ethiopians, that were important. They mostly, indeed, overlooked the things that made Ethiopia unique and significant. They almost all disliked their assignments.

This was not surprising. The capital from which the defense of the empire was directed, the capital of the ideals for which that defense was coming to stand, was not a city likely to appeal much to foreign correspondents. When they began to arrive they found it—as visitors to the coronation had found five years earlier—a disagreeable and baffling place. In the characteristic way of semiwesternized Asian and African towns, an old and poor society mingled hideously, uncomfortably, with the less attractive of Europe's exports. Opinions might, and did, differ widely about the inner character of Addis Ababa, but few Europeans were likely to find it a pleasant place of residence or to enjoy its social amenities.

There were some decided assets. The climate, at eight thousand feet, was exhilarating, healthful, and pleasant. Of course, during the period of the rains from June to September the relentless daily downpours made it oppressive, muddy, and inconvenient, but even then the sun shone for part of the day and at other seasons it was delightful. The setting was beautiful, green hillsides stretching down to a great valley on one side and up to mountains on the other, with distant ranges and peaks in the background to add grandeur and variety. It was lavishly verdant, blanketed with eucalyptus and, especially after the rains, bright with flowers. But man-made attractions were minimal.

It was dirty, it smelled bad, and appallingly deformed beggars flocked the streets. At night hyenas could be heard with their awful howls. Insects were everywhere. It was a straggling city. Even today, it sprawls interminably, punctuated by ill-kempt empty lots, with skyscrapers and imposing public buildings separated by miles of scattered clusters of squalid huts and hovels on the steep sides of valleys or across plains, roofed more often than not in corrugated steel, shaded by banana palms, facing mud lanes, engulfed in dirt and poverty. In 1935 when the population was much smaller (no one has any idea how large it was, but it may have been in the neighborhood of a hundred thousand), when there were few modern buildings, when few streets were paved, and the muddy byways were thronged with donkeys and carts, the aspect was still more emphatically counterurban. The public buildings, some of them dismal copies of European prototypes, rose like premature ruins in the emptiness. The center of town was the great octagonal church of St. George, built on a knoll by the Italian prisoners of 1896. In logical irony, it was the handsomest and most consistent of the buildings in a European style; its fine classical façades accurately recall the baptisteries of the later Renaissance in Italy. The principal roads circled the steep slopes around St. George's, in sharp contrast to the monumental straight avenues that Haile Selassie laid out for his coronation; Menelek, who had founded the city and hired Swiss architects to design it, had fostered a vaguely Alpine character. The shops and houses were mostly one-storied stucco, but a few buildings rose to chaletlike heights, with fancy wooden balconies. Near the irregular square below St. George's, called the "piazza," were the places frequented by foreigners; even those were unpretentious. The principal hotel was the Imperial, near the piazza, surrounded by verandas in what someone called a Swiss-Indian style of architecture, set back from the road and with a tremendous view across the valley. Menelek's imperial palace, a mile away on the next hill, was of traditional Ethiopian character, a compound of low buildings roofed in corrugated steel, scattered on an eminence. The unfriendly might describe them as shacks. Another two miles off, in a large park, was the new palace, a horrendous adaptation of Hohenzollern neobaroque that might have housed a wealthy but vulgar merchant in suburban Hamburg. A few miles in a different direction was the Moslem quarter, almost a separate town of more concentrated, urban aspect—but a town, in those days, of unparalleled squalor.

The foreign legations were mostly housed in what looked like modest nineteenth-century suburban villas that also recalled the more uninspired cities of imperial Germany, built further up the mountainside, safely removed from the "native quarters" (as some Europeans persisted, and persist today, in calling the places where the Ethiopians live and work in their capital) and enclosed by large walled gardens, heavily guarded. The railway station lay another few miles in the opposite direction, deeper in the valley, connected with the piazza by one of the great imperial avenues laid out by Haile Selassie but as yet, for much of its distance, purely conjectural.

It was, in short, an imperial capital of woebegone aspect, a travesty of capitals, half planning and pretense and half rustic villages, ugly, uncomfortable, and most of all unfinished. So most of the Europeans who were obliged to live there saw it, and so, even more emphatically, did the numerous foreign correspondents who arrived to cover the impending war.

The deeper effect it had on the foreigners, however, was diverse. Most of them noticed the poverty and such details as the grotesquely symbolic policemen with elaborate but torn and dirty uniforms directing nonexistent traffic in bare feet. They saw that the population was

composed, in a distressing proportion, of foreign tradesmen, petty
traffickers from Greece or Italy or the Arab world or India, and of
whores and beggars. Much of the rest of it—the native proletariat—
consisted of the retinues of rich men or people who hoped to join the
retinues, the hangers-on of households so extensive as to resemble a
combined fief, gang, and business firm. Englishmen in particular, like
Evelyn Waugh, were struck by the ruthless oppression with which the
"Abyssinians" ruled their numerous subject peoples without the com-
pensation of hygiene, education, and honest administration which he
thought the Europeans had brought to their colonies. Waugh, like most
other Europeans before and since, was emphatic about the unspeakable
brutality of Ethiopian courts and prisons and the prevalence of crimes
of violence, about the treachery and primitive hostility of the people,
the inability of Ethiopians to keep agreements, their wily refusal to
honor debts, their suspicion of modern medicine, their intractable
sloth. He noted that the radio broadcasting station and the hospital
had been built by Italians, in some cases private philanthropists.[4]

What many people of Waugh's persuasion failed to notice or dismissed as insignificant (although another Englishman, G. L. Steer,
saw deeper meanings in the scene) was that the Ethiopians were themselves running the Italian-built transmitters, that they had constructed
a modern airport for the city, that there was emerging a literate elite of
clever young men, highly resourceful and patriotic, for the most part
those whom the emperor had caused to be educated at good foreign
universities at public expense. (Waugh regarded this elite as both cun-
ning and silly.) It was easy to overlook or miss the importance of the
fact that the comic cops were Ethiopians patrolling their own streets,
that the population lived in health and affluence as great as that of
any colonial capital in Africa. Most foreigners missed what John Melly
saw: "Education, though still only for the few, is rapidly progressing,"
a fact "in great extent due to the Emperor." Or that such inconspicuous
improvements were "merely the outward and visible signs of the organization and progress which have been taking place in Ethiopia in the
last decade."[5] Certainly few visitors suspected that for some Italians,
notably Marshal Badoglio, the chief reason for invading Ethiopia was
not its intractable primitivism but the progress that was being made in

overcoming it. They saw, instead, the plausibility of the excuses, the need for a modernizing and civilizing force.

Few foreigners, generally acutely aware of a barbaric caste system and the domination of a diverse patchwork of peoples by the Amharic minority, realized that humble or non-Amharic birth was no bar to careers—that this was a society remarkably open and hospitable to talent. They found the equality of women, if they noticed it at all, a laughing matter. They generally did not take very seriously the young Ethiopians' fascination and skill with mechanical gadgets. One American observed that a fascination with machines was just another version of a fascination with brightly colored beads; she did not know that Ethiopians would one day operate one of the world's most efficient airlines. What was easiest of all to overlook was that Amharic Ethiopians lived in freedom, governed neither by spies and bullies like the Italians nor by foreigners like all other Africans.

Still, the foreign correspondents were there and were writing dispatches. In April 1935 revulsion against Italy was just beginning to become a formidable political force in Great Britain. But in that month, John Melly, the eccentric humanitarian who was trying to do something about health services in Ethiopia, reported, "There has been rather a rush of Press Correspondents lately. X.Y., of a London paper, is a funny little rabbit. . . . He said that they [the proprietors of his paper] had just discovered that their readers were pro-Ethiopian, so the paper was about to become pro-Ethiopian, therefore he got his news and local colour, and has now gone home. I think practically the whole British Press is pro-Ethiopian now, which is a very good thing. If Mussolini decides to attack, I think he will get a very nasty jar."[6]

What Melly, with preternatural percipience, was observing was a revolution in world affairs. By the time the invasion began months later, the flow of the correspondents' words had become a river rising about the bases of even such distant and solid pillars of past politics as American isolation.

Because Britain was the major power in Europe, certainly the one that had to bear the largest responsibility for dealing with Italy, the approaching election gave meaning to the roles of climate and journalism. It becomes necessary, therefore, to follow in some detail the sinuosities of British politics and policy making.

British opinion was coming to be deeply divided, although the issues on which it was divided were unclear and to some extent unreal.

There was little specifically pro-Fascist opinion. There were some small Fascist movements, one of them led by a fervid veterinarian, but not until the eve of the Ethiopian War was Fascism espoused by anyone but cranks. Then came Sir Oswald Mosley, who had been an audacious and imaginative left-wing Labourite and now organized a British Fascist party. He was an ardent defender of Mussolini, but his following, though noisy, was small.*

Another body of opinion was much more important. It represented the tired nationalism of an imperial power exhausted by war, depression, and overextension. The government and its friends seemed bent on remaining as uninvolved as possible in dangerous foreign crises and confusions. Many of the more stalwart conservatives, like Winston Churchill, saw that Hitler's Germany was a certain and dangerous enemy and proposed a spirited foreign policy to contain it. But such people thought of Mussolini not as a brutal and aggressive dictator but as a possible ally. Most were imperialists who sympathized with the idea of Europe's civilizing mission.

On the other hand, a rapidly growing number of Britons favored safeguarding the peace through "collective security," which meant supporting a strong League of Nations against all aggressors in the hope that such united action by peace-loving countries would restrain war makers. They shared the ultimate motive of the second group: they hated and feared the prospect of a second world war. But their recipe for preventing it was quite different.

The recipe in 1935 involved support for Ethiopia, and here the influence of the mass media was decisive. Ethiopia was eminently newsworthy. Evelyn Waugh was approximately correct when he wrote of the London press in the summer of 1935:

> the editorial and managerial chairs of newspaper and publishing offices seemed to be peopled exclusively by a race of anthropoids who saw, heard, and spoke no other subject [than Ethiopia]. Few

* Mosley was in the pay of the Italian government. Much later, when the British captured Mussolini's private papers, they found letters written by Dino Grandi, the Italian ambassador at London, to the Duce, which revealed that Mosley had been receiving £6,000 (about $30,000) a year from the Italian embassy. The document was triumphantly read aloud to the House of Commons by the Labour home secretary in 1946.

of them it is true could find that country on the map or had the
faintest conception of its character; those who had read [Lewis M.]
Nesbitt believed that it lay below sea-level, in stupefying heat, a
waterless plain of rock and salt, sparsely inhabited by naked, homi-
cidal lunatics; . . . the editor of one great English paper believed
and for all I know still believes—that the inhabitants spoke classical
Greek. But Abyssinia was News.[7]

The part of the public affected by these developments was demanding action to save Ethiopia; at first it demanded it, with rare exceptions, not from any knowledge of or sympathy with the threatened
empire but in the name of international morality. There were indeed
deep and ancient barriers in the minds of Europeans and Americans
to any outright alignment with the Ethiopian cause on any except
the most abstract grounds of liberal idealism. Even for those who
were not open believers in the Europeans' right to rule, there was the
inherited belief that European norms must be the norms of civilized
deportment, a form of myopia that looks today, somewhat misleadingly,
like crude racism. One American correspondent, W. D. Hubbard,
rather sheepishly admitted immediately after the war, "I admired
[Haile Selassie] immensely and wished him good luck and wise counsel in the conflict which was beginning. Nevertheless, I firmly believed
that it wasn't right that Whites should be defeated in Africa. I believed firmly that if any advance—political, industrial, or agricultural—
was to be made in Africa, it must be under the domination and leadership of the white race."[8] The admission is significant; it showed how
great the shock had been of finding Africans on the side of righteousness, as defined by western standards, how rapidly old assumptions
could be shattered.

To many of the friends of Ethiopia in Britain the cause seems at
first to have appeared in much the same light as that of the Royal
Society for the Prevention of Cruelty to Animals. Lord Lugard, the great
colonial administrator, congratulated the British Red Cross on its services to the Ethiopian armies in these terms: "You will have the
satisfaction of saving the lives and limbs of many of these gallant
barbarians fighting for their country. All good fortune attend you . . ."[9]

The myopia was thoroughly understood and exploited in Rome.
"After all," Mussolini told a French newspaperman, "England only
recently regarded Abyssinian independence as an absurdity. In 1925,

Sir Ronald Graham [the British Ambassador] and I signed an agreement that practically cut Abyssinia to pieces."[10] What the Italians failed to understand was that the myopia represented not an ultimate truth but an ophthalmological defect that their own actions might remedy.

The assumption of white, western superiority was the biggest obstacle the Ethiopians had to overcome. The way to counter it was the line they took from the beginning: to borrow the European norms and use them and so invoke an opposite prejudice. They stressed that this was a conflict between two independent states, one attacking the other, not between civilization and barbarism. As a consequence, two conceptions of decency—international law versus western civilization —were brought into collision, and a Great Debate developed. As the most distinguished American historian of these events has observed, pro-League opinion everywhere arose from systems of abstract values strongly held, and "moralistic qualities were attributed to the League."[11] There were plenty of people who continued to distrust moralism, but there were more who liked it. It grew apace. What started out as an abstract hostility to aggression and the violation of international commitments (very European notions, after all) was transformed eventually into positive sympathy with Ethiopia, respect for non-European peoples, and revulsion against colonialism.

Among the conflicting attitudes, the British government tried to steer what it thought was a realistic course: one that would avoid war with Italy and if possible save Italian friendship while assuaging the electorate with its increasing dedication to the League. The course was at first evasive, as exemplified by Simon's majestic silences and by a remark of Anthony Eden's in the House of Commons, when he parried a question about Italian aggression. He answered that Mussolini had submitted the dispute to arbitration (which was true neither in fact nor in intent) and that until the arbitrators made their decision, "the less said, the better."

But less negative prescriptions were in the making. A new cabinet was formed in June 1935, constructed to fight and win the election. Ramsay MacDonald retired as prime minister, and his deputy, Stanley Baldwin, took his place. Baldwin had led the Conservative party for thirteen years and had been prime minister twice before. He was a stolid man who presented himself as the embodiment of the slower moving virtues of the English—honesty, dependability, rustic forthrightness, the reverse of all that was clever, tricky, or foreign. He liked to be photographed in barnyards patting dogs, although his background was that of an urban businessman. His authorized biographer, years later, was to say that his most notable quality was laziness, but this is questionable. He was an active and alert politician in, perhaps, the narrowest sense. His genius was to avoid rocking the boat, his defect that he did not always notice when the boat was being rocked by someone else. He not only disliked foreign affairs but sometimes gave the impression that he thought they didn't exist. Once he asked his foreign secretary not to bother him with a world crisis at a time when he was concerned with urgent problems of party politics. He wished to assure the electoral safety of the Conservative party; but he lacked vision, and sometimes even elementary prudence, in pursuit of it.

His choice of men to handle foreign policy was an example of the odd effects of this preoccupation. Baldwin did not want the young Anthony Eden, whose name and inclinations were associated with internationalism and support of the League of Nations, to become foreign secretary when Simon left office. (Simon was transferred to the more congenial Home Office.) Baldwin could not, however, disregard Eden or flout the powerful portions of public opinion to whom Eden appealed. He made Eden minister for League of Nations affairs while appointing Sir Samuel Hoare to the Foreign Office, thus dividing responsibility among two men with different objectives.

The choice for foreign secretary was in some ways logical. Hoare was an extremely intelligent and well-educated man of the privileged classes who had been long in public life and had held several cabinet posts. He had experience in foreign affairs, and he had once served in the embassy at Rome. His latest position had been secretary of state for India, and in that taxing office he had had even more than the usual cares; he had presided over the complex and onerous work of drafting a bill—a constitution in effect—for the reorganization of the Indian government. As a result of his exertions at the India Office, his health had suffered, and he was said to be in low spirits. It has further been said that Baldwin hoped that translating him to the most prestigious of cabinet posts would cheer him up.

The trouble with Hoare as foreign secretary, aside from his alleged poor health and depression, was partly that he was an old-fashioned diplomatist, too old-fashioned to operate in a world of surging passions and ideologies. Later, when he was ambassador at Madrid during World War II, he showed his impressive talents for negotiation and manipulation. Manipulation was his forte, as it was Laval's in a less seemly way, but his office in 1935 required metaphysics. Another trouble was that he was subject to conflicting pressures from his colleagues, including Eden, from public opinion, from politicians, and from such quarters as the Royal Navy, and he was better prepared to operate as a commander than as a staff member.

The navy was particularly important. It was the most powerful in the world—it had to be, given the planetary scale of its responsibilities. It was also very efficient, the only branch of the British services that had maintained its strength and skill and reputation during the lean years of small appropriations and smaller public esteem. But it was spread thin, and in East Asia it faced a powerful potential enemy in Japan. There were other difficulties. The British service chiefs were cautious (as were the Italian, French, and German chiefs) almost to the point of timidity. They thought that pressure applied to Italy might lead to a naval war that Britain would fight on unfavorable terms. They said so, in a report from the chiefs of staff to the prime minister on July 5, 1935.[12] The ministers accepted the most pessimistic appraisals. The permanent undersecretary for foreign affairs, Sir Robert Vansittart, wrote to his chief, the foreign secretary, in August, "This country has been so weakened of recent years that we are in no position to take a strong line in the Mediterranean."[13] They were impressed when the admirals brooded out loud about the extreme undependability of the French as naval allies, the inadequacy of dockyards in the Mediterranean, the vulnerability of Malta (the chief British base) to Italian air attack, the threat of Japan.

The admirals were not defeatist or panicky. They believed that in the end they could beat Italy if they had to. They very much disliked, however, the idea of exposing *their* navy in support of a footling policy of backing the League and beleaguered Ethiopia.

The civilian leaders in various ways exaggerated (sometimes no doubt unconsciously) the importance of what the sailors told them.

Baldwin said to his private secretary, Tom Jones, after the war started, "I had repeatedly told Sam [Sir Samuel Hoare] 'keep us out of war. We are not ready for it,'" and added, "our fleet would be in real danger from the small craft of the Italians. Italian bombers could get to London . . . our anti-aircraft munitions would have been exhausted in a week. We have hardly got any armaments firms left."[14]

One definition of British national interest and purpose in the Ethiopian situation was finally made in June 1935. On the eighteenth of that month, the Maffey Commission made its report, which had been asked for in March. It was the work of an interministerial group of experts presided over by Sir John Maffey, a civil servant who was, significantly, permanent undersecretary of the Colonial Office. The report dealt with the barbarism and instability of Ethiopia. It recognized that Italy undoubtedly was planning to secure control of the country. It perceived no particular harm in this, since Italian dominion would be unlikely to injure British interests so long as Italy remained friendly to Britain. Its recommendations for British policy were concerned solely with imperial considerations. These would require frontier rectifications in favor of adjoining British colonies and control over the watershed of the Blue Nile. It would be difficult to find a purer or less imaginative statement of colonialist attitudes.

The report probably did not have much influence on major decisions, but one item in its history was illuminating. It was supposed to be secret, but it rapidly became known to the Italian government and eventually to the public—it was published in the Italian press six months later. The British soon realized that the Italians knew about it, but they had no idea how they had found out and suspected a leak in the London Foreign Office. Actually, it was photographed by a messenger in the Rome embassy. The stupefying fact was that this individual, and, it seems possible, a good many other embassy personnel employed locally, were agents of Italian army intelligence. This kind of slack security, a relic of the free and easy days in the Victorian era when Britain had nothing to fear, showed quite as clearly as the content of the report how ill British habits were adjusted to the terrible needs of the age of totalitarianism. It also, of course, showed Mussolini how unprepared the British were to resist him; he exaggerated the importance of the Maffey Report, but he did understand its basic purport.

The chief preoccupation of the cabinet, next only to saving world peace, was necessarily the General Election. The ministers* had to face the Labour party which, shockingly beaten in the previous election in 1931, had begun to recover and was in a good position to capitalize on the growing enthusiasm for the League. The party had always had a strong pacifist and internationalist tradition. It had favored co-opera-tion with foreigners, it was at least vaguely anti-imperialist, it was passionately opposed to armaments, which it regarded as likely to lead to arms races and wars and also as a form of waste that benefited capitalists and diverted public money from worthwhile social projects. The Labour party had long preached and, during its brief tenures of office, practiced all these policies. Now the traditional positions were becoming popular causes.

The situation was a trying one for Conservatives. Many of them understood better than their opponents that the League was nothing but the policies of its leading members and that League action against Italy meant British and French action against Italy. This they con-sidered, with much less justification, might in turn mean war. They thought that the opposition was muddleheaded and that to demand national disarmament while at the same time challenging Mussolini was foolish and dangerous.

Evidence of muddleheadedness as a nationwide phenomenon was to be found in the Peace Ballot. This was a survey of public opinion in the form of a questionnaire circulated on a mass, not a sampling, basis by the League of Nations Union, an eminently respectable, non-partisan organization. Eleven and a half million people returned the ballot, and, despite the random means of selection, the result was taken as indicating a powerful current of British opinion in the six months when the ballot was being distributed—November 1934 to June 1935.

Almost unanimously, those who answered the questionnaire voted that Britain should remain a member of the League. Almost three to one they voted that Britain should support the League in military sanctions against an aggressor.† It is impossible to tell how many of

* The cabinet in 1935 was called a National Government; it had originated in 1931 as a coalition of the Conservatives with certain factions of the Liberal and Labour parties. But by 1935 the word "National" was a cloak for almost pure Toryism. Practically no Labourites still supported it, and the Liberal party had almost disap-peared except for Lloyd George and his friends, who opposed it.
† Sanctions, the only real power of enforcement the League had, were to be recom-mended by the League and executed by its member states.

those who answered the questionnaire thought that sanctions were a way of avoiding war and not, as the government thought, a way of involving Britain in one. Some undoubtedly were prepared to fight in support of international law. But the ministers were sure that most people did not understand the implications of using force to restrain Mussolini. Vansittart called the Peace Ballot an idealistic fraud.

However fraudulent it may have been, the government began to realize it had to conciliate public opinion by appearing to support the League while pursuing privately what they considered the more rational policy of conciliating Mussolini and so averting disaster. The first thing that was done to conciliate Mussolini after Baldwin took over, however, was remarkably ill-judged and unrealistic. It was a proposal that Britain should concede to Ethiopia a strip of territory through British Somaliland to the port of Zeila. In exchange, Ethiopia would cede to Italy all of the Ogaden Desert, which had been the scene of the Walwal incident and which the Italians seemed to covet. But Italy was not at all interested in the Ogaden. Ethiopia, with its existence at stake, was not at the moment interested in Zeila. The proposal was more than merely unrealistic; it further convinced Mussolini that the British could be bullied.

There was another revealing ineptitude. The French were not consulted, presumably because they were regarded as untrustworthy. Eden, on his way to Rome to present the proposal, stopped in Paris to talk to Laval but did not tell him what the British government had in mind. (Mussolini, slyly, did.) He reached Rome on June 23 and learned that the purport of the offer had already been leaked to the Italian government (by the same source, presumably, that leaked the Maffey Report). The French, already distressed, were now enraged, and Mussolini rejected the proposal almost before it had been made. He was getting bolder.

On July 6 he addressed a blackshirt gathering at Eboli: "Abyssinia, which we are going to conquer, we shall have totally. We shall not be content with partial concessions, and if she dares resist our formidable strength, we shall put her to pillage and fire . . . To those who may hope to stop us with documents or words, we shall give the answer with the heroic motto of our first storm troops: 'I don't give a damn.' "

On July 31, 1935, he published another violent article in his newspaper, *Il Popolo d'Italia*. He wrote: "The essential arguments, absolutely unanswerable and such to end all further discussion, are two: the vital needs of the Italian people and their military security in East Africa . . . The second is the decisive one . . . Put in military terms, the Italian-Abyssinian problem is immediately simple, with the force of a logical absolute. Put in military terms, the problem admits of only one solution—with Geneva, without Geneva, against Geneva . . . In military domination, the policy of Fascist Italy has found its supreme historic and human justification."[15]

These sorts of statement may well have been mere blustering, but they could not be disregarded. Hoare later told Ray Atherton, the American chargé d'affaires in London, that he believed Mussolini was "mad."[16] The British, nonetheless, thought—in a sense, they *had* to think—that Mussolini's ambitions were material and finite, that they could be satisfied in some way that would leave Britain in peace and at the same time placate that growing part of the electorate that demanded an "international" solution.

A characteristic attempt to combine the two was made on July 11, when the British imposed a formal prohibition on the export of arms to East Africa. This sounded like a respectable step; it seemed plausible that any arms build-up would make the situation more dangerous than it was. But the Ethiopians were entirely dependent on imported arms and the Italians were already fully equipped.

In effect, then, the dilemma of the British ministers had produced a decision of a sort. Nothing much would be done to stop the madman. No material support would be given to Ethiopia. But the exigencies of electoral politics required support for the League, and this might serve to deter Italy.

In Geneva, therefore, a similar grotesquerie was transacting itself. When the Ethiopian government had first presented the conflict to the League, it had accepted the Council's recommendation of recourse to arbitration on the Walwal incident. For a long time nothing was done, but an arbitral commission had eventually been appointed and had commenced operations. The curious effect of the League's provision for the settlement of international disputes was to set up cumbersome machinery for settling what was, by itself, a very small dispute and one which had nothing to do with the real crisis or the intentions of the aggressor. The commissioners, despite prodding from the Ethiopians and the Council, found themselves unable to reach agreement, not only about the rights and wrongs of Walwal but also about what issue they were supposed to arbitrate: the legal ownership of the oasis or fault for the bloodshed in the encounter there. After endless debate, the arbitration commission trailed off into meaningless inaction. Laval, at the end of July, thanked the League for its helpfulness in furthering the reconciliation of Italy and Ethiopia.

Something more positive was clearly required from the British, and Sir Samuel Hoare made an important proposal in September. It was based on the theory that the real motive for Italian aggressiveness was economic, specifically a need for access to raw materials.

The Italians (and the Germans and Japanese) talked a great deal about their privations in this respect and about their need for "space" generally. These were complaints that British believers in empire understood. The consequence of thinking they understood them was impairment of will, induced, one may sketchily suggest, by guilt. The matter was clearly stated by one particularly silly and therefore candid member of the inner circles of Britain's ruling class, shortly to become a member of parliament and an important personage in the Foreign Office. He wrote in his diary on July 30, 1935: "I am bored by this Italian-Abyssinian dispute, and really I fail to see why we should interfere . . . Why should England fight Italy over Abyssinia, when most of our far flung Empire has been won by conquest."[17] Among the British ruling class, bred for generations on the notions that empires were good for the bank account as well as for the soul, it may therefore not have been perceived that Mussolini's motives were not economic and that talk about need for raw materials and space was mostly persiflage. In any case, the British chose to present, with much flourish, a new policy based on the space shortage.

It was couched in terms of lofty idealism. On September 11, 1935, addressing the Assembly of the League, Hoare proposed what he called a new approach to the problem of war. He said that Britain would support the League's guarantee of the independence and integrity of its members. But he thought that the motives for the Italian plan to attack Ethiopia were economic and that it could be averted if Italian needs were satisfied in another way. "We believe," he said, "that small nations are entitled to a life of their own and to such protection as can collectively be afforded to them in the maintenance of their national life . . . It is not enough to insist collectively that war shall not occur or that war, if it occurs, shall be brought to an end. Something must be done to remove the causes from which war is likely to arise."

This sounded sensible, high-minded, and pro-League, although collective insistence to prevent war, however insufficient it might be, was exactly what the League's business was supposed to be. And the program he went on to suggest for removing the causes of war was one quite outside the League's scope. "The abundance of supplies of raw materials appears to give peculiar advantages to countries possessing them . . . Especially as regards colonial raw materials, it is not unnatural that such a state of things give rise to fears lest exclusive monopolies be set up at the expense of countries that do not possess colonial empires. It is clear that in the view of many this is a real problem . . . The view of His Majesty's Government is that the problem is economic rather than political or territorial. It is the fear of monopoly . . . that is causing alarm."[18] And he went on to suggest that Britain would be glad to take part in a large and dispassionate study of this entire problem. There was a strong, although not much remarked, implication here; Mussolini had reasonable grounds for acquiring Ethiopia, but it would be unfortunate if he tried to take it by force. This may have been something Hoare really believed; he had already told the House of Commons much the same thing on July 11.

The proposal was irrelevant. For one thing, although many people vaguely assumed that there were untold riches awaiting discovery, in point of fact there *were* no raw materials in Ethiopia, except coffee. Before 1935 about half of Italy's coffee had come from Ethiopia. This did not constitute an appreciable drain on Italy's foreign exchange. In any case, even Sir Samuel Hoare could scarcely have supposed that a great nation was arming itself for war to assure an uninterrupted flow of *espresso*. Moreover, it was obvious that undeveloped regions, including those held as colonies, were only too anxious to sell their raw materials to whoever would buy them. The only limitation was the financial resources of the buyer, and these would not be increased by transferring raw materials from one flag to another. There was no danger, let alone any existence, of a "monopoly" by colonial powers that would exclude non-colonial powers from supplies of anything that colonies produced. If a shortage of coffee was the cause of

Mussolini's imperialist lusts, there were forty million Brazilians yearning to supply him with it at bargain prices.

Furthermore, Hoare's plan contained no mention of the thing many people thought was Italy's real interest in Ethiopia—a new homeland for surplus Italians, that other aspect of space. Many influential British observers thought this was really what had made Italy decide to fight.[19]

The program was not only irrelevant. Its envelope of support for League principles caused it to miscarry. Hoare was startled to find that what impressed people in his speech was not the idea that Italy's needs could and should be satisfied but instead his statement that the League ought to prevent aggression. In a way, he had inadvertently committed the British government to a course of action it disliked. He had said, "In conformity with its precise and explicit obligations, the League stands, and my country stands with it, for collective maintenance of the Covenant in its entirety, and particularly for steady and collective resistance to all acts of unprovoked aggression."[20] This was, in fact, a good deal less categorical than it sounded, since the Covenant did not *require* the League to impose sanctions on an aggressor but merely permitted it to do so, and since acts of unprovoked aggression could be defined only after the event. It was also misleading, since Baldwin, more than a year before, had stated government policy on sanctions before the House of Commons: "The moment you are up against sanctions, you are up against war . . . If you adopt a sanction without being ready for war, you are not an honest trustee of the nation."[21] And the government was emphatically not ready for war. Moreover, the use of the word "collective," copiously scattered through the text, had a special meaning for some people back home who, as a result of the highly charged debates of recent months, had become mindlessly wedded to the phrase "collective security," as if it were a perfectly concrete and definite and practicable alternative to war. This made the emotional impact of the speech much greater.

In short, Hoare sounded as if he were being tough. Anti-Fascists took heart. Mussolini fumed. Hoare was astonished. He may have intended it as a deterrent; he did not intend it as a commitment. But his voicing of a seemingly fearless and unbending determination of the British to support the League principles was described as a milestone in world history. League delegates rallied strongly. Haiti—

which was, with Liberia, the only independent black state in the world beside Ethiopia—greeted the initiative with exuberance. The Little Entente powers supported it. The Soviet delegate remarked that "this Assembly may become a landmark in the new history of the League."[22]

It was, then, an important speech that had far-reaching effects that were quite possibly the reverse of those that Hoare intended. The deterrent effect was negligible. Mussolini did not consider calling off the projected war, but the League and world opinion were, strongly and as it turned out decisively, emboldened to try to stop the aggressor. The world was now ready for a crisis and a turning point.

6

Crisis

By the middle of September 1935 it seemed certain that Ethiopia would be attacked and that the League, led by Great Britain, would take action to save it. A showdown looked certain to many people, and there followed a season of cliff-hanging suspense and occasional hysteria. It was all unreal, since British policy was not what it seemed to be, but the effect was to increase enormously the consciousness of, and the interest in, international—"collective"—action for stopping aggressors. When the realities began to appear at the end of 1935, the frustration, disillusion, and sense of betrayal heightened still further the tense conviction among the supporters of international morality and opponents of Fascist aggression that a crusade was necessary. The very depth of feeling that the crisis of September and October 1935 evoked was an important and formative force in world history. The terms of the crisis, and the responses of Italians, British, French, Americans, and Germans to it, were confused and inchoate, but they were, in the most literal sense, germinal.

In Italy reactions were complex. There was much alarm in some quarters, but in general the reaction was of outrage, of determination to assert the national will and destiny in the face of foreign meddling. Italians were told that the League, led by decadent, overrich France and Britain, was a conspiracy to strangle a poor but honest Italy, the virile New Italy fighting against aged plutocrats for its just rights. This line was undoubtedly very appealing to many Italians. Those in high places, however, not always convinced by their own propaganda, were imprisoned by it. They were nervous, but the people who mattered apparently felt that it was too late to turn back. Virile self-assertion in the pursuit of just rights had now become the regime's chief justification for survival. Mussolini told the counselor of the American embassy at Rome on August 19, "no one could expect that Italy would draw back now and destroy her prestige in incurring the disdain of other countries."[1]

The engine of war was tightly wound and set upon its course. A certain dynamic logic was at work, as it often is in military planning. Preparations engendered their own impetus. The buildup had been vigorously pushed since the beginning of the year. Transports and warships had been moving through the Suez Canal in steady flow and enormous numbers. In the first six months of 1935, 102 Italian naval vessels had gone through (the figure for the same period in 1934 had been three).

The venture was massive, but it was also hazardous and difficult. It was not surprising that prudent Italians, like Marshal Badoglio, should have had doubts about it. War against Ethiopia would have to be fought from Eritrea and Italian Somaliland, and these were from every point of view unsatisfactory bases, requiring huge improvements. The northeastern coast of Africa, along the Red Sea and the Indian Ocean south of it, is singularly lacking in good harbors. Between Suez and Mombasa, more than 3,000 miles to the south in British Kenya, the only first-rate port was Jibuti, in French Somaliland. The only commercial ports in Italian territory were Massawa in Eritrea and Mogadishu in Somaliland. Massawa, 2,000 miles from the nearest port in Italy, had inadequate water supplies and was equipped to handle only about 2,000 tons of shipping a month. There were no modern harbor installations and unloading was done slowly, by hand labor. Mogadishu, 3,700 miles from Italy, had no harbor facilities at all. Ships calling there—and few did—anchored in the roadstead and were unloaded onto small boats. In both cases the hinterland was dry, sparsely settled, and practically trackless. In Eritrea there were 4,000 Italians living among more than half a million local inhabitants of various races and characters, widely scattered. In Somaliland there were 1,500 Italians and an uncounted number of Somalis, many of them nomadic. Massawa was about 100 miles from the nearest penetrable point on the Ethiopian frontier. Mogadishu was some 500 miles across desert from any considerable settlement within the empire. The summer temperature at Massawa was usually about 120° Fahrenheit in the shade. In Mogadishu the summers were not quite so hot.

The Italians had built some roads in their colonies. In Ethiopia there were virtually none. The road toward it from Massawa (at that time impassable to cars) led up a steep escarpment, through Asmara, almost 8,000 feet above sea level. There was also a narrow-gauge railroad to Asmara. A distance of 75 miles, the rail trip took five hours. Addis Ababa was some 450 air miles due south of Massawa and some 600 air miles northwest of Mogadishu. Most of the land routes lay through high mountains of the wildest and most rugged sort. Since Napier's remarkable but almost unopposed march in 1868 to Magdala (a distance of some 300 miles, which had required more than three months), no army had successfully penetrated Ethiopia. The only route between central Ethiopia and the rest of the world, aside from trails, was the railroad from Addis Ababa to Jibuti.

There is no question that it required boldness verging on mania to contemplate the conquest of Ethiopia and skill amounting to genius to achieve it. The Italians, who had every reason to be deeply ashamed of the conception, had every reason to be proud of the preparations for its execution. In six months, the monthly capacity of Massawa was increased from 2,000 tons to 60,000 by the hasty extension of harbor facilities. At the beginning of 1935 it took six days to unload a troop ship. By August ships were being unloaded in a single day. In January the capacity of the port was five ships, in August fifty. Comparable expansion was taking place at Mogadishu. These were remarkable technical achievements, greatly to the credit of the Italian navy and engineers and to the local labor which was responsible for most of the construction. No less impressive was their solution of the most urgent supply problem, that of water. Some wells were drilled, but most of the water was supplied by tankers sent from Italy.

The establishment and provisioning of personnel was also a prodigious feat. In one year after January 1935 more than 300,000 troops and more than 25,000 laborers arrived in the two colonies from Italy, an average monthly rate of more than 25,000 individuals, along with about 1,500 animals and 400 motor vehicles. An entire naval base was built at Massawa in six months, with arsenals, floating docks, fuel tanks, and workshops. Radio transmitters were set up—thirty-four of them—in the two colonies by September 1935, and direct radiotelephone communications with Rome from both colonies were available. Eight floating hospitals were established at the ports, all admirably equipped; the medical achievements of Italy in the war were stupendous. Airfields were built, and airplanes began to arrive in Massawa as early as December 1934. Roads were extended or improved within the colonies—in January 1935 there were only about 125 miles that were passable for motor vehicles.

It was not possible to hide the extent of this formidable effort, even if the Italians had wished to, since what went through the Suez Canal was public knowledge. Its very dimensions meant that it was a slow process, and news of it, spread over a long period of time, began to have a cumulative effect, as newsmen hovered in increasing numbers over the corpse of Fascism's reputation; for the Italian war effort was in itself enough to convict Italy of aggressive intentions. And it practically committed Italy to continue the adventure so massively commenced.

The apparent determination of the British government to support the League of Nations in a collective effort to prevent or punish aggression, combined with the growing evidence of Italy's determination to pursue one, seemed likely to produce events so vast and ominous that they would affect the whole world. The most striking impact of the prospect of an imminent showdown was on the United States.

It was striking in particular because its effect contrasted sharply to the peculiar detachment of the American government and public opinion from affairs in the rest of the world that had long characterized them. The United States of America in 1935 was, by reason of its economic and potential military strength, the most important country in the world. But for fifteen years that strength had not been applied to international affairs. More precisely, it had been used by Americans as if the rest of the world did not—or should not—have anything to do with the western hemisphere. Americans in the 1920s and early 1930s sometimes seemed to be acting in the belief that by disregarding the eastern hemisphere they could make it go away.

Disuse of power was as decisive in its effects as leadership would have been. The world was not less affected by America for being negatively affected. The most important results of "isolation," as the

Americans called their effort to create a political planet of their own out of the western hemisphere, was that the Europeans were forced to act—and to think—as if the older age when they had run the world was still alive. It was this illusion that had made possible, among other things, the strange mistake of Mussolini in supposing that a colonial empire was still, as it had been in the nineteenth century, a test and gauge of greatness.

What was to happen to the world in the next generation was decided in very large measure by what Americans thought and did. What they thought and did was beginning, by the end of 1935, to change. The first questions about the dream of a sea-girt island, invulnerable and impenetrable, the first great controversies in many years about the desirability of isolation, began to emerge.

"Isolation" as a policy and a state of mind was of ancient and honorable origins. It had become a rigid doctrine with the disillusionment of World War I and a matter of urgent expediency with the world Depression, which sent all nations in the early thirties on quests for solitary salvation. By the mid-thirties it had become almost a religion for many people. It is difficult now to realize how complete the sense of remoteness was, how totally removed most Americans felt from the affairs of the Old World, how deep was the reflexive assumption that the United States had no concern with a crisis abroad except to remain aloof from it. To understand this aloofness, and the illusion that it could be indefinitely maintained, it is necessary to take into account American belief, difficult to recall in the 1970s, that the European powers were much stronger than in fact they were. The great powers were, as seen from America, still great masters of the world order. Europe was the home of power, not a power vacuum. There was no need for America to be drawn into its affairs; in fact, to most Americans the need was to stay out of them. Europe, which ran the eastern hemisphere, was very distant, very quarrelsome, and very dangerous.

Few in America dared publicly to question that it was both possible and necessary to remain detached. Discussion revolved around the most expedient techniques for staying neutral should a European war develop, not about the rights and wrongs and solutions of the crises that seemed to threaten war. There were dispassionate surveys in the American press and in American diplomatic correspondence about the interests, resources, and probable effects of the policies of the great powers, but so far as public discussion of the issue went, those powers might have been operating on another planet. Few public figures, of whatever ideological associations or whatever their diagnosis of the true meaning of the Italo-Ethiopian crisis, suggested that the United States should do anything about it.

But in fact it was really only the United States that *could* do anything about it. This was generally ignored in Europe and almost universally ignored in America; indeed, in 1935 the only place it was clearly realized was in Ethiopia. This perception led to a tragicomic effort by the government at Addis Ababa to involve the United States, to try to trap it, as it were, into assuming responsibilities in world affairs against its will. This effort had no chance of success, but its nature and fate illuminate the strange fantasy in which the world lived.

Since the persistence of obsolete ideas was, as it generally is in politics, the real source of the crisis that was developing, it is useful to consider the most striking exemplification of archaism that the situation provides: the reactions of the United States and its people on the eve of war.

The sense of detachment was most clearly indicated at first by lack of interest in Ethiopia. A few high officers of state, notably President Franklin Roosevelt himself, were concerned about the situation and aware of its implications, but just as British public opinion imposed on the British government the need to pretend that it was not isolationist, American opinion imposed on the American government the need to pretend that it was. In the press, little editorial attention was given to affairs in East Africa before September 1935, when it came to look as if they might possibly lead to a European war. American diplomatic correspondence about it was fairly copious by the standards of the time—before the outbreak of World War II, when the staffs of American missions abroad and of the State Department began a prodigious expansion, American diplomatic reporting tended to be spasmodic instead of encyclopedic. But the dispatches arriving at the State Department in 1935 were mostly noncommittal, reflecting a second-hand urgency.

When public, editorial, and diplomatic opinion began at last to focus upon the Italo-Ethiopian crisis, there was not at first the slightest suggestion that the United States could or should take any position. But in some ways, attitudes reflected many of the confusions and preconceptions already evident in Britain.

There was, as in Britain, a small body of opinion that showed some genuine and sympathetic interest in the fate of Ethiopia. This was lent cachet by the fact that two black Americans in succession were active in—indeed, according to some press reports, were vying for the command of—the Ethiopian air force. The first was an adventurer named Colonel Hubert Fauntleroy Julian, known as the "Black Eagle of Harlem," who in 1935 became an Ethiopian subject and was destined for a long and dramatic career in African affairs. The second, who succeeded Julian after a public quarrel in an Addis Ababa restaurant, was an interesting Alabaman named John C. Robinson, who used as a *nom de plume*—and *de guerre*—the name of "James Wilson" and was called the Brown Condor of Ethiopia. He was a graduate of Tuskegee, a highly educated and intelligent man and a good pilot, who was serving simultaneously as an officer in the Ethiopian air force and as correspondent for the Associated Negro Press. He was the subject of some interest—less than he deserved—as an indication of the interest of black Americans in the fate of the only considerable independent black state. But the Ethiopian air force was negligible, Wilson's activities in it had little practical effect, and he never attracted much attention among white Americans.

In August there was organized in Alabama a black committee called "Friends of Ethiopia in the United States," and many others followed. Although they were viewed chiefly as picturesque by the white press, the black press in America gave them full publicity. It appears that black Americans were intensely interested in Ethiopia and unanimously hostile to Italy. There were anti-Italian riots by blacks in a few cities. The Ethiopian War came at a time when black pride and self-awareness were on the rise, and antipathy to Italy was already marked. In June 1935 the heavyweight fight between the black boxer Joe Louis and the Italian former world champion Primo Carnera had been the occasion for a sort of American preface to the war in Ethiopia. Italian shops in Harlem were wrecked, Italian bars boycotted. When Louis knocked out Carnera, Italian Americans promised that Italy would have revenge in Ethiopia.[2] When war was approaching, there were telegrams of support from the National Association for the Advancement of Colored People to Geneva, and efforts were made to raise recruits for the Ethiopian army. W. E. B. Du Bois presciently observed that the war would be "the last great effort of white Europe to secure the subjection of black men."[3]

But black opinion did not yet count for much in America, and most whites were uncommitted. Some Protestant groups, inclined to be anti-Italian because they *were* Protestant and solicitous for the welfare of Ethiopia because of the numerous American missions there, showed sympathy for the oldest Christian nation in the world. But the *Christian Century,* their spokesman, was as rigid as possible in its support for "neutrality."[4] Catholics were divided in their attitudes. One writer (a strongly anti-Catholic one) on the Vatican later said, "Almost all the Catholic press the world over came out to support Fascist Italy, even in such countries as Great Britain and the United States of America."[5] But this alleged unanimity is not borne out by facts. The organ of the archdiocese of Boston, for example, was passionately anti-Fascist, although the liberal Catholic papers *Commonweal* and *America* were vaguely sympathetic to Italy's "needs."

Neither black nor Christian periodicals proposed any American action, even in the form of co-operation with the League should it adopt sanctions. A white-led Committee to Aid Ethiopia, organized by the Episcopal bishop of Albany, did not have much effect, and little attention was paid to the statements of Professor W. H. Kilpatrick that the protection of Ethiopian independence was a matter for both moral and national concern to the American people. Small efforts to interest the country in the real issues passed almost unnoticed, and no more positive proposal was made than for the sending of medical supplies to Ethiopia.

There was not much explicitly pro-Italian opinion, with the considerable exception of Italian-American circles and their press. The situation of Italian Americans was complex and for many of them uncomfortable. They had always been divided about Fascism, and several anti-Fascist organizations were active. The oldest, AFANA (Anti-Fascist Alliance of North America) had been organized in 1923 and was closely associated with American labor and socialist groups. There were anti-Fascist Italian-language papers in major American cities, representing various shades of opinion, including the Catholic *Voce del Popolo* in Detroit. There was also an English-language paper in Boston, *The Lantern*, which spoke for advanced radical opinion. But anti-Fascists among Americans of Italian origin were deeply split by faction, and the ambiguous attitudes of American labor and leftist leaders toward Mussolini had deprived them of outside support. Since most anti-Fascist leaders were leftists in the red-baiting age of the 1920s, they were disliked and harassed by much of the American press and officialdom. Several distinguished refugees from Fascism had been deported as undesirable aliens.

The strongest Italian-American organizations and newspapers, and probably the great majority of Italian Americans, were pro-Fascist. There were many clashes in the Little Italies of American cities, and Fascists and anti-Fascists had had a fight beside Rudolph Valentino's coffin in 1926 when Fascists tried to mount an honor guard (although the star had been anti-Fascist and his films were banned in Italy). But overwhelmingly, it was pro-Mussolini papers like Generoso Pope's *Il Progresso Italo-Americano* in New York and pro-Mussolini organizations like the Sons of Italy that dominated Italian-American opinion. They became sponsors of ardent support of the war against Ethiopia.[6] Their espousal of the cause placed them in a new and difficult situation. Until 1935 American opinion as a whole had not been for the most part unfriendly to Fascism. Mussolini's policies had provoked no great interest or antipathy. His regime had had a good press, generally speaking. Men like the former American Ambassador Richard Washburn Child had had considerable influence in presenting the New Italy in a favorable light. Many liberals and progressive Americans in particular, like their counterparts in the British Labour party, were inclined to sympathy with Fascism. Roosevelt himself had called Mussolini "that admirable gentleman."[7] For most Italian Americans there was until late 1935 no cause to suffer the discomfort of divided loyalties. But now the situation changed, as Americans began to change their minds.

When war seemed imminent, support for Italy among Italian Americans was enthusiastic and widespread, and active propaganda from the Italian government strengthened it. Italian-American women contributed their wedding rings, and several hundred male Italian residents sailed after hostilities began, to fight for the cause. This enthusiasm became for a time a powerful weapon of Italian policy, although later it backfired, like everything else connected with the

Ethiopian War. At first its chief use was to fortify the already overwhelming support for a completely neutral United States. The Italians
wanted America to stay away, which the Americans, for quite different
reasons, were determined to do. While Italian Americans, urged on by
the Italian embassy and consulates, gave massive support to the Italian
cause, everyone else treated it as none of their business. This was
what Rome wanted, but it gave rise to misapprehensions in Italy.
There, both government and press were led by reports on Italian-
American opinion into supposing that American opinion as a whole
was positively enthusiastic about Italy's colonial venture. Italian correspondents reported that Americans' acquaintance with their own black
population, the long experience with the need for holding blacks in a
subordinate position, gave them a particularly friendly understanding
of Italian aspirations in East Africa. White Americans knew, the New
York correspondent of the *Corriere della Sera* wrote, that seventy years
of freedom had not altered the "semi-barbarism" of American Negroes.[8]

The Italian appraisal was deeply misleading. Outside of Italian-
American circles there was almost no positive support for Mussolini's
colonial policies. There was at most—and that only in the early stages—
some tendency to regard them as understandable. What existed was an
ineffable detachment from the tangled affairs of European power politics. Papers like the Chicago *Tribune*, which positively supported the
Italian cause in the summer of 1935, were exceptional.

Leaders in America reacted with characteristic brands of detachment. The chief organ of responsible American opinion, the *New
York Times*, was the most detached of all. Its news stories were on the
whole detailed and not incorrect, although they show a high degree of
irrelevance to the significance of international aggression—for example,
exhaustive attention was given to whether the Italian public was reacting favorably or unfavorably to British moves, which, since Italian
opinion was either controlled or manufactured, was a largely unreal
issue. But the *Times*'s editorial attitudes were vacuous. Until September the chief editorial reference to the crisis was mostly in the form of
brief, humorous paragraphs in the column "Topics of the Times." In
September a few prominent editorials appeared. None expressed judgments on the crisis between Italy and Ethiopia, and none suggested
that the United States had any direct concern. They all dealt in

stately detachment with the question of whether the League would prove successful in achieving a solution to the difficulty. The tone was decorously pro-League but in a most distant way. They were full of rhetoric signifying remarkably little: "Not only the fate of the nations involved but the fate of the League itself will be hanging in the balance" (September 1). "Would sanctions mean war? Sanctions would be different from making war, although, it must be admitted, there would be a great danger of their leading to war" (September 17). And when the League debates seemed to be promising action, the *Times* decided that it was "rising to the full height of its power and dignity." The tendency to exaggerate the importance of the League was understandable, but it meant that the real problems were disregarded.

The casual reader in the 1970s might conclude from the series of editorials that their chief strength was the correctness of their punctuation. But the empty double-talk undoubtedly had a larger meaning. It was the decorous voice of wish-fulfillment. Foreign affairs, for the *New York Times*, as for most Americans (and for Stanley Baldwin), should be kept foreign and, if possible, tranquil, and the way to keep them that way was to tread majestically toward them on pussy-feet.

The attitude was, in different forms, characteristic of most American commentary in the weeks before the fighting started, although less authoritative papers took somewhat less vacuous positions. Interestingly, the Philadelphia *Inquirer*, a mediocre paper of conservative and luridly anti-New Deal cast, expressed about the most forthright condemnation of Mussolini to appear in any important publication. As early as August 16 it was denouncing him in unmeasured terms and calling the League "lily-livered." It incredulously asked two days later whether Mussolini would dare "to rush into this mad venture in utter disregard of solemn treaties, international obligations, and the rights of other peoples?" and later predicted that his defiance of morality and the League would prove his undoing. But the *Inquirer*, in common with the rest of the American press, showed little interest in Ethiopia itself and none whatever in possible American action.

The business community, at least that part of it whose views were reflected in *Business Week*, was similarly detached. Almost the only concern was about the effect that international "complications," such as might arise from the crisis, would have on the world demands for American materials and munitions. (*Business Week* foresaw disorder and disadvantage should there be a sudden rush to buy war materials from the United States.) The editors were on the whole hostile to Mussolini ("Italy is a threat to the peace of Europe")[9] and were sure he was bluffing. With more understanding than most Americans, they saw that the League was nothing more than the sum of the policies of its principal members and correctly anticipated that Britain would not dare call the bluff. They also saw that the East African crisis was connected with Italy's domestic economic problems, which were much more thoroughly understood and documented in *Business Week* than in most United States publications. The extreme precariousness of the Italian budget and balance of payments, the mounting unemployment (still considerably underestimated), the heavy pressures on the Bank of Italy resulting from deficits and gold flows, were all appraised, accurately, as portending major economic and political troubles for Mussolini. The editors also perceived, almost uniquely, that the conquest of Ethiopia would not lead immediately to the establishment of a docile colony but would provide Italy merely with a morass into which money and power would be indefinitely drained. Still, *Business Week*, despite this percipience, shared the general inclination to suppose that Mussolini's motives were both rational and economic; its editors thought he was wrong in supposing that Ethiopia would solve his economic problems, but they were sure that that was his supposition. On September 21 *Business Week* printed a long article about Ethiopia's minerals, which were supposed to be the attractions to conquest. It spoke of rumors about fantastic wealth in copper, gold, mica, and oil and of the value of Ethiopia's cotton crop to Italy's textile industry. It reported, although only in passing, that the mineral resources were entirely speculative and none of the supposed resources had ever been found in exploitable quantity. Even the agricultural riches were largely potential; aside from coffee and skins, Ethiopia's production was negligible by the standards of world trade. Nonetheless, the conjectural treasures were regarded as the motive, and a plausible motive, for Italian ambitions. Sir Samuel Hoare was not alone in his misapprehensions.

They were shared by the organ of another group of opinion, at the other end of the political spectrum. *The New Republic*, then as now, was the voice of left-wing, educated, skeptical people who saw

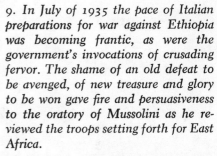

9. *In July of 1935 the pace of Italian preparations for war against Ethiopia was becoming frantic, as were the government's invocations of crusading fervor. The shame of an old defeat to be avenged, of new treasure and glory to be won gave fire and persuasiveness to the oratory of Mussolini as he reviewed the troops setting forth for East Africa.*

10. *On July 7, 1935—celebrated as the 2,688th birthday of the city of Rome—with the invasion of Ethiopia near, Mussolini invoked the Augustan past and called on Romans to display their classical warlike skill and spirit.*

11. In the same month of July, in terms no less fervent than those used by Mussolini, Haile Selassie stood on the balcony of his palace and called on his people for a crusade of national defense against Italy.

12. Ethiopia, with its proud civilization, faced a European power that it regarded as in no way superior—Ethiopia's culture was ancient and rich, and the Fascist version of European culture was deformed and corrupt. Ethiopia was armed with spears and outdated rifles against Italy's planes and machine guns.

13. Haile Selassie inspects a machine gun.

14. The heraldic lions of Great Britain's coat of arms symbolize the power of the English crown and nation. In Ethiopia, lions had a similar symbolism, but the lions were not heraldic—they were real. In 1935 a former minister of war wore a lion's mane on his ceremonial war dress.

15. Prince Kassa was the greatest of Ethiopian personages after the emperor; he was commander in chief of the imperial armies because of rank, seniority, and his considerable talents. While the archaic splendor of his costume was impressive, his armies were also archaic, and his field communications consisted of foot messengers and a single wireless set.

16. The Ethiopian artillery, meager and obsolete, made a brave show of demonstrating that Ethiopia was a modern state equipped to fight in a modern war.

the western world as corrupted by an unscrupulous capitalism. But *The New Republic* was so much imprisoned by its ideology that skepticism was drowned in suspicion. In 1935 it paid very little attention to the Italian-Ethiopian dispute, and when it did pay attention it was of an oddly random sort. At one point it explained the failure of Britain to oppose Italian expansion by observing that Britain no longer had any interest in Ethiopia because it had already lost its markets there to Japanese competitors (a theory without basis in reality) and it explained Italy's concern by saying that the Ethiopians had been armed to the teeth by Japanese munitions makers and thus presented a real threat to Eritrea and Italian Somaliland (a theory also without foundation). As the crisis grew more acute, *The New Republic* grew more thorough and more rational in its treatment. It supposed, without going into the matter in any detail, that Mussolini's motives were the product of Italy's need for markets, raw materials, and an outlet for "overpopulation"; it said that Britain was prepared to concede Mussolini's real need for such facilities. But *The New Republic* was certain that such concessions would not provide any real stability in European international relations, since the need of capitalism for expansion was infinite, and the world could never be carved up among competing capitalisms in a way to satisfy any of them. And it accused the American government of selfish meddling in affairs that did not concern it when Secretary of State Cordell Hull reminded Ethiopia and Italy in July of their obligations to abstain from war under the Paris Peace Pact (Kellogg-Briand Pact) of 1928. *The New Republic* suspected that the State Department's attitude was based upon a desire to defend (contrary to the interests of the American people) the concession that five years before had been given to an American company, the J. G. White Engineering Corporation of New York, to build a dam on the Blue Nile near Lake Tana (which it had never exploited).

Like the conservatives of *Business Week*, the leftists of *The New Republic* were doubtful whether Mussolini would derive from Ethiopia, once conquered, the benefits he expected. The Italians, it sagely observed, exaggerated the importance of Ethiopia as a potential market for Italian goods.

What was most striking of all was the agreement of *Business Week* and *The New Republic* in their prescription for American policy. They were both resolutely opposed to any American initiative of any sort. Ironically, *Business Week* thought that no one but a few liberals in the big cities were opposed to the "Keep Out" sign which should be posted against this, and any other, foreign entanglement, while *The New Republic* thought that big business interests were conspiring to involve America in a foreign quarrel. Its writers saw the League as a sinister instrument of decadent nationalism, doomed from the beginning, and they particularly resented the implication that it was American isolation that accounted for the League's weakness: "It is nonsense to say . . . that this is all America's fault, that if we had joined the League years ago it would now be an effective international policy."[10] And when war was finally seen to be imminent, it denounced any possible American co-operation with the League action against the aggressor: "America should remain aloof at all costs."[11] At no point did either the conservative or the leftist weekly suggest that America might make a useful contribution to peace by using its power or that the fate of Ethiopia was to be considered as anything but an incident in the European situation. At no point did either suggest that Fascist Italy was pernicious, as the antithesis of freedom and progress. *The New Republic* limited its remarks on the state of Ethiopia to quoting Maxim Litvinov, the Soviet representative at the League, when he felicitously remarked upon the indictment of Ethiopia by Italy's representative, Baron Pompeo Aloisi, that the Ethiopians might be guilty of barbarous practices but it would not improve the situation to have the Italians shoot them.

The constant reiteration of the view that the Italian-Ethiopian crisis was none of Americans' business showed that it was really in the forefront of Americans' minds and was frightening them. What worried them was that it might lead to a European war. This was the age of revulsion against World War I and of pacifism among young people and reformers. The prospect of another 1917 frightened some Americans to the point of angry hysteria. And by midsummer it was making a dent in high politics. There were signs that politics was responding to the pressures of opinion in the way that had become traditional since the election of Warren Harding.

The most important of these signs was the Neutrality Resolution passed by Congress and signed by the president in August 1935. Its hasty enactment was speeded by the Ethiopian crisis and the fear of a

general European war, although its history was long and deeply en-
meshed in both domestic politics and the long-standing debates about
what had caused the Great Mistake of 1917, as it was seen in 1935. Its
immediate background was the investigation, carried out by a committee chaired and inspired by Senator Gerald Nye of North Dakota,
into the role of the munitions industry in the United States and its
role in American foreign policy.

The Nye Committee's findings and the attitude it represented
blended the traditional American distrust of foreign entanglements and
the vaguely Marxist belief widely held throughout the world in the
thirties that wars were made by capitalists seeking markets and particularly by munitions makers—"merchants of death"—desirous of sell-
ing their wares. There emerged the conviction that America could most
conveniently isolate itself from the lethal conflicts of the Old World by
embargoes on money, men, and materiel to belligerent powers—the
notion, like the word, had a Jeffersonian association that commended
it to both conservatives and progressives.

The Administration, or at least the principal authorities in foreign
affairs—the president and the secretary of state—were much more internationalist in their outlook. Roosevelt's attitude is difficult to define.
He always bowed to realities; he was a man of principle in a personal
rather than a general way, and he did not like to commit himself to
abstract positions. But he undoubtedly disliked the Italian policy. Mussolini's compulsive inclination to adventure in the name of shopworn
slogans was precisely incompatible with the president's temperament.
When Mussolini told the American counselor of embassy in Rome that
considerations of prestige prevented him from abandoning his plans to
attack Ethiopia, Roosevelt characteristically suggested telling Mussolini
that if he did back down his prestige would be *increased*. He should
appeal, Roosevelt wrote, "to the higher and not the lower ideal."[12]
The president was outraged, when the war began, by Italian under-
handedness and brutality.[13] But his reactions were those of a distant
observer. He was interested principally in his domestic programs, and
like the National Government in Britain he was inclined to concern
himself with foreign affairs only when they impinged on domestic affairs.

The executive branch in 1935 was concerned mainly about its
ability to make foreign policy without rigid congressional guidelines.
The constitutionality of legislative interference might be subject to

doubt, but public opinion and the western senators did not think so. The American Administration, like the British, was going to have to face an election, and the fate of Roosevelt's domestic program depended on the support and co-operation of many of the congressional leaders who were most rigidly dedicated to isolationism and neutrality legislation. The Administration tried to induce Congress to make the neutrality law discretionary: to allow the Administration to withhold arms shipments to aggressors while continuing to supply the victims of aggression. But this was precisely the line of thinking, it was said, that had led to American involvement in 1917. And the only definition of aggression available was that provided by the Covenant of the League. From the isolationist standpoint, the kind of legislation the president wanted would mean that American policy would be associated with, maybe even *defined by*, the League. This was what isolationists had determined to avoid ever since 1919. With threats of filibusters impending, the Administration accepted as inevitable the temporary legislation passed in August, which imposed upon the president the very limited option of finding that a state of hostilities existed and withholding all arms shipments or of shipping arms equally to all purchasers.

Since Roosevelt's domestic policy and success in the 1936 presidential election depended upon soothing a public opinion that seemed to be almost unanimously opposed to any involvement in European politics, the public diplomatic acts of the United States and the State Department's public statements were aloof and cautious to the point of nullity. The Department equalled the *New York Times* in the majestic mumbo jumbo of its convoluted prose, conveying sentiments about as compelling as those on a Christmas card. (State Department style always tended to consist of sonorous assertions of principles that nobody could possibly quarrel with.) The nullities precisely met the wishes of the governments of Britain, France, and Italy. As some American commentators like Elmer Davis observed, they disappointed those sectors of public opinion in Britain and France that were demanding international action to stop the aggressor and support the League. They disappointed, too, the government of Ethiopia, which was trying its best to invoke some sort of United States support.

The Ethiopians, in particular the emperor, had long been inclined to regard the American republic as the most reliable, indeed the only reliable, possible friend among great powers. The United States had practically no commercial interests in the country—the only American firm with any considerable dealings in Ethiopia was Singer Sewing Machines, and even its market was very small in comparison to its other vast overseas interests. The United States still had in that part of the world a reputation for honesty, fairness, and complete disinterestedness—the old reputation that had, a century and more before, brought American power into the Mediterranean as a supporter and supplier of the sultan of Turkey. The presence and influence of Everett Colson, and in fact of an American legation in the capital of a country that had no political or economic connection with the United States, were testimony to Haile Selassie's admiration for the United States and his desire to engage the interest of its government in Ethiopian affairs.[14] When he welcomed the American chargé d'affaires, W. Perry George, in October 1934, the emperor remarked that he had "worked very hard to secure American diplomatic representation in Ethiopia. We cherish our relations with the United States, understanding that their friendly character is undisturbed by any political aims in this part of the world, and realizing our great need for politically disinterested cooperation in our economic development."[15]

It was a moment of singular symbolism. Perry George was a career Foreign Service officer, a man who represented both personally and professionally the traditions of the white ruling class in the United States. And he represented, by instruction, the insularity, indeed the insulation, of American foreign policy. When the emperor appealed for disinterested co-operation, he was unknowingly contributing to the destruction of insularity—and, in the end, of disinterestedness and of the dominance of the traditions that the American diplomat stood for.

The emperor was deceiving himself; or, more precisely, his invocations were ten years premature. But he persisted in the hope that the United States might somehow help. The recurrent efforts to achieve this co-operation, and the response they met with, form a peculiar and illuminating tale.

The instrument that Haile Selassie first tried to use with the United States was the Paris Peace Pact of 1928. This was simply a general statement to the effect that the signatory powers each renounced war as an instrument of national policy and agreed to settle their disputes by peaceful means. It was interpreted as "outlawing war." In June, Addis Ababa formally requested the United States to examine means of "securing Italy's observance of engagements as signatory of the Kellogg [Paris] Pact."

The secretary of state replied promptly on July 5. The crux of his answer was characteristic of the Department's prose style, its tendency to cloak its policies in conventional sentiments: "my Government would be loath to believe that either [Ethiopia or Italy] would permit any situation to arise which would be inconsistent with the commitments of the Pact."

Beneath this propriety lay the fact the Administration *had* to avoid anything that could be construed at home as a willingness to meddle. The Ethiopians (correctly interpreting it) despaired; the Italians (drawing inferences that were only half correct) construed it as approval for their projects. Everywhere it was assumed that the statement of July 5 was, as the Boston *Evening Transcript* put it, a "brusque refusal of the American government to invoke the Pact to prevent the Italo-Ethiopian conflict from developing into open war."[16] Secretary Hull then said that it regarded the Paris Peace Pact as binding on all the sixty-odd countries that had signed it. American policy consisted in asserting that no one had a right to invade anyone else, but that the American government would not resort to any action beyond high-sounding admonition to prevent its doing so.

A much stranger effort to prevent war was made by another American official. As early as February, Breckinridge Long, the American ambassador at Rome, had reported that preparations for an extensive military campaign in East Africa were underway and he believed himself that the regime would be endangered without a success in Ethiopia. Failure to win, he said, would "bring about a change of government,"[17] and he reported Mussolini's frank personal statements that he was "absolutely and irrevocably determined on his Abyssinian venture."[18] In September, Long made his own essay in peacemaking. He was a skilled diplomat, very much in the European tradition of manipulative diplomacy. It is plausible to suppose that he viewed the security of the Fascist regime as something to be hoped for; he was certainly much concerned at the prospect of an adventure that might lead to a European war. He suggested that Mussolini could make a great gesture to save the peace and secure his reputation as a constructive statesman by limiting his ambitions to objectives that could be secured without war. Incredibly, the particular objectives that the American ambassador proposed as appropriate were annexation of Ethiopian territory "as far as Addis Ababa," leaving "the original kingdom of Ethiopia" more or less intact.[19] To these proposals Mussolini replied that the fate of Ethiopia was "purely an Italian colonial matter." Long's proposal had been made as a personal initiative, and it shows more about the American Foreign Service than about American foreign policy. But it is another illustration of the confusion that arises when a major power fails to formulate a plan for handling a crisis.

The Ethiopians did not know that the principal American diplomat concerned was recommending the partition of their country. They responded to Hull's platitudes about the Paris Peace Pact with a stratagem. It was based on the belief that America might be ensnared into supporting them whether the Americans wanted to or not. The incident is remarkable, both for its complexity and as another example of the extraordinary unreality that pervaded the entire statesmanship of the period.

One basic fact to be noted in considering the "Rickett incident," as the Ethiopian stratagem was called, is that there was not known to be any oil in Ethiopia. There is still, more than thirty-five years later, not known to be any, although oil companies were investigating the possibilities in 1935 and have been investigating them ever since. (Ironically, the only promise of oil, and that highly speculative, that the oil companies have found after years of surveys in contemporary Ethiopia has been in its Red Sea province, which was in 1935 the Italian colony of Eritrea, while Italy itself has turned out to have large oil resources.) Still, in 1935 it was widely accepted, even in Ethiopia, as probable, or at least conceivable, that an appetite for oil was one of the chief motives for the Italian venture.

A second fact, contributing to a scarcely greater measure of unreality, was that the incident was an attempt to resurrect "dollar diplomacy." The Ethiopians—and possibly Colson himself—supposed that a large American business interest in any part of the world would ineluctably attract American diplomatic protection and thereafter the United States Marine Corps. This was an anachronism; it was the very sort of adventure that American opinion and policy had been most concerned to prevent since 1919. But in threatened Addis Ababa it was deemed logical to invoke the old diplomacy.

In July 1935 the African Development Exploration Corporation of the United States had received a charter of incorporation in the state of Delaware. The affairs of the corporation were complex and obscure in the extreme—an "amazing story," as *Business Week* observed, "so complicated as to be unbelievable."[20] The obscurity was due to another anachronism. It was the familiar kind of venture that had flourished, often yielding returns on the order of 50 per cent annually to investors, in the nineteenth century. Most of its directors were British, including its chief agent in Ethiopia, Francis W. Rickett.

Rickett was an adventurer on a very high level, a privateering capitalist of the old school who was also an English gentleman of the hunting and shooting persuasion, of genial manner. His connections and principles were cloaked with the mystery of one of E. Phillips Oppenheim's naïve stories of international agents; no one knew exactly where he came from or how he came to play the odd role he did. He had excellent connections with Haile Selassie and with Everett Colson, however, and he was a willing and skillful operator at the particular job which he undertook. But he was in this case an entrepreneur in the narrowest sense. The backers were Socony-Vacuum Oil Company and the Standard Oil Company of New Jersey, which, as their officials later explained to an outraged secretary of state, had long been interested in the possibility of oil in East Africa.

It was not, however, an interest in business opportunities for American oil companies that had prompted the formation of the African Development Exploration Corporation; it was a political calculation of the Ethiopian government. As early as January 1935, Rickett had been in touch with the Ethiopian authorities. It was he who had solicited support from the American oil companies by dangling very favorable terms offered by the emperor. The concession was to give exclusive rights to exploration for oil resources and their development in eastern Ethiopia, the part of the country bordering Eritrea and Italian Somaliland. Generous royalties for Ethiopia were provided, against an immediate payment of $25,000,000 that would have permitted Haile Selassie to finance the purchase of American arms. The terms were announced on August 29, on the eve of the meeting of the League Council. There is no doubt—the emperor shortly admitted it—that the concession was intended to give an American company and therefore, he hoped, the American government, an interest to defend *within* Ethiopia, in the area most immediately threatened not only by Italian arms but by the various compromise proposals under discussion. It was the counterpart of the similarly byzantine diplomatic calculation in Addis Ababa that had brought the British commissioners and escort to the gates of Walwal ten months before.

The initial effect was to implicate Great Britain as well as the United States and to create a brief sensation. There was outrage and anxiety in London and Washington—in London because the predominance of Englishmen in the concession might seem to suggest that the lofty tone the British government was taking at the moment in Geneva veiled a low-grade commercial interest of its own; in Washington because it suggested United States involvement in a foreign fracas that the government was determined to stay out of. Both governments instantly denied all knowledge of the concession. Hull summoned the chairman of the board and vice president of Standard-Vacuum (which owned the African Development Exploration Corporation and was itself owned by Standard of New Jersey and Socony-Vacuum) and ordered them to cancel the concession. It was an unprecedented demand; the board chairman at first demurred, but eventually he agreed.

The cancelling of the concession was announced with considerable éclat, and the fact that the State Department had caused its cancellation was given wide currency. The American government was pleased; it had demonstrated that it was not only not responsible for the concession but that it had rejected the dollar diplomacy of bad old days. Most of all, it demonstrated its determination to remain unentangled in the Ethiopian crisis. The British government was exculpated. The Italians, who had been loud in their burst of outrage, were pacified. The Ethiopian government expressed its regret that it would not be able to benefit from the capital and technical skills of experienced oilmen.

This curious four days' incident helped focus American attention upon the crisis in East Africa in an American context, and it came at a time when there was more and more clearly emerging what looked like a deadly engagement between an aggressive Italy and the keepers of the world's peace. There began to appear, in both the press and the government, increasing signs that the Americans regarded Italy as a sinister troublemaker.

The Italian government was sufficiently concerned about the evolution of American opinion to send a special agent, Bernardo Bergamaschi, to study and report upon American attitudes. The Italians were not concerned about the possibility of any direct intervention by the United States, for that was unthinkable. What they worried about was the possibility that American opinion against them might develop to the point where the United States would co-operate with sanctions if the League were to apply them. They knew well enough that the *prospect* of American co-operation would itself be a powerful factor in encouraging the League to adopt them. The Neutrality Resolution forebade precisely such a policy, but it was a stopgap, a temporary act, and it could be changed.

Bergamaschi found the climate in America to be anti-Italian. There was no positive support at all for the Italian aspirations in East Africa, outside of Italo-American groups. He attributed this antagonism to the skill of British propagandists and proposed that it be changed by hiring a public relations firm in New York to plan a pro-Italian advertising campaign. His proposal was ill judged—the efforts of Italy to present its case were to produce a backlash effect—but his appraisal was correct. Opinion in the United States, while remaining for the most part stolidly isolationist, was being engaged on behalf of the League and Ethiopia. Once war was begun, this evolution proceeded rapidly. Eventually it was to engulf isolationism in a raging sea of anti-Fascist opinion and to lead toward full participation in world affairs and eventually to the overextension of the post-World War II decades.

Further stages in this development will be examined later; it is important to note here that it was Italian actions, as presented to the American public in September of 1935, that marked the first beginnings of the development of a general anti-Fascist opinion in America and a general association of the Italian dictatorship with irresponsible international conduct and vicious aggressiveness. The war that was now to begin saw this development profoundly affected and deepened by two other developments that accompanied it: the failure of Britain and France to back the League of Nations and the association of Nazi Germany with Fascist Italy. By the time the Italians had reached Addis Ababa, the Americans had formed the impression that an ideological union of Facist aggressors threatened world peace and that the European democracies were unwilling or unable to stop them. It was a fateful impression.

The attitude of the German government toward Italy's Ethiopian venture was not generally expressed in public. Its concealed realities would have astonished a great many people, although they would not have surprised Pierre Laval or Sir Samuel Hoare.

To understand the development of Germany's view it must be recalled that the Ethiopian policy seems to have been undertaken by Mussolini partly as an anti-German venture. German-Italian relations were at their worst in the winter and spring of 1935, when Italy was co-operating in the French effort to contain Nazi Germany. Aside from a few displays of ideological affinity, the only component of Italian-German relations was enmity. And so far as Mussolini went, the affinity counted for almost nothing. He feared and resented Hitler and certainly entertained no feeling of comradeship. He may have seen that a "Fascist International" was a logical contradiction in terms, since nationalism was the chief component of Fascist doctrine.

On the other side of the Alps, reactions were different. The affinity had meaning. With the curious sentimentality of which he was frequently capable, Hitler admired Mussolini as his maestro and frequently referred to himself as the Duce's disciple. While he despised Italians, he admired Fascism. He also believed that a collapse of Fascism would threaten Nazism in Germany, since people commonly associated the two. On the other hand, Hitler's most immediate need was to break up the encircling ring of the Versailles powers and the "Stresa Front."

Under these circumstances, German policy opposed the Ethiopian venture in its early stages, when it appeared that it had the blessing of the British and the French. There were plenty of indications of hostility to Italy. The Germans knew and said that the threat to Ethiopia was the price the French were paying for the containment of Germany. It was noted in the German press that the economic survival of Austria (always rather precarious) was helped by the arms the Italians were ordering, in preparation for the Ethiopian invasion, from an Austrian munitions factory in the winter of 1935, and Hitler had long intended to annex Austria. The German press bristled with denunciations of Italy for its oppression, undoubtedly real, of the quarter-million German-speaking population in the South Tyrol. (At Christmas time

1934 the Munich press declaimed against the Italians with particular fervor for outlawing *Christmas trees* in the South Tyrol, an insult to German *Volkstum*.) The attacks became so strident by the spring of 1935, at the time of Stresa, that the Munich *Neueste Nachrichten* was banned in Italy. At the same time, a German documentary film called *Abyssinia Today,* applauding Haile Selassie for his enlightened rule and modernization program, was distributed throughout Germany and enthusiastically greeted in the German papers. Articles appeared ridiculing the Italian army, predicting a fiasco if the invasion of Ethiopia took place. Since all published expressions of opinion in Germany were government controlled, these items obviously reflected high policy. The Italian ambassador in Berlin, Vittorio Cerruti, who was inclined to be anti-German anyway, found the climate of opinion so hostile that he was barely on speaking terms with the foreign office officials.

But as the summer went on, this strained situation began to change, in precisely the measure that dislike of the Ethiopian venture in France and Britain became more noticeable. Opposition in Berlin to the Italian attack on Ethiopia existed because it seemed to be being undertaken with French and British approval. When it began to appear that the British and French did not approve and that the League of Nations might be invoked against Italy, then the attack was warmly welcomed as contributing to the break-up of the anti-German Front.

There were other concerns, on the Italian side, that led to improvement in German-Italian relations. Italy was largely dependent on German coal and had become its leading importer during the period of military preparations. With mounting evidence that Mussolini had exaggerated British and French complacency, German coal sources became more important; later they were to become indispensable. Cerruti was replaced by Bernardo Attolico. He was, like his predecessor, a career diplomat unconnected with the Fascist movement, but he left for his post with new instructions: to display as much cordiality as possible. He set out to do so by going to Hitler's mountain retreat in Berchtesgaden in September 1935 to present his credentials instead of awaiting the German dictator's return to Berlin, and he attended the enormous annual party rally at Nuremberg, which Cerruti had boycotted. Moreover, Mussolini's determination to squelch Nazi operations in Austria began to weaken. By October, when the formal hostility of the League and of France and Britain were clearer, the Italians allowed the Austrians to begin negotiations with the Germans to ease some of the more painful tensions arising from underground Nazi activities.

The attitude of the people who made policy in Berlin was still very tentative. From their point of view, good relations between Germany and Italy depended entirely on the existence of bad relations between Italy and France and Britain, and they were chronically suspicious that Mussolini would rebuild the Stresa Front if he could. They affected an outward air of neutrality in the Italian dispute with the League. They may have suspected what was undoubtedly true, that Mussolini's mild show of amicability toward Germany was an attempt to frighten Britain and France with the threat that opposition to his venture would cause a breakup in the anti-German front. But it was the Germans, not the Italians, who were in a position to call the tune, and Mussolini's advances were the beginning of a process that ended in dependence on Germany. He later said that the Rome-Berlin Axis had been born in September 1935, and he was probably right.

By the time the war began, then, the reactions of the United States and of Germany had been fatefully directed into the courses they were to follow until the destruction of the Axis in 1945, and in complementary ways, the British and the French were preparing their own destinies and that of the League of Nations.

It is instructive to note that none of the governments concerned were doing what their own and foreign peoples thought they were doing. Not in the United States, where the Administration was, in effect, trying to think of ways to evade the more stringent orthodoxies of isolationism; not in Britain, where lip service to collective security and the League concealed the conviction that the only safe course was to negotiate with Mussolini; not in Italy, where Fascism's fire-eating talk about national destiny, the civilizing mission, and irresistible power concealed both petty jobbery and a bad case of nerves; not in France, where Laval was now presenting himself as a loyal if reluctant supporter of internationalism; not in Germany, where Hitler's real intentions were curiously veiled in discreet disapproval of Italian activities; not in the Soviet Union, with its world-wide following of loyal Communists, for whom a profound lack of interest in Ethiopia, Africa as a whole, and the transactions at Geneva was covered by a formal air of zealous co-operation and formal sympathy for Ethiopia. There were a few people who, by reason of superior perception or special interests, saw through some of the frauds. One interesting example was that of American black leftists, who denounced the Communists and the Soviet Union in most unmeasured terms for their cynical failure to support or even discuss the crime that was being committed against a black nation. But generally speaking it was a time when, even in democratic governments, citizens took, and were counted upon to take, their statesmen's utterances at face value. The situation was about to change, suddenly and drastically, as a result of what happened in Ethiopia.

The question of what, decades later, would be called "credibility" was one that men of good will had worried about during World War I, and President Wilson's insistence on open covenants openly arrived at —what was called the "new diplomacy"—was intended to harmonize methods of conducting governments with the requirements of an age where for the first time in history mass opinion was literate, partly informed, and politically influential. The new diplomacy had failed disastrously, and the comedy of the Ethiopian crisis demonstrated its failure with stunning totality.

It was a result of these misleading appearances that by the end of the summer of 1935 a major world crisis seemed to have developed, in which the League might for the first time try to impose its collective will upon a great power and the British and French might find themselves fighting to support it. Hopeful and well-intentioned people believed that the lost promises of 1919 might at last be made good, that international action and morality might now prevail. Others feared that League action might precipitate a second world war. Almost everyone, even those few who knew what was really going on, was tense, excited, and apprehensive. There was talk of possible air raids in Britain.

What induced this atmosphere of fateful crisis was the belief that the British and French could not "back down"—the phrase was widely used—in their commitment to collective security. The British public was now noisily enthusiastic about League action, and the machinery had at last begun to work. The Ethiopians had been trying since January to get the Council to take up their case as a threat to peace. On September 4 it had finally done so. The Ethiopian representative, Gaston Jèze, had made the most of his opportunity. He drove home the legal point that the very existence of a member state was threatened, in violation of several articles of the League Covenant. But the moral point was more heavily emphasized. "The League," he said, "is the conscience of mankind. Ethiopia makes a supreme appeal to that conscience."[21] The Council had agreed to order a committee of five representatives, including those of France and Britain, to study the situation. Then, on September 11, had come Hoare's dramatic speech. It was generally taken to mean that Britain would support League action to protect the threatened victim of aggression. At the same time, Italian blustering was more vociferous than ever, and Italian intentions more massively obvious. The atmosphere of crisis, and expectation, mounted.

But behind these external manifestations there was no world crisis at all, not in the sense that the public imagined, the sense of a turning point in the history of ways of settling international disputes. The awareness of climax was the result of mistakes, ignorance, and deliberate concealment of intentions. On the very day that Hoare delivered the speech that so many people regarded as a clarion call to virtue, he was completing quiet conversations in Geneva with Pierre Laval. They agreed on one definite point. They would not apply military sanctions, whatever action the League might take, whatever appearance of opposition to Italian aggression that they might feel obliged to present. Italy would not be blockaded by the British fleet, and the Suez Canal would not be closed.

In retrospect, it looks like unholy deceit and cynicism, like a gruesome farce in which cynical old men were deliberately misleading their nations and betraying a great cause. But it was not. Both Hoare and Laval were serious men, badly frightened by what they believed to be a serious threat of war. And they thought that their own people were confused and misinformed about its character. The supporters of the League, Hoare and Laval thought, simply did not understand that military sanctions might mean a major war. Enthusiasm for League action they saw as a new and sudden fad, characterized by little lucidity and less staying power. It was a weak foundation on which to build a national war effort. Transcendently, they clearly saw the real danger that Germany, unprepared to take on a coalition of the three great powers, might judge it possible to move if two of them were involved in a struggle with the third. In this, the troubled ministers in Paris and London were prophetically correct, and it contributed to the general atmosphere of hand-wringing that now prevailed. Neither government was prepared to assume the awesome responsibility for an action that—they feared—might produce in Italy a suicidal military resistance. They were probably wrong in their judgments. They were certainly unadventurous. They were very narrow in their view of how diplomacy could and should be conducted. They had no real understanding of what ideology meant. But they were not hypocrites or villains; they were merely obsolete.

What still looks shocking is the vast duplicity into which they had been led. The hard, secret decision to eschew military sanctions meant that at the moment when world opinion was growing anxious to stop the Italians and the British and the French were sanctimoniously placating that opinion publicly, they were privately agreeing not to use the one weapon that *could* surely stop them. They were determining in advance that there would be no showdown. They were—it was made clear in the secret conversations—determined to persevere in their efforts to preserve the friendship of Italy as the cornerstone of their European policies. They hoped, in short, to square a circle, and this they proposed to do by an appearance of judicious support for the League's machinery to discourage and punish aggressors. They hoped that it would prove a deterrent, while at the same time they would privately seek a settlement acceptable to the Italians. This policy could be stated in terms that sounded respectable, scrupulous, and even logical.

But the circle could not be squared. The *appearance* of support for the League looked publicly more categorical than Laval and Hoare intended. This was in part inevitable; it is difficult to moderate a tidal wave by discretion. But it was partly fortuitous. For one thing, despite (or perhaps because of) the timidity of the British naval authorities, their aversion to fighting on behalf of the League, and their distrust of the French, the British had decided in August to strengthen their Mediterranean defenses. The Admiralty ordered ships from vulnerable Malta to Alexandria and strengthened the garrisons at the Mediterranean stations. It then ordered units of the Home Fleet, including *Hood*, the largest battleship in the world, transferred to Gibraltar, where it arrived on September 12. These naval movements were publicly known. Their timing seemed too significant to be anything but deliberate. They convinced most of the world, including the Italians, that Great

Britain meant business. And they contributed powerfully to the quite fictional impression of a major European crisis and the belief, accepted in such places as the *New York Times* editorial offices, that the full naval power of Britain might be brought to bear in support of the League of Nations and its covenanted defense of victims of aggression.

The Admiralty and the Foreign Office, acting separately, unwittingly galvanized world opinion. There was now the exciting expectation that the League would take action against a great power if that power did not abandon its obvious intention to attack a small member state. Pro-League circles throughout the world were enormously heartened, and the isolation of Italy at Geneva was noticed as a sign that, at long last, international morality had finally triumphed in politics.

In Italy the effect of the fictional crisis was naturally also seismic. Responsible people were appalled at the prospect—punishment by all of the League nations, perhaps a war that must surely prove catastrophic. Apprehension was greatest in military quarters. The general staff, reacting in the way that Hoare and Laval presumably hoped it would, tried to convince Mussolini of the folly of his course of action. The cautious, secretly anti-Fascist Badoglio prepared a long memorandum for the dictator demonstrating that Italy could not possibly hope to survive British opposition. Dino Grandi, in London, passionately advised abandonment of the Ethiopian invasion. There was even, in some circles, a tendency to suppose that the venture *must* be called off and that Mussolini must resign. Roman gossips already speculated on his successor.

Mussolini himself was much alarmed. But he was now *personally* totally committed; the compelling reasons that had contributed to his initial decision were more compelling than ever. If a distraction, an international triumph, had been necessary to divert attention from a grave domestic situation to save his own prestige, it was even more so now. Withdrawal, as he had repeatedly told the American diplomats, would ruin a regime already compromised. Having exploited the notion of Italy as a brave young nation resolutely dedicated to the fulfillment of its just ambitions and having actually profited from the situation in which the Italian David seemed to be facing the fat and decadent British Goliath, retreat or even compromise appeared out of the question politically, as it probably was psychologically. Moreover, the monarchy was associated with this dilemma. Victor Emmanuel's chronic caution dictated, now, not a surrender, which would certainly have endangered his throne, but a resolute pursuance of the policy already adopted. The only person in Italy who was *constitutionally* capable of stopping Mussolini was frightened into support of his policy.

As a result, the Italian press responded to the British naval movements with bravado and counterthreats, and to Hoare's speech with silence. Mussolini was announced to have told the council of ministers on September 15 that Italy would "reply to any threat whatsoever, from wherever it may come" and shrewdly observed that he was sure France would not permit Franco-Italian collaboration in European affairs to be disrupted by a colonial conflict or by any delusory dedication to the League of Nations. And on the same day, in an interview with a correspondent of a French paper, he went further in trying to appeal to French concern about Germany by suggesting that Britain's "monstrous" behavior was leading Europe to an unnecessary war. "Never," he said, "from our side will come any act of hostility against a European nation," but "we shall go straight ahead" in Ethiopia.

On September 18 the League's Committee of Five issued its recommendations. They were an attempt to meet Italy's announced grievances against Ethiopia by establishing extensive League controls to assure a more civilized conduct of affairs in Addis Ababa and to make sure that no offensive actions were undertaken against Ethiopia's neighbors. Mussolini merely rejected the proposals as irrelevant. Indeed, the scheme was both far-reaching and vague enough to threaten Ethiopian independence. The Ethiopian government itself hesitated to accept the proposals, until it was clear that Italy was not going to do so. But the proposals never had the slightest chance of acceptance in Rome, although some Italian foreign office people were prepared to use them as a basis for peaceful extension of Italian influence. Indeed, even before they were made public, Mussolini had told the American ambassador, "It is too late to talk of compromise. It is too late to withdraw any of my plans for operations in East Africa."[22] And Long observed, "He is irrevocably determined and serenely calm and is riding into the face of a storm which will either ruin him and bring disaster to his country, or raise him actually to that pedestal where he is sentimentally placed by his fanatic admirers." The ambassador was wrong in supposing Mussolini to be calm; that he never was, although he was skillful at giving the outward impression of it. But the rest of the observation was astute and accurate, perhaps more deeply so than the American realized.

The British, out of their compelling need to appear to be doing something they had no intention of doing and being something they had no intention of being, created the appearance of a world crisis and with it a moment of misplaced hope that the forces of good might be armed with British battleships and thus, for once, made to prevail over evil. They had, at the same time, gradually created a situation in which Mussolini was forced, for his own salvation, to defy them. Thus there began to take place the first steps toward a gigantic realignment of the world's conscience and the world's power. For much of the world there now emerged a picture that was presently to take on a certain parallel to reality, of a clear division between the forces of evil and those of good, between aggressive Fascist dictatorships and peace-loving democracies (among which, rather oddly, the Soviet Union was to be classed), between aggressive nationalism and beneficent internationalism, between collective security and gangsterism, between a decadent appeasement of the dictators and a forthright opposition to them, between imperialism and freedom. The conscience of the world was beginning to awaken, to the embarrassment of all the governments of Europe.

7

Appointment in Asmara

A war had been arranged and would shortly take place. It had been concluded that the Italians would attack when the rains ended. Few wars in history have been attended by so much advance publicity.

By the time it began, everyone was ready for it. Ready, that is, psychologically. No one abroad supposed that Ethiopia was ready militarily. Still, among those who favored its cause there was hope that geography and fighting spirit might long postpone defeat. The judgment was entirely reasonable; the Italian project was an immensely difficult one, as the Italian and foreign military experts were fully aware. They tended, indeed, to exaggerate the defensive powers of the Ethiopians; many of them were sure that the campaigns would last two years. Many European experts thought it would take even longer. Almost nobody in Europe anticipated a quick Italian victory.

In Ethiopia, however, informed persons, foreigners and the more up-to-date government officials, believed that Ethiopia could not win, and some expected a rapid disaster. A few optimistic observers vaguely thought that Ethiopia could put an army of a million men into the field (official sources had permitted this figure to be made public), but this was a wild exaggeration, and in any case, anyone who had seen the Ethiopian army knew that numbers meant very little. Even if there had been anything like a million soldiers available, it would not have helped much. Men who were present say their most vivid recollection of the beginning of the war was the sight of the forces assembling in Addis Ababa, villagers in bare feet armed with wooden pitchforks, enthusiastically prepared to march against the machine guns of Italy. The gap between the technologies of the two countries, unimaginably vast, mattered much more than manpower. The more perceptive also thought it mattered more than geography or morale.

Except for the well-trained and well-equipped imperial guard, there was no modern army at all in the western sense. The imperial guard consisted of a few thousand men. The regulars consisted of about 100,000 men, but their training varied from the negligible to the non-existent. Few of them were uniformed. While the organization was theoretically that of a European army, it was in large degree a tribal assemblage, with personal loyalty to a chief replacing hierarchical discipline and the command function. Even in the modernized units, old traditions were strong, and the titles of officers were startling: the officer who was supposed to lead an attack was called The Front of the Rhinoceros. There were about 50,000 rifles and several hundred machine guns but mostly they were old. Sixteen thousand new rifles had been bought early in 1935, but some of the others were said to have been used in the Boer War, and even in the Franco-Prussian War. In many cases the ammunition carried by a soldier was for other firearms than his. There were a few artillery pieces, including one French 75 from World War I. Some of them had been captured at Adowa in 1896.

Besides the regular army, an uncounted number of local levies were available, but these were organized on principles even more primitive and often armed with spears. The provincial forces were under the command of local princes and governors. Their headquarters and armies were widely separated. Their reliability was in some cases dubious and their efficiency minimal. Some of them were units of subject and dissident ethnic and religious groups. Most of them met the European standards for savages: the Gofas smeared their faces with ochre and pink and were both democratic and licentious; they did not believe in officers, ranks, or commands, and they practiced rape as a matter of course. Abebe Dimta, their chief, marched with three lion cubs on leashes. Sometimes the soldiers were females who rode mules to battle. Some carried curved swords that recalled the arms of Islam during the Crusades.

There was no air power. Despite the emperor's efforts and the zeal of John Robinson, the air force apparently consisted of eleven planes, eight of which were in flying condition, and they were equipped neither for combat nor for bombing. There were thirteen anti-aircraft guns, widely dispersed. The Italians had about 400 planes, bombers, and fighters (few fighters, since there was nothing to fight), and they had good pilots.[1]

However great the pessimism of informed people, the average Ethiopian seemed to foreigners crazily optimistic. Optimism arose from their almost complete ignorance of European arms and warfare, from the legend of Adowa, from what was said to be a certain disposition to extreme conceit as a national characteristic. There were, indeed, some meager but real grounds for hope. The crude forces available could operate without the communications and supplies necessary for a modern army, and they were judged well qualified for guerilla operations, harassment, and forays. The Ethiopians were traditionally skillful in tactical exploitation of terrain, and they had a reputation for wild courage in combat. The basic strategy adopted in Addis Ababa were sensible; to attack unexpectedly; to expose a narrow front; to move by night and spend the days in caves and covert; to make no major effort to hold the border provinces in the path of the invaders; to avoid open battles, withdrawing to impenetrable mountains from which attacks could later be launched upon Italian bases and supply lines. A fairly detailed defense plan had been worked out for the northern front, although putting it into effect required the co-ordination of the efforts of local princes and a dependable system of communications, both of which were highly speculative. In the south, where a wide desert separated the heartland from Somaliland, it was planned to try to hold the river valleys along which the attacks would have to come.

Given these objective grounds for hope, given the reassuring sight of the towering mountains visible from the capital, illusions were possible even in the government. They existed in some military circles, notably in the person of the old war minister, Prince Mulugeta, who disdained all foreigners as incompetent. Many sensible people, indeed, expected that terrain, weather, and health conditions would mire the Italians.

The government obviously had to encourage optimism; its success in doing so had the important consequence of making it impossible to consider British or French proposals that were aimed at satisfying Italy by concessions of non-Amharic territories. In October Sir Sidney Barton, the British minister, emphatically told London that the attitude of the princes and chieftains was so intransigent that the emperor could not consider concessions even if he wanted to.[2] Ethiopia was at least as completely committed to a war of total defense as Italy was to one of total conquest. A reappraisal of realities might have dictated another course, but the emperor and his advisers hoped that if the invasion proved slow, the League of Nations might be forced by a developing anti-Italian opinion in the world to act. The best informed of the foreign correspondents in Addis Ababa, George Steer of the London *Times,* observed, "Haile Selassie never thought of his army as anything but a delaying force."[3] The real hope, for the ruler, lay not in his armies but in Geneva and in world opinion.

The war began on October 3. There were hysterical scenes in Rome and Addis Ababa and tense alarm everywhere else. Something sudden, dramatic, titantic, cataclysmic was expected to happen. What happened was a large-scale manipulation of symbols on both sides. The Italians advanced across the Ethiopian frontier with trumpets, flags, and a large display of national honor and met no resistance. Then they stopped advancing.

This anticlimactic beginning was mainly the result of the emperor's determination to be a martyr—martyrdom being, under the circumstances, the most practicable path to salvation. He had ordered all the Ethiopian forces, except for a few reconnaissance agents, to withdraw 20 kilometers back from the frontier facing Asmara, where the armies of General de Bono were assembled. On September 28 he sent a telegram to the secretary-general of the League of Nations notifying him of this pacific precaution.

> Earnestly beg Council to take as soon as possible all precautions against Italian aggression since circumstances have become such that we should fail in our duty if we delayed any longer the general mobilization necessary to ensure defense of our country. Our contemplated mobilization will not affect our previous orders to keep our troops at a distance from the frontier and we confirm our resolution to co-operate closely with the League of Nations in all circumstances.[4]

To his own people he spoke in rather different terms.

> Italy prepares for a second time to violate our territory. The hour is grave. Each of you must rise up, take up his arms and speed to the appeal of the country for defense.

Warmen, gather round your chiefs, obey them with a single heart and thrust back the invader.

You shall have lands in Eritrea and Somaliland.

All who ravage the country or steal food from the peasants will be flogged and shot.

Those who cannot for weakness or infirmity take an active part in this holy struggle must aid us with their prayers.

The feeling of the whole world is in revulsion at the aggression aimed against us. God will be with us.

Out into the field. For the Emperor. For the Fatherland.

Announced by drums, Haile Selassie read the proclamation in person from the steps of the palace. The crowd went mad.

The ascending enthusiasm of the Ethiopians had been in course for some time; this was merely a climax. Appeals to the memory of 1896, to glorious native traditions, to the ideal of service to fatherland and monarch, all had been much stressed and with great effect. Excitement, and fervor, climaxed in the celebration of the Maskal, the Feast of the Holy Cross, which is both a religious and a national holiday. It coincides with the end of the rains in Addis Ababa. In 1935 it therefore also coincided with the approach of invasion. Maskal festivities are always a wild and exuberant affair. There are vast crowds, floats, costumes, lions conveyed down boulevards in pick-up trucks, attended by priests. Thousands of soldiers parade at a dead run, carrying torches and shrieking their weird and terrifying war whoop. Bonfires are a major feature, and the principal one is lit by the emperor himself. In 1935 the Maskal became an orgy of patriotism and warlike excitement. Old Mulugeta, xenophobic and traditionalist, was a hugely popular figure as he rode with the parade, surrounded by prancing horsemen, wearing his princely crown and gorgeous robes, and carrying a silver-headed spear. There was much more than foolish optimism in the ardor; there was a sense of national destiny, deliberately called forth. The emperor was using every ounce of charisma, of power and prestige and Ethiopian tradition, to mobilize the national will.

There was a certain inconsistency. In Geneva he was cautious, correct, co-operative, pacific. In Addis Ababa he was ferocious, warlike, even aggressive with his references to the fruits of victory in the Italian colonies. But the inconsistency was doubtless necessary if Ethiopia was to survive, and in a certain sense it cohered into a harmony. He was being a good prophet and a good Ethiopian.

It illuminates this coherence to know that mobilization orders were prepared on the same day as the message to Geneva but were not issued until the Italians had crossed the frontier. Technical, like emotional, preparation for defense was necessary, but the announcement of concrete measures had to wait until Italy had consummated the Ethiopian martyrdom. The Italians played into the emperor's hands. On October 2, the day before the frontier was crossed, Mussolini harangued *his* people, and the world, in a way that revealed *his* need to appear an invincible war lord. Both governments were telling their citizens to be fierce and promising them rewards for ferocity adequate to the needs of the country. But Haile Selassie was urging ferocity in defense and Mussolini in gratuitous aggression, and no similarity of rhetoric and stage-managing could conceal the difference. The Italian shrieked that forty million of his countrymen would march in unison "because there is an attempt to commit against them the blackest of all injustices, to rob them of a place in the sun." He said that Ethiopia was "a country without a trace of civilization" and that his patience was exhausted. It was patience that Haile Selassie was so resolutely and impressively practicing; and that difference, too, was profound.

The Italian attack came, as everyone knew it would, in the north, where Asmara provided a better base and Massawa a better port than any in Somaliland. Eritrea was much nearer Italy. It was also much nearer Addis Ababa, and the capital was of necessity the ultimate objective of the Italian attack. If the Ethiopian defense lasted that long, it was hoped—probably it was assumed—that when Addis Ababa was taken, resistance would cease. There was only one practicable route to it from the Italian base: across the rugged country south of Asmara and through the terrible but passable terrain between the high mountains on the west and the intolerable desert on the east, south 300 miles to Dessie; then southwestward another 200 miles into the highlands and to Addis. There was no other way. Any other line of approach would lie through towering and trackless mountains, or through the life-destroying desert.

Traversing this route, everyone knew, would be a formidable undertaking. No detailed preparations had been made for it when the invasion began. It may be that the Italians hoped the initial assault would lead to a crumbling of Ethiopian resistance. It is known that they expected that many of the provincial governors would support them. They thought some of the populace would. Suitable arrangements had been made to this end.

The first stage of the advance, however, was very thoroughly planned. Three columns were to advance from the frontier before Asmara in a generally southern direction, to establish themselves on a line from Adowa to Adigrat, about 30 miles east. This was the country that had been fought over in '96, and the soldiers who marched to the border from Asmara passed a monument to those who fell in the earlier war. It was a statue of a soldier pointing toward Ethiopia, and it bore the inscription, "Italians, remember we died for our country, and one day will cancel this defeat by victory."[5]

Available for this initial phase of the campaign were three corps, mixed units of Italian regulars, Fascist militia, and askaris, the well-trained and well-equipped Eritrean soldiers who generally led the advance against their cousins the Ethiopians. (The I Army Corps, on the left heading toward Adigrat, was commanded by General Ruggero Santini. He was familiar with the country; he had fought there in 1896 as a second lieutenant and had taken part in the evacuation of Adigrat after the defeat at Adowa.) The three columns and supporting troops included almost 100,000 men and were supported by planes, including nine heavy bombers which took off at dawn on October 3 to bomb Adowa, where they killed a woman, a child, and three cows, wrecked several buildings, and frightened the population into the hills.

The countryside was appallingly difficult. It is a high plateau, broken by steep peaks and ridges. There were no roads, only tracks, in 1935, and the only inhabitants were in lost villages of a few poor huts clinging to hillsides. Because of the topography, there was no communication among the Italian columns.

They met little opposition. None of the main Ethiopian forces was committed. The border itself was unmanned except for a few customs officers, and no Ethiopian forces were encountered until the Eritrean Corps met a brigade of 500 men on high mountains just short of Enticcio. The Ethiopians were dispersed by aircraft, which machine-gunned them from low altitudes. On the right, where the terrain was wooded and especially rugged, General Pietro Maravigna's II Corps, a 23,000-man column led by askaris and Fascist militia, took part in several skirmishes, and the Italian lieutenant commanding the vanguard was killed. As the column approached Adowa, stronger resistance was met, but only from isolated units that were soon dispersed. By afternoon on the third day all three columns had reached their objectives.

Early on Saturday morning, October 5, General Santini raised the Italian tricolor over Adigrat, where he had seen it hauled down in '96. By five in the afternoon General Maravigna was on the outskirts of Adowa, and at 10:30 on Sunday morning the 2nd Battalion of the 84th Infantry of the Italian army entered the town with colors flying.

Adowa could scarcely have seemed to the invading soldiers to measure up to the explosive political and emotional power its name had generated for the past forty years; certainly it could not have looked like a prize to endanger the peace of the world. It was much what it had been in 1896, a provincial market center of six or seven thousand people, with its poor huts, its pleasant stream, its eucalyptus trees, its two picturesque churches on knolls high above the meadows. Prosperous by Ethiopian standards, since Adowa lay on the trail that was northern Ethiopia's only outlet to the sea, it was appallingly poor even by comparison to the most squalid village in impoverished Calabria in southern Italy, the ultimate in humbleness and obscurity. But names of insignificant places—Valley Forge and Waterloo—can, simply as names, become great forces in history. With a due sense of his role as vindicator of his nation and his race, Maravigna made his triumphal entry, and at noon on October 6, 1935, he hoisted the flag of Italy before the Church of the Savior of All the World; he kissed the cross which the frightened priests held out to him and avenged the humiliation of Italy, of Europe, and the white race.

There had been only 5 Ethiopian soldiers to resist the Italian capture of the town. (That was the result of the emperor's decision to withdraw from the frontier to avoid provocation and incidents. It may have been both a political and a military mistake, since it gave the Italians a moment of triumph, but he had judged it a moral and diplomatic necessity.) One of the five had been shot to death by the patrols. In the whole campaign, Maravigna had lost 31 men—6 Italians and 25 askaris. The Ethiopians were estimated to have lost 100 killed and 500 prisoners. It is said that the inhabitants of the few villages on the line of march welcomed the Italians as friends and liberators and were generously provided with hot meals by the Italian supply units, but this detail was provided by official reports and is open to question.

A week later General de Bono arrived in Adowa to unveil a marble monument to the dead of 1896 (previously shipped from Italy) and to proclaim in the main square the annexation of the province of Tigre to the dominions of Victor Emmanuel III. The local population, or that part of it that had returned from the hills, are said to have received these solemn rites without hostility or interest. A number of notables, including priests and a few Moslem holy men and some chieftains, attended the ceremony. The bishop of Tigre, in the name of all the priests in the province, made his submission to Italy, although (as one very pro-Italian British historian of the war has pointed out) there was considerable doubt as to the sincerity of this episcopal defector, since a few days earlier he had been urging his diocese in most unmeasured terms to resist the Italians.[6] A second proclamation was then read, outlawing slavery in the province. It had the effect of leading a number of Tigrine slave owners to turn their slaves off their land, thus condemning them to starvation. With the same dedication to the manipulation of large-scale symbols that had led them to arrive in Adowa armed with a marble monument, the Italians immediately dismantled one of the gigantic steles at Axum, the ancient capital seventeen miles from Adowa, and shipped it to Rome, where it still stands.

The occupation had been as carefully organized as the campaign. The new civil authorities brought with them engineers, who immediately, and with incredible skill and speed, set about the construction of highways. They brought too an abundant supply of 1780 Maria Theresa dollars (freshly minted from the original plates in Vienna, just as Napier's occupation money had been). The government of occupation seems to have been, at this stage, reasonably efficient, humane, and thorough and to have secured the acceptance of the inhabitants. It was, like the emancipation of the slaves, intended to dramatize Italian civilization and good intentions. Mussolini had told De Bono just before the attack that in view of world reaction, "The strictest orders should be given by you personally to all commanders: Inexorable decision against the armed forces, respect and humanity for the unarmed and defenseless population."[7] The orders at first were well executed.

The early stages of occupation might show the Italians at their best; but good conduct, while it may have achieved its immediate purposes in Tigre, did not go very far in achieving its larger purpose, which was to impress the world with the humanity and efficiency of Italian aims and methods. The emancipation of slaves went largely unnoticed in the western world, outside of Italy, and so indeed did the whole occupation. For most of the world was receiving its news from what was now a regiment of western correspondents in Addis Ababa.

The Ethiopians, while not always skillful at giving correspondents the kind of treatment they expected, were glad to disseminate news of a sort that, duly reported to hungry editors, drowned the press releases of the Italians in a sea of sensationalism. The correspondents were told of atrocities committed by the Italians. The death of two citizens and three cows in Adowa was elaborated into a tale of deliberate massacre by air of the defenseless populace, involving the deliberate bombing of a hospital. (There was no hospital in Adowa.) The story may have been the result of an honest mistake occasioned by the panic in the town on October 3, or it may have been a deliberate invention; in any case, it was what hit the headlines in London and New York, and no one noticed the abolition of slavery in Tigre.

Despite these sensational events, real and imagined, nothing of major military importance had as yet happened. The occupied territory was an infinitesimal proportion of the country, and none of the places had been seriously defended. But Ethiopian morale, a few days earlier so dizzily high, was shaken by several ominous developments. The loss of Adowa shook the confidence of many of the Ethiopian soldiers and chiefs who believed that 1896 was evidence that fate was infallibly on their side. The acquiescence of the local inhabitants, including the bishop and the local notables, suggested that *popular* resistance to Italian conquest was not likely to be a serious delaying factor. And the battle at Mount Augher before Enticcio had shown that the air power of the Italians could be decisive. One Italian soldier writing home in the euphoric aftermath of the entrance into Adowa noted: "With our Air Force, Italy can never lose. As the planes go forward and explore the ground not even an ant can escape them."[8] He wrote not much more than the truth; aerial reconnaissance and low-level machine-gunning certainly damaged both the morale and the military plans of the Ethiopians.

And there was treason. Prince Haile Selassie Gugsa was governor of the province of East Tigre. He was a person of great consequence and small virtue. He had been married to the emperor's daughter, who had died some time before—there had been and still are the sorts of rumors about her rather mysterious death that are usual with the decease of any member of the imperial family, in the absence of public information—but he had retained the emperor's trust. He ruled from his capital at Makale, some 60 miles south of Adowa, in the old-fashioned manner of a local despot who combined the least efficient and attractive features of a feudal lord and a tribal chief. He was, moreover, both debauched and discontented, for he was accorded at court a standing that seemed to him insufficient, and his province was a small one (separated administratively from the larger province of Tigre proper to provide him with a governorship). Since early in 1934 he had yielded to the blandishments of the Italians and had made numerous trips to Asmara. This fact was known to the government at Addis Ababa, but it was believed—the emperor was inclined, in this case as in some others, to a rather naïve confidence in the morals of those he liked—that he was accepting Italian money without intending to deliver anything in return. De Bono was not so naïve as the emperor, and he had not only well and truly bought Gugsa, but had worked out a strategem of treachery that, if it had come off as planned, would have been very devastating indeed. Gugsa had told the Italians that the Ethiopian defense plans involved the withdrawal of the Tigrine forces, under Prince Seyum, the governor of Tigre, from the Adowa area. Seyum (the Italians had also tried to subvert him, but unsuccessfully) was to unite his army of 16,000 men with Gugsa's 10,000 men in the neighborhood of Makale and, thus consolidated, the two Tigrine governors would together make a stand against the Italians at a point of their own choosing. It was a sensible plan, but it played into the Italians' hands. They intended that at the moment of attack Gugsa, true to his treasonous undertakings, should surrender his army, thus making impotent the forces fighting with him under Seyum's command and permitting the Italians to destroy at one blow and with little cost the major Ethiopian resistance in Tigre and the whole northeast.

This plan was discovered by the efficient Ethiopian consul in Asmara, Wodaju Ali. He became aware of the flow of communications between the Italians and Gugsa, and he went to Addis Ababa with copies of the receipts for deposits made in Asmara banks to Gugsa's account. This was only two weeks before the hostilities began, but Haile Selassie, believing that Gugsa was merely mulcting the Italians with skillful duplicity, declined to alter the strategic plans that depended upon Gugsa and his 10,000 men.

The Italian plan went awry because Gugsa lost his nerve. Learning of Wodaju's visit to Addis and the evidence he carried with him, Gugsa reasonably concluded that he would be arrested by imperial agents. Instead of waiting for the Italian advance and the union with Prince Seyum's army, he decided to defect as soon as Adowa was captured. On the day the Italians reached Adowa, October 5, he set out from Makale to join them. He took the precaution of cutting the telephone line behind him, the only communications link between Seyum and the capital; then he marched north with such of his men whom he could induce to accompany him. On October 8 he reached Adigrat and placed himself and his few troops at the disposal of the Italians. He also brought with him a Swiss engineer, who had been building a new road from Dessie to Makale and who later proved useful; his maps were much more recent and detailed than any others available and the Italians used them during the rest of the war. They greatly assisted the Italians in their most spectacular achievement, the building of roads.

The effect of this treachery was of some military importance. The way to Makale was open to De Bono, although he did not advance along it for another month, and Prince Seyum's forces were left without plans or communications. As an incident in the political and psychological struggle, it was much more significant. The treachery—its miscarriage concealed from them—was taken by the Italian people as evidence that Ethiopia was likely to disintegrate and that most of the provincial authorities were, as they had been told earlier, anxious to accept Italian rule. In Ethiopia the spirit of resistance among some of the Tigrine chieftains was much weakened. In Asmara Gugsa was received with honors and made governor of the whole of Tigre, now annexed by Italy although most of it was as yet unconquered.

After these events a long lull intervened. The government at Addis Ababa was assembling its forces gradually, in an almost leisurely way—

an army of some 80,000 men—to march northeast to support Prince Seyum and to prepare an attack on the occupiers. The war minister, the venerable Prince Mulugeta, who represented the most conservative elements in Ethiopian ruling circles, was still convinced that the enemy could be conquered by traditional, tried and true methods such as had availed in the days of his sovereign Menelek. His men were inspired by his example: barefoot, relying mainly on their spears, "they thought," Steer wrote, "that they could do everything." (Mulugeta disapproved of the emperor's modernism—he wanted him, as a suitable preparation for war against white men, to expel white men of every nationality from the capital and the empire.) His methods were obsoletely deliberate. Not until more than two weeks after the invasion did the army set off to meet the Italians, proceeding toward Dessie (to which there was a passable road) some 200 miles northeast of the capital and more than 200 miles south of the nearest point of Italian penetration.

In Asmara there was a similar delay, though for different reasons. Behind the Italian lines, the magnificent engineers were at work on roads and telegraph lines. Until they were completed, De Bono would not take the next step in his southward march. European civilization, in its technical and military aspects, was being installed as the Europeans went along. It was perhaps a necessary way to fight a campaign in such savage country, but there were risks; Prince Seyum's 16,000 men were somewhere to the south and west and there were other forces on the Italians' right flank.

There was another reason for the delay besides the leisurely command of Mulugeta and the caution of De Bono. It had nothing to do with the commanders. It was what was happening in Geneva.

Anti-Italian opinion among League members, already strong, turned to passion with the outbreak of war. The conduct of Ethiopia as a wronged and innocent victim was exemplary. The Italians did not improve their case by claiming as a pretext that Addis Ababa had ordered mobilization when in fact it had not done so. On October 2, the day before the assault on Adowa began, French pilots from Jibuti reported that the Italians had already violated the frontier at the extreme southern end of the Eritrean border on a patrolling mission. Haile Selassie's last peacetime message to the League had drawn attention to this incursion, and at the very time it was being considered in Geneva, Mussolini was making his appeal to the Italian people, stirring for many in Italy but insufferable to everyone at Geneva.

So the news of the invasion came at a time when Italy had flouted all attempts to forestall war and was evidently determined to make it, without provocation and without cause. By the time the invasion started, Mussolini had not only been placed in the position of an aggressor but acted like a man glorying in his role. This was in some ways misleading. He was now very nervous indeed and was already telling Aloisi that he might be prepared to settle, after all, for some such formula as had so often been suggested, of cession to Italy of the non-Abyssinian provinces while leaving the "old kingdom" intact. The governments of France and Britain would have been, and continued to be, only too glad to settle for something like this. But the League had now been roused to action, and most League members, expecting British leadership, were determined to punish the aggressor. On October 5 the Ethiopian delegate demanded that the Council of the League vote the application of Article XVI of the Covenant, which provided the only substantial weapon of the League against an aggressor—sanctions to be imposed by the member states.

There could be no doubt that the requirements for the application were fully met: Italy had clearly resorted to war in defiance of its obligations under the Covenant. The Italians said their action had been defensive, in response to the Ethiopian mobilization order which they said had been issued on September 30, but this was untrue and was known to be untrue. On October 7 the Council announced that "we are in the presence of a war begun in disregard of the obligations in the Covenant." When the Assembly met on October 10, fifty of the delegates (out of fifty-four voting) voted that Italy must be considered to have committed an act of war against all members of the League. (The only votes against it came from the delegates of Italy itself and of the governments under Italian influence: Austria, Hungary, and Albania. There were three abstentions.) The Assembly at once commenced discussions of what form the sanctions were to take. It was a solemn moment. The purpose for which the League had been brought into existence was now being fulfilled; a new age of international law was seen to have been born; for the first time, a collective action to keep the peace and punish the aggressor had been taken.

What was not known, of course, was that Britain and France had already agreed to try to prevent anything in the way of military, as distinct from relatively harmless economic, sanctions and to try to salvage the friendship of Mussolini. They had agreed, in short, to prevent the League from taking any action that might be effective. Their efforts to reach a compromise settlement, entirely unknown to anyone else, were to continue during the coming months behind the mask of support for sanctions. Eventually they developed a coherent proposal, which leaked out to the press three months later. When the news of this proposal burst upon the world, it was staggeringly unexpected, and it was seen as a complete reversal of policy. It was nothing of the sort; in fact their negotiations had begun while the League was voting. On October 8 Laval ordered the French ambassador at Rome to tell Mussolini that he deeply regretted the necessity of consenting to brand Italy an aggressor. He warned that if war should actually develop among European powers, France would be obliged to stand with Britain, but he hoped that the friendship of Italy and France could be preserved through all vicissitudes. The message was characteristic of the curious dilemma of the French and British statesmen: to try to warn while simultaneously reassuring. Throughout the succeeding months, there was no interruption of the discussions. Indeed, the British and French were trying harder than ever to overcome privately the dangers which their public policy of support for the League had incurred. By the end of October serious negotiations were underway, and British and French foreign office officials were working hard together to devise an acceptable settlement.

There was warrant for these actions in terms of the pro-League policy, since the Covenant did not forbid, and in fact might be construed as demanding, the exploration of all possible paths to peace simultaneously, and the British and French were careful to see that the notion of simultaneous exploration was written in to the sanction resolution. There was, moreover, a good deal of what might be called autonomous logic in them: the efforts at negotiation were reasonable enough if considered in isolation, if no importance were attached to the humbugging of the public, the countenancing of aggression, the carving up of non-European countries to satisfy European needs. But by contemporary standards it was very immoral not to attach importance to these considerations, and as is usually true in history bad morality made bad politics. There was troubled awareness of this in Paris and London, and so the original immorality was of necessity compounded, and the secret conversations, designed to achieve a compromise that would save everyone's face and perhaps a portion of Ethiopia, were concealed behind the tragicomedy of sanctions. Sanctions, which turned out to have very limited real significance, were endlessly discussed and debated in the world.

There has seldom been a clearer example of the fact that in public affairs the subjects that the public knows about, talks about, and thinks are important are usually irrelevant to the issues that are actually being decided. It was a myth that the League ever could or would ask its members to punish Italy and save both Ethiopia and peace. But the myth in itself became more important in the end than the facts. The big topic for people in Britain, America, and France, and in most of the countries that were members of the League, was what sanctions should be applied to stop Mussolini. Despite its categorical wording, it was immediately clear that there was nothing automatic about the deterrents provided in Article XVI. There was no automatic embargo severing even commercial relations. Nobody withdrew his ambassador from Rome. Everything had to be worked out in the brave new phony world of collective action for the restoration of peace and the preservation of international law and order.

The potential effectiveness of economic sanctions was questionable, certainly in the short run, although it was known that an embargo on certain products, notably oil, would have a large impact. The one sure and quick anti-Italian measure would have been the closing of the Suez Canal; this would certainly have put an instant stop to Italy's war effort and would have saved Ethiopia. But the British were determined not to close the Suez Canal, on the legalistic grounds that it was operated by a private corporation with which the British government had no right to interfere. Of course, the real reason was that they feared its closing would so enrage Mussolini that he might be led to attack the British navy in the Mediterranean. All other kinds of embargo were problematical. For one thing, Germany and Japan had resigned from, and the United States had never been a member of, the League, and it was alleged by the British leaders that none of these countries would co-operate with the member states in the League's attempt to harass the aggressor. Still, some 70 per cent of Italian for-

eign trade *was* with the member states, including some in materials that
were militarily or economically indispensable. It was generally supposed that a rigorous prohibition on this trade would eventually have
the effect of forcing Mussolini to negotiate, if not to call off his war.

Despite the general excitement and the violence of anti-Italian
feeling, the initial and almost unanimous agreement among the governments represented at Geneva was that Article XVI could not be
construed as meaning what it obviously did mean. The appointment
of a Co-ordination Committee to discuss the whole thing indicated the
unwillingness of governments to endanger their own economies or
their own safety by any wholesale rupture with Italy. The realization
that France and Britain would lead no crusades brought a quick revival
of prudence. It was Eden who made most of the proposals that were
eventually adopted by the Co-ordination Committee and later translated into action. They were of a sort skillfully designed to achieve
the ambiguous British purposes. The embargo on arms shipments to
Ethiopia was revoked and the export of arms, munitions, and imple-
ments of war to Italy prohibited. No loans or credits were to be made
to the Italian government and no exports purchased from it. Certain
raw materials, including aluminum (of which, alone among minerals,
Italy had a sufficiency within its borders), were to be withheld from
the aggressor. Coal, oil, iron, and steel might still be shipped, however.

It appeared to some that this curious list of prescriptions was an
open avowal that nobody wished to do anything except more token
gestures. But it was taken very seriously by most of the world, not only
by the people at Geneva who worked with endless industry at sculpting
a jaw with false teeth but also by so much of the world's press. Troubled attention, for example, was given the long list of abstentions and
exceptions on the part of member states. Paraguay announced that it
would not adopt sanctions at all. Liechtenstein announced that it
would permit Ethiopia but not Italy to order arms from its manufactur-
ers (of which, of course, it had none) but that it would not ban loans
or commodity exports (of which there were also none).

Sanctions were voted and adopted by most of the fifty-four member states on October 19, to take effect a month later.

Some people at Geneva, including the British leaders, hoped that
limited sanctions might induce Mussolini to negotiate. They thought

that the threat of a slow, long-term squeeze might force him to do so, without incurring the danger of a sudden confrontation. They may have been right, for eventually the Italians did begin to feel the pressure. But events would not wait upon a squeeze play, and bolder men felt the need for stronger measures. Some of them were on the Co-ordination Committee. They formally proposed embargoes on oil, coal, pig iron, iron, and steel on November 6. There was resistance from the British and French. The matter remained open, however— the people who really wanted to force Mussolini to give up had won that much. Token concessions had been made to Morality; the question of whether Morality was really to be enforced continued to be discussed.

The real effects of the League's actions took place far beneath the surface of the day's news, and they were deeply paradoxical. The Italian dictator privately reacted to sanctions with a mixture of relief and apprehension and—as Hoare and his colleagues hoped—an increased willingness to engage in negotiations. He reacted publicly, however, in the opposite way, by ordering his delegates to abstain from participation in League activities. The government knew the sanctions voted would not immediately damage the Italian economy very seriously, but it also knew a good propaganda point when it saw one. The Italian press thundered about the iniquitous attempt to suffocate the Italian nation, which would be met with frugality, sacrifice, and gallantry; an outraged Italian nation would certainly, in the end, prevail in its youthful vigor, whatever the cost. Sanctions were taken as final proof of the argument, which the Fascists had long preached, that any nation determined to find its destiny must be self-sufficient. As applied to Italy, which was almost wholly lacking in the raw materials for an industrial economy (so far as was known at that time), the argument was preposterous. But what was important was that the noble mission in East Africa, coupled with the hostile response of the satiated and selfish powers at Geneva, provided a patriotic motive for demanding the sacrifices which the Depression and the stagnation of the Italian economy had already imposed. What had been a danger to the regime was thus converted into an asset, a triumph of national vindication. The queen of Italy journeyed to the Victor Emmanuel Monument, that fantastic white edifice combining on a gigantic scale the more vulgar features of a necropolis and a wedding cake, and gave her wedding ring to be melted down for the war economy. She was followed by a quarter of a million other Italian women who tossed gold rings into flaming braziers. It is said eighty million dollars' worth of gold was procured in this way.[9]

Ever since it had become clear, back in the spring, that Britain would not, openly anyway, support the Italian aims in Ethiopia, a degree of enthusiasm for it in Italy had been stirred by ingeniously presenting it as a declaration of Italian independence from the tutelage of selfish and decadent competitors. It is interesting that the enthusiasm had been almost wholly lacking when it looked as if the French and British were complaisant. The American ambassador at Rome had reported in February that most Italians were indifferent or hostile to a war of conquest. But opposition changed that. Now sanctions, combined with the news that the shame of Adowa had been turned at last into victory, brought excitement, even jubilation, to the considerable portion of the Italian people that had no knowledge of the risks or of the extreme doubts of men like Badoglio. Sanctions provided a tangible cause for massive patriotic outrage. Nor was all this an entirely superficial excitation contrived by Fascist polemical skill. There really was *élan* in Italy. Italians had long been bred to cherish the dream of new frontiers, and this provided the emotional foundation for the world's last essay in the old sort of colonizing. Genuine enthusiasm, now called to life, was noticeable among the Italian soldiers on the front as well as at home for building a new Rome in Ethiopia's green and pleasant land. The impulse to adventure in conquering new worlds, neighboring, distant, or in cosmic space, may be naïve and troublesome, but it is extraordinarily persistent; later, it was to take Americans to the moon as earlier it had taken them to the Mississippi and the Pacific. A sheepish, and very anti-Fascist Italian judge of the adventure, in which he took part, wrote years later, "the hundreds and thousands of Italians who flocked to Ethiopia between 1935 and 1940 responded to a call that had nothing to do with the directives of the Fascist regime or geopolitical laws. It was the stimulating, enthralling call of the Far West, with its unexplored riches, its unknown hazards and dangers."[10] Mussolini ingeniously captured and exploited this call, and it was perhaps not surprising that foreigners should mistake it for signifying a vital national impulse, an almost irresistible new dynamism, a wave of the future.

The impulse to conquest was shared by quite improbable people, including Benedetto Croce, Italy's most distinguished philosopher, and Luigi Albertini, its most distinguished journalist. They had tolerated Fascism in its earlier days, but they had become the leading anti-Fascist intellectuals to remain in the country. Both publicly supported the national cause against European attempts to "throttle" their country. Among exiles, the Socialists Arturo Labriola and Mario Bergamo, who had excoriated Mussolini and all his works, rallied to their homeland in its terrible trial. Herbert Matthews, the *New York Times* correspondent who believed that the imposition of sanctions was an unmixed disaster, wrote, "Sanctions unified Italians behind the Duce by providing a motive for patriotism and a common grievance against the world. Sanctions started Italy on the path that was to lead to the Axis."[11]

There was no doubt that doom was being approached with real fervor, that sanctions provided Italian war spirit with greater motive and power. They were a national insult, and they vindicated the xenophobia that Fascism had always preached. Glory was, for the moment, restored to the Fascist regime.

Italians were being told that the pro-League policy in Britain was the instrument of a decadent and privileged aristocracy determined (as an Italian supporter of Italian imperialism put it) to use the occasion of "a final solution of the Abyssinian problem" to force Italy "either to humiliate herself and the white race's honor before a black people who had committed the first act of war or go to war with fifty-two nations." A situation which, he went on to say, "the Whigs" (meaning the ruling class of England) "appear not to have appreciated . . . or rather, they seem even to have enjoyed it."[12] Italy was also informed by its press of what seems to have been believed by Mussolini and other government officials—that *real* English national sentiment remained pro-Italian. Conservative London papers like the *Daily Mail* were strongly inclined to support Mussolini, and liberal papers like the *Manchester Guardian* were strongly opposed to anything that might lead to war; both were quoted, to suggest that sanctions were unpopular with most people in Britain.

The immediate material effect of sanctions was an increase in Italian trade with the United States and Germany. The exports of those two countries rose rapidly, approximately 20 per cent, in the first weeks of the war. While the attitudes of the two governments were very different, indeed opposite, the impact of the events of October 1935 were seismic, perhaps decisive, in both capitals.

The German government was not yet overtly enthusiastic in its support of Italy. It's public posture was reserved, and for good reason. At the moment the invasion started, an American newspaperman observed that the Germans were "delighted." The reason for delight was logical, if tortuous: if Mussolini were stopped or defeated, Italy would disappear as an effective obstacle to German expansion, Austria could be annexed, and German influence in central Europe indefinitely expanded. If Italy were triumphant, it would be at the expense of France and Britain, and Hitler's freedom of action in the west would be enhanced.[13] There were corresponding problems, however. Hitler still believed that humiliation of Italy would be a humiliation for German fascism as well. On the other hand, a clear victory for Italy might prevent him from annexing Austria, oblige him to accede in the enthrallment of the Germans in the South Tyrol, and limit his influence in Central Europe generally. Hitler indeed tried to give the impression of co-operating with the League and he imposed restrictions on increased exports to Italy of a long list of strategic goods including oil. It is possible that Hitler was, as Eden thought, so doubtful about Mussolini's fate at this juncture that he did not wish to be associated with it.[14] In any case, there was nothing to be gained through overt support for the outlaw, and by a show of neutrality Germany could underwrite either outcome. But still, as events developed, the Ethiopian crisis was pure gain, and to cash in, all that was needed was for Hitler to fold his hands.[15]

The pose of scrupulous neutrality did not at all prevent the Germans from covertly encouraging expanded trade, and there was a rapid diminution of anti-German editorials in Italy. Despite public restrictions, every effort was made to ease the payments difficulties. The Germans asked in payment neither gold nor exchange (which the Italians did not have) but goods which the Germans did not need or want—sulfur, olive oil, and silk. Meanwhile, the Germans untruthfully told the League that they would not permit exports to Italy to rise above their normal level. Hitler was on the verge of winning his struggle to break up the Versailles coalition, and exports for the moment were his most useful weapon.

The position of the United States was precisely the opposite of Germany's: the government had to appear *not* to co-operate with the League in order to assuage isolationist opinion, while becoming more and more inclined to do so. The Neutrality Resolutions had been implemented on October 5, 1935, with a ban on a list of exports of "war materials," previously drawn up, to either belligerent. There was some effort to warn, or even to threaten, Mussolini: the State Department had fought for delay and had suggested that it was legally possible for the government to decree an embargo on the sale of raw materials to Italy, and Ambassador Breckinridge Long was rebuked for having suggested to the Italians that any embargoes the United States government imposed, in case of a spread of hostilities, would apply equally to the opponents.[16]

There was strong opposition to any one-sided embargo from the isolationists in Congress and also from exporters who were beginning to realize that the League's sanctions might become a gold mine for American business. Roosevelt used the isolationists to frustrate the exporters. The former believed that *any* trade with *any* belligerent portended American involvement. The president was therefore able to denounce (if not to outlaw) the expanding trade with Italy. He asked that businessmen sacrifice "tempting trade opportunities" in exports that might prolong the war, and he said that the American public would not approve activities causing "the struggles on the battlefield to be prolonged because of profits accruing to a comparatively small number of American citizens."[17] When the Institute of American Meat Packers inquired whether such statements indicated the Administration's desire to stop meat shipments to Italy, its representatives were told by the Department of State that they should avoid entering into commitments for increased exports because policy in the matter of trade with Italy "might be changed"—which meant that trade might be prohibited. An American shoe company, with orders for military boots from the Italian government, was told by Roosevelt that he would not take the contract if he were the owner of the company. The president used powers provided under other statutes to prevent the transfer of ships to Italian ownership and to threaten to foreclose government mortgages on shippers who were trading with Italy. American citizens were warned that they would travel on belligerent ships (meaning Italian ships, since Ethiopia had none) at their own risk and by doing so would forfeit the protection of the government.

Within a few weeks after the war started, then, a "moral blockade" had been imposed. The government was trying, and in limited spheres managing, to support the League without appearing to do so.

And the League had vocal American supporters now. A sea change was beginning. American opinion, if still overwhelmingly dedicated to non-involvement, was becoming in many ways strenuously anti-Italian and anti-Fascist. Italy was getting a bad press. The Italian papers were, to be sure, able by careful selection to make it seem that American opinion was on the whole—as they claimed British opinion to be—sympathetic to Italian aims. The sympathy, which could hardly be concealed, that many Americans, including the Administration, seemed to feel for the League was said to be the result of British propaganda (a supposition also constantly advanced by the more extreme isolationists). But Anne O'Hare McCormick of the *New York Times* said that suspicion of the reality was filtering down through Italian opinion.[18]

The Italian government acted promptly and energetically to deal with hostile American opinion by invoking Italian-American support of the Fascist policy. From the very beginning of the war, efforts had been made by the Italian embassy to mobilize the Italian Americans. On October 2 a hundred leading Italian Americans in Washington had met to organize a United Italy Association, to encourage support for the war and to aid the Italian Red Cross (which they did with a contribution, out of hand, of almost $20,000 the first day).[19] Italian-American organizations and papers stridently denounced Roosevelt's implementation of the Neutrality Resolutions which they said (correctly) was discriminatory, since Ethiopia could not have benefited from American exports in any case. Letter-writing campaigns to the State Department and to members of the Congress were encouraged by *Il Progresso Italo-Americano* (the State Department was sure it was sponsored by the Italian consul-general in New York), and it is said that a million letters were actually sent, denouncing all acts favorable to the League and harassing to Italy. They may have had some effect in reinforcing the isolationist positions of members of

Congress, and even of Mayor Fiorello LaGuardia of New York, who had large numbers of Italian constituents, especially those who were themselves of Italian origin. Representative Peter Cavicchia from Newark went so far as to assert that "the Golden Rule required" that Italy be supplied with anything it needed short of guns.[20] It may, in fact, be that the proposal for a discretionary neutrality law, which the Administration wanted, was doomed by the dramatic mobilization of Italian-American pressures.

Such pressures, however, produced reactions. The State Department was enraged by what amounted to meddling by Italian diplomats with American affairs. The president was reported to be seriously annoyed. Among ordinary Americans, an ironic reaction, unmeasurable but clearly present, began to take place. One of the reasons for the zeal with which Americans of Italian origin responded to the efforts of the Italian government seems to have been a sense of social inferiority. The tangible evidence of glory for their fatherland provided by the capture of Adowa stirred some Italian Americans with new pride. But the United States was an unmelted pot with a very well-defined pecking order; Italians were still "immigrants" and their wish to identify themselves with national glory, even Mussolini's, provoked among some other Americans disdain, suspicion, even hatred. The inferiority that attached, subjectively, anyway, to Italian Americans made their efforts to convert America to a pro-Italian attitude seem to many either funny or sinister. It was an unpleasant and discreditable situation, which undoubtedly contributed to the rapid growth of anti-Fascist feeling in the United States. The emancipation of Italian Americans from the disdain of many of their countrymen, paradoxically, would have to wait for Italy's defeat in the greater war to follow.

Geneva debated. In Ethiopia Prince Mulugeta was still mobilizing his army. Soldiers from all over the empire were collecting in the capital. On October 17 they were reviewed by the emperor. On October 21 the exodus began. The odd and cumbrous force went forward. It reached Dessie on November 4, and then began to move north toward the Italians 150 miles away, picking up recruits as it went. Beyond Dessie there were no roads, only a track, and the Ethiopians could move only at night for they had come into range of the Italian air force. Still, they proceeded with remarkable speed and safety, considering the circumstances. They arrived at Mount Alaghi, two-thirds of the way, on December 10, and not until almost at the end of their journey were they found and bombed by the Italian airmen.

After the fall of Adowa, the only action for a long time was in the south. There General Graziani commanded the Italian forces that had assembled in Somaliland. He had a much smaller army than De Bono's—his role was designed to be diversionary, and his lines of supply were much longer and more vulnerable. Nonetheless, in the first days of the war he had crossed the border at its extreme southern end, along the Juba River, and taken the town of Dolo a few miles inside Ethiopia. Three hundred miles to the northeast the Dubats also under his command had moved out from Walwal toward the Fanfan River, which offered a passable corridor north toward Harar. The chief objective on the river was the settlement of Gorrahei. Like Walwal, it dominated a large region of the Ogaden, being the only watering place for miles around, and a road ran through it.

The chief defense of Gorrahei was a fort that had been built there a generation before by the Mad Mullah, when in the early 1900s he had contested the whole region with Ethiopians and Europeans alike. The Italian air force demolished the fort, along with most of the town, with 20 tons of bombs; in the process, they mortally wounded the able Ethiopian commander of that front, General Afewerk, whose loss caused panic and demoralization among his men. The Italian ground forces entered Gorrahei on November 8. There were other skirmishes in the neighborhood, and an Italian force advancing north was ambushed and decimated at Anale. Thereafter Graziani's advances stopped, and although the road to Harar could probably have been quickly opened action in the south ended.

The Ethiopians were relieved, but there were some ominous notes in the Ogaden. Some of the scattered Moslem tribes—including one whose chief was a son of the Mad Mullah—went over to the Italians with their arms. The Italians gave the defectors a well-publicized welcome as liberated victims of barbaric Ethiopian enslavers. Their motives and their allegiance, however, like those of the Tigrines in the north who had welcomed De Bono, cannot possibly be measured by European standards. The Somalis were certainly innocent of all notion of national affiliation. It says nothing about the relative merits of Ethiopian and Italian rule that the chiefs forswore their extremely hazy allegiance to Haile Selassie while the native troops fighting for the Italians—Dubats in the south and askaris in the north, fought with zeal and substantial loyalty under their Italian officers. The most conspicuous element of the allegiance of these people, as with most peoples organized in local and traditional societies, was to the local leader. In many cases, it was their only allegiance, except that dictated by immediate expediency. Both personal loyalty and expediency worked for the winner; both now worked for the Italians, with their tanks and planes, and against the emperor of Ethiopia.

The Italians zealously offered the chiefs attractive bargains in fealty and frequently sold them. But the picture that they then attempted to draw for the world—of people suffering under the yoke of intolerable tyranny—had no reality. And the defections had little importance. The population was so scant and the strategy of the Italians put so little importance on the Ogaden that what happened there was of no consequence.

Nevertheless, Graziani's brief advance, culminating in the fall of Gorrahei, left many of the foreign correspondents convinced that the southern front would be the scene of the decisive action. In the Ethiopian capital they were bored and starved for news, and some of the most distinguished correspondents moved to Harar early in November. It was the second city of the empire, an entirely different sort of place from Addis Ababa and for most westerners a much more attractive one. It was a genuine city in the European sense, a compact town with tight streets and picturesque city walls which it had never outgrown. Its houses were attractive and had lovely Arabian gardens. Harar had for centuries been the seat of a Moslem kingdom and a great trading center, and it had the patina of past importance. Seen from a distance, surrounded by very rich and fertile countryside, crowning its hilltop with minarets and church towers, it was beautiful; inside the narrow streets with their lively shops and markets and the houses with their closed gardens, it was charming, if rather insanitary. The population was only partly Amharic and largely Moslem, and the whole atmosphere was of a civilization wholly remote from that of sprawling, shapeless, ugly Addis Ababa. It had been annexed to Ethiopia within living memory, and some Europeans, like Waugh, found the characteristic eastern, Islamic flavor familiar and congenial and were delighted by it, and they professed pity for its citizens enthralled by an alien and barbarous tyranny.

There the journalists assembled, an oddly incongruous island of western intellectuals. Most of them stayed in the best hotel, L'Impératrice, which had no bathrooms, or the leading pension, Mademoiselle Hall's, which was run by Germans and was said to be the cleanest spot in Harar. The representatives of the French news agency Havas and of *Le Journal* and *Paris-Soir*, an elite of French correspondents, were there, with Waugh and Steer of the London *Times*, Lawrence Stallings, the great American authority on wars past, present, and future, who represented the North American Newspaper Alliance and Fox Movietone News, and Herbert Ekins of the United Press, along with many other newsmen and photographers. Harar, certainly had never seen anything like it; it was as if a company of medieval mandarins had descended on the city of Council Bluffs, Iowa.

As in Addis Ababa, the journalists' professional purposes were frustrated in Harar that November. The nearest fighting was 200 miles away, and by the time they reached Harar it had trailed off into skirmishes. The correspondents waited for a nearer battle, but the Italian offensive was not renewed. There was no news to report except for the arrival of a few Ethiopian casualties from the south and a brief visit by the emperor on a morale-building trip to Jijiga, the headquarters a few miles east of Harar. So once again the correspondents filed thousands of words of background and local color, and the world learned from them not about the battle which had not happened but about Harar and the strange ways of the men who lived there and those who were preparing to defend it.

For those who stayed in Addis Ababa there was frustration no less perversely fruitful. They had to perform in a professional vacuum. One of them, a Spanish correspondent, filled it by translating long passages from a German history of Africa and sending them to Madrid as his own stories. Journalists hovered disconsolately in quarters scarcely more inviting than the Hôtel de l'Impératrice in Harar; the leading hotels of the capital, the Splendide and the Imperial, were not lavishly equipped with modern comforts. The Deutsche Haus, the equivalent of Mademoiselle Hall's, was better, but it could accommodate very few guests. Diversion was sought at Le Select and Le Perroquet, combined bars, restaurants, and movie theaters managed by competing

Frenchwomen who provided fair food and impossible wines to their suddenly expanded European clientele.

They complained about their treatment by the Ethiopian authorities, who combined a suspicious reluctance to let them file stories—strict but rapidly changing limits were put upon the number of words they could send—with bureaucratic inefficiency. They were much harassed. Permission to leave the capital for places where, it was hoped, action might be expected was granted, if at all, only after long and confusing delays. They fought with the incompetent and whimsical Belgian youth who, mysteriously, had been put in charge of imperial censorship. They formed groups to elect representatives to make complaints to the authorities. They spent long, boring days in gossip and drinking in the dismal, crowded, lethargic city. They talked to Everett Colson twice daily. They "dashed frantically about in cars," as Steer recalled, "between the Legations, the Foreign Ministry, the Palace, and the radio, scratching together from the barren rockeries of Ethiopia a few frail seeds from which we hoped would flavor exotically a story."[21]

But they continued to send out dispatches, on an average of 30,000 words a day, even when there was nothing that met the conventional definitions of news. The American correspondents (whose readers, Waugh loftily thought, were so voracious as to swallow any information, however fraudulent, vulgar, and irrelevant) sent home a copious flow of background pieces, stories about the Ethiopians' fighting spirit and picturesque military establishment. There was a great deal about the peculiar characters who gathered, vulturelike, under the war clouds: an ex-member of Al Capone's bodyguard in search of new employment; a fraudulent Monégasque viscount who designed to offer his services to the emperor as a sort of one-man suicide squad; a South African revolutionary who hoped to use the war as the occasion for a crusade to exterminate the white race.*

Tension ran high. No one knew what to expect, or what the Italians were planning, or how long the war might last. The state of mind of the Ethiopians and the rather elementary apparatus of government were such that many foreigners began to fear that the regime might lose control and that the populace, thoroughly imbued with defiance of the Italians, might massacre all the white men who were

---

* These items are all from Waugh's account.

rapidly drifting into town. The British legation imported a Sikh regiment from India as a legation guard—a precaution that would save lives later. The families of foreigners were sent on the long and uncomfortable train journey to French Somaliland and safety.

The most peculiar position was that of the Italian legation. The situation and function of a diplomat is minutely covered by international law which has been, on the whole, scrupulously observed by even the most unscrupulous governments. But the Italians were in an unprecedented position, since their government was engaged in large-scale hostilities with the receiving state without being legally at war against it. Moreover, they regarded Ethiopia as an un-state of barbarous proclivities and were deliberately designing to embarrass it as much as possible by placing the Ethiopian authorities in an impossible and ridiculous situation. The minister, Count Luigi Vinci-Gigliucci, was a small, chubby, stubborn man with the kind of volatility and sentimentality that could be turned off and on at will. He was well-liked in the *corps diplomatique,* and he was both witty and amiably quixotic: his fondness for animals verged on the intemperate, and he kept a menagerie, including several cheetahs, in the legation.

The natural and correct thing for Vinci would have been for him to ask for his passports and depart at the moment the invasion started, since Ethiopia had become, in obvious fact if not in law, his country's enemy. But Vinci insisted that he must remain until all Italian personnel in the empire were safely accounted for, and the Ethiopian government, intensely desirous of acting according to the rules of civilized intercourse among states, hesitated to eject him. It took some time for the numerous Italian consuls and commercial agents (who had proliferated greatly in recent years and had been clearly agents of political warfare and attempts to suborn local authorities) to make arrangements to quit their posts. Even after the invasion began, Vinci and his entire staff were still in their legation, and he was holding regular press conferences and attending meetings of the Fascist club of local Italians. He was under vague surveillance, but he was free to come and go. He led an active social life during the period when Italian armies were advancing on Adowa and Adigrat, dining with friends at other legations, where he was always a welcome and entertaining guest.

A week after Adowa fell, the Ethiopian government ordered him to leave. He agreed. Preparations were made. The ciphers were burnt in the legation garden in an enormous bonfire that fascinated Vinci's pet monkey, who tried to put out the flames by sitting on them—an amusing incident much discussed in foreign circles in the capital. A special train was arranged and a formal farewell ceremony with official honors organized, with Ethiopian officials and other diplomats present at the railroad station to bid the departing Italians goodbye. All was to be in accord with the most strict demands of western protocol.

But Count Vinci did not show up for the occasion. He announced that he had changed his mind and that he would remain in his legation unless removed by force. He refused to accept his passports from the foreign ministry—an act unprecedented in diplomatic history—and locked himself with his staff inside the legation. He said that he felt obliged to remain, like the captain on a sinking ship, until the last official Italian personage was safely on his way. This was a man named Agostino, who had been serving as commercial agent in Mogalo (a town where Italy had no commerce). Agostino had not yet completed his mission: he was a naturalist engaged in making a collection of butterflies. Vinci said he would stay in Addis Ababa until this important lepidopterological work was complete.

All this was bizarre as well as improper, and it was quite clearly intended to be provocative. Vinci may have been hoping that the Ethiopians would lose patience and forcibly deport him, which would have been just as improper and even more outrageous than his own conduct. Not until October 26, more than three weeks after the war began, did the minister finally agree to go; Agostino's butterfly collection was complete, Vinci said. He had been partly successful, if his aim had been to annoy the Ethiopians into abandoning their thin-crusted European decorum. He had been harassed in minor ways and publicly insulted. But his own conduct was so much more indecorous than theirs that he had, in a wider sense, defeated his own ends. Italian diplomacy was made to appear both swinish and silly; it was, as was so often true that year, Italy that seemed to be making a travesty of civilized practice.

The perplexing situation of Ethiopia was illuminated in this preposterous incident. The emperor and his advisers were trying to show the world that they had a claim on its conscience, and the Italians were trying to make monkeys of them. The slightest yielding to reasonable reactions of annoyance could only serve the Italian cause. But on the whole, the Italians damaged themselves and the Ethiopians succeeded in looking like dignified martyrs. Even Waugh admitted that as the voice of a wronged nation Haile Selassie spoke with genius: "The public utterances of the Emperor . . . were drafted for him by his professional white advisors, but it is probable that he took a large share in their composition. They were designed entirely for foreign consumption and were quite admirable. They were repeated throughout the world and more than any single feature of the situation stirred the women, clergy, and youths of the civilised races, conservative and socialist alike, to that deep, cordial, and altruistic sympathy which has been his reward."[22]

Waugh was premature, of course; the emperor's reward was not to be the sympathy of "women, clergy, and youths," but the restoration of his nation and his throne. And he was wrong when he implied that it was dishonest for the emperor to appeal to the world's conscience as a defense for Ethiopian independence while at the same time approving of Mussolini, who called his war a civilizing mission. He erred in a moral and historical sense in seeing one form of propaganda as a lie while mistaking another for the truth, but his error was more basic than that. He thought it was wicked for the Ethiopians to defend themselves by outwitting the Italians. He correctly ascribed a good deal of conscious skill (and some falsehood) to the Ethiopians' propaganda, but he missed (or was confused by) the fact that irredeemable savages must by definition be incapable of outwitting their civilizers.

The Ethiopians were incompetent at managing administrative matters such as censorship, but they were more persuasive than the Italians and on the whole quite as accurate in their dissemination of news. When news was unavailable, Addis Ababa accepted rumors as truth if they seemed useful. All propagandists do. Such was the origin of the stories about the destruction of a hospital and the death of scores of innocent patients and nurses and other civilians in the bombing of Adowa. (There was, as noted above, no hospital at Adowa, no nurses or patients to be killed, and the civilian "massacre" had evidently consisted of two casualties.*) The useful rumor was

* Waugh attributed the story of the massacre to an American Negro pilot (obviously "James Wilson," although he was not named) who claimed to have been present at the time of the bombing. There is no other evidence to support this attribution.

circulating, and the Ethiopians aided its circulation. But in general, little propaganda was actually manufactured (in contrast to the Italian practice); the available news was generally judged by the correspondents to be fairly accurate.

The correspondents found it impossible to get anywhere near the main front in the north or any nearer the Ethiopian army than they could get by standing on the streets and watching it march through Addis Ababa. A few of them set off, more or less on their own, in the second week of November, toward Dessie, where the Ethiopians established their headquarters. They passed with difficulty and discomfort along the half-built road through the dramatically wild and varied country, through peaceful Galla villages, past army stragglers, into towns where obstinate, suspicious, and confused officials prevented or delayed their efforts to send stories back to the capital and sometimes threatened them with arrest. They were frequently threatened by angry tribesmen, brigands who detested white men as much as they detested the Amharas. Several times the correspondents were turned back. The weather was cold. The road deteriorated. Maps were unavailable or inaccurate. Some local leaders were friendly, but they seemed naïve and absurdly optimistic about the war. One provincial governor told Waugh that "the Italians were a poor sort of people . . . one of his friends had killed forty of them, one after the other, with his sword . . . They disliked fighting so much that they had to be given free food before they would do it."[23] The Europeans thought him a rather sympathetic representative of a doomed society.

On November 30 the correspondents reached Dessie and were received by the mayor, who wore a traditional cape, while the rest of his costume consisted of English soccer shorts and socks with red and white stripes. Like their colleagues who were simultaneously waiting in Harar for something to happen on the southern front, the correspondents in Dessie found nothing to report there. There was no evidence of military activity, let alone action, aside from a crude field hospital that was crowded with soldiers suffering (Waugh said) from syphilis. It was not feasible to send any stories at all. The telegraph was reserved for the military. The only event of interest in Dessie was, as it had been in Harar a week earlier, the arrival of the emperor. He came to set up his headquarters (in the Italian consulate) and to take command of the northern armies. Nothing else happened. The days dragged on. Evelyn Waugh gave up his losing struggle against boredom and dislike of Ethiopia and returned to Addis Ababa, where he caught a train for Jibuti and civilization.

On the Italian side, inactivity was scarcely less complete or cor-rosive. In Asmara the commanders were waiting, after the fall of Adowa and Adigrat, under orders from Mussolini not to continue the advance until the effect of sanctions was clearer and until "Anglo-Italian relations were settled."[24] They had contemplated the possi-bility of continuing the southward thrust to Makale, Gugsa's capital, which was about 50 miles south of Adowa, but Mussolini at first advised against further operations.

This delay must have coincided with De Bono's inclinations. He was preternaturally reluctant to move. His dispatches dealt endlessly with supply difficulties and the dangers of possible counterattack, and he emphasized the huge size of the forces that would be necessary to ensure a safe advance. When Mussolini changed his mind and decided that the delay would embolden rather than disarm his opponents in Europe, a serious conflict immediately developed between the dictator and his old friend. From Rome there now came hortatory instructions to start moving. De Bono refused, still writing interminable dispatches about supply problems and the fatigue of the army mules.

Judgments on his command are divided but predominantly criti-cal. He was, as Gaetano Salvemini, the very distinguished anti-Fascist scholar, crisply observed, "no genius."[25] Moreover, his caution was in sharp contrast to his reputation, for he had always liked to boast of his audacity and rashness, and he had publicly deplored soldiers who "do not feel the joy of risks."[26] The extreme irritation produced by Mussolini's enjoinders to advance may have owed something to dis-illusioned self-knowledge.* But his caution is defensible. The problems of supply *were* enormous. Time *was* needed for the consolidation of positions won, the building of roads, the pursuit of political warfare through attempts to placate the populations of the occupied areas and make deals with local leaders. And De Bono (like some people in

---

* De Bono published summaries of these interchanges soon after the war; they con-stituted a strongly implied rebuke to Mussolini for irresponsibility. Badoglio was to publish similar implied reproaches. Mussolini permitted both publications and even wrote forewords to them; it is possible that he mistook the implications and regarded them as tributes to his own ardor and audacity.

Rome) may have hoped to take the country by guile and not by storm, once the initial victories had been won. Still, he was making prodigious exertions. Advanced supply bases were being set up, for 40,000 troops and a like number of mules, in each of the three corps. Supplies of bread for I Corps alone required a bakery with 48 ovens in Adigrat, and these supplies were sent by pack across the mountains. No fewer than 33 field hospitals, with their personnel and equipment (which was superb), were transported at enormous cost and effort. The Italians depended heavily, not merely for their military success but also for their safety, on planes, gasoline, guns, and transport. One hundred and fifty tons of gasoline was the daily requirement for aircraft; suitable reserves had to be provided. Moreover, the tactical situation of the occupiers was tricky; Prince Seyum's considerable forces were maneuvering freely on their right flank; the Ethiopians' superior mobility and the furtiveness with which they could move made them an unknown and unnerving menace.

De Bono's *conception*—massive and ponderous preparations accompanied by a campaign to secure the collapse of the imperial authority without more serious fighting—was in some ways plausible. It resembled in its major outlines the strategy of Sir Robert Napier, which had proved staggeringly successful sixty-seven years before. But De Bono's *actions* were less defensible. His troop dispositions were doubtfully conceived; he concentrated more men than were really needed for his advances and left his flanks underprotected. And he was preparing the kind of campaign that could succeed only in political isolation—if the war were left, as it were, undisturbed by foreign distractions and pressures. It was a cautious soldier's war, not the war of a nervous and impetuous dictator. Mussolini, by contrast, had come to believe that after Adowa quick and daring advances could win the day.

De Bono's caution received vindication later; his successor, Pietro Badoglio, an abler soldier and one not afflicted with temperamental indecision and reluctance to commit himself, was almost as much preoccupied with preparations and supply lines as De Bono, once he took command. The weight of opinion of military experts in Europe supported the belief that conquest would be very slow and difficult. But De Bono's critics say he squandered his advatage; and it was true that he was in some ways very favorably placed immediately after the fall of Adowa. Prince Seyum's forces amounted to not more than 16,000 men, all badly equipped, and the main Ethiopian armies were still slowly assembling. There were no considerable forces to oppose a forward march within hundreds of miles. While fuel supplies were indeed a difficulty, the Italian control of the air was so telling and decisive that adequate air support could probably have been provided with minimal supplies. In Italy, anyway, some people thought that if De Bono had moved with speed after Adowa, the kind of preparations he was making might have been quite unnecessary.

Mussolini thought so. He brusquely disregarded De Bono's dispatches and ordered him to begin the advance to Makale, Gugsa's capital 60 miles south of Adowa, and thence to the Tacazze River, another 60 miles further on, not later than November 3. De Bono agreed to move to Makale, but he refused to consider a further advance until he had had time to build roads.

The three columns that had taken Adowa, Enticcio, and Adigrat now set out again toward the south. They were more than ample; they were, indeed, ponderous, and De Bono's critics say that one of them should have been sent to try to find Prince Seyum's troops and eliminate the threat to the right flank. The left flank was likewise exposed, although only to isolated groups of Ethiopians. It was to be covered by a unit that would cross the Danakil Desert from the Eritrean port of Massawa into the mountains, to meet with the main forces just north of Makale. This unit was under the command of General Oreste Mariotti.

The main forces encountered scattered opposition, some of it fierce but none of it strong enough to do more than hold up the three corps. A few miles before Makale, a substantial Ethiopian force was encountered. A few Italians and an estimated 300 Ethiopians were killed, but the town was entered on November 8 without further resistance.

As at Adowa, the priests presented crosses to be kissed by the Italian generals, and it was reported that there were enthusiastic cheers for the invaders from the townspeople. It is possible that the local people were in fact somewhat relieved to see their conquerors. The town was in a desolate state, for Galla tribesmen, marching through it to join Prince Seyum's forces in the mountains to the west, had looted it on their way. The occupiers soon put things to rights, or said they did.

Within a few moments after the first troops went in, Italian planes were landing on the airstrip with food supplies for the civilian population (so the Italians claimed). Municipal services (there cannot have been many) were immediately restored. There was a great deal of self-congratulation in Makale and in Rome on these efficient and humane achievements. One Italian soldier wrote home, "There are now the first signs of civilization in this land where, until a few days ago, there were raids and barbarism. The natives, who asked for protection, are enthusiastic about the rapidity with which we brought Latin civilization."[27] It is likely that the soldier thought he was writing the whole truth; it is possible he was writing part of it. As with the Ogaden tribes in the south, in a place like Makale, a remote village of a few thousand, allegiance was obscure and variable—it had nothing of the character of the Italian villages occupied ten years later by the Germans. The inhabitants were of mixed ethnic and religious character. Nationalism, if it existed at all, was certainly overshadowed by local allegiances and by urgent expediency. But what was not true in the letter of the Italian soldier was that "Latin civilization" could reasonably view the natives' enthusiasm as a justification for the war.

A different and much more striking illustration of the peculiar conditions that made the Ethiopian situation so hard to understand in the rest of the world was the extraordinary experience of General Mariotti's column, advancing from Massawa to rendezvous with the main forces before Makale. It shows in lurid ways the contrast between the customary western notions of what is expected in war and the reactions of a people trying to defend themselves against forces mysterious to them.

After a trek through incredibly difficult conditions of climate and supply, Mariotti's column reached a gorge not far from the place of rendezvous and there was ambushed by an Ethiopian force. For a time the Italian position looked serious, indeed calamitous. Herbert Matthews, who was accompanying the Italians—the only American correspondent on the scene—reported that the Ethiopians were in a position to exterminate them utterly. The Italians could not advance, withdraw, or attack the enemy hidden on the cliffs above them. They were shut off from supplies for four days. Matthews noted of the moment of crisis what people who have never been near fighting can never understand—that he felt "moments of great exultation" and the "joy in battle and danger which sweeps away fear, and those are great moments in a man's life."[28] He expected death, and destruction of the entire column certainly was possible. While their numbers were small, their fate affected far more people. The wiping out of the column would have been a catastrophe for Italian morale and prestige. It would have been a triumph for the Ethiopians. It might have improved Ethiopian morale, although lack of self-confidence was not, in general, among their handicaps. Throughout the world the effect of the extermination of an Italian force would have been considerable.

During the night, when the Italians were hovering hopeless in their chasm, the Ethiopians abandoned their positions and withdrew. It is the judgment of the most recent and careful historian of the operations that the Ethiopians withdrew simply because they had lost interest in the battle. Having had a brief encounter on incredibly favorable terms, they got tired of the fighting. If this interpretation is correct, and it seems plausible, it showed one of the disadvantages of trying to resist a modern army with men accustomed to manners of fighting that belonged to the *Iliad*. In the morning, General Mariotti resumed his march without hindrance or losses and reached his rendezvous in safety. Italian prestige went unmarred, Italian morale unshaken.

De Bono, having successfully and quickly reached Makale, refused to go farther. More local chiefs offered their submission as soon as the Italians appeared in the neighborhood. A few isolated groups of resisters were wiped out. But in the Tembien hills and along the Tacazze, to De Bono's right, Prince Seyum's army was still ominously intact and presumably preparing to strike. Supply lines, longer than ever, obsessed Italian headquarters. De Bono, partly through his own mismanagement of his forces, was precariously exposed. He flatly refused to obey orders to continue beyond Makale.

On the morning of November 16, 1935, by telegram, he was dismissed from his command.

The action was intensely characteristic of Mussolini. He had undertaken the whole Ethiopian venture, it is said, partly at De Bono's urging, with a romantic wish to gratify the old man's vanity and enable him to end his mediocre career in glory. Now he fired him, and De Bono's subsequent honorable reception and elevation to the rank of marshal could not conceal the fact that he had been fired in disgrace.

It may be, however, that De Bono was glad to be dismissed. He was the kind of man for whom a marshal's baton might well have compensated for the disgrace. He is said to have been deeply worried about his own competence as a field commander and moved by a real dislike for battle. His long career had been spent almost entirely in political and administrative posts. Warfare in Ethiopia was undoubtedly daunting. Matthews, who tried to be impartial about the Fascist regime and who admired the Italian army, wrote:

> Abyssinia gave me its peculiar trials, as well as the normal ones. Most of the war was fought on the plateau at heights of 6,000 to 11,000 feet. So near the equator, the rarity of the atmosphere is so intensified that in terms of strain on the heart, lungs, and nerves, the effect was comparable to that of an altitude of 10,000 to 15,000 feet in the temperate zone. The difference between midday and midnight was often as much as 70 degrees. In Dankalia and on the seacoast I was to encounter temperatures as high as 140 in the shade; it was so hot that one gasped for breath, but I never minded heat very much. The intense cold of the nights on the plateau was much more bothersome to me.
>
> So was the dust. One hears much about the role of mud in wars, but the other extreme of dust is equally common and very distressing in its way. The campaign in Abyssinia was fought in a constant cloud of dust which choked and blinded one and covered clothes in layers. One has to live through wars to discover what an astonishing amount of punishment the human body can take. I often wondered how lungs could stand up under the quantities of dust that have to be swallowed.[29]

There were better men than the cashiered commander who were daunted.

De Bono must be recognized for what he was, a vain and foolish man, but he must be given credit for his inhibitions and his impulses. His caution was criticized by some military experts as well as by Mussolini, but most of the foreign experts thought that years, not months, were needed. And his caution displayed itself in a lavish extravagance of time and money and a strict economy of men. He treated his soldiers well; and he treated the Ethiopians, both soldiers and civilians, not only with humanity but with generosity. He believed that he was bringing civilization to them and that the war could be won by converting them rather than killing them. Subsequent events make him appear, by contrast to other Italian generals, a hero of philanthropy. But neither the conditions of war nor the political situation in Italy and Europe nor the temperament of Mussolini permitted so leisurely and kindly a strategy. The same thing that made token sanctions designed for a long-run effect unworkable made De Bono's plans unworkable. Outside complications interfered. It was as if a chess game were being played in a burning house.

De Bono's dismissal was in one sense self-defeating. His successor, Badoglio, required time to prepare for his very different kind of war, a time perhaps almost as great as De Bono himself would have needed. For two months after De Bono returned to Italy little happened in Ethiopia. It was a momentous delay.

The long interruption of the Italian advance counted for a great deal in determining what happened to the world in the years to come. If De Bono had been less reluctant to advance, the war might have ended much sooner, and had that happened, it may be conjectured that the Hoare-Laval deal would never have been made; the British policy of trying to save Mussolini's friendship might not have failed so disastrously; the League of Nations would not have been discredited; Hitler would not have marched into the Rhineland, and Mussolini would not have become his ally. Then there would have been no appeasement, and no second world war; Haile Selassie would never have made his appeal to the League of Nations; and Ethiopia would not exist today.

8

Intermission with Thunder Storms

The war had begun, but it was nowhere near ending. The lull, continuing after Marshal Pietro Badoglio's appointment as commander in chief, gave Ethiopia a remission; elsewhere it brought a climax of tensions and a revolution.

If Badoglio had immediately advanced and won, Mussolini might have had all that he hoped for: Ethiopia; restored friendship of France and Britain; containment of Nazi Germany; and a glorious record of invincibility to fortify Fascism, impress its peers, and sanctify its subjects with the charisma of greatness. The Italian dilemma was obvious. Delay would endanger these aims; an unsuccessful advance would wreck them. Recasting the image of Italy needed more time than was available. There is no clearer evidence of the dilemma than the frantic telegrams with which Mussolini urged Badoglio, vainly, to greater boldness. And by the time that the reputation for crushing efficiency and military glory had been at last won, so much had happened that the other objectives were lost. Germany was aggrandized, Mussolini's prestige and government shaken and his freedom of action diminished, and the efforts of the British and French to save their friendship with him had exploded in a sensational disaster that hastened the maturing of anti-Fascist sentiment throughout the world.

Pietro Badoglio, who was thus in a way responsible for both the salvaging of Fascism and its ruin, was less interesting as a man than he was as a historical force. Thoroughness, so necessary and so dangerous to Mussolini, inhered in his temperament, his background, his professional training. His methods were logical, as his role was paradoxical; he was old-fashioned, unimaginatively competent, distrustful of Fascism—all of the things that Mussolini despised. His mind was conventional to a degree. He had an eminent past as a political personage—and was destined for a far more eminent future—but he was and remained a pure example of the genus soldier. He was a Piedmontese, born of the lower middle class. Like many of his class in Europe in the later nineteenth century, he had chosen an army career as a way to social advancement, a way out of the stultifying semipoverty and futility of the dead-ended *petit bourgeois* world. He was evidently driven by what enemies would call ambition and admirers devotion to the service of his country. His private life was austere, aside from an excessive dedication to playing bridge. He kept no mistresses, a fact surprising to his countrymen, who called him a "lay priest." As with army officers elsewhere in his time, dedication to soldiering involved dedication to a moral code based on great, undefined abstractions: loyalty, courage, honor, and expertness. He was devoted to his monarch, and like those of most monarchist generals (a common type in his day, even in republican France) his notions of monarchy and nation were inextricably intertwined. For him, as for many members of the European military caste, the religious sanctity of oaths was important; they were people who defined themselves in somewhat archaic terms—in some respects, officers' corps were medieval. But they had so convincingly associated themselves with the greatness of the nation that they commanded respect approaching awe in patriotic quarters that were by no means exclusively conservative, and they had often shown themselves remarkably flexible in their adaptation of railways, airplanes, and machine guns to their professional purposes.

Born in 1871, Badoglio had fought in 1896 and in the Libyan campaign. He had fought again in 1915, when the efficacy of his command had been seriously in question. He had been at Caporetto, and like many of the officers involved in that disaster had had to face accusations of incompetence and even of cowardice. But his career was not impaired, and at the end of the war, when he was forty-nine years old, he became Italian chief of staff. At the beginning of the Fascist regime he supported Mussolini, and Mussolini had much confidence in him—more than did some of his fellow generals, who thought him mediocre, or than some ranking Fascists, who thought him politically unreliable. Although many old-line officers backed Fascism, the more ardently ideological Fascists suspected their old-fashioned ethics, their royalism, and their snobbery; and Badoglio was a model of the officer class.

With Mussolini's backing, he remained as chief of staff until 1940, with interruptions for political posts. In 1924 he went to Rio de Janeiro as ambassador, and from 1928 to 1933 he served as governor of Libya. He was made a marshal of Italy (and a marquis) in 1926 and so was Italy's highest ranking officer. He was pro-Fascist in the sense of being willing to serve the regime and in the larger sense of favoring an authoritarian state. But in other ways he was anti-Fascist. He disliked the vulgarity of the party-state, its infringements on tradition, its odor of mobs and privateers. Most of all, he distrusted its leader. Mussolini's confidence in him was not reciprocated, at least not after the early years of the dictatorship. Badoglio was deeply skeptical of his chief's whimsies and follies and amateurism. The experience in Ethiopia was to contribute largely to his distrust, and it grew rapidly thereafter. In May 1940, when Mussolini finally decided that Germany had won World War II and that it was safe for Italy to enter it, Badoglio knew better. He told the dictator, "We have no arms, we have no tanks, we have no aeroplanes, not even shirts for our soldiers. It is suicide."[1] He resigned his post in October, in protest against the foolish and, as it turned out, calamitous attack on Greece. Thereafter he conspired against Mussolini as a confederate of the king. Both men were pro-British and anti-German; both believed that ultimate victory in World War II was impossible. When the crash came he played a large role in unseating Mussolini, and Victor Emmanuel called him in 1943, to be prime minister. He was, in that later period, admired by conservative people like Winston Churchill who saw in him not merely a staunch anti-Fascist and anti-Communist but an honorable man and able soldier, a true patriot standing above partisan politics.

It was a fair judgment, although an obsolete view of an obsolete kind of person. Badoglio's difficulties were those of a man out of phase —German soldiers of similar character were suffering from similar, and more desperate, dilemmas. A man who, from sense of duty, put himself in the service of a state whose leader he knew to be irresponsible and imprudent, who attempted bravely to carry out instructions he knew to be absurd, was an example of the anachronisms of patriotism and the military caste in an age of ideology. His obsolescence had another aspect similar to those of his German counterparts. He was ruthless, but in ways unlike those of new-fashioned Fascism. He had not the slightest hesitation in making full use of strategic bombing, or poison gas, or aerial machine-gunning unarmed men for military ends. But he disliked the brutal trivialities of the vulgar Fascists, as he hated their impetuous military and diplomatic adventures. Ruthlessness was, for him, a part of calculation, not of self-expression.

His position was so strong after his appointment as successor to De Bono that he could afford to defy his Duce now dependent on him for success in Ethiopia, upon which the regime depended. Badoglio could try to call the tune, and did. In answer to Mussolini's impetuous orders to advance, he wired, "Leave me alone."[2] And he is said to have remarked, "What fool in Rome is telegraphing this rubbish?" Since he had advised against the campaign in the first place, his position was the stronger. He could say, "Leave me alone"—he could imply, "I told you so."

Badoglio was deliberate where De Bono had been hesitant, but their problems were identical and identically perceived; they were the problems of bringing modern military organization and equipment to bear on a primordial terrain and an almost primordial enemy. The characteristic strength of a modern fighting force is equipment, and this requires modern transport. The efficient institutional organization of a modern army could overcome great difficulties, but the outstanding examples of this—the military successes of the Germans in 1940 and 1941 —depended on speed, and speed depended in turn on road and rail systems and relatively short distances. Even the German military machine broke down in Russia. To avoid such break-down in the far less developed and fantastically rugged land of Ethiopia, a very, very long period of preparation was required.

The time was used for both political and strategic preparation. The air force, otherwise unoccupied, was ordered to put in its time with strategic bombing, a good deal of which (since there were no industrial or communications targets) was aimed at demoralization. Some of it combined military and morale objectives, for example, the imperial headquarters at Dessie, which suffered heavily. It was first bombed on December 6, 1935, and repeatedly thereafter. (John Melly, the organizer of the British Red Cross unit, dryly observed, "The inhabitants had become wary after the first dose of frightfulness. Sorenson, the missioner from America, was a little bitter about the bombardment of his hospital."[3] It was this sort of preparation, systematic and comprehensive, that set Badoglio's command apart from De Bono's. He was moving slowly, but he was neither inactive nor humane.

He had reasons for alarm. The only significant actions during the lull were a number of Ethiopian attacks on his army's exposed flanks, including one quite serious one, on December 15, led by Prince Imru. The new commander had to consolidate the exposed advanced positions that De Bono had been forced by Mussolini to occupy (evacuation, however sensible militarily, would of course have been unthinkable politically), to fend off incursions, and to fight minor engagements in order to displace Ethiopians from strategically important points on his flanks. His attempt to meet these problems showed Badoglio at his ablest; simultaneously it revealed some serious weaknesses in his army.

For example, Mount Tzellari, which commanded the village of Abbi Addi, which in turn commanded a crossing place of the great Tacazze river valley that formed the main strategic barrier to the west of Makale, was attacked and taken by the Italians on December 19. Low-flying airplanes intervened to machine-gun the Ethiopians who had managed to hold off the enemy force in hand-to-hand fighting during most of the day. But the success was made possible largely by Eritrean troops; there were 13 Italians killed in the battle and 370 Eritreans, a suggestive fact of the sort that public opinion in Europe generally did not notice. An even more suggestive fact was that the mountain, having been captured with considerable difficulty, was immediately abandoned by the local Italian field commander (without the knowledge or approval of headquarters), apparently because of alarm at the probability of the Ethiopians' returning to it by stealth. It was reoccupied by the Ethiopians, who were then in a position to threaten Abbi Addi, which the Italians had to evacuate.

So time was measured in different ways: for the soldier much was needed, for the dictator, faced with world politics, none was available. Mussolini impertinently urged his generals to advance. The clash of two needs infuriated the only man who could defy the dictator, and if his defiance was cloaked with respectful public relations and consummated dilatorily, nonetheless, it added another thread to the rope that was to strangle Fascism. Delay produced effects of the most momentous sort.

If Mussolini measured success by the degree his behavior affected others, as persons of his psychological make-up often do, he might have congratulated himself on creating, during the lull, major political changes in the United States, producing dramatic crises in Britain and France, forcing the resignation of a British foreign minister bringing down the government of the French republic, and contriving the ruin of the League of Nations. These results, however, were not immediately evident. Instead it looked in the autumn of 1935 as if the delay in Italy's advances into Ethiopia were allowing the League time to organize itself for effective resistance. So, for a time anti-Fascists hoped, and even the Italian government feared. The apparent stalemate before Makale, the change of command, and Badoglio's failure to march strengthened the hands of those at Geneva who thought that Mussolini might be stopped. The League Co-ordination Committee recommended, as its mandate required, an extension of sanctions, and on November 6 it approved, on a Canadian motion, a prohibition on shipments of oil. This was—everyone realized it by now—the crucial issue. And what seemed the greatest obstacle to oil sanctions had been weakened: the American government, with its plea on October 30 for a "moral embargo" against any increased shipments of goods to Italy, had shown its readiness to try to co-operate. On November 15 it went further. Not without trepidations about the effects on American isolationist opinion, the secretary of state specified that the export of oil (among other articles of military importance) in more than normal quantity would be "contrary to the policy of this government" and "to the spirit of the recent Neutrality act."[4]

From the Italian standpoint this looked ominous indeed. American policy now looked to be a real policy, not a mere publicizing of placative platitudes such as American policy so often consisted of. It was ingeniously devised to win the support, or at least disarm the hostility, of those numerous Americans who were allergic to the mere mention of the words "League of Nations." The curbing of profiteers, who could develop a large interest in a foreign war by increasing exports to a belligerent, was an aim that many isolationists approved of. They read the history of profiteering in 1914–17 as just such a baleful entanglement. Moreover, public opinion polls were beginning to indicate a plurality of Americans in favor of co-operating with peace-loving nations to restrain aggressors.[5]

Specific legislation to enforce the State Department's policy was lacking, but indirect methods of enforcement were available. The Shipping Board could threaten to foreclose mortgages (of which it owned a great number) on ships carrying abnormally large cargoes destined for Italy. It did so with considerable éclat on November 13, in the case of a heavily mortgaged tanker named *Ulysses* which was planning to sail with oil for Italy. The Italian government protested, and the Italian ambassador, Augusto Rosso, called the threatened foreclosure an unfriendly act. He told the secretary of state that the whole American policy was discriminatory and was in return treated to one of Cordell Hull's classic, sulfurous tirades, which is said to have shaken Rosso considerably.

Little of this appeared in the Italian press or was known to the Italian public, although Roosevelt was beginning to be denounced as a British stooge. Opinion in America still provided the men who ran the Italian press with a wide selection of quotations suitable to allay anxieties. Opposition to Roosevelt's policy came from diverse sources which could be usefully quoted. Among them were two men who aspired to replace Roosevelt: Father Charles Coughlin, the "radio priest" of Royal Oak, Michigan, whose sensational anti-New Deal, anti-Wall Street, anti-foreign, anti-intellectual imprecations were attracting immense radio audiences and giving some nervous people grounds for seeing him as a sort of American Mussolini (he was to back a third-party candidate in the election of November 1936 and suffer humiliating defeat); and Norman Thomas, the scholarly, judicious humanitarian voice of academic leftism, a perennial Socialist candidate for president. They included the now obnoxiously strident Italian language press, which was losing friends for Fascism every day. They included conscientious pacifists, at a time when pacifism was attracting many young people, and know-nothing isolationists, who still represented a noisy and numerous body. It was more than enough to provide reassurance for the readers of Italian newspapers. In the process of providing it, the editors laid down one of the lines that would be basic to Axis propaganda until World War II was finally lost a decade later: there were two Americas, a good America of sturdy, honest, white, "little people" and a bad America led by Roosevelt, bankers, and some decadent intellectuals.

The impression of dedicated isolationism, still current in 1935, was misleading, and its falsity was to prove the undoing of the dictatorships in both Italy and Germany. The real tendencies of American opinion, slowly coalescing, were in the end what brought American troops to the Elbe and the Tiber and turned back what Anne Morrow Lindbergh called "the wave of the future." But all that the development of anti-Fascist opinion and policy in America could mean in the fall of 1935 was a willingness to give limited support to the League, and all that the League could do was to reflect the wishes and policies of France and Britain.

What was happening to opinion in France and Great Britain was, therefore, of more urgent interest, and there prosanctions opinion was becoming unmistakably more powerful. It was ironic that the activities of Roosevelt and Hull were depriving the British government of one of its more useful pretexts for avoiding effective sanctions—that sanctions could not work without the co-operation of the United States. The Opposition was quick to note this, in both France and Britain. In France, the Socialist and Communist press pointed out that there was now little question but that sanctions would be surely and quickly efficacious. Even some of the British government's supporters saw things the same way. The London *Times* observed that Roosevelt's policy would "make practicable the prohibition by the League Powers of the supply of oil to Italy,"[6] and other progovernment papers showed signs of having taken the Conservatives' election campaign too seriously. Within the government several ministers, notably Neville Chamberlain (who was the cabinet's strongest supporter of rearmament) welcomed the American policy. Everywhere in France and Britain people were more determined in their support of the League, now that it looked at last as if the League might act; but some, in British Liberal and Labour circles, questioned the bona fides of the government.

There was reason to question them. There had been talk ever since the League first denounced Italy about efforts to negotiate with Mussolini, and the government leaders did not exactly deny them. They spoke instead of a "two-pronged peace policy"—one prong being sanctions, the other efforts at a compromise solution. The Co-ordination Committee's recommendation for oil sanctions was made on November 15.

The day before, Britain had had its General Elections, and the government—still called the National Government, but now over-whelmingly and simply Conservative—had won some 430 seats in the House of Commons over a combined Opposition of Labour and Liber-als of fewer than 200. With the election fought and won, the cabinet was freer to follow its own instincts while still showing solicitude for the League. As a result, one of the turning points of history took place. It was not the consequence of any real change in attitudes or efforts among the people who decided things, still less of any peculiar wicked-ness on their part. It was chiefly the product of the gap between the way things were and the way that electoral exigencies had made them ap-pear. The crisis that followed was the result of this and it created a deep and disillusioned conviction of duplicity and cynicism, and a failure of idealism.

A case can be made for what looks, in absolute terms, like duplic-ity. The men who made the policy, most notably Hoare, and those who acceded in it, most notably Baldwin, saw their roles in a different way from the way that the Opposition or later generations saw them: they were, in their own view, the agents of a government which was "repre-sentative" and "responsible," but their mandate for national security was absolute: they must do what seemed to them prudent and wise in the national interest. For few in the inner circle really doubted that public opinion was irresponsible, ill-informed, and volatile or that it was necessary to try to save peace, and the British empire, by actions both unpopular and secretive. They believed in the "two-pronged pol-icy." The continuity of their policies demanded a measure of conceal-ment and that was, after all, also part of their civic responsibility. Their dilemma was one of the great dilemmas of representative governments in free societies.

Uncertainty and what now looks like confusion were, however, general among Conservatives. Churchill, for example, usually in op-position to the cabinet's foreign policy, took a complicated stand. He favored an understanding with Italy, but he also favored vigorous rearm-ament *and* support of the League as the best ways to achieve it. He was sure that Mussolini would back down, and the peculiarly personal char-acter of his view is summarized in a passage from a speech in the House of Commons, delivered in mid-October. "When we separated in August . . . the story was that economic sanctions meant war . . . But what has happened? . . . Signor Mussolini—I think it is a sign of his commanding mind; it seems to me one of the strongest things he has done —says 'Italy will meet [sanctions] with discipline, with frugality and with sacrifice.' That is a great saying in the difficulties in which he stands. So I say that we are not only in the presence of an assertion of the public law of Europe, but of its recognition by the State affected and by the historic figure at the head of that State."[7] He went on to pay tribute to the struggle of Ethiopia to save itself and said that it would not be made a matter "for compromise or barter. But no one . . . can justify the condition that prevails in that country." He concluded by a ringing expression of confidence in the efficacy of sanctions, the graceful yielding of the Italians, and the future of the League.

In this, Churchill was probably influenced by a widespread Conservative attitude which, sound enough in its assumption, was short-sighted, and confusing and paralysing in its effect. It had been effectively voiced by the Anglican pundit, Dean W. R. Inge: "I think all friends of the League should beware of their involuntary association with Socialists who care nothing for Abyssinia . . . but who wish to embroil us with Italy because they hate and fear Fascism."[8] He may also have been influenced by Eden, who was a protégé of his, in some ways Churchill's agent within the ministry. Eden's attitude, even more confused on the face of it, *also* reflected a certain credulousness about the secret diplomatic discussions *within* the cabinet. Hoare kept his views to himself, so that some of his colleagues were not clear what was going on. They all probably hoped that by negotiating they could save both world peace and the independence of Amharic parts of Ethiopia. Ever since the previous summer the ministers had pursued the notion that the proper policy was to ascertain Mussolini's minimum demands and to try to negotiate. They were alarmed and annoyed when Mussolini forced their hand by actually invading Ethiopia, but they were not any more pro-League. They continued to believe that Italy's demands were negotiable. And they saw sanctions *both* as a campaign device to win an election (which it was) and as a way to force Mussolini to negotiate (which it might have been).

The prospective imposition of oil sanctions may have forced the hands of those in London and Paris who were inclined to negotiation. In Italy it was apprehended that oil sanctions would force a crisis. Years later Mussolini told Hitler's interpreter, Paul Schmidt, that he would have had to withdraw from Ethiopia within a fortnight had they been imposed, and that this would have brought disaster to the regime.[9] Mussolini's ineffable impulse to self-dramatization suggests caution in accepting the verity of such retrospects, but something like this was probably the case. In any event, the prospect of oil sanctions made Sir Samuel Hoare anxious to reach a quick settlement.

The pressures on him were strong. Laval was being very difficult indeed, combining obstinacy with private threats. The Italians were bombarding the world with public *and* private threats that could not, at the time, be entirely discounted as bluff. Eminent Italians—including General Garibaldi, grandson of the Liberator and an old friend of Hoare's, warned him that oil sanctions might lead to an Italian-British war.[10] Similar intimations were ostentatiously thrust upon Hoare from all quarters. The Italian press fortified these ominous impressions with rich vituperation. On December 5 he told the high commissioners of the British Dominions that it was essential that threats by "the mad dog," Mussolini, must not deter the League in its sanctions policy, but for several weeks his representative, Maurice Peterson, head of the Foreign Office's Ethiopian division, had been working with Laval to provide a formula that would be satisfactory to the mad dog.

The formula Hoare at first envisaged was unrealistic. It revived the previous summer's proposal of cession of Zeila, in British Somaliland, to Ethiopia and proposed that Italy cede one of its own ports, Assab, in Eritrea. In return Italy would get Adowa and Adigrat and a number of deserts. (The tendency of people to try to placate Mussolini by giving him deserts was ineradicable; it is not surprising that Mussolini, who disliked deserts, should have been infuriated by it.) Then, on December 7 Hoare left for a vacation in Switzerland, and he stopped overnight in Paris to see the French prime minister. There ensued one of those conversations ending in secret and outrageous agreements that were Laval's characteristic contribution to the conduct of international affairs. The discussions of December 7–8, 1935, form a symmetrical counterpiece to those in Rome the previous January, where the awful mess had originated.

The proposal that evolved (it was to be presented immediately for approval to Mussolini and only after that to the League and to Haile Selassie) apparently went a good deal beyond anything the cabinet in London had discussed. All thought of asking Italy to cede part of Eritrea was abandoned, and most of the province of Tigre was to be given up by Ethiopia, along with much of the eastern part of the empire. The southern half, up to a line only seventy miles south of the capital, was to be reserved for Italy's exclusive economic sphere. It was the old heartland project revived in a rather extreme form. Zeila was still to be given to Ethiopia, but with the remarkable provision that no railway be built to connect it to the Ethiopian hinterland (without which its value, in any case problematical, would of course be nil). When the agreement was made known to the cabinet, Eden expressed himself as astonished and says he thought of resigning, and even Peterson was surprised.[11] Baldwin's first reaction was to hope that it would all come to nothing. There was some feeling that Hoare ought to come home to explain and defend his agreement, but according to Eden (and here again the curious, comradely procedures of British policy making are illumined) no one thought it would be fair to ask the fatigued minister to cut short his Swiss holiday. With some reluctance, the cabinet decided it must support its absent member's policy. Eden, reflecting later, blamed himself for excessive sensitivity "about apparent disloyalty."[12] His record of events suggests the transactions of a small-town congregation contemplating plans for a covered-dish dinner.

The cabinet did so far emend the Hoare-Laval agreement as to insist that Haile Selassie's approval be solicited at the same time as Mussolini's. Laval, when the matter was raised with him, refused. The Ethiopians, he thought (undoubtedly correctly), would certainly refuse, particularly in view of the possible imminence of League approval of oil sanctions.

At this point, British public opinion took a hand in events. The substance of the agreement was printed in the papers.

The idea that some kind of deal was urgent, before oil sanctions could be adopted and produce their expected fatal results, had been strongly pressed for some time in conservative papers in both Paris and London. There had been a good deal of speculation about what terms *might* satisfy Italy. The *Morning Post* and *Daily Telegraph*, both ultra-Tory, as well as the Liberal *Manchester Guardian* and the *Observer*, were at the beginning of December discussing the partition of Ethiopia as a basis for settlement. The projects bore a remarkably, indeed a suspiciously, close similarity to those which were being considered, presumably in the utmost secrecy, in the French and British foreign offices.

There were similar discussions in the Paris press. Perhaps people in high places were trying, by means of leaks to journalists, to begin preparing public opinion for a peace plan. It has been said that both Hoare and the permanent undersecretary of the Foreign Office, Sir Robert Vansittart, a passionate devotee of conciliating Italy, had been so engaged. It was standard operating procedure, although it had rarely been applied to so startling a change of public policy. But now quiet speculation was drowned in stupefying revelation.

A generally accurate summary of the proposals Hoare and Laval had agreed upon were on front pages before the cabinet in London met to consider them. The question of how they got there is perplexing,* but, whatever the source of the leak, its effects were sensational. They demonstrated with agonizing clarity the dilemma of representative government and the related difficulty that neither public opinion nor statesmen were able to maintain a grasp of realities. Just as the public generally had not realized that their leaders had wanted negotiation *instead* of confrontation, Hoare and Laval had not realized that their nations would not accept their agreement—even if Mussolini and Haile Selassie had been inclined to do so. The League and the ubiquitous formulas of collective security, of peace through international action, were too popular and too powerful to allow Hoare and Laval's act of brokerage.

The fact was immediately evident. What a recent and detached chronicler of the episode has called a "fantastic political tornado"[14]

* The *New York Times* got the story from its London bureau on the night of December 8, 1935. The next morning three right-wing Paris papers, *L'Oeuvre*, *Écho de Paris*, and *Le Petit Parisien*, carried it. Laval claimed that the leak was engineered by disgruntled officials of the French Ministry of Foreign Affairs who hoped to discredit his policy. It seemed plausible, since French opinion was much agitated, and in left-wing and anti-government circles, pro-sanctions pro-League feeling was running high. Foreign ministry officials (although rather unlikely to be sympathizers with the leftist critics of Laval) might well have disliked the furtive Fascist sympathies of their chief. They might have calculated that the best chance of wrecking the deal with Italy was to publish Laval's betrayal of the League and thus mobilize public opinion. The plausibility of this theory grew in the weeks that followed, and most subsequent British historians have accepted it. But other authorities, including no less a one than Arnold Toynbee, believed that Laval himself leaked the secret in order to force the British ministers to consider in undue haste a plan that, if time had allowed for calm reflection, they would in their high-mindedness have rejected. Some observers have perceived a third, equally plausible, explanation: that the wickedness was as much British as French in its inception. (It is certainly interesting that the first leak, to the *New York Times*, originated in London.) Salvemini, for example, believed that both Hoare and Laval wanted the proposals made public so that favorable press reception in Paris and New York could be used for leverage in Britain.[13]

struck Great Britain. The cabinet had at first loyally stood by the absent foreign secretary (his absence was forcibly prolonged by an episode that mixed the dramaturgy of Euripides and Walt Disney: he had a fainting fit in St. Moritz and broke his nose falling on the ice). Immediately after the storm broke, it disavowed him. However, it pursued further diplomatic manipulations; these were also not known to the public. With Eden as acting foreign secretary and Vansittart as its agent in Paris, it tried to get Laval to agree that the proposal should be presented simultaneously to the governments of Ethiopia and Italy. Laval, also manipulating to the last, insisted on terms for this alteration in the agreement: that the Ethiopians be told that if they did not accept, then oil sanctions would not be adopted. There was a great deal of discussion back and forth on this delusory point. In the meanwhile, in London, Paris, and Geneva all hell was breaking loose.

The House of Commons met on December 10—the day after the newspapers printed the first reports and the cabinet approved the agreement—for the purposes of debating the Speech from the Throne, the cabinet's annual message to the legislature. It debated instead the newspaper reports. The members of Parliament were already being subject to strong pressures and violent expressions of opinion from their constituents. To those who supported the League were added those who disliked, to the point of hysteria in many cases, what seemed to be government duplicity. Baldwin attempted to handle the situation with evasiveness. He told the Commons that he had not read the papers and that the proposals that had been reached were tentative. He also said—and became notorious for saying it—that weighty considerations of state of the most secret sort were controlling government policy. If they were known, all opposition would dissolve; but they could not be made public. His lips, he said, were sealed. (He later told his son that he was talking about Laval's absolute determination to give Mussolini anything he wanted, but he made it sound like some awful secret weapon.) This portentous nonsense did not go down at all well. He was hooted by the Commons and excoriated the next day by much of the press. Nor did it avail anything for Eden to try to explain that the Co-ordination Committee of the League had authorized attempts to achieve a settlement while at the same time recommending oil sanctions; so it had, in the most general and unofficial way, but it had not authorized the kind of betrayal that was conceived to have taken place. When the

17. Camels, which were useful in the desert but died in the highlands, were almost the only transport, except for donkeys, that the Ethiopians had.

18. The Ethiopian army was in large part tribal, in lesser part feudal, and in very small part modern. The soldiers were often wildly self-confident, counting on providence, numbers, and their own bravery. On a few occasions these strengths sufficed to threaten Italian forces with defeat, but the Ethiopians won no single battle in the war.

19. One of the most remarkable figures of the war was an American black named Hubert Julian, known as the "Black Eagle of Harlem," shown on horseback. He trained a squadron of pilots to defend the last independent country of Africa. In 1935 he became an Ethiopian subject and, briefly, leader of the Ethiopian air force. A passionate man and an able pilot, he caught the imagination of Ethiopians and American blacks alike and became, for a time, their hero.

20. The Italian legation in Addis Ababa, where Count Luigi Vinci-Gigliucci, Italian minister, barricaded himself and refused to leave the capital with the rest of his staff.

21. Pierre Laval, premier of France, pictured here in 1940, negotiated agreements in 1935 that aimed at saving Franco-Italian friendship at the price of the existence of both Ethiopia and the League of Nations. He was a shrewd, calculating, shady manipulator who did not realize that morality can be a powerful political force.

22. Anthony Eden, the handsome young British minister for League of Nations affairs in 1935, had a reputation for internationalism and high principles; his position on Ethiopia represented the British cabinet's concession to a public opinion that demanded support for a pro-League, anti-Fascist policy. Sir Samuel Hoare, the foreign secretary, had much more influence in policy making. He was a skillful statesman of the old school, a subtle negotiator who thought that peace and the safety of the British empire required that Mussolini be bargained with, not opposed. They were both decent English gentlemen and in different ways good specimens of the small club that ran the empire.

TIME
The Weekly Newsmagazine

Volume XXVII   MAN OF THE YEAR   Number 1

23. *Broadcasting to the nation in December 1935, Franklin D. Roosevelt looked dignified, benign, high-minded, responsible. More than any other national leader, he was responsible for identifying Fascism as an aggressive world force that, if not stopped, would threaten the whole free world, including the United States.*

24. *In January 1936 Time carried on its cover its annual portrait of the "Man of the Year," chosen by its editors—it was Haile Selassie. This choice marked the beginning of a revolution in American attitudes: it was the first time an African had been chosen, and it indicated the sudden awareness of Fascism as a threat to morality and world peace.*

official text of the Hoare-Laval agreement was released three days later, the British public had already made up its mind with singular unanimity that the policy was unacceptable, impractical, dishonest, and generally abhorrent.

Still, the government persisted in its efforts to make the agreement work. Eden was despatched to Paris and Geneva to reason with people. Although Baldwin denied it, instructions were sent off to Sir Sidney Barton in Addis Ababa and Sir Eric Drummond in Rome to present the agreement with strong recommendations for its acceptance to Haile Selassie and Mussolini. But it became clearer and clearer that this was all unreal. Parliamentary opinion was more and more agitated, and so, Eden found in Switzerland, was a great majority of League members. There was no longer any hope of negotiations along the lines that Laval had insisted on.

Eden now at last asserted himself. He insisted that Hoare return to London (Hoare was reluctant to do so and postponed his departure until practically ordered back by the cabinet). Eden also prepared a speech to be given to the League, which said that the British government had intended the proposals merely as a tentative suggestion "in order to ascertain what the views of the two parties and the League might be upon them . . . ," and he added, with professional redundancy, "If, therefore, it transpired that these proposals . . . do not satisfy the essential condition of agreement by the two parties and the League, His Majesty's Government could not continue to recommend or support them."[15] The cabinet approved the draft and so, with a bare minimum of dignity, saved its face. Hoare, when he reached London, received the prime minister, who asked him how he felt. "I wish," the foreign secretary said, "I were dead."

His wish was not fulfilled, but he did cease to be foreign secretary. His resignation was announced the next day, December 18, and Eden was appointed to succeed him. It later came to appear that Hoare was thrown to the wolves by the rest of the cabinet, which saw that it was necessary to provide some sustenance for a ravening public. But he was not, if the figure may be extended, actually consumed: six months later, presumably restored in health and spirits, he returned to the cabinet as first lord of the Admiralty. The dismissal evidently represented no disavowal of the man and his policy. Baldwin was desperate or at least (as his official but very unsympathetic biographer put it) "feeble, toneless, and unhappy," as if "crushed by some appalling disaster."[16] If no placation of public had been achieved, the Baldwin government might well have been forced out of office.

Even so, some people thought it was a near thing. Sir Austen Chamberlain, a former foreign secretary and a Conservative member, said in the House the day after Hoare's resignation,

> There is the question of the honour of this country, and there is the question of the honour of the Prime Minister. If, as is suggested in some quarters, the Prime Minister won an election on one policy and immediately after victory was prepared to carry out another, it has an extremely ugly look.[17]

It did indeed, and for many people neither the honor of the country nor that of the prime minister would ever quite recover. But the cabinet had survived.

It was in France that the most sensational and significant shocks were registered after the Hoare-Laval earthquake. There, not only was the ministry discredited—it was destroyed. The republic itself was shaken, and a whole train of stupendous social and political effects were unleashed.

Some of Laval's motives were comparable to those of Baldwin: notably, it may be supposed, his desire to remain in office. But this was much more difficult for Laval than for Baldwin, for several reasons. For one thing, his ministry, like all ministries of the Third Republic, depended on a shaky parliamentary coalition. For another, elections still lay ahead, not triumphantly behind as in Britain. They were to take place in the spring of 1936. And the domestic political situation was complex and alarming and rapidly becoming more so.

There had been less pro-League sentiment in France than in Britain, and more support for a deal with Italy. But France was not so stable as Britain, and it was now approaching the verge of civic disintegration and, some thought, revolution. The Depression had come late to France but by 1935 had struck with even more shattering force than in Britain. In February of 1934 the republic had—or so contemporaries thought—been almost overthrown by violent riots. The polarization of French politics between a frustrated, desperate Right and a vigorous and no less desperate Left, was proceeding apace. The Ethiopian crisis and the conduct of Pierre Laval combined with these seismic disturbances to produce a still larger disarray. The biographer of Léon Blum, the French Socialist leader, observed that the Ethiopian crisis was a real turning point in French affairs."[18]

Protofascist groups, splintered but fast-growing, were so closely identified with Italian Fascism (some were subsidized by it) that any threat to Mussolini was a threat to all that they held most dear. Sanctions represented precisely such a threat, and French militants, along with some of their old-fashioned right-wing allies whose militancy consisted of obscene vituperation in papers like *Gringoire,* had responded to the notion of collective security with desperate baffled rage that exactly matched Mussolini's own response. Their inability to convert the mass of Frenchmen to their point of view and the growing tendency to united action by the French Left increased their bafflement and their desperation. Street fighting developed rapidly. The militants had been Laval's most frenzied backers, and their backing, not disavowed, helped to convince the Left that fascism was indeed a universal phenomenon, even a universal conspiracy, backed by the state. Anti-fascism was being turned against the whole French social order.

The swing to the Left that now was becoming a landslide may in part be charged to the appearance of ineffable cynicism of Laval himself. His very willingness to conciliate the paramilitary fascist outfits infuriated many people who would otherwise have counted themselves moderate. Some right-wing republicans were appalled equally by the immorality of Laval's international policy and his placation of the militants. Catholics were divided. Spokesmen for enlightened Catholic opinion, very distinguished men like Paul Claudel (perhaps France's best living poet), François Mauriac (perhaps its best novelist), and Jacques Maritain (perhaps its best philosopher) passionately denounced the betrayal of the League and morality. But much conservative, pro-Catholic opinion was pro-Italian.

There were divisions on the other side as well. Some leftists supported Laval, most of them pacifists who distrusted the capitalist League. But most of the Left, dedicated to anti-Fascism on principle (and for reasons of political expediency as well) saw capitalist imperialism as a trait of Laval's policy rather than of sanctions; and since the Soviet Union was supporting the League, so did the French Communist party. "The cleavage over the Abyssinian question," one British historian of France remarked, "ran through all sections of the country."[19]

A nation-wide taking of sides with passionate commitment, something like a Dreyfus Affair, looked to be shaping up.

Among the parties that had supported Laval's cabinet was the one confusingly entitled the Radical and Radical-Socialist party—the name dated from the time when Radical meant democratic and Socialist meant approval for social reform. It was led by highly professional and often rather uninspiring and uninspired politicians, supported by stolid middle-class voters as well as more libertarian groups; but it was still a party of the Left in its dedication to traditional freedoms (as defined in its own vocabulary), and it didn't want to be associated with the malefactors of great wealth who were supposed to dominate everything to the right of it in the Chamber. The Radicals were indispensable to Laval; without Radical support, it was impossible for a cabinet to survive. In the Chamber of Deputies elected in 1932, whose unhappy mandate was now approaching its end, they controlled 156 seats and were much the biggest single group. There were five Radical ministers in Laval's cabinet, including its most respected member, Edouard Herriot. And these ministers resigned after the publication of the Hoare-Laval agreement.

It was quite a long time after. Whatever crises of conscience the Radicals had suffered, conscience deferred to tactic. The elections would take place in April 1936, and if the Radicals were to succeed in holding their own, they had first to be sure that Laval's policies *were* discredited with their constituency and then to find new electoral allies among the anti-Laval, pro-League Left. It took several weeks to do so, and then, early in January 1936, the five ministers withdrew from the cabinet and the Radical deputies withdrew their parliamentary support for the government. Laval resigned as premier on January 22, and his place was taken by Albert Sarraut, a reliable if rather uninspiring Radical whose experience was mainly in colonial administration. He lacked, to an even greater extent than most premiers of the Third Republic, fame or magnetism; and like many of them he was selected for precisely that reason. His was to be an interim ministry, without program and without a reliable parliamentary majority, holding office only until the elections could provide a new Chamber with what would certainly be a very different political complexion. For the Radicals had proceeded to successful negotiations for an electoral alliance, called the Popular

Front, with the Socialists and Communists. It was an old Radical tradition to be on the winning side when public opinion shifted.

Much was to happen before the elections, almost all of it favorable to the Popular Front. The most dramatic of these events was the attempt to assassinate Léon Blum—the Socialist leader and the future premier—by student followers of one of the protofascist groups, on February 13, 1936. Blum was an intellectual, a Jew, an internationalist, and a stern anti-fascist. He had from the beginning of the Ethiopian crisis taken a consistent line toward it. He had argued that the League must be strengthened and that any attempt to conciliate Mussolini would only divide the enemies of fascism. His editorials in Le Populaire, the Socialist daily, had been the most intellectually impressive and politically influential of the denunciations of the Hoare-Laval deal, and they had contributed powerfully to the weakening of the government and the withdrawal of the Radicals. He was therefore the very embodiment of all that the protofascists hated and feared most, and the attempt to murder him was logical. But it was a political mistake. It discredited the people who had done it and made a martyr of their opponent. The left-wing press exploited Blum's martyrdom to its fullest.

All attention focused on the elections. But they were months away, and during those months France was governed by Sarraut's caretaker cabinet, which meant a long postponement for a new foreign policy to replace Laval's. By the time the elections were held—in May—the French had lost their freedom of action. The timing of the French elections, no less than that of the British, was an important element in giving the Ethiopian crisis its lasting importance.

The attitudes of the Sarraut cabinet were purely negative; they were against what Laval had been for, tending vaguely to the leftist prescription of ecumenical anti-fascism and solidarity with the Soviet Union. But these attitudes were overshadowed by the transiency of the government. A ministry whose ultimate aim was self-liquidation was bound in some measure to be dedicated to self-defeat.

In Italy it appeared that a golden miracle had saved Fascism from embarrassment, perhaps from mortal danger. The League Council had been scheduled to consider oil sanctions on December 12. In theory the League might now proceed to the measure that could, it was understood, stop the invasion before it had gotten beyond its preliminary stage. But this was as illusory as Hoare's hopes of calling off the war by judicious concessions; for now the real nature of the League was revealed to the world and to its own more hopeful members—it was a forum for great powers, and nothing more. Two of those great powers seemed to have indicated with lethal clarity that the policy of the League, as an independent entity, did not coincide with their policies. There was little possibility that the League could now pursue an independent course, and there did not seem, even for the credulous, much chance that Britain and France would accept oil sanctions. Baldwin flatly stated the facts to the House of Commons a week later when he said that "no responsible government could disregard that Italy would regard the oil embargo as a military sanction or an act regarding war against her."[20] If Britain's cabinet felt this way, then the League could not act.

Baldwin's statement was an epitaph to hopes for the League that had mostly been interred when the Hoare-Laval agreement first reached the headlines. The burial, however, was not immediately perceived as final by everybody. It was still believed by some that the League might be resurrected. Discussions of oil sanctions dragged on for some time afterward, and the dismissal of Hoare and the subsequent resignation of Laval raised false hopes for the reversal of Franco-British policy and a resuscitation of the League. But most people thought now that this was outward show.

They did in Rome. Mussolini showed himself, as he so often did, a competent tactician. It is not clear whether he would have been prepared to consider the Hoare-Laval plan or not, had it been presented in secrecy. It seems conceivable that he might have, despite his earlier categorical remarks about total victory. Oil sanctions were unquestionably a menace. Badoglio's delay in Ethiopia was deeply disturbing. Mussolini was, as he recurrently was, frightened. Even *without* secrecy, even in the face of the domestic outcries in Britain and France, the Italian government apparently did seriously consider a settlement along the lines of the Hoare-Laval proposals. As late as December 18, when the British government had already decided to abandon Hoare, the Grand Council of Fascism (according to a communiqué that was never published) expressed "its sincere appreciation of the friendly spirit inspiring the communication made by the two governments with the object of finding a solution to the Italo-Ethiopian conflict. It decides to consider the verbal proposals as a possible basis for the negotiation."[21]

Such a decision would in fact have been natural; the Italians would have gotten most of what they wanted immediately with all the rest in prospect, and without cost; and the alternatives were dark indeed. On the other hand, there are subtleties that rule out a straightforward explanation. It was obviously desirable to negotiate while Badoglio was still preparing his attack, in the hope that negotiations would obviate or postpone oil sanctions. But by December 18 it was obvious that Geneva was in such disarray that action was unlikely to be taken, and negotiations, being harmless and possibly protracted, might well reverse the very unfavorable opinion that was burgeoning so rapidly in so many quarters. They would serve to rebuild abroad Mussolini's reputation as a conciliatory statesman while not endangering his domestic reputation as a heroic defender of Italy against predatory and decadent dogs in manger.

The communiqué of the Grand Council meeting was not published, apparently, because news of Hoare's resignation reached Mussolini during the night of December 18-19. This put a quite new light on the situation. Aloisi at Geneva (as a non-participant in League procedures, though Italy was still a member and still maintained its delegation) told the French that they would have to wait to see what happened in Britain.

The French were in close touch with Rome up to December 19. Laval had kept Mussolini informed of consultations with Hoare. Afterward he had done all that he could to keep the path to negotiations open. It is likely that Mussolini thought there was a possibility that he might succeed. Since he thought Laval was a good sort of friend and wanted to keep French friendship, he might have been prepared to negotiate. But we may assume that when he saw the mounting confusion in Britain and France he worried less and decided that the wisest course was to let Badoglio's plans mature. He knew that action could be expected before long.

On January 12 Graziani began a major attack in the south; a month later Badoglio's offensive opened in the north.

It was in Germany that reactions to the Hoare-Laval agreement and its aftermath were most surprising and also most subtle and most immediately significant. They contributed to the growing popular belief that Germany and Italy formed a new force in world affairs—massive, monolithic, and frightening to partisans of the existing order. The belief may have been an illusion, but it prophesied a fact.

Italy was still, at the end of 1935, seen in Berlin as more probably an enemy to Germany than an ally. Most Germans regarded it with distrust and distaste, as the press campaigns and the peculiar spasm of pro-Ethiopian sentiment in Germany in the summer of 1935 had shown. Hitler was later to display on several occasions a retroactive enthusiasm for the Italians' Ethiopian adventure: "The Italians," he told Field Marshal Albert Kesselring in 1942, "are first-class colonizers. Given ten years of Italian rule, Addis Ababa would have become a most beautiful city."[22] At the end of 1935 his enthusiasm was not noticeable. Nevertheless, the Axis was being made. Coal imports from Germany into Italy had doubled in 1935, to reach more than half of Italy's total, while those from Britain had fallen by a quarter. A cautious cordiality toward Italy had been shown in the press after the adoption of sanctions.

The publication of the agreement in Paris caused momentary consternation in Berlin. It was exactly the kind of compromise, aimed at saving the friendship of Italy, France, and Britain and perhaps the Stresa Front against Germany, that the Germans most feared—it was exactly the kind of compromise that the Nazi regime itself excelled in and was able to achieve in a way that democracies with press freedom were not. The Berlin press gave ample testimony to the logic of Laval's attitude: if Italy could be bought off, Germany would be isolated and enfeebled. It was exactly this that the Nazi papers were openly warning their readers of on December 10, 1935. The theme was weirdly paradoxical: the papers in Germany, as in London and New York, denounced an ignoble plot against the League of Nations and the independence of Ethiopia. Hitler actually went so far as to *apologize* to the Polish ambassador for allowing the increased exports of coal to Italy. (If Britain and France made an amicable settlement with Italy, then Poland's friendship became important to Germany, and Poland had supported sanctions.) The only possible line for the Germans, if the deal worked, was a high-minded backing for the League (from which Germany had resigned with contumely two years before).

But the deal did not work, and both of Hitler's hands were suddenly freed. With Italy divided from the French and British, he had much less to fear from any of them. There was no obstacle to trying to make a friend—or servitor—of Fascist Italy, and no reason to conceal his enmity toward France. An historian of the Rome-Berlin Axis wrote years later, "History has perhaps never played a stranger trick upon Man than to allow British indignation against international lawlessness and imperialist and racialist bullying to have smoothed the path of Adolf Hitler."[23]

Three months later the Germans, not without grave apprehension, sent their troops into the demilitarized Rhineland, which since the end of World War I had been the bulwark and symbol of French safety and European peace.

In the United States the Hoare-Laval agreement created almost as much of a sensation as in Britain and France. As a result of it, more Americans, with stronger conviction, began to leave the familiar avenue of isolation, turning at the fork they had approached the summer before. The new route was crowded as 1936 began, and its travelers included the president of the United States. The change was of a sort that could be—and was—misread; at first, on the surface, news of the agreement seemed to fortify the arguments of those who, from differing points of view, opposed any involvement at all in world affairs. This was natural. The most conspicuous of isolationist arguments seemed thoroughly borne out by the British-French plan: that European politicians were cynical and untrustworthy. *Realpolitik* of the sort Laval dealt in ranked in American political mythology with hostility to motherhood. And aversion to *Realpolitik* had always been the stock in trade of Americans who favored an "American system" as distinct from the "European system" of international affairs. The Hoare-Laval agreement gave to all isolationists a comfortable sense of vindication. But this was a superficial reaction, a conditioned reflex to an unexpected stimulus. In fact, the motor reflexes of America were being remade.

There were two easily distinguishable brands of isolationism. The first was old-fashioned, associated politically with an odd combination of now rather parochial Populism—William Jennings Bryan's kind of democracy—and strong conservatism. It was embodied, in most people's minds, in Senator William E. Borah of Idaho. He wanted to stay aloof from the quarrels of foreigners, but he also insisted on the God-given right of American traders to trade as much as they pleased with whomever they pleased. Of a very different sort was the liberal isolationism, associated at the moment with the name of Senator Gerald P. Nye of North Dakota. (Isolationism was looked on by its opponents as an obscurantist product of midwestern provinciality, although Borah was a hero for eastern reactionaries and Nye for eastern radical college students.) Nye thought that wars were the product of the very kind of free-wheeling capitalism that Borah seemed to be sponsoring.

Borah's brand of isolationism would remain for a time rocklike, but Nye's was beginning to crack. Progressive people, especially progressive pacifists or quasi-pacifists, who supported the view that wars were produced by munition makers and traders, were having second thoughts after news of the Hoare-Laval agreement and of Italian atrocities reached America. (Second thoughts were also encouraged by the obnoxious propaganda tactics of Italian-American groups which, palpably mouthpieces for a foreign government, were denouncing the liberals' demands for an absolute embargo to warring nations. Such an embargo, it was said, was a British plot to starve Italian babies.)

The New Republic, The Nation, and other periodical bellwethers of progressive thought were changing their line. Up until November or December, they had been resolutely isolationist in the old way, hostile to capitalist and imperialist Britain, distrustful of the League, uninterested in the fate of Ethiopia, detached about Mussolini's Italy. At first the worst they said of the East African venture was that it was no worse than what the British and the French had been doing for centuries and that Mussolini could not be criticized for trying to capture markets and raw materials. (Nobody ever troubled to inquire whether there *were* markets or raw materials in Ethiopia.) Adversions in the liberal American journals to Ethiopia had sounded sometimes remarkably like those of the Italian press: "Haile Selassie and his Amharic nobles wish to continue to exploit the Ethiopian peasants, unmolested by white men,"[24] *The New Republic* had observed on the eve of war. It was the kind of neat simplification that when uttered by Fascist dictators sounded sinister to most Americans. Uttered by American liberal intellectuals, it sounded, at first, high-minded.

The old liberal tradition of sympathy for Fascism still lingered toward the end of 1935, but it had begun to change. In November *The*

New Republic proposed a more sophisticated explanation of the war, one that showed a much clearer and more hostile understanding of the nature of Fascism. "The primary reason for the war seems to lie [not in commercial or economic motives but] instead in the unsettling effect that extreme nationalism and limitless power have upon the sanity and sense of balance of a dictator." Fascism was referred to as a "disease."[25] By January, Italy's methods of making war were being called "shocking," and in February *The New Republic* gave great prominence to a passionate anti-Fascist manifesto by Italian exiles, including Max Ascoli and Gaetano Salvemini.[26] This change of line may be ascribed partly to the Hoare-Laval agreement, which made it appear to the kinds of people who read the liberal journals that the League was the victim of an imperialist plot and therefore deserving of approbation. Approbation began to rub off on Ethiopia, despite its regrettable internal arrangements.

The effects of the Hoare-Laval shock were strengthened and made more lasting by a fortuitous but influential occurrence: the publication, in rapid succession, of three books excoriating Mussolini and Fascism in the most unmeasured terms, written by people of sound credentials. The three were *Mussolini's Italy*, by Herman Finer, a political scientist at the University of London, which appeared in the United States in December 1935; *Sawdust Caesar*, by George Seldes, an American journalist, published in the same month; and *Under the Axe of Fascism*, by the very distinguished Italian exile Gaetano Salvemini, who was teaching at Harvard, which came out later. Finer's book was scholarly and detached, but it left no doubt that Mussolini was a tyrannical dictator and his social reforms a sham. Seldes' book was a sensational but well-informed account of the sordidness of Fascism and its very reactionary aspect. Salvemini's was judged at the time a masterpiece, and it remains today a powerful indictment of both Fascism and its foreign admirers. It was intensively documented, leaving nothing but squalid shreds of the glittering legends that had surrounded the New Italy. All three were reviewed with admiration and indeed effusion by the liberal journals and by much of the rest of the American press. Vera Micheles Dean, the respected Cassandra who directed the Foreign Policy Association, gave Finer unmeasured praise in her review in *The Nation*. In the *New York Times Book Review* William MacDonald praised Seldes' book lavishly: "What Mr. Seldes has done, and done with marked success, is to sharpen the lines and deepen the shadows of a tragic and unlovely picture."[27]

The tragic and unlovely picture was being more and more copiously documented. The *New York Times* judiciously alternated G. L. Steer's dispatches from Addis Ababa with those of Arnaldo Cortesi, its correspondent in Rome. The latter were not, on the whole, unsympathetic to Italy, but in the months of the lull Cortesi was reporting the hesitations and despondency that inaction was producing there, while Steer, flamingly pro-Ethiopian, was writing sensational and evocative stories. In superb, emotional prose he dramatized Ethiopia's role, that of an innocent and high-minded victim, which had been skillfully prepared earlier by the Ethiopians and by Steer's friend Colson. Italian barbarism made big headlines in the *Times* and other American papers. New Year's Day 1936 saw great play given on the front page to the Ethiopian accounts of the bombing of the Red Cross headquarters in the south and the killing of the Swedish Red Cross repesentatives.* The next day Cortesi sent in the Italian version, the murder and mutilation of Italian pilots, but his story appeared on page 9. The immediate result of all this was to induce hatred of Fascism, which gradually became the hallmark of American liberals. By March, Paul Douglas, who would much later be a distinguished senator from Illinois, was writing quite violent anti-Fascist articles for *The New Republic* with titles such as "Mussolini and the Workers," based upon information in Salvemini's book.

The books by Finer, Seldes, and Salvemini had actually been written before the war began. Seldes', indeed, had been written six years before, after the Fascists had expelled him from Italy; the manuscript had been rejected for publication in both France and Britain following warnings to the publishers from the French and British foreign offices. None of the three books owed anything to the Ethiopian venture; all were expressions of the well-informed and long-standing anti-Fascist convictions of their authors. But their impact would have been much smaller had they appeared a year earlier. It was the background of the war, of Haile Selassie's splendid posture, of the atrocity stories from Addis Ababa, of the Hoare-Laval agreement, that made them molders of opinion and contributors to a large conversion. They helped assure

* See below, Chapter 9, p. 242.

that the Italian-Ethiopian War should become what it was later called, "The first liberal bugle call."[28]

The conversion, although as yet limited, was seminal. The actual volume of news and comments was not so great as to make the issues consistently conspicuous. During the lull there were weeks when the Ethiopian War did not appear on front pages, but attitudes were nonetheless being strikingly affected. There is no clearer indication, perhaps, of the birth of a new climate of opinion than one of Helen Hokinson's superb, satiric cartoons in *The New Yorker*. It showed a favorite scene of hers, a meeting of a suburban women's club. The assumption of this series of cartoons was that the lady members were fumblingly echoing the major tendencies of eastern middle-class opinion; in this one Madam Chairman was saying to the members: "The vote is now fifteen to one that we deplore Mussolini's attitude. I think it would be nice if we could go on record as *unanimously* deploring Mussolini's attitude."

A mental set was melting, and the bases for one kind of isolationism was disappearing. One historian has observed, "The isolationists attacked the League powers and defended Italy during the Ethiopian crisis because they feared America could be involved in a war of Great Britain and France against the Fascist state and wanted to demonstrate that no logical reason for such a step existed,"[29] but this was ceasing to be true for what had been the most fecund and influential group of isolationists, the progressives of the Nye and *New Republic* sort. The alignment that was to emerge with lines clearly drawn in 1939, with the great debate between isolationists and anti-fascist interventionists for control of the American mind, was perceptibly taking form. Omens, some too small to be appreciated and some too flagrant to be overlooked, were appearing on every hand. American boys played that year with toy soldiers that had black faces and the uniforms of Ethiopia. All unknowing, white school children giggled over a couplet that combined the flavor of an old universe with the token of a new one: "Haile Selassie/ He's dusky but he's classy."[30] *Time*'s Man of the Year was the emperor of Ethiopia. And on January 3, 1936, Franklin Roosevelt delivered to the Congress his annual State of the Union message.

Half of it, exceptionally, was devoted to foreign affairs. Embedded in the president's characteristic flourishes, at once cautious and flamboyant, was a denunciation of the European dictators as a threat to human values and world peace. "They have impatiently reverted," he said, "to the old belief in the law of the sword," and he cautiously criticized the attitudes of his countrymen, saying that the United States "must take cognizance of . . . marked trends toward aggression . . . a situation which has in it many of the elements that lead to the tragedy of general war."[31]

Considering the circumstances, it was a remarkably forthright rebuke to both American isolationism and the governments of France and Britain. It set forth ideas now so well worn that it is hard to realize that to many in 1936 they seemed dramatically new: that American safety and the world's peace and freedom required not aloofness but participation and leadership; that autocracy and aggression were inseparable phenomena. Enough time had passed since Woodrow Wilson had set forth these themes for people again to view them as novel. The *Times*, majestically noncommittal as ever, observed in the closing sentence of its editorial on the occasion that the importance of the speech "will be instantly recognized."

The *Times*'s minimal salute to the new era faintly echoed the facts: Mussolini's adventure had defined in many minds the idea that fascist dictatorships meant international danger. It had made many people aware that virtue, gallantry, and civilization resided in a nation of blacks. And it inaugurated the mobilization of America's world power.

Throughout the west, throughout the non-fascist world, a fateful chemistry had begun to work. The strategy of containing Germany was breaking down; Germany and Italy were both about to be freed to contemplate new aggressions. Pacifism and genteel internationalism began to be transformed into militant anti-fascism. The illusion of an impregnable, all-conquering, all-cunning fascist monolith paralyzed governments like that of Sarraut in France and military leaders in both France and Britain. But among intellectuals in particular, and among many ordinary people too, hatred of war was beginning to dissolve in hatred of fascism, and a new *mystique*, the *mystique* of the fight for freedom, was being born. Nowhere is this clearer or more significant than in Great Britain. The state of mind revealed in the Peace Ballot was transformed within a single year into militancy. The young men at Oxford who in 1933 had put their signatures to an oath that they would never fight for king and country were now beginning to be ready, indeed eager, to fight—not for king and country but for international democracy. When the opportunity came in Spain in 1936, the intellectuals of Great Britain angrily marched to support the cause of Spanish democracy. Poets like Herbert Read, who had struggled since 1918 to find a rationale for pacifism, gave up the search and turned with zeal to war to save Spain from fascism, and some of their younger contemporaries went to fight and die in the cause.

It was a sudden and radical revolution in attitudes, and it had its counterpart in France and the United States and everywhere else. It generated enthusiasm for the Soviet Union and world Communism. It supplied, for men of the Left, a substitute for the imperatives of patriotism—the imperatives of ideology, belligerently espoused. By the time Badoglio's army began its long advance to Addis Ababa, Mussolini had produced a world revolution.

The strange destiny of Ethiopia had begun to realize itself. It was paradoxically creating the Rome-Berlin Axis and making it terrifying and therefore strong. But it was also commencing the work that would eventually invoke the conscience of the west and bring an end to fascism and the world power of European states.

9

The Machine in the Mountains

The long lull ended at last. Graziani and Badoglio were ready to begin their advances. A fine road had been built from the Eritrean border to Makale, and men and supplies were rolling down it. The extinction of the last free state in Africa could proceed; the last colonial empire could be built.

It was none too soon, even from Badoglio's narrow professional standpoint. For his schedule had inescapable limits: he could not begin until he had summoned his array, and he had to finish before the rains came. After May the terrain would become impassable, and further action would not be possible before autumn. There was great anxiety in Italy. A victory delayed until autumn would, quite aside from international complications, be very dangerous. During the lull there had emerged signs of disaffection within the Fascist regime despite the inverted diplomatic victory of the Hoare-Laval agreement. There was concern in loyal circles. It was, Mussolini observed, a "speed contest."[1] And military experts everywhere were skeptical that Italy could conquer the country before May. Most of them overrated—as did Badoglio—the difficulties of the task the Italians had undertaken, or at least they overestimated the time it would take to do it, once the panoply of twentieth-century power had been assembled. The military experts of the powers supposed that the war would last for months, perhaps for years. The Italians themselves, or some of them, supposed so, too. Because of this, the impact of Italian successes, when they came, was much exaggerated. Fascism would, as a result, build the myth of a military might that had so far existed only as a fear or fantasy.

The anatomy of the myth is in itself interesting, if only because of its peculiar fraudulence. Fascist Italy might appear as a mighty, indomitable nation, but it was not. It was a paper eagle. The things that gave rise to the misleading impression were important, for they illustrated very clearly the forces that were ruining Europe and the peace of the world. They included gullibility and wishful thinking and fear. They also included profound ignorance of East Africa and what a war there meant.

The terrifying picture of a nation in arms that had been displayed before the war began, the victories that De Bono had won, the larger victories that Badoglio was still to win, were all meaningless in European terms. Never again, after 1936, would Italian successes be repeated; never again would Fascist arms prevail. In the Alps in 1940 even staggering France won a crushing victory against the Italians. In Greece, later that year, the Greeks humiliated them. In Libya in 1941 beleaguered Britain inflicted a military disaster on them. Later a strained British navy in the Mediterranean would command the surrender of the Italian fleet. Not until Fascism was gone and Italians at home were fighting with their fists did they display against their peers the real military skill they were capable of, which propaganda had dazzlingly simulated in 1935 and 1936.

The persuasive Fascist pose of omnipotence was due to a misunderstanding. The Italians had certain highly developed skills useful in the war in Ethiopia: road building, flying, solving problems presented by an almost impossible topography, tropical medicine. These special talents enabled them triumphantly to defeat their most important enemy, which was Ethiopian geography. But false inferences were drawn. They were strikingly summarized by an English army officer, Major E. W. Polson Newman, a most careful chronicler of the war from the Italian side. He held the conventional view that Italy was heroically performing a useful mission that would serve both Ethiopia and the world; he had no sympathy whatever for Ethiopia as a nation or a culture, and this disdain, irrelevant to Italian military power, blinded him to some facts that lay within his realm of expertise. His commentary, often perceptive, is as a result an odd blending of vision and myopia. He wrote, shortly after Haile Selassie's defeat, an analysis of the Ethiopians as fighting men which may be taken as a tolerably accurate summary of an informed European's view.

. . . one is inclined to ask what moral force was behind these courageous men who stood up time after time to the shattering fire of modern weapons, and then seemed to take to flight when they had suffered sufficiently. While some fought gamely against the Italians, others tamely submitted in comparatively large numbers. The fact is that in the European sense of term there is no "Abyssinian army." The term "army" is quite out of place when applied to a feudal system such as prevailed in Abyssinia . . .

Unlike his European counterpart, the Abyssinian soldier has no sentiment or idealism about his calling, and did not go to war to defend his country. He did so as a faithful servant or slave of his feudal master. . . . when confronted with an enemy of superior numbers, the idea would not occur to him to fight, or continue fighting . . . Similarly, taking to flight in such circumstances was not regarded as cowardly but as the natural thing to do.[2]

Some of this was both accurate and perceptive. But the author's conclusion, a hundred pages later, was illogical:

All thinking people readily admit the strength of modern Italy in being able to succed in a great military effort of this kind. There are no longer any doubts about the fighting qualities of the Italian soldier or the efficiency of the Italian airman. These have both stood the most exacting test in a war on modern lines, and Italy has the unique advantage of having first-hand experience in the use of modern armaments and up-to-date equipment . . . This being so, there is no reason why the British people should not live on the most friendly terms with a Mediterranean neighbor, who is a staunch supporter of order and good government . . . with Italy established in Ethiopia it will be advisable for Britain to revise her imperial strategy . . . it may well be that the whole future of Europe and the world will hinge on the ability of Britain to cooperate with nations from which she differs in many respects.[3]

One important thing he did see clearly, the most important difference that emerged from the clash of cultures: the nature of the command function. The contrasting positions of Haile Selassie and Mussolini were clearly illustrated.

They were both trained soldiers, but neither of them was an experienced strategist. Haile Selassie was a better one than Mussolini. He had a more coherent notion of what was needed in a strategic situation. He was nearer the scene of action, he was more patient, and he was much less affected by fancies, whims, and impulses. On the other hand, neither of them was in a position to act as a general, for their responsibilities as political leaders distracted them from the sort of purely military conception with which Badoglio approached the campaign. The need to take politics into account impaired their purely military strategy.

But there the resemblance ended and sensational differences began. Polson Newman saw them clearly enough: the war was a war of two organizations. Each organization embodied, and was limited by, the particular conception of what the civilization *was* that had created it. Fascism was, or professed to be, based on the idea of "everything within the state," as Mussolini had said, "nothing outside the state, nothing against the state." That was what totalitarianism was all about, a state carried to the final perfection of control, through twentieth-century kinds of organization and technical equipment, over its environment, its citizens, its enemies. The Ethiopian monarchy was a semi-religious suzerainty that still presided over but did not control—the idea of control was repugnant—a sprawling, diverse congeries of communes, tribes, regions, princes, churches. In Ethiopia everything was traditional, static, and endowed with inalienable rights. And in war this enormous contrast translated itself into a difference on the two sides of the function of command.

Mussolini had at his disposal the machinery of state and the kind of allegiance that made the dismissal of De Bono and the appointment of Badoglio a simple matter of a policy decision. The emperor of Ethiopia was imprisoned in the labyrinth of inherited seniorities and rights supported by personal loyalties that often made it impossible for him to entrust military commands to the best qualified men.

Haile Selassie had tried valiantly to amend this archaic state of things, and it is possible that the beginnings of success had been one of the things that motivated the Italian attack. Badoglio naïvely wrote:

The development of the Abyssinian situation brought one important fact home to military minds: that the tendency of the Negus to concentrate the entire imperial authority in himself, eliminating gradually and by any means in his power the authority of the local chiefs (if not actually the chiefs themselves), had as its principal aim the concentration of military power, his object being thus more readily to organize and arm his troops, as far as possible, in an up-to-date European manner.

The problem was neither easy, nor one that could be speedily solved; yet it is certain that it remained simply a question of time.

The passage of time, that is to say, would work only to our disadvantage.[4]

This statement may owe something to retrospect and something to propaganda. Still, it disposes, so far as Badoglio goes, of the Italian argument that the war was necessary to bring the benefits of modern institutions to Ethiopia. For Badoglio, the war seemed rather to be a way of preventing Ethiopia from developing modern institutions. His attitude supported the argument that the Italians were fighting in defense of their colonies against future Ethiopian aggression, but it precisely contradicted most of the other arguments they habitually produced.

During the intermission in the north, while Badoglio was making ready for his great offensives, there were spasmodic side shows in the south. The southern front was much less important, although many people thought that the decisive action might take place there. But Graziani was a long way from Italy and a long way, too, from the centers of Ethiopian authority, and the wastes he was occupying were unimportant. But he was in a position to threaten the city of Harar and the railroad from Addis Ababa to Jibuti. More important, his operations were to supplement Badoglio's demonstration that the invaders were invincible, and the prospect of invincibility would in itself make a crack in the fragile apparatus of the central administration and command.

General Rodolfo Graziani was to play an eminent role in the later history of Ethiopia and, like Badoglio, in the later history of Italy as well. He was a very different sort from the northern commander, a Fascist general and a popular and ebullient figure who ingratiated himself with his troops and with correspondents. He was eleven years younger than Badoglio and his career had been much less notable. He first appeared as a prominent figure as commander of the army in Libya starting in 1930. He was to be Mussolini's chief of staff and in the end his minister of defense in the republican-Fascist government formed in northern Italy under German occupation, and he would have the honor of surrendering the last pitiable army of Fascism in 1945. Graziani had neither Badoglio's caution nor his professionalism. He was anything but distrustful of Mussolini, although as chief of staff during World War II he would show a more realistic appreciation of Italy's fighting capacity than the dictator. He was, by most accounts, trivial-minded, mercenary, flamboyant, and brutal. He had successfully crushed the rising of the Senussi tribesmen in Libya against Italian rule, and in doing so he had made a reputation for singular ruthlessness coupled with brilliance and panache. It was a combination that precisely recommended itself to many young Italians. Those whom Angelo del Boca (he included himself) described as "horrid little beasts,"[5] young men like those of Graziani's army, adored him. He is quoted as saying, when he was appointed to his command in Somaliland, "The Duce shall have Ethiopia, with the Ethiopians or without them, just as he pleases."[6]

Graziani faced a trying situation for a general who liked panache. The Ethiopians were estimated to have 80,000 men facing him, while he had only one division—and a huge front, some 500 miles of Somaliland-Ethiopian border between Kenya in the south and British Somaliland in the northeast. In the first round of fighting, in October and November 1935, he had occupied Dolo and advanced into the Ogaden, taking some oases and several miles of the track that led north toward Harar. But although he had defeated the considerable army of General Afewerk and taken some towns, he still was threatened by Prince Desta, leader of Sidamo province, a wild and obscure land of hills and coffee, northwest of Dolo. Desta was reputed to be a wily general and to have a large and capable army whose existence constrained Graziani. Until it was disposed of, the Italian did not dare advance further toward Harar.

In fact, Prince Desta's army was already in difficulties. In November he had conceived an ambitious plan to invade Italian Somaliland and had moved imprudently from his base at Neghelli, two hundred miles away, toward Dolo. His supplies were grossly insufficient, and his men were exposed to the few but efficient planes that Graziani had at his disposal. By the end of November, the advance had stopped short, and Desta's men were reported by Lieutenant Frère, the emperor's Belgian military adviser who was with Desta's army, to be subsisting on a cupful of flour a week. Frère reported that bombing, starvation, and disease had reduced the effective strength of the Sidamo army to four or five thousand men. But the Italians knew nothing of his attrition. They were worried, and Graziani prepared to attack. First by air. There were attacks on Desta's supply lines. Graziani included, on December 30, an attack on the Swedish Red Cross base, almost the only medical service available to Desta's army, explaining in a leaflet that the Ethiopians had forfeited the usual immunity given to the Red Cross by decapitating an Italian pilot who had been taken prisoner. The chief Swedish doctor was killed along with several of his assistants and twenty-eight patients. The retaliation did not stop with the Swedes; bombs and also gas were used on January 5 against an Egyptian Red Crescent camp and a British missionary hospital.

News of this raid set another milestone on the avenue that world opinion was traveling. Reports prepared and widely disseminated by the authorities in Addis to the news-starved correspondents made headlines throughout the world. They contributed very substantially to the wave of indignation that was solidifying as an anti-Fascist ideology.

It is true that an Italian pilot *had* been decapitated—also castrated and cut into pieces, the pieces being distributed as mementi among his captors. This was apparently not done by Desta's Ethiopians but by Somalis. It is said that they were trying, by this act of ritual butchery, to give evidence of their loyalty to the Ethiopian cause; they offered the head as a trophy to an Ethiopian officer. The Italian press, reporting the incident, did not draw the distinction; but the newsmen in Addis Ababa, in particular Steer, who was partial to Ethiopia, gave this version to the world, and the Italian story received little attention outside of Italy.[7]

On January 12, having done much to discredit his nation and his ideology, Graziani began his attack. He had by now 14,000 men, 26 artillery pieces, 3,700 animals, and several tanks—at least these are the figures Graziani gave in his book, *Fronte Sud.* The Italians tended to exaggerate since the impression they wished to give was of overpowering force. By comparison with Badoglio's operation it was very small. But the outcome of the attack was the same. It resulted in a massacre.

The attack on Desta's forces began with gas and bombs. The defenders had no strong point and no caves; only the thick palms that edged the rivers offered a hiding place from the pilots. In the four days that followed, the Italians' communiqués announced the killing of 4,000 Ethiopians, a liberal estimate (nobody knew, not even Desta, how many there were still fighting when the assault began). Graziani could use tanks, which Desta tried to stop with horsemen. At the end of two days his men gave up and began to retreat. By January 20, 1936, the Italians had reached Neghelli, Desta's base and principal town, whose name was to be that of marquisate granted to Graziani by the grateful king of Italy.

This success in the south, in itself of small strategic importance, meant that there was no longer a threat at one end of the frontier, and Graziani could concentrate his forces for an advance on Harar at the other. It meant the end of one of the most esteemed of the six principal armies with which Ethiopia had hoped to thwart the invaders. But neither of these advantages was immediately acted on. Graziani, an unhappy junior partner in the invasion, was still starved for materiel. The crossing of the Ogaden was not seen in Rome or Makale as having much importance. Graziani complained bitterly to Badoglio, and asked for more men. Badoglio, disregarding the request, urged him to attack, and so, from Rome, did Mussolini. Graziani's actions in the next two months were confined to complaints. While he was complaining, Badoglio won the war.

There were also spasmodic operations in the north during the lull. Ahead of the northern armies, in Makale when Badoglio took command, lay the road to Dessie and Addis Ababa, across which the main Ethiopian army, 80,000 men, had installed itself on the top of the vast, vertiginous plateau called Mount Aradam. To Badoglio's right, on a long line running some 50 miles northwest from Aradam, in the Tembien mountains, were the armies of Prince Seyum and Prince Kassa. Before an assault on Aradam could be undertaken, the flank had to be made safe and through some of the most daunting terrain in the world.

The prefatory campaign, called the battle of Tembien, is an illuminating example of the nature of warfare and of the contrasting methods of Italians and Ethiopians. It is illuminating because nobody knew what happened. It is a truism of battlefields that nobody knows what is going on, but usually people find out soon afterward. Here the situation was different, because the methods of fighting and particularly communications were so different on the two sides. The two main Ethiopian forces, the armies of Kassa and Seyum and that of Prince Imru some 60 miles away, communicated by messengers who took two weeks to cover the distance on foot. While the Italians had full radio equipment, Kassa, commander in chief, had a single radio with which to communicate with the imperial headquarters at Dessie and the main force at Aradam. And the forces were widely dispersed; individual units had no idea what their fellows were doing.

Correspondents, who have provided the most impartial and vivid reports on many twentieth-century battles, were not at Tembien. Badoglio disliked reporters, an attitude usual and natural among professional soldiers. What was unusual in this case was that he had actually barred them from the front. It was a point of violent difference with Mussolini, whose attitude was the opposite of a soldier's. He was recruiting writers in droves—two hundred Italian correspondents had been sent to East Africa after being given stirring speeches by the ministry of information on the desirability of sending back copy that would ennoble the image of the Italian soldier. But they were not at Tembien. The only first-hand report on the battle by a writer was that of Filippo Tomaso Martinetti, a well-known futurist, then an ardent Fascist, whose coverage consisted of an enthusiastic poem. (Later, some Italian newsmen were allowed to visit the fronts, but their reports were scarcely more informative, since they followed closely the official line and dealt almost entirely with the remarkable achievements of the Italian army and the depravity of the foe.) And none of the foreign correspondents in Addis Ababa succeeded in reaching the Tembien battleground either.

Certain things, however, including some horrifying facts, are clear enough about Tembien and the battles that followed. Badoglio sent the III Army Corps on January 19 to advance along a trail between Mulugeta's army to the south and the armies of Prince Seyum and Prince Kassa to the west. The next day, two other units, the II Eritrean Corps and the Blackshirt "28th of October" Division advanced to the west, to disperse the princes' forces. The mountainous terrain was cut by steep-sided canyons of immense depth. In places it was heavily wooded. It held unpleasant associations for the Italians; here they had advanced a month earlier on Abbi Addi, on the great Tacazze River, captured it, and then abandoned it under embarrassing circumstances.

The Eritreans and the Blackshirts advanced rapidly at first, occupying the Warieu Pass in the mountains above the Tacazze and moving in the direction of Abbi Adda. On January 21 the Eritreans and part of the Blackshirt Division were attacked by Ethiopians and surrounded. Prince Kassa called up reinforcements to exterminate the Italians and to force the pass. There were heavy fighting and casualties.

It was a moment of horror for the Italians. The enemy, often completely unarmed except for spears, advanced into gunfire without hesitation. As they fell, they were replaced by even larger numbers from the seemingly endless supply of manpower. As the panicky Italians and Eritreans precipitately drew back, they abandoned their arms; so technical superiority lay for a while with the Ethiopians who picked them up.

The psychological horrors were even greater than the measurable military ones. Italian soldiers had been told that if they were captured they would be tortured and castrated. They had been informed that the enemy was not only inhuman but subhuman, and the ineffable courage and ferocity of the Ethiopians made them appear, indeed, very different from any species of human the Italians could imagine. So did their war cry; as anyone who has ever heard it can testify, it is unlike any sound ever made by a human voice.

Steer painted a most graphic picture of the Italians' situation:

> Every Amba [mountain] was swarming with Kassa's Gondaris: when they were near the Pass, the Diamenti Group were surrounded on every side . . . this was [the Ethiopians'] most irresistible mass charge of the war. Wave after wave descended on the dusk from the rocks, racing up to the artillery crews with the drawn sword and wrenching machine-guns out of the hands of the men who fired them. They lost men in swathes, but it was impossible to stop the black cataract. The mountain air, fresh and darkening, rang with the high battle-shriek of the Ethiopians whipping themselves to risk any kind of death. The black men ran forward shooting straight in front of them and boasting in a wild falsetto of the number of people they had already killed.[*]

The Ethiopians issued a triumphant communiqué, announcing a great victory. But triumph was premature. The Italians and the askaris were also fighting with courage and ferocity, and with incredible endurance as well. Endurance, and the air force, saved them. Reinforcements—70,000 men, Badoglio said—came to their relief. When the new troops reached the pass, the Ethiopians abandoned the battle and

* Steer, p. 253. The description, not an eye-witness account, was based on careful investigation.

retreated. They simply stopped fighting. The explanations have been numerous and varied. It has been said that with reinforcements of their own the Ethiopians could have exploited their advantage and won the decisive victory that had already been announced. Reinforcements were available; the road was open for Mulugeta with his vast army to the southeast to relieve Prince Kassa, and it is said that his failure to do so arose from pique at Kassa's superseding him as commander in chief. But Prince Kassa himself later said that this was not true. His retreat, he wrote, was decided by his own refusal to expose his men to the horrors of poison gas, which he said was used very lavishly by the enemy. It contaminated the whole countryside, he said, killed more than 2,000 animals, as well as uncounted men, and made further offensive operations impossible.

There seems to be no doubt whatever that poison gas was used by the Italians. Any number of observers confirmed it, and the Ethiopian delegation to the League presented a very circumstantial report giving details. Angelo del Boca, a hostile but extremely well-informed and on the whole careful authority, says flatly, "I can state with *absolute certainty* that . . . the lower regions of Tembien were drenched with yperite [mustard gas] on several occasions."[8]

The retreat was a preface to disaster. While no one questioned the courage and skill of the Ethiopian warriors, discipline and efficiency in adversity were not among their qualities. The defeat was disorderly and precipitate. Their armies remained, for a time, in being, but there had already begun a process of dispersal that was to preface disintegration. Losses, uncounted, were very great and in some respects crucial. It is a characteristic and important detail that Kassa's field radio, operated by two Czechs, was lost, so that there could be no contact even with the rapidly moving units of his own army. He suffered an estimated 8,000 casualties—if the guess was near the truth, this meant more than one man in five. Supplies, temporarily augmented by the capture of Italian materiel, were gone. The Italians suffered much less, since their arms supply (once the siege was lifted) was comparatively speaking infinite and their casualties were only a few over a thousand. (These were relatively heavy, to be sure, considering that the gas, the planes, and the artillery were all on their side, but their losses made no real dent on the available manpower. And both psychology and the powers of discipline and command enabled *them*, instead of the enemy who had run away, to fight another day.)

It had been a near thing, though, and the terror on the Warieu Pass had been matched by terror of a different sort at Italian headquarters. At one point Badoglio had prepared plans for the abandonment of Makale, the point of furthest advance and the base for future operations against the main Ethiopian army. Then a general retreat would have been necessary, for Prince Kassa could have advanced to cut the road from Adowa and Makale. It would have been a crucial and humiliating loss, and Badoglio must have wondered whether the offensive could ever be renewed and whether the regime itself could survive. Some writers have said his distress reached the verge of hysteria, but this seems out of character.[9] In his dry, cautious memoir he called it "an unfortunate episode[10] and unreservedly, if with some air of surprise, applauded the incredible gallantry of the Ethiopians. General Quirino Armellini, a master of meiosis, later told Del Boca that "certain difficulties did arise in the first battle of Tembien.[11]

Now Badoglio had to contemplate the next obstacles. His chief hope for quick results lay in bringing to bear overwhelming military force to disperse Mulugeta's army while at the same time contriving the political disruption of the empire. There was a vigorous prosecution of political warfare of a sort already well begun before the war and upon which De Bono had relied, perhaps, for ultimate success. The Italians, although they probably miscalculated the fragility of the empire, were skillful in their use of terror, bribes, and threats. The use of gas was undoubtedly partly psychological in purpose; along with high explosives, it intensified the Ethiopians' reaction to battle—to fight with great vigor for a time and then to quit. Terror weapons were accompanied by the subversion of local leaders. De Bono claimed later that Ethiopia had lost the services of some 200,000 fighting men in the retinues of chieftains who had been successfully subverted.[12] There was also a leaflet war. Pamphlets in large numbers were dropped by air over armies and civilians. Like so many other developments in the Ethiopian War, this one foreshadowed World War II, in which the preparation and distribution of airborne propaganda became a major operation.

Steer quotes one of the leaflets used in the north during this period of the war, and he comments:

> It did not matter much to the whites whether high-explosive or literature struck the individual; it was the picture of force driving home the lesson into the whole community that satisfied them.
>
> The pamphlets read: "People of Eritrea and the Tigre, listen. War brings both good and evil, even churches being sometimes damaged and destroyed. But do not think that this damage or destruction causes the least care to the Italian Government. When by the Grace of God peace is restored, every church which has suffered harm will be renovated and improved."[13]

The themes, in the complexity of their appeal, would have done credit to the much more sophisticated psychological warriors of World War II: threat, promise, and a lordly assumption of the victors' power and riches. And political warfare may have catalyzed the decomposition of the empire. The most devastating effect of it was among the non-Amharic peoples. It had been practiced, with certain although unmeasurable effect, among the Somalis of the south and the Tigrines of the north. In the next stage of the invasion it was the evocation of Galla hostility to the Amharic overlord that was to have the most sensational and atrocious effect.

The Galla peoples were numerous and widely scattered, with concentrations in many parts of the empire. There had been numerous clashes at various times between Galla and Amhara. The Azebe Gallas, who lived in the region south of Makale, were particularly antipathetic to the Amharas, as well as being of remarkably fierce disposition. Their hostility was exploited by the Italians. Evidently, they were provided with guns from Makale; they had certainly gotten them from somewhere. The Ethiopian government's efforts to recruit among them had been for the most part unsuccessful, and when Prince Mulugeta arrived in the region north of Dessie he punished this lack of loyalty by floggings and the wholesale destruction of villages. It was, predictably, an error. The Gallas of the region came to regard him and the authority he served as their most conspicuous enemies. By the time of the Tembien battles, they were conducting a fairly large-scale guerrilla warfare in the region where the Ethiopian main army was trying to organize its defense and supply lines. Their harassment of the imperial armies was to add the awful epilogue to what was about to happen.

In an important way, Italian political warfare was aimed at the emperor personally. It was largely his semi-sacred position that gave Ethiopia such coherence as it had. He was, or seemed to observers to be, impassive in the face of the threat; his confidence in his own power and popularity and destiny at least looked unshakable still. His courage certainly was; and courage was much needed, since the Throne itself was a logical target for the Italians, and they might be expected to use weapons more direct than subversion.

It seems possible they may have tried to destroy the sovereign both by the direct method of trying to kill him and the indirect method of finding a complaisant pretender to replace him. Nothing is certain, but some of the facts are suggestive.

The matter of the pretender is obscure indeed, and has ever since given rise to speculation and rumor. The ex-Emperor Joshua had disappeared from view in 1916 and had been (it was supposed) in captivity ever since, probably in the neighborhood of Harar. He would have been still a fairly young man—probably under forty—in 1935. When the war began, there were stories of efforts by the Italians to secure his person. In November 1935 quite definite reports reached Addis Ababa that he had died and his body been brought to the capital and hidden there. An account by an aged slave who attended him[14] gave a circumstantial account of his assassination. Others have claimed that he died of natural causes. Still others have said he didn't die until much later. But the Italians had frequently charged Haile Selassie with being a usurper, and they used the rumor of Joshua's murder to accuse him of killing the true emperor. (It was used, years later, for the same purpose, by Ethiopian revolutionaries.) The fact is that nobody knows what happened to Joshua. Some anti-Fascist writers have tended to argue that he was indeed murdered, but only to frustrate persistent Italian efforts to release him and re-install him. It is rather appealing theory; and there is nothing whatever in the previous practices of either the Italians or the Ethiopians to make it impossible. What is particularly tantalizing is the suggestion made by several observers that the Gallas in the region of the northern battlefield were adherents of Joshua and that this accounted for their receptivity to Italian bribes and their extreme hostility to the government and armies that they suddenly found in their midst.

The idea that the Italians attempted to kill Haile Selassie directly is not in fact less speculative, but it rests on known facts that had real consequences. The emperor had reached Dessie early in December with a large staff, including several ministers and his son, the duke of Harar. In the little town he established a full court in some state (he had brought his French chef and his wine cellar with him). He administered justice and the affairs of state, which included the displacement of Mulugeta by Kassa as commander in chief, and distributed decorations.

A principal, and illuminating, problem was the aberrant conduct of the local authorities. They reacted in natural but regrettable ways to the abrupt incursion of alien dignitaries from the capital. They had already tried to arrest some of the visiting correspondents, and it is said that they also detained two English missionaries in the province for violating the curfew regulations, chaining up one of them with a dog leash. The emperor was obliged to give his attention to these and other details.

No particular effort had been made to keep the presence of the court at Dessie a secret: it was, indeed, rather conspicuous. Almost immediately after its arrival, Dessie and the road leading to it were heavily bombed—it was in the course of this "blanket bombing," as the Ethiopians called it when they presented protests to the League, that the British Red Cross camp had been hit. At the same time, the Italians dropped leaflets on several places claiming that Haile Selassie had been killed.[15]

Whether or not there was a deliberate effort to kill the emperor, the Italian bombings had a side effect that quite by chance accomplished a part of what might have been accomplished if Haile Selassie had indeed been hit. It was in keeping with his role as a personal leader of his peoples and his armies that he participated actively in the defense against the Italian planes. On January 18, 1936, during one of the attacks, he was personally firing at the planes from a hill at the edge of the town. Everett Colson had come up from Addis Ababa to Dessie to confer with him. He was to return that morning, but before leaving he went to watch the emperor's participation in the anti-aircraft operation. He ran up the hill.

Colson had been living under incredible tension and, in his dedication, overworking. Addis Ababa was some 8,000 feet above sea level, and Dessie about the same. Colson suffered a heart attack. He

was seriously incapacitated thereafter, and his health deteriorated stead-
ily. He lived another six months, but he had to leave Ethiopia in
March before the final decisions were taken about the high policies of
the imperial government.

It was one of the innumerable factors that contributed to the disarray of the empire. The poison gas, the bombings, the leaflets, the
subversion of the Gallas, the suppositious attempt to wipe out the
sovereign and the court, all were aimed by the Italians at transforming
a single successful attack on Mulugeta's army into a final decision.
These were ways in which the Italians exploited the essential facts of
Ethiopian history; they also belied the claim that Italy was bringing
civilization to barbarians.

It was not only a false crusade but a game of paradoxes. The
Italians played it skillfully, but the battle of Mount Aradam[16] fulfilled
with exactitude the requirements for winning a game whose stakes had
disappeared. The vast anachronism proceeded according to plan.

The main Ethiopian army was 12 miles south of the Italian
position at Makale on the road to Addis Ababa, in a superb strategic
site. Mount Aradam has been compared (both historically and topo-
graphically) to Masada on the Dead Sea, where Israel made its last,
heroic stand against the Romans in A.D. 73. A high plateau with steep,
rocky sides, the mountain overlooks a river valley on the north and a
vast plain on the south. It is of irregular shape, more than 5 miles at its
greatest length from east to west. The highest point is 9,000 feet
above sea level and 2,000 feet above the country around it. The top
and sides are largely bare rock. There are sheer cliffs around most of its
circumference, but to the south five gorges and valleys cut irregular
paths to the summit. The entire area is much eroded and punctured
with caves and grottoes.

This vast acropolis sheltered the principal fighting force and defense of the empire whose lifeline they surveyed from its heights. Their
numbers are disputed and unascertainable. Badoglio thought—or said
—that there were 80,000, but this probably is too high. It is likely that
even Mulugeta himself did not know. However great their number,
they were poorly armed with few and obsolete artillery pieces and
limited munitions even for their rifles. Their food supply was uncertain.
They had no air support.

Against them the Italian marshal had 70,000 men in seven divisions, as well as vast back-up forces of medical and supply units, 280 cannon, 170 planes, and munificent supplies including 10,000 gallons of brandy and 700,000 lemons. The preparations and planning had been careful, thorough, and extravagant.

On the eve of his great offensive, Badoglio, recently frightened and normally laconic, was confident and even magniloquent when he addressed the correspondents in one of his rare press conferences. Luigi Barzini, present as a correspondent, recorded his concluding words: "You will have the privilege of witnessing a tremendous, indeed a stupendous spectacle, gentlemen. We shall win this war with a campaign of the utmost brilliance, a campaign unequalled since the days of Napoleon. In less than two months, beneath the weight of our assault, you will see the Ethiopian empire crumble to dust."[17] It took a little longer than two months, but compared to the predictions of military experts in Europe, his was astonishingly accurate.

The planning was based on the careful cartography of the pilots. For once, as a result of their meticulous (and unopposed) aerial photographic reconnaissance, the Italians knew the country better than the Ethiopians, and Badoglio had been led to the correct conclusion that a frontal attack on the north, eastern, or western face of the plateau was unfeasible. An attack from the south, where the five gulches provided precarious but passable routes to the top, was more practicable, and if properly contrived it would take the Ethiopians by surprise from the rear. To clear a path to the plain on the south, and at the same time to feint with a simulated attack to distract the Ethiopians' attention, two army corps were to advance on either side of Mount Aradam at a distance of several miles, intending to reunite on the southerly plain, while units of each would feign diversionary advances toward the plateau from north, east, and west. And in the meanwhile the utmost air and artillery power would be brought to bear upon the scores of thousands of defenders crowded on the summit. Great quantities of high explosive were to be dropped on the plateau. It was to be incessantly strafed by machine-gun fire from fighter planes.[18]

On February 10, 1935, the 70,000 men of the Italian forces advanced, marvelously equipped and supplied with all the ingenuity and technology that twentieth-century Europe could provide. It was a climactic moment in the history of mankind, where more than 100,000 men were fighting, one force armed with spears and staves and the shoddy cast-offs of the western world and with reflexes and creeds and bravery little changed in two thousand years, against another armed with the product of what its members called civilization, who had come two thousand miles to a strange and lunar landscape. Thereafter the technological gap would close, and nothing like it would ever happen again.

There was never any serious doubt about who would win.

While the I Army Corps advanced on the east side of the plateau, moving ostentatiously to attract the attention of the defenders, the III Corps advanced to the west under cover and with stealth. By the third day, small forces were attacking on the eastern and western cliffs while the main forces continued their furtive movement toward the south. The Ethiopians were deceived as planned; they responded to the feints with vigorous rifle fire and launched some counterattacks to the east and west. By February 15 the encircling movement was almost complete. The advance units of the two corps were within a few miles of each other to the south of Mount Aradam, and they began to advance on it up two of the valleys.

The Ethiopian defenders were stunned and at first barely reacted. They had been subject to incessant attack from the air and from artillery. To escape from this appalling ordeal they had sought shelter in the caves; and they were apparently unable to emerge long enough to find out what was going on or where the main attack was to come from. Their counterattacks had been isolated actions, led by small groups under leaders of great resolution. The main force was trying to save itself from extermination under the rocks. Steer wrote that in response to the bombardment, "not a shot was fired from the tremendous amba [mountain]. Not a man remained on sentinel. They lay, wrapped head and foot in their grey shammas, like immobilised pools of mercury in every hole and depression."[19] Mulugeta had wondered from the beginning how long they could endure it. Starting on the second day, some of the men and their leaders, fighters of doubtful loyalty, including Gallas, began to run away; there is no way of telling how many on the plateau had already fled or been killed by the time the Fascist "23rd of March" Division reached the crest late in the afternoon of February 15.

There were enough defenders left to put up a fight, once they realized what had happened—that the unassailable fortress had been scaled. The Ethiopians shouted their terrible battle cry, and there were skirmishes. But by the time darkness had fallen to provide cover, it was clear to Mulugeta that the position and the battle were lost, and he began the descent through the narrow gap the Italians had left between the two attacking corps. He would have served himself and his men better if he had stayed to surrender.

The retreat, which lasted for three days, was more costly and horrible than the battle that preceded it. An even heavier weight of bombs was used against the fleeing Ethiopians than had been dropped on Mount Aradam: it is said to have been the most intensive aerial bombing the world had known until that time. In the three days, Badoglio said, 396 tons of explosives were dropped from aircraft. Gas was also used; one Ethiopian leader, whose older brother and father had died on the plateau, told Steer that his effort to defend Mount Alaghi, which protected the escape route, had been "gassed out."[20] It was one of the great slaughters of modern times.

The Italians were not alone responsible. For now, in defeat, the Ethiopians faced another enemy, not less terrible, whose weapons were not bombs and gas but hatred and atavism. The Gallas fell upon the survivors. They robbed, castrated, and killed all of the soldiers of the imperial army they could find. Prince Mulugeta had left the plateau in the greatest haste, abandoning all his equipment and his personal luggage in an effort to lead his men south to safety. He was accompanied by his foreign adviser, a strange, quixotic Cuban-American named Captain Del Valle, and a British Red Cross officer, an army major with the evocative name of Burgoyne, who had gone up the plateau with Mulugeta's army as head of a small medical unit. In the midst of their flight they learned that the body of Mulugeta's son, mutilated and killed by Gallas, had been found by scouts. They went to search for the corpse, and a few hours later were themselves surrounded by Gallas. While they were trying to fight them off, the Italian air force discovered them and machine-gunned them. They were almost all killed—by Italian machine guns or Galla spears—and so were most of the attacking Gallas. Survivors among the latter stripped the bodies of the Ethiopians including Prince Mulugeta, and of the British officer, and castrated them.

It was an incident that added in lurid ways to the awful catalogue of ironies that was the history of the war. The Italians had allied themselves with the Gallas against their common enemy and had massacred both. The Ethiopians had been set upon by countrymen who, at the moment anyway, saw no difference between Italian overlordship and Ethiopian rule. The Italians publicized the outrage, believing that world opinion would draw no fine distinctions between Galla and Amhara and that the barbarism of Ethiopia would thus be illuminated. But it was not chiefly the Galla and Amhara whose reputation in the world was scarred; the Italian reputation for atrocious conduct was already established, and as word about Badoglio's methods came out, opinion elsewhere reacted in expectable ways. The Italians' definition of civilization—and the west's—received a blow from which it would not recover. The Italians might succeed in some quarters in blackening their victims' names; they did not succeed in whitening their own. Reports of their use of gas and of indiscriminate air attacks were already current, and there was corresponding skepticism about their allegations concerning the barbarities of the Ethiopians.

In one interesting example of the process in course, the Italian government, in an effort to counter the impression made by stories of Italian atrocities, announced that the Ethiopians were using dumdum bullets supplied by Britain. Dumdum bullets were illegal under the laws of war; they were also singularly disagreeable: they flatten out inside the body after penetrating the flesh, tearing the victim apart. Their use, unanimously and vociferously publicized by the Italian press to the accompaniment of screams of outrage, has never been proved, and most later writers have doubted it. It is excessively unlikely that the emperor, solicitous of the reputation of Ethiopia as a civilized nation, should have authorized it, and there is no known place the bullets could have been obtained. The British government was at pains to deny the charge that they came from Britain. It issued a long and very thorough memorandum on the subject, proving the claims baseless, and the chairman of Imperial Chemical Industries, charged by the Italians with manufacturing them, specifically denied the accusation. The British reputation for "decency" and the thoroughness of the refutation convinced most of the world, although, as Eden plaintively noted, "The Fascist press, with undistinguished unanimity,

lightly dismissed our carefully documented reply."[21] But few people in
the rest of the world worried much about dumdum bullets. It was the
savageries of the Italians that left a lasting impression.

This impression was later gratuitously fortified when Vittorio
Mussolini, the dictator's son and an air force pilot in Ethiopia, published a book about his experiences. It came out soon after the war
and immediately received the flattering attention of the world press. It
was written as propaganda along two characteristic Fascist lines: war is
fun and builds character; Italian power is invincible. It was judged in
Italy particularly suitable for reading by young boys and was assigned
in schools. *Voli sulle Ambe* was full of philosophical reflections, such
as "A war fills a man with a longing to fight another."[22] But the passage that was most widely quoted abroad dealt with the author's
aesthetic pleasure in the effects of bombing. He released an aerial
torpedo on some Galla tribesmen. "The group opened up just like a
flowering rose. It was most entertaining." It became a text for those
who preached that Fascism was satanic. It summed up the kind of
rhetoric that made the Ethiopian War a moral issue as surely as the
opposing rhetoric of Haile Selassie.

Moral judgments on world affairs are always subjective; morality
is in the soul of the beholder. The men who fought at Aradam were
all of them in some sense barbarians. It is absurd and provincial to say
that the Italians, the sons of Dante and Mazzini, were more to blame
because they should have known better—it was the humane and generous Mazzini who had talked of Italy's responsibility to extend the
blessings of Dante's culture to the backward peoples of the world. They
were, like everyone else, acting according to imperatives. It is even
more absurd to say that their proclaimed purpose, the civilizing of
people who fought with spears instead of airplanes, justified the means;
the means they used showed that they were incapable of civilizing
anyone by warfare. It is absurd to claim that since the Ethiopians
fought with spears they were either more or less civilized, more or
less moral. The impulse to make such judgments is often a provincial
one; it must in this case arise from one of two ethical fallacies: either
that European civilization was inherently superior and therefore imposed upon its members an obligation to demonstrate it *and* extend it
by any means; or the converse, very similar, fallacy, that Europe's states

were inherently racist and imperialist and therefore immoral and that all who resisted them were by definition good.

The battle and its aftermath had been very destructive. The Italians, by their own count, which was almost certainly low, had 800 in dead and wounded, including 145 African troops. The Ethiopians, they said, had 20,000 casualties. The latter figure was probably inflated, but it was true that the destruction of the Ethiopian army was far advanced. There now began to be evident a process of military decomposition. All but one of the Ethiopian armies in the north had been defeated and partly destroyed—the exception being Prince Imru's army far to the northwest of Aradam. Something like a rout was beginning.

It was accompanied by decomposition of the administrative apparatus of the state and the demoralization of the whole society. In places where the defeats of the imperial forces were visible, Ethiopia began to go to pieces. But it was going to pieces in a peculiar way, which the Italians misjudged. They thought the whole empire would fall into their hands as a result of the collapse of authority, but in fact authority was not really collapsing. It was changing hands. From beneath the thin crust of western institutions were emerging the ancient components of the society. Villages, princes, chieftains, tribes began to rise from the ruins and along with them the familiar habits of localism: raiding, looting, and endemic civil war. The new authority was archaic by Italian standards, but it was very deep-rooted and very vigorous, and in the end it would defeat Italian efforts to build a colony.

In the neighborhood of the battlegrounds, bandits were already beginning large-scale operations. Sacking and pillaging were frequent, and Alan Barker, a British officer who took part in the liberation of Ethiopia in 1941, and a distinguished writer on military history, says that some of the Ethiopian regulars sent "to quell their activities had either been defeated or had thrown in their lot with the trouble-makers."[23] There were riots and rebellions in other places as well, and the impression given by all accounts is one of widespread breakdown of civil discipline and of looting and brigandage rapidly spreading. There also were mass desertions, often of organized groups. It was not quite all one way; Somali and Eritrean soldiers were also deserting the Italians. A thousand of the Somalis had fled from Graziani's army in the south in a single day, some to take refuge in Kenya, some to join Desta's army. In the north, groups amounting to some 2,000 Eritrean soldiers defected to the Ethiopians, some of them *after* the battle of Mount Aradam had shown the hopelessness of the Ethiopian cause.

The destruction of Ethiopian unity had not yet, in any case, proceeded so far that, with the victory at Aradam, Badoglio could safely commence his march to Addis Ababa. The armies of Kassa and Seyum still existed, although much depleted by defeat and dispersal. Imru had to be defeated. The court still had several battalions of imperial guards, the best-trained and best-equipped part of the army, south of Aradam, along with other forces as yet uncommitted, and supplemented by such of Mulugeta's men as had avoided slaughter by Italians or Gallas and the temptation to desert. The shape of what was to happen was already clear, but much fighting and marching remained.

Badoglio had already occupied Mount Alaghi, the most important position on the road south from Aradam toward Dessie, on February 18. Then he turned to deal with the depleted armies of Kassa and Seyum, on the hills above the great valley of the Tacazze. The III Corps and the Eritrean Corps, which had seen much of the fighting at Aradam, were despatched northwest to attack them. The same methods were used: bombing, machine-gunning from the air, and gas. The Ethiopians faced the same problems: shortages of arms, ammunition, and food. They displayed the same wild heroism as in previous battles, but the same outcome was assured. On February 27 the Ethiopians attacked the advancing Italians with enormous *élan* and—armed mainly with cudgels and scimitars, it is said—moved against the machine guns. They made some breakthroughs. As in the first battle, they reached the approaches to the Warieu Pass and were driven back only with enormous efforts and at considerable loss to the Italians. But by evening the attack had failed, at the cost (the Italians said) of 1,000 dead, and Seyum ordered a retreat, back toward the Tacazze valley. An Italian correspondent who was in one of the planes that harrassed them reported in the *Corriere della Sera*, "The Ethiopians straggled along in disorder. There was only one road open to them, and the fords were so narrow, the rocky walls of the ravine so precipitous that they were soon jammed in a solid mass. Even though we were flying at a 1,000 meters, we could see them quite plainly. Our plane swooped down, zigzagged along the defile, sowed its seeds of death, and zoomed upward."[24]

The slaughter continued. At the emperor's orders the entire surviving mass of Kassa's and Seyum's armies began to abandon what was left of their positions in the Tembien. The two generals reached headquarters, now established at Quoram, north of Dessie and not far from the advanced Italian units south of Aradam, after two weeks of marching. There was almost nothing left of their armies. It was said they lost 8,000 men in the whole operation, in contrast to Italian losses of under 600. The figures are to be regarded with the usual skepticism, but whatever they were, the effect was of annihilation, for many of the survivors disappeared.

There remained the army of Prince Imru, and to this Badoglio now turned his attention. The attack began on February 29—the day before the fortieth anniversary of the battle of Adowa, which the Ethiopians celebrated with solemn religious ceremonies and fasting in Addis Ababa and the Italians in Rome with wild rejoicing and a message from the ancient D'Annunzio, who wrote, "On this day, the entire nation draws a profound breath . . . What I hear is the panting of destiny."[25]

Imru has generally been regarded as the ablest of the Ethiopian generals. He was one of the emperor's new elite, trained in modern warfare and European methods of government, the only one of the generals who owed his command not to seniority in an antique system but to professional qualifications. He had been a very efficient administrator of provincial governments. He was, for example, the only general in Ethiopia who paid his men regularly in the field—Kassa, Seyum, and Mulugeta had practiced the traditional policy of holding out the prospect of payment after victory as an incentive to loyalty and hard fighting. He understood and had trained his men in guerrilla warfare. Well-situated to harass the enemy rear and the supply lines from Eritrea, he had done so with effect. Although he was still appallingly underarmed to face the enemy in open battle, the harassment had netted considerable supplies of guns. His position was, however, converted from an asset into a serious danger by the disaster to Kassa's and Seyum's armies. Isolated, too close to the Italian bases, exposed to encirclement and extermination, he had begun to retreat on February 29, pulling back under strong pressure.

The emperor had written to him advocating withdrawal. The letter fell into Italian hands when the messenger carrying it was captured, and Badoglio published it. It was an act typical of the marshal and of Italian policy, for the purpose of publication was to demonstrate the invincibility of the Italians and the folly and fate of those who opposed them. But the effect on those who read it at the time, as upon those who read it today, was very different from that intended; it suggested pathetic gallantry in the face of appalling odds. The characteristic defect that the old European military caste shared with the upstart Fascists was revealed by the fact of publication: they could not understand that to outsiders the position of the underdog was appealing or that helplessness may make more friends than invincibility. The letter read:

> To Ras Imru.
> How are you? We, thanks be to God, are well.
> Before we had been informed of the defeat of Ras Cassa, thinking, it was simply a matter of the defeat of Ras Mulugheta, as soon as we arrived at Quoram we wrote certain letters.
> Since, however, in the meantime we learnt that Ras Cassa and Ras Seyum had already arrived at Socota, after their armies had been defeated, and as we wished to make quite certain of the truth of these reports, our letters were not sent.
> As you will certainly have understood, an army so numerous that it had already thrust back and intimidated the enemy and had succeeded in retaking Macalle went to pieces without having suffered serious losses and without any attempt whatever at resistance.
> This is a grievous matter.
> Our army, famous throughout Europe for its valour, has lost its name; brought to ruin by a few traitors, to this pass is it reduced. . . .
> In order to push forward our front, we have arrived in the neighbourhood of Aia; since the enemy has been the first to occupy the position of Dubbar, we have placed ourselves where we, in our turn, can watch him. Within a week we shall certainly know what is going to happen.
> Ras Cassa and Ras Seyum are with us, but have not a single armed man with them. For yourself, if you think that with your troops and with such of the local inhabitants as you can collect together you can do anything where you are, do it; if, on the other

hand your position is difficult and you are convinced of the impossibility of fighting, having lost all hope on your front, and if you think it better to come here and die with us, let us know of your decision by telephone from Dabat.

From the League we have so far derived no hope and no benefit.

Badoglio added:

This document is of remarkable interest. It reveals, among other things, the mind of the Negus and of the Rasses, who, although their defeat was mainly attributable to their own incompetence, blamed with impunity their troops, whose courage, on the contrary, had proved itself in all circumstances to be of the highest order.[26]

For a time it looked as if the retreat might succeed in saving Imru's army. Some 8,000 troops who were covering the withdrawal of the main force, which the Italians estimated at 20,000, were occupying strong positions on surrounding heights called the Shire Ridge, which gave its name to the battle that followed. General Maravigna failed to take the precaution of sending out patrols, and he did not know they were there. Advancing down the track between two hills, the Italian division found itself, at noon on February 29, caught in a murderous crossfire. For once the antagonists were not entirely disparate in their small arms. As General Dante Bonaiuti later said, "The Ethiopians were mainly armed with 77-87 rifles that even predated our old Mannlichers, but they were crack shots and they soon inflicted heavy casualties on us."[27] But the Italians had artillery. Imru dealt with this disadvantage with audacity and skill: when his positions began to be pounded by shells, he ordered his men to *advance* to attack the Italian guns. The Ethiopians showed, this time, that they were capable of as much endurance as the Italians. Despite bombings and shelling, they continued their forays long after the Italian morale had begun to crumble and the Italian officers were trying desperately to rally their men. There was much hand-to-hand fighting, and the Ethiopians seized machine gun after machine gun literally from the grasp of the invaders. It was the hardest fighting that the Italians experienced in Ethiopia, and for two days they lived in a hell made more unbearable by the possibility that they might at last be defeated.

But the inevitable exhaustion of enemy supplies saved them. By

March 3 Imru had run out of ammunition. The fighting had cost him 5,000 men killed, and it is said that the Italian II Corps alone had fired as much ammunition as the entire Ethiopian army had possessed at the beginning of the war.[28] And now the IV Corps, which had not taken part in the encounter, appeared to take over the advance from the battered II Corps. The Italians tried, and failed, to surround the Ethiopians, and the IV Corps undertook the familiar work of pursuit, with the familiar consequence of wholesale massacre. The Ethiopians were trying to cross the Tacazze to escape into the mountains on the far shore; at the crossing there were very heavy bombings, and small incendiary bombs—used as *anti-personnel weapons*—were dropped on clusters of the fleeing men at the fords. Gas was also extensively used— as it had done before, it destroyed what was left of Ethiopian morale, for no amount of bravery or skill availed against it. Prince Imru said years later:

> I succeeded in leading some 10,000 of my men across the river to safety. But they were so demoralized that I could no longer hold them together. It had been my intention to carry on a guerilla war in the mountain regions . . . ideally suited to such tactics, but when I told . . . one of my few surviving chiefs of my plan, he would have nothing to do with it . . . Day by day my ranks thinned out; many were killed in the course of air attacks, many deserted. When I at last reached Dashan, all that remained of my army was my personal bodyguard of 300 men.[29]

Other survivors were similarly dispersed and destroyed. Attacks by insurrectionists and brigands complemented the hazards of the awful terrain. By path, Prince Imru made his way back to Addis Ababa and reached it alone, a month later. There was nothing left of his army.

Ethiopia had been defeated, its armies massacred and dispersed. With the small and temporary exception of the encounter on the Tacazze in December, they had won no battle and successfully defended no position. Only on the southern front, which no longer mattered, were there sufficiently coherent forces left to fight effectively. The people's morale was beginning to collapse; the fierce pride of September had availed nothing and was dying.

At imperial headquarters the facts were understood. But to the court the situation appeared, while desperate, less hopeless than it would have to detached observers. There were certain aspects that were a little encouraging, and hope might be put in various strategies of last resort. Retreat to the capital and preparation for a siege. Guerrilla warfare. In the end, a fugitive government rallying its people from inaccessible mountain strongholds. There was no disposition to give up.

For this resolute state of mind the emperor was evidently chiefly responsible. The disasters had led to despair among some of his staff, but Haile Selassie was determined, full of ingenuity and schemes, confident of his power to control the country and to incite the fighting spirit of his citizens. There was delusion in this, but it was true that he still could count on the loyalty of the men around him, whatever their misgivings. And it may have seemed, as some of his advisers insisted, that he was personally almost the sole barrier remaining to total Italian victory. But his position was precarious. The administration in most of the Amharic provinces anyway had not disintegrated and civic discipline had not completely dissolved, but they might do so soon.

From Badoglio's standpoint, Haile Selassie stood symbolically as well as literally astride the path to Addis Ababa and must be disposed of before the component parts of Ethiopia could be seized and the capital taken. The deadline of the rains was still the principal autocracy in Ethiopia: if the human autocrat could parry the Italian invasion until natural forces came to his aid, the conquest must be long delayed, and the role of invincible conqueror would elude the Fascist state.

Badoglio was afraid that the emperor might withdraw to Dessie and toward Addis, preparing delaying actions that would have to be dealt with far from the Italian bases, with supply lines dangerously exposed to guerrilla operations and without the roads that bulked so large in Italian calculations and Italian imagination. A very small and badly equipped force, if it had the magnetic leadership of the Crown, might under such circumstances slow down the Italian advance to the time when it would sink into the bottomless mud of the rainy season.

But the emperor was more romantic and in a way more realistic than Badoglio. The decay of the authority of the state, he thought, could be arrested only by a personal victory for the sovereign. It was

strategically necessary to prevent the discrediting of the emperor. Badoglio hoped and suspected that this was the case, and he wrote later,

> The idea of an offensive seemed in the meantime to be gain-
> ing ground; the Negus was perhaps drawn toward it not so much
> by a genuine will to attack, as by the advice of the chiefs, the digni-
> taries of the Empire, and even of the Empress herself, all of whom
> now, in accordance with Ethiopian tradition, saw a possible solu-
> tion of the conflict only in a great battle directed by the Emperor
> in person.[30]

From his point of view, it was the best possible circumstance.

Whether the emperor's decision to attack was either necessary or
wise is open to doubt, if it is judged by European standards. The
means for an offensive were meager. No forces were available except
the imperial guard and the survivors from Tembien and Aradam. For
one thing, the proposal contradicted the sensible prescriptions of the
emperor's European military advisers, that all direct encounters with
large Italian forces must be avoided. There was an element of *Götterdämmerung* in the decision that was being made, but the twilight
was so rapidly approaching anyway that a gamble was urgent; and in
the character of Ethiopia and its emperor there was something that
makes it seem, in retrospect, inevitable.

The Italians were exploiting their victories in the north with
prodigious speed. It was not now simply a question of delaying the
main advance; the defeat of Mulugeta, Kassa, Seyum, and Imru had
opened the way into new provinces. It now, indeed, became possible
to conceive an approach to the capital from a direction other than the
Dessie road. The Tacazze had been crossed; the II Corps was moving
through the most dizzying part of the highlands, west and south
toward Gondar, the third city of Ethiopia. In the east there were advances from Eritrea into the Danakil toward the railroad, the life line
and escape route from Addis Ababa to the outer world. On all the
lines of advance—particularly among the nomadic Moslems in the
Danakil—Badoglio's forces were arranging deals with local leaders and
meeting a reception that varied from indifference to welcome. In
Dessie itself, behind the imperial headquarters on the road to the
capital, there was a rebellious conspiracy, organized by deserters from
Aradam and encouraged by leaflets dropped from Italian planes. The
crown prince, who was in command, used a traditional Ethiopian

method of dealing with it: he offered a free pardon to the soldiers if they would simply go home and invited the chiefs to a banquet where he arrested them. The conspiracy dissolved, but for a moment it was a knife held to the jugular vein of the only retreat route left and a symbol of the decomposition. There was, clearly, no time to be lost. It was these causes that determined that the climax should come when and where it did.

And so the battle of Mai Ceu was fought. It was fought under the most adverse circumstances, partly with remnants of armies hastily assembled under defeated generals (Kassa and Seyum were both in the field again) against very strong Italian positions. As always, there were insufficient arms and no aircraft at all. Defensive battles had invariably been lost; it was likely that an offensive would be a disaster. And adversity imposed a further liability. All the precautions had to be taken, and they included a desperate effort to win the support of the hostile Gallas, the same who had harassed the retreating Ethiopians and, with fine impartiality, the advancing Italians after Aradam. This took money, which was available, and time, which was not. The delay enabled the Italians to find out what was going on; indeed, they could hardly avoid noticing the assembling of forces, even if their intelligence had been less accurate than it was. The only real advantage the Ethiopians might conceivably have had, that of surprise, was lost.*

The battle was the product of necessity, not of calculation. The emperor sent a telegram to the empress in Addis Ababa on March 20. The Italians intercepted it and Badoglio published the text:

> We are drawn up opposite the enemy and observing each other through field-glasses. We are informed that the enemy troops assembled against us number, up till now, not more than approximately ten thousand men. Our troops amount to exactly thirty-one thousand. Looking at them closely, one might think they were about twenty thousand men [perhaps the Negus was referring again to our troops].
>
> Since our trust is in our Creator and in the hope of His help, and as we have decided to advance and enter the fortifications,

---

* Del Boca thinks that Badoglio was "completely taken by surprise" by the numbers and quality of the attackers, but he is so anxious to discredit the marshal that this may be questioned. And he does not doubt that the Italians knew when and how the attack would come.

and since God is our only help, confide this decision of ours in
secret to the Abuna, to the ministers and dignitaries, and offer up
to God your fervent prayers.

EMPEROR[31]

Mai Ceu was a fertile valley surrounded by high hills, some 40
miles south of Makale, the Italian base and headquarters. It was less
than 20 miles north of Quoram, where the Ethiopian command was
installed, on the trail that led all the way from Asmara to Addis Ababa.
The Italians had occupied it soon after Mount Aradam and were
strongly entrenched there and in the mountains that surrounded it.
Badoglio had at his disposal in this area two army corps and several
additional divisions. The engineers had been at work with their usual
efficiency and speed, and the road from Makale reached almost to Mai
Ceu. Supply routes at the southernmost end were still by mule train—
the engineers had not been able to make the last stages passable to
motor vehicles as yet. They passed over the Dubar Pass, 10,000 feet
above sea level. It imposed great hardship on men and animals. Still,
supplies were flowing. In the meanwhile, at Ethiopian headquarters,
where no supplies at all were coming in and munitions were desperately short, officers were shooting off guns out of high spirits.[32]

The chief asset of the Ethiopians was the imperial guard. It consisted of six infantry battalions and a brigade of artillery, all of them
well-trained and relatively well-equipped—they had 5,000 rifles—the
nearest thing to a modern army that the empire could produce. But
the rest of the men (Badoglio said 30,000 to 50,000) at Haile Selassie's disposal consisted either of irregulars or battered survivors of earlier defeats, none of them even minimally equipped. They had no
radio communications at all and no gas masks. Their morale was un-
derstandably poor, and it must have been worsened by the delays involved in attempts to negotiate with the Gallas. The original date
fixed for the offensive was March 24. It was put off until the twenty-
eighth, a Saturday, and then to the thirtieth—since the Ethiopians
would not fight on Sundays. It was finally launched on March 31. It
was a surprise in reverse for the Italians, who had been expecting it
earlier.

The night before, the emperor—supported by his aide and adviser, Colonel T. E. Konovaloff, who had been an officer in the imperial Russian army under not dissimilar circumstances—addressed the

princes who would command the forces—chosen, as Konovaloff observed in his memoirs, by seniority. He explained the plan of attack: it recalled Badoglio's at Mount Aradam, a small frontal assault with the main forces marching around the flanks in an attempt to surround the enemy. Leonard Mosley, the emperor's biographer, says that the plans had been given to the Italians in detail several days before by the Galla tribesmen with whom the emperor had spent precious time negotiating. A few days earlier, with a good tactical plan unknown to the enemy, there might have been a smaller likelihood of catastrophe. Badoglio made no mention of information from the Gallas and said that his intelligence was provided by the emperor's imprudent telegrams to Addis Ababa; but he knew what was going to happen, and he had built defenses in the right places.

What had happened so often before now happened again. Early in the morning the Ethiopians attacked. The imperial guard surged forward with great *élan*, "giving proof," as Badoglio wrote, "of a solidity and a remarkable degree of training combined with superb contempt of danger."[33] They succeeded in advancing a short distance on the eastern flank against very heavy opposition—"an avalanche of fire," as the Italian commander said. To the west there were larger advances in more favorable terrain, but these too were held. At four in the afternoon the attacks were renewed on both flanks, but no further gains were made. The Italians, with everything in their favor, seem to have fought hard. So did the Eritreans, and so did "the irregular units," as Badoglio called them—the Gallas whom he had enlisted and who, he said, "rendered signal services to our cause."[34] If so, it was in striking contrast to their services to the emperor, who wired to the empress before the battle was over, "The Galla helped us only with shouts, not with their strong right arm."[35]

But what was quite as characteristic of the Ethiopians' response to battles as this courageous advance, against impossible odds and availing little, was their conduct immediately thereafter. Frustrated, they gave up. By nightfall on March 31, they had begun to disappear from the battleground, leaving their equipment. As Konovaloff wrote: "No one had given them orders. They just drifted in behind their chiefs, and many of them came back empty-handed."[36]

The emperor had taken part in the fighting. According to some, he had deliberately put himself in danger, courting an heroic death

with his men. Now, by night, with a heavy rain falling, he returned to
the cave where the command headquarters had been set up, to watch
the disintegration of his forces and of his nation. The paths back from
the battlefield were crowded with fleeing men refusing to obey their
officers, and Haile Selassie observed, "What a disgraceful disorder."[37]
But in a typical gesture he decided to distribute his personal supplies—
clothing, liquor, food—to them. As Konovaloff told the story, the cave
was instantly filled with soldiers, fighting their way to the gifts. And
when the imperial party moved out, to start the terrible trip south,
they saw the men seizing the munitions and setting fire to them, a
fearful orgy of defeat. The track was jammed; the emperor reached
Lake Ascianghi, 7 miles to the south, after twelve hours of march.

The rout became another nightmare. The Gallas, now that they
knew who had won, abandoned the last pretense of allegiance to their
Ethiopian overlord and set upon the refugees with great ferocity. They
would hide in hills above the road, fire blindly into the throngs, and
then, as survivors ran for safety, descend on the dead and dying to
castrate them and rob them of their clothes and whatever else they
possessed. And as after the other battles, there was a no less terrible
threat from above. "The army of the Negus," Badoglio wrote, "de-
moralized, decimated by its heavy casualties and by the numerous
desertions during the battle . . . continued to be harassed by the activity of our aircraft."[38] And on the next day: "Hard-pressed by our
troops, waylaid along the road by bands of Azebo Galla . . . ham-
mered by our entire Air Arm—prompt and bold as always, it had sent
up its aircraft regardless of their type, even to the last machine, in
order to carry the attack to the utmost limit and pour down their part
in it from above—the enemy hastened his retreat, which changed
gradually into precipitate and disorderly flight."[39] Badoglio estimated
his losses in the encounter at Mai Ceu and its aftermath as "68 officers,
332 Italians, and 873 Eritreans" and the Ethiopians at more than
8,000. If this was accurate, it would mean a quarter of the imperial
force. On April 2 the foreign office in Addis Ababa cabled the Ethiopian legation at Paris, "The military situation will become impossible . . . Impossible to find reinforcements. The Emperor will remain where he is till death. Then, collapse of the Empire."[40]

On April 1 Gondar had fallen without resistance, and there could
be no doubt that the end was near. That day Badoglio cabled Musso-

lini, "The battle upon which the fate of the Empire depends is over."[41] The emperor was at the holy city of Lalibele where, hundreds of years earlier, Ethiopian monks had carved churches from the solid rock. He stayed, praying and fasting for forty-eight hours, and then set out for Dessie. He reached it on April 14 and hurried on. The next morning the Italians entered the town, and by noon the tricolor of Savoy was flying there.

The victory seemed conclusive, the capture of Addis Ababa a matter of time and road building. What had happened was, beyond question, an impressive achievement by the Italians. Their warfare, if atrocious, had been effective; their courage, their quartermastering, their medical services, their engineering, redoubtable. Later anti-Fascist writers have attempted to belittle the conquest, pointing to the inaccuracy of the bombings, the undoubted weaknesses in the command, the poor morale of many units, the immeasurable odds against the Ethiopians. But it was not surprising that Europe should have been indeed dazzled. The French, the British, and the German general staffs had all expected the conquest to take several years. So had many skeptics in Rome, including Badoglio himself. The foreign experts had no doubt overrated the difficulties; still, by any standard, the Italian performance was startling. It contributed powerfully to the exaggeration of Italy as a military power in the European sense, which now assumed a great role in the network of mythologies that was soon to destroy Europe. The encomiums of Major Polson Newman, betokening a brief world reputation for Italy as a nation of warriors, were one consequence. The moral reputation of Fascism had been wrecked, its military reputation temporarily made.

In the rest of the world the war was producing large headlines (although at irregular intervals) and strong emotions. There was no longer, in any responsible circles, any hope or expectation that anything could be done to stop an Italian victory. Indeed, responsible people in Britain and France were becoming concerned for the safety of their own countries. Anthony Eden, the new foreign secretary, was despondent. He quoted a dispatch from the embassy at Belgrade that seemed to him to sum up the situation: "It is not exaggeration to say that the Paris proposals [for oil sanctions] caused British prestige in

Yugoslavia to slump to zero." There were few illusions left, and he went on to write, "While there could be no going back on the policy of sanctions, I could not believe that Geneva would be, for at least some time to come, an adequate guardian of peace. The Abyssinian conflict had brought into prominence the working scope and limitations of the League of Nations."[42]

Whatever Eden's personal attitudes, the domestic political pressures on him to remain inactive, in keeping with the honored tradition of the National Government, were very strong. Still, having been brought to office to rescue the government by showing that it really had good intentions after all, he went through the motions of trying to impose oil sanctions. On January 22 the Committee of Eighteen at Geneva (a subcommittee of the Co-ordination Committee) with British backing, voted again to consider them and appointed a committee of experts to study their effect—a means of asserting a principle without actually acting on it.

A reason for not imposing oil sanctions was found in the formula that Eden presented in the House of Commons: the British would co-operate in such sanctions if everyone else was willing to do so. It was a familiar formula: Britain's inaction was due to the lack of co-operation among other League countries and, more especially, the United States. In his memoirs, the foreign secretary was at pains to show that foreign countries were unwilling to help, and he attributed his own failure to secure oil sanctions to lack of support from France and the United States.

Lack of support or at least uncertainty of it was undoubtedly evident, and in France it was very marked indeed. The new foreign minister, Pierre Flandin, was a man of ability and conformed more closely than Laval to the usual notions of integrity, but his views on Italy were not basically different from Laval's. He saw the only real enemy as Germany and every other power as a potential neutral or ally in the struggle to contain Nazi aggression. Mussolini warned the French ambassador at Rome that if further sanctions were adopted, he would finally resign from the League. This would have little practical meaning, but it would symbolize in a definite and dramatic way his enmity to his erstwhile friends. So Flandin had no choice of policy in dealing with Britain and the League: if Italy was to be thus further estranged, France must at least be able to count on Britain's support if Hitler moved. It was a point the French had repeatedly made, and it was reasonable enough. Flandin offered it as part of a bargain: France would support oil sanctions if Great Britain would enter into what amounted to an unconditional alliance. This was regarded by the British as a kind of extortion. When Flandin proposed it, on March 3, 1936, after extensive and inconclusive debates at Geneva, Eden replied with a polite promise to consult his colleagues in London.

Before he had time to do so, Hitler had entered the Rhineland and announced that the Locarno Treaty, which guaranteed France's eastern frontier, was void. This was precisely the situation that the French had foreseen and for which they had wanted a promise of British support. The Germans had done just what everyone feared, seizing the opportunity presented by the decay of the Franco-British-Italian front. Coming when Italy's decisive victories in Ethiopia were beginning to be won, it effectively ended discussion of how to thwart Mussolini.

Not only in France were attitudes toward oil sanctions reluctant and conditional. Other countries in the League had lost their taste for an action whose sponsors were so conspicuously reluctant to undertake it. The most important of these was the Soviet Union. The Soviet government had been, before December, at least publicly zealous in its devotion to the League, to sanctions, and to the Ethiopian cause. This attitude harmonized well enough with the traditional Communist aversion to imperialism; it harmonized even more precisely with the very new Soviet policy, which had emerged in 1934, of trying to build up a "popular front" against Fascism and which had already led to a Franco-Soviet alliance and to Soviet entrance into the League. But after the Hoare-Laval agreement Soviet enthusiasm (never manifested in anything more definite than speeches at Geneva) cooled. Western ambassadors at Moscow found the commissariat of foreign affairs unwilling to discuss the matter at all. In smaller countries a similar discouragement was evident.

What was happening in the United States was more complicated. After Roosevelt's message to Congress proposing a new American role and a new diagnosis of European affairs, Congress was wrangling interminably about the terms of neutrality legislation. The Administration tried to translate its concern for international action to stop aggression into a "discretionary" law, which would save the independence of the executive branch by allowing it to decide when and against whom to impose embargoes on United States exports. The proposal met with general hostility in a Congress still largely dominated by isolationists of various stripes, and it eventually had to be abandoned. On the basis of the American wrangling, it seemed clear that no transatlantic support could be looked for in the west if stronger sanctions were to be adopted in Geneva.

But there are certain reservations to be made. For one thing, it is said that Roosevelt's abandonment of his effort to try to get legislation that would permit him to back the League was due not so much to congressional hostility as to what the British themselves were doing. Information was reaching the State Department from the American embassy at London that indicated that the British did not seriously intend to impose oil sanctions; at the same time, Eden was saying that the decision not to press for oil sanctions was made largely because of information reaching London from the British embassy at Washington indicating that the Americans would not support them. The sequence of events is confused, but the confusion itself is interesting. Despite the Administration's efforts, American exports to Italy *had* mounted, but Eden exaggerated the increase when he used it as an explanation of the effective abandonment by Britain of the effort to secure oil sanctions. The League powers, and especially Britain, tended to talk as if the efficacy of oil sanctions would depend entirely on the immediate and total stoppage of oil exports to Italy by the United States. But the experts appointed by the Committee of Eighteen did not support this argument; on February 12 they had made their report suggesting that the effectiveness of oil sanctions would be only very slightly reduced if the United States continued exports at the prewar level and that even if the United States permitted unrestricted exports the Italians would be placed in a difficult and dangerous position by embargoes on the part of the League powers. In fact, Eden's placing the blame on the Americans, if it reflected anything more than an attempt to get Britain off the hook, was based on the appraisal of its ambassador in Washington, Sir Ronald Lindsay, that American opinion would not tolerate support of the League and of sanctions.

It certainly looked that way, and perhaps it was that way. American isolationism had begun to change and to weaken, but there was no national inclination to support a system of international peace keeping that the British and the French had themselves discredited and destroyed.

The Rhineland crisis of March 1936 contributed to this development, as it contributed to all aspects and all consequences of the Ethiopian crisis. The events that led up to it, in the history of German-Italian relations, are significant in this way. They are also subtle and unedifying. There was no desire in Rome to see the aggrandizement of Hitler. But with victory in East Africa deferred, there must be no alienation of Germany either. Mussolini would have preferred, certainly, to have kept the friendship of Britain and France, even after their reluctant opposition became noticeable. His virulent anti-British polemics of the summer of 1935 had been, it is probable, partly a sort of shriek of frustration and of outrage at what he thought was a betrayal, partly a tactic to excite Italian national solidarity. From what is now known, he still seems to have felt at the beginning of 1936 that Hitler was a menace and a potential enemy, whose temporary appeasement was a regrettable necessity. It must be recalled that part of the purpose of the Ethiopian campaign, as it was first conceived in 1934, was to achieve a quick military victory, a sort of instant reputation as an irresistible power, in order to intimidate the Germans. Shreds of this purpose remained, and it had certainly not been vitiated by the Germans' extreme coolness, not to say pro-Ethiopian attitude, in the summer and autumn of 1935, when they were affably co-operating, or appearing to co-operate, with the League. The tenor of the diplomatic dispatches exchanged between Berlin and Rome in the latter part of 1935 and early 1936 shows a mutual distrust and suspicion. In October 1935 the German foreign minister, Baron Konstantin von Neurath, had solemnly advised the Italian ambassador in Berlin that Italy ought to try to make a suitable compromise to liquidate the Abyssinian undertaking.[43]

In the winter of 1935–36 distrust persisted, but German-Italian relations were changing. They were changing, first, because of the effect that sanctions made on the Italian economy. Italian dependence on German coal was increasing rapidly; and while Hitler's directive at first ordered that German exports to Italy be held to the prewar level, this was later revised to permit them to rise to the highest, rather than the average, prewar monthly figure. In fact, they rose much higher. Moreover, in December Hitler eased the way to increased export by approving negotiations for a credit of 40,000,000 reichsmarks to Italy to strengthen the rapidly deteriorating Italian balance of payments. Considering the Germans' reservations about Italy, there was a suggestion of blackmail in this. It was the beginning of dependence; and it was made much more compelling by the extreme impatience and alarm that Mussolini undoubtedly felt in January 1936, induced by Badoglio's cautionary telegrams. On the last day of the month, Arnaldo Cortesi of the *New York Times* reported from Rome (on what evidence is not made clear) that Mussolini had told his cabinet that they must prepare for the possibility of a second winter of fighting—that is, that the war might last into 1937. On the eve of Badoglio's great victories there was a good deal of despondency in inner circles in Rome.

Indeed, there was more than despondency, and some people felt the regime was in danger. Loyal followers were beginning to murmur. And indeed to shout. On the day of Cortesi's dispatch the German ambassador at Rome reported a conversation between the German consul general at Naples and Italo Balbo, one of the early Fascist leaders and at that time governor of Libya. This eminent personage exploded with rage at the Duce. He was a friend of Badoglio's; he knew Mussolini all too intimately; and he thought that the latter had lost all sense of reality and begun in a quite pathological way to think of himself as "infallible." The war Balbo described as a disaster, and the German ambassador, Ulrich von Hassell, commented in his report that his remarks "amount to a criticism such as had certainly never before been uttered by any Fascist leader, especially to a foreigner."[44] Mussolini's "speed contest" was, in the ambassador's opinion, a matter of the utmost urgency. The deadline of the rains had presented itself as a deadline for survival of Fascism.

Hostility to his leadership was Mussolini's greatest weakness but it was also, in a paradoxical way, a source of strength, for the destruction of Fascism was something the Germans did not at all desire. They distrusted Mussolini's policies (as well they might); vivid recollections of 1915 made them doubt Italy's loyalty as an ally (as well they might); they suspected that Mussolini harbored a nostalgia for the Stresa policy and would have liked a reconciliation with France and Britain (as well they might). Nonetheless, Fascism was the proto-type of National Socialism. Too much had been made of their ideolog-ical affinities, of the harmony of the two, great, youthful, virile, expand-ing nations of Europe, to sacrifice it. More specifically, the Germans were interested in two things: freedom of action for the Nazi party in Austria, which Mussolini was in a position to give them through his domination of the Austrian government and, most urgently, assurances that if the Germans remilitarized the Rhineland Italy would not honor its obligations under the Treaty of Locarno to come to the support of France.

There was, then, an element of *reciprocal* dependence in Italo-German relations in January and February of 1936, and there existed the possibility of a deal not entirely dissimilar to that which Laval and Mussolini had worked out a year earlier. Repeated enquiries about Italian intentions regarding Locarno were made by the German government. All sorts of ingenious arguments were used to encourage Italian co-operation. Ambassador von Hassell and some of the officials in Berlin, however, were very doubtful; they repeatedly warned that Italy's heart lay in the Stresa policy. But Hitler had decided to occupy the Rhineland in spite of his own misgivings and the opposition of the German army general staff—the generals regarded the venture as excessively risky, certain to bring strenuous French reaction, which the German army could not hope to resist, and perhaps the destruction of the German regime. So Hitler *required* Italian co-operation, and what he required he usually got. At the end of January, he summoned Hassell to Berlin, and there Hassell had a long conversation with Attolico, the Italian ambassador. Attolico was friendly; he denied that Mussolini felt any longings to return to the Stresa policy. But he was defensive in his attitude, and he was attempting to bargain with the Germans. In Hassell's words:

> Finally, with regard to the military situation, if the pessimism of which I had spoken referred to the question of achieving a de-cisive success before the rainy season set in, then he [Attolico] could not but share this pessimism. If, however, this pessimism consisted of thinking that Italy was not able and perhaps even did not wish to carry her military undertaking further, but would have to liquidate it before the rainy season, then he could only state

most explicitly that this view was quite without foundation. Italy was resolute and entirely capable of fighting on. . . . From the economic angle, too, they were definitely in a position to go on holding out for many months yet. On the other hand, it would be foolish for him to attempt to deny that Italy's overall politico-economic situation was most difficult. He would be betraying no secrets if he said that if anyone were to offer Italy acceptable compromise proposals, Italy for her part would not "spit in their face." . . . It would, in my view, be wrong to assume that Mussolini was doing this in order to lure us into taking action against Austria and thus diverting world attention from him to us.[45]

Later Hassell saw Hitler. The ambassador wrote a memorandum on their talk. Hitler, he reported,

said he has no illusions at all about the fact that Germany was at present as good as completely isolated. We possessed no really reliable friends. No real trust could be placed in Poland's policy and Italy was herself in a very difficult position. It would be highly undesirable if this isolation should, as the result of a collapse of Fascism in Italy, become a moral isolation too. We must do everything to prevent the manifold opponents throughout the world of the authoritarian system of government from concentrating upon us as their sole object. But apart from this it was also in our interests that Italy as a piece upon the European chessboard should not be weakened too much. There was a time, especially after Mussolini's well-known demonstrations on the Brenner, when perhaps we might not have wished to see Italy emerge from the conflict too great or too victorious, but nowadays this danger surely no longer existed to any great degree. . . . He had therefore resolved to continue our benevolent neutrality towards Italy. . . . he could only welcome it if relations of mutual trust between Italy and Germany were restored. It was a mistake to pursue a policy of emotion in such questions; regardless of what one's own personal feelings might be, it was politically correct to treat the events of 1934 [the Nazi assassination of Austrian chancellor Dollfuss, which had so frightened and affronted the Italians] as a closed chapter.[46]

The elements of a deal were abundantly present. Just as Laval had bought Italy's support for an anti-German policy by countenancing its plans in Ethiopia, Hitler now bought Italy's support for a pro-German policy, including the betrayal of the Locarno powers and abandonment of the Italian dominance in Austria, for the same consideration. It was in its mechanics a very old-fashioned kind of bargaining, recalling the elaborate colonial arrangements and alignments of the later nineteenth century. The fancy ideological packaging in which it was enveloped was in large part irrelevant. (In one way, though, the ideology had importance, although it was not of the kind that appeared on the surface. Mutual distrust and dislike remained, but the Germans and Italians both had a kind of regime and ambitions wholly unlike those of the nineteenth-century governments.) The important fact was that Mussolini's whimsies and volatility had placed him in a position of dependence. The fascist bloc now became, despite his original intentions and the better judgment of most Fascists, the cornerstone of Italian policy. Although Mussolini did not realize it, Italy had lost its freedom of action. It was the first step that was to lead toward the final humiliation of the abjectly servile puppet republic at Salò in the last years of World War II.

The picture of a world divided into flaccid democracies and aggressive autocracies, which Roosevelt had sketched out in January, was beginning to correspond to the realities of power. When the Rhineland was occupied, at the moment when Badoglio's great victories were presaging the end of Ethiopia, the lines for the coming world war were drawn.

10

End of a Beginning

With the failure of the emperor's attack at Mai Ceu, Ethiopian society began to turn into what the Italians had claimed it had always been—a chaos. Decomposition became anarchy and released impulses that were perhaps not so much primitive as merely human. It was anarchy in the most literal sense, for the authority of government dissolved, and in some places a Hobbesian state of nature immediately appeared. Life in Ethiopia was thereafter for many both brutish and short and was to remain so for years. It was instantly clear that if anybody had a civilizing mission, it was Haile Selassie and not the Italians. But what emerged in the end was not barbarism: it was on the one hand a very archaic world of the complex organisms of village life; on the other, it was "resistance" movements that were very modern, indeed prophetic. An old world was reborn, a new world was a-borning.

At first, however, it was the tortured rubble, human and administrative, that was most conspicuous. It was a terrible sight, and few saw beyond it.

The destruction of Haile Selassie's edifice was far advanced by the time he reached Dessie on his way back to the capital. Even his personal staff and the remnants of the imperial guard had become insubordinate. Along the mournful road south, insubordination turned to mutiny and then to treason. Konovaloff reported that when local chiefs asked Haile Selassie where his soldiers were, the sovereign replied, "Soldiers? Today there are no more soldiers; they are all brigands for whom we no longer exist." The great chiefs, the Russian wrote, "were losing little by little all their prestige,"* and the soldiers were engaging not merely in brigandage but rape and gratuitous murders—as if, Mosley said, "to show that they too could be as savage and blood-thirsty as the Azebe Gallas who still dogged their footsteps."[1] Along the track, villagers failed to bring the customary gifts of food or even to come out to meet their sovereign. "The Emperor himself," Konovaloff wrote, "was losing a great part of his authority . . . The disintegration of Ethiopia continued at galloping speed . . . [but] everywhere the villagers had live-stock and lived in peace."[2]

The imperial party received by messenger a report that in the capital the authority of the regime still held and in the south Graziani's advance had been halted. Dissolution was not yet total. But there were also reports of spreading revolts in the northern provinces. Rumors, like an epidemic, assisted the disarray. In the capital it was believed that huge armies of "shiftas," armies of Italian-organized brigands, were overrunning the country and moving toward Addis.[3]

The emperor hurried along the impossible road. He was much alone and, Konovaloff noted, very tired. But he was planning for the future, for guerrilla war to be fought in the Nile Valley and the south, with the help of Prince Imru. The very weaknesses of the empire as a modern state could so be turned to advantage, to the harassment of the Italians.

His party reached Addis Ababa on April 30, 1936. The capital had already been bombed. It was being showered daily with leaflets and on one occasion by Fascist pennants. (Mussolini's son-in-law, Count Galeazzo Ciano, his minister of propaganda, soon to be his foreign minister, and, at the last, to be shot by his order, had performed this act of aerial virtuosity, dropping the flags on the market places.) Badoglio was in Dessie, and the engineers were at work on the road, the main street of the empire that the emperor had traveled, making it passable for motorized units.

---

* From a lengthy memorandum describing the flight, which Konovaloff prepared for G. L. Steer and which was included in the latter's *Caesar in Abyssinia*, p. 336. Konovaloff's is the only available eye-witness account on the Ethiopian side of the emperor's attack at Mai Ceu and the return to Addis Ababa afterward; it should be noted that the loyal colonel was greatly shaken and his reporting may be open to question. It is, nonetheless, not only the main source for what happened but also superbly written in great and graphic detail.

It was a formidable task for Badoglio, moving with massive bodies of men and materiel that the road could not, in its existing state, accommodate. Such large numbers as the marshal was bringing might have seemed unnecessary, since there was no force to oppose their march to the capital. But he wanted them for characteristic reasons: it would, he wrote, be "useful to make an immediate demonstration of force along the road, especially in the Shoa region [the province in which Addis Ababa lay], where the inhabitants might not all be immediately favorable to us. It would be especially useful to make our appearance in Addis Ababa with an impressive contingent of troops."⁴ The capital was sprawling and large forces would be needed to pacify it. And he wanted to be able to take immediate control of the railroad to Jibuti as well.

Such plans meant long delay for his three columns, one mechanized and two of infantry, a total of 20,000 men (half Italian and half Eritrean), with 1,725 motor vehicles. Fifteen days were needed for the journey of 400 miles. At times, "in some parts at every few hundred yards, the column was obliged to halt, while the troops dismounted and the battalion of engineers, which marched with the advanced guard, had to take steps to improve the trace of the road, to build bridges, and to make passable fords and long stretches of marsh, tasks in which they were assisted indefatigably and with the utmost zeal by the troops of the other arms."⁵ The capital, and in particular the foreigners who were still in it, were to pay very dearly for his massive march.

In the south, a sickening comedy was transacting itself.

Graziani, who would shortly have an opportunity to prove his reputation as the cruelest and the most foolish of proconsuls, had had no opportunity to prove his reputation for martial boldness. He was anxious to do so by reaching Harar before Badoglio reached the capital. He was, indeed, frenziedly eager to do so, and insanely indignant at the frustrations he encountered. The adverbs are not entirely metaphorical; his conduct in these days certainly verged on the pathological. He was the embodiment of Fascist folly, but he was also its victim. Or thought he was. The general who liked to picture himself as the very symbol of dash was stalled in the Ogaden while in Rome his Duce was petulantly

berating him for the absence of those particular qualities that he supposed himself to stand for.

The rebukes were, evidently, justified. According to most observers,
there was practically nothing to have stopped Graziani from marching
on Harar after—or even before—he had liquidated Desta's army in the
southwest in January. The defending forces were sparse and scattered
until the beginning of April. The terrain was appalling, but it was not
going to get less appalling with the passage of time. From December
to April, as Steer observed, Graziani had done nothing aside from the
"side-show" in which Desta's army had been destroyed. But Graziani,
for all his swagger, was as reluctant as De Bono and Badoglio to act until his resources were so large that he could be sure in advance of a triumph.

By April things were changing, from his point of view for the
worse. The rains began, turning the country before Graziani into a
checkerboard of marshes and mudholes. And the Ethiopians before
Harar were collecting reinforcements and armaments. They were even
in a position to contemplate an offensive. Ten thousand men under the
command of General Nasibu and of Prince Desta's brother Abebe
(who was always attended by three leashed lions, the almost mystical
ensigns of Ethiopian power), had taken up positions on the hills south
of Harar, where the Ogaden Desert met the eastern spurs of the highlands. The force had several tough old Turkish soldiers as advisers
(along with some young Belgians who were, apparently, less helpful;
one of the Turks said of them, "They included lawyers, shopkeepers,
and comedians."[6]) Morale was, for a time, high and the defensive positions excellent. If Graziani had been able to move earlier, the new
army would never have come into existence.

Telegrams to Graziani from both Badoglio and Mussolini were becoming more impatient. He answered one from Badoglio, sent early in
March, with illuminating words: "I am bitterly aware that had I been
believed a year ago when I pointed out the advantage of an offensive
on the southern front, I could have annihilated both the Ethiopian
armies in the Ogaden and so have brought the Italo-Ethiopian war to
an end. History will attribute this failure to its proper source. My own
conscience is completely clear."[7] Badoglio and Mussolini continued to
demand action. (Badoglio wired him, "My old comrade-in-arms . . .
bring us yet another victory.") In reply, Graziani ordered Harar and

Jijiga heavily bombed. The measure was without military utility but very destructive. The secretariat-general of the League was informed by the Ethiopian government:

> This morning at seven-thirty-seven enemy planes bombed and machine-gunned the open city of Harar for an hour. The number of victims is not yet known. Among the numerous buildings destroyed were the Catholic Church of Saint Savior and several buildings of the mission, the French hospital, and the French consular agency, the radio-telegraph station and the prison. In addition, fifteen bombs struck the Egyptian Red Crescent ambulance hospital. The hospital of the Ethiopian Red Cross was struck by several bombs, and two fell in the compound of the Swedish hospital. All these hospitals prominently displayed the Red Cross sign.[8]

On April 14, the day Badoglio reached Dessie, Graziani at last began his advance. (On that same morning he had another hortatory telegram from Rome: "There is not a moment to lose, my dear Graziani.") On the 15th the Italians reached the Ethiopian lines on the rocky, sheltered cliffs above a flooded stream. For days no progress was made; the Ethiopians fought with sustained courage and great skill. Not until April 23 was the defense line broken. Graziani's army had suffered the most prolonged setback and the most serious losses (2,000 men) of any Italian army in any single battle. Del Boca quotes the diary of one of them: "They tell me Graziani is in a nervous state. I'm not surprised. The rain that kept him inactive at Hamanlei for four days and another four days at Daggahbur has held up his advance on Harar, which should have been in our hands by now. If it hadn't been for the rain, we'd have entered the city on the day Badoglio entered Addis Ababa, or even earlier. All this delay threatens to cast a shadow over Graziani's glorious campaign."[9] There were further embarrassments. During a visit to a church in Jijiga, Graziani stumbled and fell, seriously injuring himself. And at the end of the campaign, in Diredawa, there was humiliation. Badoglio was there to greet him. He had come by train from Addis Ababa.

If his frustrations did indeed affect his reason, it was a matter of importance. For Graziani was to be very intimately connected with the fate of Ethiopia and the reputation of Italy; he was to become "the Butcher of East Africa," a rival in contemporary minds for the garland of odium that attached to the names of Reinhard Heydrich and Heinrich Himmler. The future destruction of other colonial empires was per-

haps in some degree, anyway, his work; he, as much as any individual
in the twentieth century, wrecked the pious picture of the Europeans
as civilizers. He was already a man with an established reputation for
butchery, but somewhere on the road to Harar he may have crossed
the line between harshness and fury.

While Graziani was being maddened at his own slow advance and
Badoglio was making his painstaking march to the capital, despairing
decisions were taken in Addis Ababa. Along his Via Dolorosa from
Dessie, the emperor had been considering plans. The empress and the
rest of the imperial family would leave at once for Jibuti—a train was
prepared and awaiting their departure at the Addis Ababa station. But
he had decided to try to defend the city, at least to delay its fall. He
summoned its array, a garrison of 5,000 men under the command of
Prince Getachu. Later, he planned to set up his government in Gore, in
the western mountains, with Prince Imru as the commander of a
national guerrilla war against the invaders.

It was a rational program, based upon what turned out to be a correct assumption: while the Italians might quickly conquer Ethiopia,
they would not conquer the Ethiopians. An elusive, fugitive government could provide leadership to (if not authority over) a resistance
movement that would reduce the occupiers to impotence. So long as an
Ethiopian imperial government still directed resistance on Ethiopian
soil, it would have a legal and emotional reality at home and abroad
that would automatically confer upon it both legal rights and political
magnetism. Ethiopia could not then be forgotten by the rest of the
world or be written off as an Italian colony whose affairs were nobody's
business except the Italians'.

Accordingly, on his weary arrival in Addis on April 30, he called a
meeting of the imperial council and summoned the French and British
ministers to tell them that the capital would be defended. There are
varying accounts of his mood and of the reasons for what happened
that day. Konovaloff said he was frenzied, tearing down curtains, breaking furniture, and at the end wildly ordering the population to loot
and burn so that nothing might be left for the Italians. Steer gave a
very different account: "His face, always sensitive, was haunted now
. . . the eyes seemed to have lost their quiet resolution . . . Fatigue and
spiritual misery had done their work. The one man in Ethiopia, capa-

ble of always taking the right decision, had lost his gift."[10] Steer's is the more convincing picture, and there is a third account by a westerner to supplement it. The emperor found time to receive the credentials of the newly appointed American minister, Cornelius Engert. Engert knew him well, and his report of the meeting bears out the impression of calm. Haile Selassie, he said, showed "remarkable sangfroid." He seemed frail, "but his handshake had its usual firmness and his unscrutable features were lit up by the same winsome smile." He expressed his esteem for President Roosevelt's clear perception of the threat of the fascist countries and said, "Tell him the fate of my country may serve as warning that words are of no avail against a determined aggressor."[11]

The emperor's sentiment coincided with the president's; and it was becoming the sentiment of a large part of the world. But it was voiced in those days by only two heads of state—the heads of isolated America and of the last embattled nation in Africa.

The emperor's gift for knowing the right decision had not perhaps left him, but the power to enforce it had. Very strong pressures were brought to induce him to abandon his plans. The French minister advised in the strongest possible terms against defending the capital— Steer thought that he, like most other foreigners in Addis Ababa, was anxious to have Italian authorities there as soon as possible to protect the lives and property of Europeans.[12] Barton, the British minister, told the emperor that he thought there was no possibility that sanctions would be extended in support of a fugitive government fighting a guerrilla war against the Italians. The empress pleaded with him to leave Ethiopia with her while there was still time. The local authorities were panicky, inefficient, anxious to give up. No effective preparations could be made to defend the approaches to the city. The army of Shoa, some 6,000 men based in Addis Ababa, had been ordered to hold the dizzy pass of Tarmaber that the Italians would have to cross. The army of Shoa never left the city. The only forces that had been sent were 350 young boys from the Imperial Cadet School under the command of a Swedish military adviser, and they withdrew without offering serious resistance.

The most important of the pressures came from the imperial council, the assembly of notables, great princes of the realm, which Haile

Selassie had set up years earlier in an effort to convert a congeries of chieftaincies into a modern state. There was a significant difference between their response and those of the ministers and civil servants who represented the new elite. The ministries, following imperial orders, were already moving their files westward. A young American adviser on administrative practices named John H. Spencer was zealously organizing mule teams and trucks to carry the physical apparatus of the Ethiopian state into the western mountains. The foreign minister, the distinguished and determined Hirouy, with some of the other westernized leaders, strongly backed the emperor's plan to remain in the country. But the princes were opposed. Prince Kassa, the loser in the north and the greatest man of the empire after the sovereign, presented cogent arguments. He pointed out—what was undoubtedly true—that the Gore project was threatened with more than the expectable risks that any guerrilla government must encounter. Gore was in Galla country, and the support of the populace was not to be counted on. The horrors of the retreats from Aradam and Mai Ceu had shown that a hostile countryside could destroy an army. The only hope, Kassa and his supporters said, was to mobilize European opinion, to try again to invoke the Covenant of the League. And the chieftains backed this view. On the afternoon of May 1 the imperial council voted—twenty-one to three—in favor of flight, to Jibuti and to exile.

Steer says that the emperor was still undecided that night. He—and Steer—thought that the people, the people of the capital anyway, did not look on what had happened as final defeat. He did not believe that the western Gallas were disloyal. Censorship had disintegrated, and journalists, several of whom had spoken to the emperor that day, were sending back free dispatches, in none of which was the possibility of exile mentioned. But final pressures were brought to bear at the very end. The emperor made one more gesture when Italian planes were flying low over the palace and the ladies of the court were huddling in fright: he ordered the drums beaten and the men of the capital to march against the approaching enemy. Then he withdrew to take counsel with himself and his conscience and with the commanders of the forces in the city. The ministers waited outside the empress's pavilion in the palace gardens. And while he was thus engaged, messengers came to say that the commanders of the garrison had refused to obey his orders to call out their men. The emperor then came out to meet his court, and Steer left a famous description of his appearance:

> He was dressed in khaki as a general. His aspect froze my blood. Vigour had left the face, and as he walked forward he did not seem to know where he was putting his feet. His body was crumpled up, his shoulders drooped; the orders on his tunic concealed a hollow, not a chest.[13]

If he had not finally abandoned his resolution then, he did so sometime that night. The train that had been prepared to take the empress and her children to the coast was waiting. When it left at four-twenty the next morning, the emperor, with most of the men like Kassa who advised flight and a few like Hirouy who had not, joined it at a station a few miles outside Addis Ababa. It was a large party; a number of court servants were included and so were the emperor's numerous dogs, of which he was extravagantly fond. It was also, in monetary terms, a very rich party. In the baggage were gold ingots from the Treasury—their value has been variously estimated and probably generally exaggerated, but it was considerable. Later these would be used to support the resistance movement, although the British press sometimes described their removal as embezzlement for personal gain.

In the city, where the departure of the court was instantly known, shooting and fires and looting had already begun.

The trip to the coast was harrowing. The Italians were approaching the railroad both from the north across the Danakil Desert from Eritrea and from the south across the Ogaden, and the line was open to air attack. And the emperor was already regretting his decision; he said so to the British consul at Harar, Edwin Chapman-Andrews, whom he received in the station at Diredawa. He told the consul that even then he was thinking of leaving the train to try to organize resistance at Harar, which Graziani would not reach for another week. Chapman-Andrews argued against it. The train went on with its full party. A few hours later it crossed into French territory and presently reached Jibuti. The cruiser H.M.S. *Enterprise*, which had been offered by Eden as transport for the empress and the princes and princesses, was waiting there, and on May 4, 1936, the party embarked.

Haile Selassie's passage to exile on a British man-of-war was the sign and symbol of the difficulties of the action that had been forced upon him. He became a protégé and ward, something like a prisoner, of the British, and in this daintily exercised bondage he remained until long after he had returned (in the train of the British army in 1941) to his country and his throne. The *douce violence* of British imperial power enveloped him; almost all the assets he still possessed were under British control. The policy of Great Britain toward Ethiopia, with respect to his semi-captivity as with the entire crisis, looked to many discreditable: not only parochial, it also seemed to comprise an element of a colonial dog-in-the-manger. In fact, it was the product of the same forces that had led the British government to support the League while it was negotiating with Mussolini. For a government that saw itself as trying desperately to save world peace by retrieving Italy from the Nazi embrace, Haile Selassie was a major embarrassment.

Prince Kassa had argued that the emperor's presence in Europe would force the British to end their tergiversations. But the reverse turned out to be the case. There was no chance that exiled Ethiopians could, by themselves, call forth a crusade for liberation. For four years the aim of Britain was to prevent the emperor from disturbing delicate balances. Until those balances collapsed, Haile Selassie was a prisoner; after that, for a time, he was a pawn.

Still, it would be bold to say that the alternative—remaining in the country to lead a government of national resistance—would have been wiser. Some of the prestige of the crown might have been salvaged, but some had already been lost by his failure as a warrior-leader of his peoples. And as events turned out, voluntary exile probably did not permanently damage the efficacy of the crown's symbolism. That would happen much later, but it would happen because of the liberation of forces involved with the growth of African nationalisms, not because of their betrayal. The resistance to the Italians might have been sharpened, but it grew so rapidly anyway that the presence of the emperor could hardly have speeded the process. A legal government on Ethiopian soil might have annoyed the Italians; it would certainly have embarrassed the British and the French statesmen who wanted to bury the whole incident in oblivion. But it probably would not have made much real difference to the course of events. In retrospect one may say that the choice that was so agonizingly faced by the emperor in his palace on that terrible night of May 1, 1936, had not much reality beyond his own conscience. One course was based on false reasoning and false hopes; the other would have yielded only futile sacrifices.

In Addis Ababa the worst happened. "Civilization" suddenly acquired a peculiar meaning, not unprecedented; it meant, for foreigners, preventing the local citizens from murdering them. This some of the Ethiopians clearly meant to do. Xenophobia and racial arrogance had always been noticeable among the Amharas. They were fortified by the belief that European governments had betrayed the country. Now they were released with the flight of the monarch and the collapse of authority.

Badoglio was waiting, 30 miles from the city, preparing for his entry. The foreigners, even those who had most strongly supported the Ethiopian cause, were desperately hoping for his prompt appearance. The citizens ran amuck. The four days that followed the emperor's departure were a story written in blood. Upon everyone who experienced and survived them, they left an indelible mark. For some foreigners they provided evidence in support of the theory that the Ethiopians were savages. No one could foresee that the Italian occupation would exceed by a wide margin the savagery that showed itself in the awful days of May when the government of Addis Ababa went to pieces.

The odd anatomy of public disorder is today better understood— or at least the difficulty of understanding it is more fully realized—than in the 1930s when most westerners reflexively assumed that law and order were the beneficent accessories of an advanced culture. Some of the things that happened in Addis Ababa have since happened in places like Milan and Chicago, and savagery is not always seen as the exclusive trait of rioters. In Addis in May 1936 the public authority collapsed. It did not abdicate. The police tried for a while to keep order. But they failed, and the capital city went up in flames. Since authority disappeared, *it* could not be charged with savagery. As in every large public disorder, aspirations and animosities that had nothing to do with the crisis were set free. Xenophobia was conspicuous, but it was not the motive of most of the rioters. People were expressing themselves in random murder, rape, and arson. By contrast, under the occupation, the Italian authorities, or some of them, ordered murder, rape, arson, and theft for deliberate ends. The definition of savagery, too, has changed since 1936.

The troubles began just before the emperor left early on May 2, and they lasted until the morning of May 5. When the Italians marched belatedly into the ruins that day, they found them silent and deserted in a downpour of rain. It is impossible to count the costs in any way that means anything. There are plenty of eye-witness accounts giving a vivid but a fragmentary picture, and most of them are highly colored with horror. There seem to have been four major kinds of disturbance: looting, which was on an enormous scale; a race war on foreigners, which may have been exaggerated since it was mostly foreigners who described it; a class war between the very poor and the comparatively rich; violent collisions between different ethnic groups of Ethiopians. The last were apparently the most devastating. Disbanded soldiers fought against "shiftas," the self-organized irregular forces. Gallas attacked Amharas. Christians attacked Moslems. Whole neighborhoods where people of one or another ethnic group lived were burned.

Major trouble began when a rumor spread that the two imperial palaces had been thrown open and that the emperor had ordered that his possessions be distributed to the populace—that anyone should take anything he wanted. It is not clear whether this was true, but Konovaloff thought it was, and it is in keeping both with the emperor's character and with the *Götterdämmerung* atmosphere attending his departure. In any case the palaces were stripped—Steer reported seeing old women stumbling under the weight of huge tapestries. So were the caves where the government had been storing arms for the defense of the city. What brought the greatest horror was looting of liquor. Wine shops were the first to be attacked, and drunkenness—which even sympathetic Europeans regarded as not merely a chronic vice of Ethiopians but one that produced a sort of madness among them—ruled the city. The police perceived early on their unpleasant position; not only was it dangerous, but it excluded them from the spoils. They joined the rioters.

Steer and a few other intrepid men scouted the streets in cars to find and save foreigners. One paragraph of his description summarizes the state of the city late on May 2:

The streets were filled with smoke, the flames were running from shop to shop, cars which had crashed or been abandoned at the roadside were burning, hot black refuse in our way could be seen through the level glare of the descending sun and the harsh irritating breath of the furnace which started tears from our eyes. A few Ethiopians, in bands, hacked at the side of [our] lorry. In the waste setting of broken and flaming Addis Ababa with the telephone wires in tangled black nets dangling across the roadway, to the tune of shattered glass under our lorry wheels, their faces and the horrible lie of the straddled corpses looked too unbearably horrible.

Order here had been a flimsy thing, sustained by the superb will of a single individual. Its destruction, in a welter of fire, dirt, explosions, was suddenly visible in every sordid detail. The bodies were beginning to stink . . .[14]

Most of the foreigners reached safety. The British were admirably organized, and the legation compound was well defended by Indian army troops. They searched arriving refugees for firearms (priests of the Greek mission were found to be harboring pistols under their skirts) and assigned tenting sites on the cricket field, laid out to provide suitable segregation of inimical national and religious groups. The more eminent refugees were permitted to sleep on sofas and carpets in the legation residence. By the time the siege ended, there were over 1,500 people in the compound, including 300 Asians and a few Africans.

There were heroic and hair-raising episodes while people were being herded into safe quarters. The emperor's private pilot, a German named Weber, with incredible skill and audacity rescued missionaries in outlying stations by plane. (On the other hand, the British sent an armed convoy to fetch the staff of the American legation, isolated on the other side of the city. They found it undefended and un-attacked, with the Americans calmly eating roast beef hash; the British were annoyed for their wasted gallantry and hazard. The Americans rode out the storm; the vice-consul's residence was looted, but the legation personnel survived without defense or injury.) The most conspicuous heroes were the men of the British Red Cross unit. The emperor had assigned them the Empress's School, in the palace grounds, as a hospital. There, after the defeat of the armies had ended their work in the field and forced them back to the city, they tried to help the few among the enormous list of casualties whom they could reach.

The moving spirit, as in all the works of the British Red Cross during the war, was John Melly, the odd young doctor who had gone to Ethiopia years before and whose personality and career deserve, by any definition, the term noble. He was a compulsive adventurer and something of a religious fanatic; he exulted in danger and philanthropy alike. He and his colleagues had saved hundreds of lives on the battlefields; now, in the last days, they were to save many more in Addis Ababa. In the reports of the unit, a sort of official diary regularly kept, their exploits in collecting wounded from the streets are recorded in dry, effective prose. And for May 3, one of his colleagues wrote this entry:

> At approximately 10 a.m. Dr. Melly decided to take out a convoy of three lorries to collect wounded, leaving Dr. Schuppler and myself to carry on with the operations. The convoy consisted of Dr. Melly, Mr. Gatward, and Mr. de Halpert with approximately three armed native personnel in each lorry. There had been no diminution in the continuous shooting from the previous day, and the looting was as rife as ever . . .
>
> Mr. Gatward describes the incident as follows: "We were proceeding slowly looking for wounded and at a crowded part of the main street we saw a man on the road at the side of my lorry who appeared wounded. I stopped the lorry to go to investigate. Finding that he was wounded, I turned around to call Dr. Melly and was just in time to see a man thrust a revolver into the cab of the lorry and shoot Dr. Melly. The latter collapsed on the seat and shouted to be taken back quickly. I, therefore, jumped into the driver's seat and drove back quickly to our hospital. I recollect a shout in the crowd of 'ferengi' [foreigner] just as the shot was fired."[15]

Melly had been shot through the lung. He died on the evening of May 4 and was buried in the British legation garden. The irony of his death was much stressed: he was shot by one of the people he had devoted his life to help. It was a deceiving irony—the identification of an individual with the collectivity he happened to belong to—and might well be perceived in the murder of any useful citizen by any individual of his own nationality. The only thing that makes Melly's death seem ironic was the assumption that Ethiopians could be held collectively guilty for the shooting.

Such judgments inform almost all accounts by foreigners of the terrible days of May, and in reverse they informed the actions of some of the rioters. The French, intensely unpopular because they were blamed for having encouraged the Italians, were singled out for attack, and the French legation was besieged. It was not implausible to lay blame at the door of the French government, but the French personnel in Addis Ababa were certainly guiltless. And the Turkish and Belgian legations were also attacked, although no more blame could attach to their governments and people than to any other white men. On the other hand, many Ethiopians risked their lives to save foreigners, and the besieged white men behaved with signal courage and with the discipline which they regarded as the peculiar virtue of their civilization. It is said that the Turkish minister submitted to the military orders of his chauffeur, who was a superior officer in the ranks of the Turkish army reserve. These were field days for instincts and moral principles of every sort.

By Tuesday, May 5, the citizens themselves were fleeing in hordes from their own countrymen as well as from the oncoming Italians. The city, still burning, began to quiet down as thousands of people moved westward into the mountains. They were still leaving when the Italians entered late in the afternoon. By then, according to Italian estimates, more than 700 people had been killed. It was of course to the Italian interest to put the worst light on what had happened, and the figures were probably high. Still, the terror had been intense and the casualties large.

That evening Addis Ababa was filled with the immense display of mechanized might that was Badoglio's army. Endless columns of trucks roared through the streets carrying men who had stuck geraniums in their caps and helmets. Half the buildings still standing showed white flags, drooping in the heavy rain, and the remaining officials of the empire and municipality came out to make their submissions. A group of customs officers, the only organized force remaining, presented arms. Some of the more knowing citizens gave the Fascist salute. Sixteen hundred trucks passed the British legation, and some of their occupants stuck out their tongues at the Union Jack. At the Italian legation the tricolor of Savoy was raised, and there were cheers for the king of Italy and Mussolini as Italian planes performed aerobatics low overhead. On the legation steps Badoglio, his eyes filled with

25. *Winston Churchill, like Eden and Hoare, was a member of the clublike governing class of Britain that decided the destinies of the world. Like them he was a conservative supporter of kings, empires, and the supremacy of Europe. Unlike them, he was belligerent, determined, and energetic. Out of power in 1935, he nonetheless supported the policy of making deals with Italy while simultaneously sniping at the cabinet's timidity and ineptitude. Five years later, when he came to power and war between Italy and Britain was at hand, he undertook the liberation of Ethiopia and the restoration of the exiled Haile Selassie.*

26. *Marshal Pietro Badoglio (center) was a highly professional soldier who won the war against Ethiopia more rapidly than most people thought possible and thereby saved Fascism in 1936. Seven years later he would succeed Mussolini as prime minister and would surrender Italy's armed forces to its enemies.*

27. Italy's greatest military strength lay in its superb engineering skill. Road and bridge building had been an Italian skill since the time of Julius Caesar. In 1935 it was used with decisive effect against the Italians' most formidable enemy in Ethiopia, geography.

28. Badoglio was always a soldier of the purest sort. Mussolini was a chameleon who dressed for his numerous roles—general, admiral, Fascist trooper, common soldier, working man, devoted father. Here the sober, responsible statesman, in top hat, congratulates the soldier on his victory.

29. By June of 1936 Ethiopia's armies had been defeated and the empire was proclaimed an Italian province. Mussolini, the Man on Horseback, proclaimed to the world that Italian arms were invincible.

30. The Ethiopian armies had been defeated, but the people had not. At first, in places where the Italian army was in control, many Ethiopians accepted Italian rule, and some paid obeisance to posters of a singularly porcine Duce. But acquiescence did not last long; lion and pig faced each other, and the lion rapidly recovered his self-confidence.

31. On June 30, 1936, after his armies had been destroyed and he had gone into exile, Emperor Haile Selassie delivered his greatest speech. Before the League of Nations Assembly in Geneva, he pleaded for aid against his Italian conquerors. He got none, but he changed the history of the world. It was the most moving moment in the history of the dying League, and the emperor, the conscience of the world, called forth a new hatred and fear of Fascist aggression and a new militancy among those who were to fight it.

32. Mussolini

tears, embraced the commander of his air force, General Vincenzo Magliocco, and cried out, "We've done it. We've won."

He had magnificently achieved what he sought. For all his caution he had moved much faster than most people had thought possible. The entrance had been an imposing, orderly, ceremonial display of overpowering force. Steer, a prophet, wrote: "It was the largest mechanized column thrown out by history, but because the world so feebly withstood it there will soon be much bigger ones."[16]

The world, outside of Ethiopia, had in fact not withstood it at all, feebly or otherwise. And now the world was unresponsive, except in Italy, where jubilation naturally reigned. The enthusiasm that had shown itself at the beginning of the war recurred at what appeared to be its end, and the serious misgivings that had shaped Italian policy and shaken the regime in the months of the lull were for one glorious moment gone. It looked as if Badoglio's talent had procured exactly what Mussolini had hoped for from the beginning: a reputation for his countrymen as exemplars of the hard virtues of the warrior, the Nietzschean virtues, after several hundred years of humiliation and foreign contempt.

If Fascism had any real core of consistency, one may guess it lay precisely in this: Mussolini and many of his colleagues were men who needed—in Mussolini's case, it was perhaps a psychopathic need—to be, and appear, strong and virile. *Personal* achievement did not satisfy them. To command the respect, the awe, and the fear of others for the Italian fatherland was the compelling purpose of Fascism, made (one may suggest) the more compelling because the Italians, in stereotype and in fact, were such unlikely materials for Nietzschean supermen. The very humanism of their national traditions produced for some of them the need to dehumanize the nation.

It had now been achieved. Foreigners like pro-Italian Major Polson Newman were shortly to testify to the fact. Italy might now, for awhile, be regarded as tough and formidable. The impression so created was a trap in which the whole world would soon be caught.

Mussolini thought he had forged a new and brutal Italy. He seemed also to have saved his regime. It was a classic example of the proposition that foreign success can divert attention from domestic problems. Unemployment and budgetary deficits were, in such a setting, small and technical matters, glory a large and impalpable one.

Tangibilities disappeared for the moment into a large, golden, enveloping cloud of national euphoria. It was a second trap.

There were very many Italians who knew better and who, in their dislike of the tinseled fraud, regretted the victory that prolonged it. But some of them were converted and all of them, for the time being, were silenced. On the evening of May 5 it was announced in Rome that Badoglio had entered the Ethiopian capital; the Italian capital went wild with joy. Never had one of Mussolini's frequent appearances on his balcony of the Palazzo Venezia evoked so passionate a response. He spoke now to the depths of the Italian national consciousness:

> During the thirty centuries of our history, Italy has known many solemn and memorable moments—this is unquestionably one of the most solemn, the most memorable. People of Italy, people of the world, peace has been restored.[17]

He was as usual wrong. Peace had not been restored and never would be so long as he lived. But the crowds were wildly eager. The Fascist Youth sang the newly composed "Hymn of Empire" while he was called back ten times to his balcony by their acclaim.

The government moved rapidly to make its triumph formal. On May 9 Ethiopia was incorporated by proclamation into the Italian state, and King Victor Emmanuel III assumed the imperial title. He must have had doubts, cautious, skeptical, Victorian-minded Anglophile that he was. He frankly told the British ambassador, when it was all over, that the victory had been fortuitous and unexpected; that if the emperor had not attacked Mai Ceu the war might have dragged on humiliatingly through the rainy season.[18] But he accepted the new crown with outward enthusiasm. It was something to be an emperor. The monarchy, its radiance long dimmed by the blinding light of Fascism, was also to have its day of glory, and loyal monarchists—who tended sometimes to private antipathy to the Fascists—were undoubtedly beguiled. Augustan undertones were audible.

On the hospital ship *Cesarea*, returning up the Red Sea from Eritrea with wounded Italians in the care of the Italian Red Cross, one of the nurses was Marie José, daughter of Albert, king of the Belgians. In 1914 Albert had defied the German invasion of his country and become the martyr-champion of the rights of small nations attacked by great ones. His daughter had married Crown Prince

Humbert of Italy and for the moment she forgot her heritage: in her diary she wrote on May 5 that the injured men in her care had greeted her as the future empress of Ethiopia and added, "The Italians on board the *Cesarea*, like all the Italians, are thrilled to think that their sovereigns are now emperor and empress. Their princess, who is tending to sick and wounded soldiers, will one day be an empress."[19] Her effusion, like that of many Italian subjects, was pure romance. Marie José had always loathed the Fascists and one day would conspire against them. But for many Italians, Ethiopia was above ideology. They would pay a price, as Marie José did, for exuberance. A decade later she would reign for a few months as queen of Italy, but she would never be an empress.

In those days no Italians mentioned the costs of the war or the fact that none of the pressing problems of the Italian economy and society had been alleviated.

The costs in manpower had been—at least according to official statistics—remarkably small. About 2,300 Italian soldiers and 500 civilian workers had lost their lives (there were much larger losses among the Eritreans and Somalians in the Italian Army). The smallness of the figure was a triumph of medical skill and organization, but it might have been cold-bloodedly observed that manpower was the one resource with which Italy was adequately endowed—endowed, indeed, to the point of demographic disaster—and that the war had been very wasteful indeed of scarcer resources. The greatest stringency was budgetary. The Fascist government was skirting financial collapse in 1935, and the war had cost what was for its time the prodigious sum of 12.1 billion lire. That would amount to something like $10 billion at the values of 1970, a sum to ruin a poor country. And there was more: sanctions, while of small military consequence, had been of considerable economic consequence, for they distorted Italy's shrinking foreign trade. The flow of exports and imports had been disrupted, and to meet the need for supplies it had been necessary to buy in expensive markets. The balance of payments, already very precarious, had now approached the point of insolvency.

These were short-run liabilities. Ethiopia itself was to prove a long-run one. The economic advantages for Italy that it was supposed by some people to harbor would, if they were ever to be realized, require capital investments on a scale that Italy was wholly unable to contrive. As a home for an emigrant population, to relieve the pressure on Italy's own insufficient land and industry, it would require still more capital—to finance houses and equipment for the settlers and to transport and market facilities to enable them to make a living. The wealth of raw materials, which the uninformed imagined might make Ethiopia a treasure house, would have required (had they existed) huge financing before they could be discovered, exploited, refined, transported, and sold. In point of fact, the new empire offered neither a home for emigrants—few would go there, and they rarely found subsistence when they did—nor a treasure of raw materials, which had never had any reality at all. What did have reality was the terrible drain on the budget that continued unabated for the five years while Italians, with enormous effort and sometimes heroic sacrifice, were trying to build roads and dams and public services and trying, with courage and futile cruelty, to subdue the recalcitrant Ethiopians.

There had never been in Rome any serious expectation of any immediate economic advantage. Italy's past experience with colonies gave ample omens of the reverse. Empires were very expensive. None of the colonies had proved profitable, and efforts at economic and political development had cost Italian taxpayers dear. Somaliland, for example, had never come near to paying its way, and in some years Italy had had to contribute *five times* as many lire as were raised in local revenues to pay the cost of running it.[20] Ethiopia was thought to be richer. Still, the imagined benefits to Italy were at best long-run, and all were illusory. It was an illusion that was widely held outside the government. But it was not the basic fallacy in the moment of elation in May 1936. The most important mistake was the belief that the defeat of Ethiopia meant the defeat of the Ethiopians. It was a mistake of incredible magnitude.

But even this was of less importance to the Italian nation than what the adventure was doing to the constellation of world power. It was here that Italy's false display as a great military power had the largest impact. Mussolini, in his more practical moments, might have realized how misleading it was to proclaim that Fascist Italy had now gloriously accomplished what imperial Rome and invincible Islam had failed to do. Fascists in high office might still have realized (as skeptics like Ciano frankly reported in his diary) that Italy could never be a match for the other great powers. But they could not act upon such privy realism. They could not admit that the effect of the war had been to make not a great world power but a satellite of its opponent, Germany.

This was a fundamental consequence of the war, concealed beneath the conquering panoply. There were others. The appearances of invincibility beguiled the west and led the British and French into a long and futile diplomatic love dance.

The first thing that had to be done from the point of view of the British government was to try to turn back relations with Mussolini to the Stresa days. This meant interring the unfortunate episodes of the intervening year with as much haste as was decently possible. Haste, barely decent, was noticeable in the earliest stages of the exile. H.M.S. *Enterprise* carried the Ethiopian sovereigns from Jibuti to Palestine. Palestine was a British mandate. There Haile Selassie was—as he would be for five years, except for one brief moment—a muzzled guest. The British government hoped that friends of Ethiopia and the League might rapidly forget. Oblivion must cloak the quiet normalization of relations with Italy.

It was not an unexpected policy, and in its motives it was not as contemptible as the friends of Ethiopia thought. It aimed at peace, and it had one justification: even after what he regarded as the indignities and treacheries he had suffered at their hands, Mussolini did—as the Germans shrewdly suspected—hanker after his Stresa friendships. He had, at least spasmodically, a wholesome respect for the British navy and for French military power, and (also spasmodically) he still nourished deep distrust of Germany. These were shared, often more definitely and more consistently, by almost all the responsible people connected with the regime, the king, Badoglio, Grandi, and many others. Even before the entrance into Addis Ababa, Mussolini had given unmistakable indications of a desire for reconciliation with his nervous tormentors. On April 23 he had instructed the press to end its year-old campaign of vituperation against Great Britain, and he began to send polite messages. Grandi had told Eden that the revival of the alignment—which the Italians had agreed to destroy in the winter desperation when they agreed to approve the Germany march into the Rhineland—was still an aim of Italian policy. Mussolini, on May 28, told a correspondent of the London *Daily Telegraph* that he would do anything in his power to

secure the "necessary" restoration of Anglo-Italian friendship. It was
not surprising that the British should have decided that the best hope
for peace lay in pursuing these suggestions.

But other forces conflicted powerfully with Italian hankering for
British friendship. The very costliness of the war, the very nature of the
elation it produced, imposed upon Mussolini the appetite and need for
further adventures. Before it was over he was involving himself in Spanish politics, encouraging and aiding the conspiracy of generals and
protofascists against the leftist Spanish republic. He seems to have had
an ill-formulated hope of bringing forth a Spanish satellite that would
be an Italian pawn in the wild game of turning the Mediterranean into
"an Italian lake." This was an ambition that was incompatible with
British friendship. Ethiopia marked a real change in the nature of Italian Fascism: from now on, dynamic adventures were essential to it.
These were precisely what British policy was directed at discouraging.
The British wanted to preserve the existing order.

And so the force inimical to British policy arose from the moral
and ideological foundations of politics in the thirties. The reason for
wooing Mussolini was the containment of German power. But Germany and Italy did possess an inner affinity, as both Hitler and Roosevelt perceived. They were both autocratic and both aggressive. While
Mussolini might have been detached from Hitler, he could not be detached from aggressiveness. In any case, it was not sure that Hitler
could be detached from Mussolini. The survival of Fascism was deemed
essential to the success of Nazism. And in the "western democracies,"
as they were coming to be called, another aspect of this was showing
itself. Awareness of the opposing and inimical force of international
fascism was spreading rapidly. The extent to which "international
fascism" had substance, even whether it was plausible to speak of it at
all, was open to question before 1935, and it is now, again, in the
writings of scholars and publicists, endlessly argued. But in the decade
that followed 1935 few people in the democracies doubted its reality
and not many doubted its solidity.

There was ample and alarming evidence for its existence on all
sides. Fascist movements were appearing in almost every country in the
western world, from Brazil with its green-shirted Integralistas to the
congeries of fascist and protofascist groups in France. They were extremely conspicuous and mostly extremely violent. They demanded

total destruction of The System, of trafficking parties and politicians, of uncontrolled capitalism, of parliaments and constitutions and the permissive traditions of freedom of the press and civil rights. Often they were anti-Semitic. Always they favored an authoritarian, highly organized, militaristic kind of world in which the institutions of society— religion, education, unions, families, everything—would be absorbed into the state, to the point where state and society were indistinguishable. They had taken over Germany, and it looked as if their Spanish version, the Falange, were going to take over Spain. They seemed to be on the verge of power in places like Romania and Greece and Hungary. International fascism, the polar counterpart of International Communism, was bent on conquering the world and it looked in the later 1930s as if it might do so.

There was no doubt that these movements, however spontaneous some of them might be, were frequently patronized and encouraged by the Italian and, after 1933, the German governments. Almost all of them were very pro-Mussolini and usually pro-Hitler. They were, however, extremely diverse, often divided, often in conflict, although their authoritarianism often permitted (as it had in the matter of German-Italian relations since 1933) their rifts and diversities and factionalism to be hidden. In a country like France, however, where competing fascist groups abounded, their true character was easily discernible. Some were veterans groups, some were merely instruments of personal power for picturesque politicians. Some were proletarian movements of disenchanted socialists and communists. Some were openly the tools of Big Business. Some, in France, were royalist. But the disunity was not particularly reassuring to their enemies, since a similar inner disunity had existed in both the Fascist and Nazi parties and had precluded neither of them from triumphantly establishing its iron and apparently permanent dictatorship. The real weaknesses of fascism as an international force were quite different: the successful parties had the absolute leadership of a special kind of personality, which people like Sir Oswald Mosley notably lacked and which, when it was available, by its very nature made collaboration among the leaders very difficult; and its only universal component was the intense, exclusive, ambitious nationalism of each fascist movement. Again and again, when fascist power did briefly rule Europe, the impossibility of reconciling the ambitions of fascist Spaniards, Italians, French, Slovaks,

Croats, Bulgars, Romanians was demonstrated. International fascism necessarily meant, in the end, a world empire for one nation, and that nation was to be, also necessarily, Germany.

The inner contradictions were clearly perceived by many people, but it was apprehended that so long as international fascism had non-fascist enemies to concentrate on, it could maintain a terrifying and efficacious unity. For many more people there was a natural tendency to conceive of international fascism as a monstrous, menacing monolith. The events in Ethiopia, in the Rhineland, later in Spain, suggested, quite misleadingly, a blueprint. Enormous emotional power was generated by anti-fascism. And men like Franklin Roosevelt had begun to believe that any policy designed to contain Germany must be based upon the recognition that German and Italian fascisms were inseparable.

The kind of diplomatic manipulation that the British experts specialized in, in the interests of separating the two, an aim based on one aspect of reality, suffered from a rapidly diminishing *constituency*. It had no base and no allies. It evoked no emotion. It did not appeal to the Soviet Union or to European Communist parties basking in the growing, glowing prestige of a Communist International that now displayed itself in the guileful garb of anti-fascism. It had the paradoxical effect of persuading many people of the notion that communism and democracy were one pole of a sphere whose other was fascism. Anti-fascism might have been an immensely powerful weapon in the containment of Germany. The British succeeded not only in throwing it away but also in handing it to the Soviet Union.

The makers of British policy believed that they had no course but to accept the *fait accompli*. Eden, however righteous his protests, on April 20, 1936, told Aloisi, the Italian representative at Geneva, that Italy should not misunderstand his public statements. He was, he said, personally opposed to continuing sanctions but, he frankly added, the pressures of public and parliamentary opinion obliged him to pretend that he wasn't.[21] The British persuaded the French of it, too. France was now, for the first and last time in many years, led by a great man, a man of the highest and firmest principles and the most profound perceptions. Léon Blum, the first Socialist to be premier, came to office in June 1936 at the head of a Popular Front ministry composed of

Socialists and Radicals (the same Radicals who had once supported, then abandoned, Laval's government) and dependent on a parliamentary coalition that included the Communists. The parties of the Popular Front had won a huge electoral victory; the Right had met disaster, and the Communists had become for the first time an important group in the Chamber of Deputies.

Blum was determinedly anti-fascist and firmly (although of necessity quietly) anti-communist. He was a humanist, a lover of peace and of people, and an extremely intelligent social reformer. Three years later he was to lead his party, uncertainly divided between doctrinaire pacificism and dislike of fascism, into a militant anti-fascist stand. Ten years later, after spending five years in a German prison, he would be premier again and begin the enormous work of equipping France with the administrative apparatus for a modern and humane society. But in 1936 he was in a difficult and, as it turned out, an impossible position. He was a Jew in a nation where anti-Semitism was growing and virulent and had become the most explosive weapon in the armory of French fascist movements. He was a socialist in a society of frightened magnates and small-property holders. He was an internationalist in a nation whose dying greatness aggravated to the point of madness the imprecations of superpatriots. He was the head of a coalition whose members passionately disagreed and some of whom were determined from the beginning to discredit and destroy it. He was in short premier of a country where civil war seemed an imminent possibility. And he was leading, in an impossible international situation, a nation whose spiritual and physical defenses were weak, a nation which was, or thought it was, almost wholly dependent for its survival upon the support of Great Britain.

Eden visited Blum in Paris in late June to discuss the liquidation of the Ethiopian incident. Blum made a favorable impression on him, and Eden rejoiced in the Frenchman's evidently sincere desire to co-operate with Britain and his deep dislike of the dictatorships. But he was embarrassingly attached to international and collective action to secure peace—and to the League of Nations. The British minister was obliged to explain to Blum that it was too late to try to force Mussolini to his knees, that the continuation, let alone the extension, of sanctions "would almost certainly lead to war, and in view of the collapse of Abyssinia and the Emperor's flight, the task of restoring the *status quo ante* in Abyssinia would be prodigious."[22] Blum reluctantly agreed. He had very little choice.

In Britain the conciliators were coming out of the caves where they had hidden the winter before. It was urgently proposed that sanctions be abandoned at once, that efforts be made to recover Mussolini's friendship, even that British naval strength in the Mediterranean be reduced to conciliate him. Dino Grandi, the Italian ambassador in London, was hopeful that something could be done to improve relations, and Neville Chamberlain, chancellor of the Exchequer and the most energetic and perhaps most influential of the British ministers, warmly backed the project in the cabinet. On June 10, 1936, he did so publicly in a speech. Since the policy of *rapprochement* and the ending of sanctions had not yet been agreed to by the cabinet, his statement was of dubious constitutionality and was certainly tactless. He spoke in no uncertain terms of the idea that sanctions and a strong pro-League policy might yet force the Italians to abandon their new empire:

> That seems to me the very mid-summer of madness. . . . Is it not apparent that the policy of sanctions involves, I do not say war, but a risk of war? . . . Is it not also apparent from what has happened that in the presence of such a risk, nations cannot be relied upon to proceed to the last extremity until their vital interests are threatened?[23]

The resulting uproar in the House of Commons and the country was considerable; it resembled, on a much smaller scale, the uproar at the time of the Hoare-Laval agreement seven months earlier. The parallels were given a certain piquancy by the fact that Hoare had re-entered the cabinet the week before, in the office of first lord of the Admiralty.

Eden made a temporizing statement to the House. It amounted to a more mollient version of Chamberlain's. He said that the decision was up to the League, but that nothing short of military action could reverse the decision already reached in Ethiopia. He also said that so far as was known in London no Abyssinian government survived in any part of the emperor's territory.[24]

The decision to abandon sanctions had already been made, or at least arrived at, by the British cabinet. There had in fact never been any question of doing anything else; it was merely, as Eden frankly observed, a question of how to time it to minimize ructions in the press. There had already been ructions in the House of Commons. Old David Lloyd George, the World War I prime minister, had called the members of the cabinet "poltroons and jellyfish." Such opinions meant, for the cabinet, that an effort had to be made to back down with as much dignity and as little attention as possible.

Help came from abroad. During the course of the month public statements favoring the withdrawal of sanctions were forthcoming from the French and the Canadians, and then from the smaller countries that had been the most ardent supporters of the League as an instrument for preventing aggression—the Scandinavian governments, the Netherlands, Switzerland, Spain. The Union of South Africa was recalcitrant—the government insisted publicly that it would never vote to withdraw sanctions or desert another African state. But it was in a small minority. The position of the majority was certain to prevail.

Sanctions could not now save Ethiopia or stop the aggressor. But the abandonment of sanctions, even if in practice meaningless, was the abandonment of a principle. Of this principle, Haile Selassie was a most oracular defender. He appeared dramatically in Geneva, to defend it before the world forum of principles. He addressed the League Assembly on June 30, 1936, and the world was never quite the same afterward.

The road to Geneva had been a hard one. The *Enterprise*—ill-named—had arrived at Haifa, the port of Palestine, after two days' voyage from Jibuti. The emperor was said, by people who saw him then, to be tired and worn, a pathetic figure now, with no trace left of the epic hero. Some thought he had given up, that he had no will or wish to go on fighting, or ever to return. They may have been right, but if they thought pathos and despair were final they misjudged a complex personality. He had always been moody and sometimes melancholy and irresolute. He had never been without resource or tensile strength.

The imperial party proceeded to Jerusalem. The rulers piously wished to visit the shrines of their faith, the homeland of the founder of their dynasty. Their reception was less than imperial. The Ethiopians were treated like private citizens. They were put up at the King David Hotel—it must have seemed an act of sardonic fate to be guests in a hotel named for the emperor's ancestor. The British high commissioner of Palestine was ostentatiously out of town, and the British consuls in Haifa and the capital did not trouble to meet the emperor. There was no official recognition whatever given to his presence. But treatment as a dethroned exile could not be total, since his position as head of a friendly state was still recognized by almost everybody. And Ethiopia was still a member of the League. That fact was his only trump card.

On May 10 he dispatched a telegram to Geneva saying, "We have decided to bring an end to the most unequal, most unjust, most barbarous war of our age, and have chosen to take the road to exile in order that our people shall not be exterminated and in order to consecrate ourselves wholly and in peace to the preservation of our empire's independence."[25] He called upon the League members to "continue efforts to secure respect for the Covenant" and to refuse to recognize "the exercise of an assumed sovereignty resulting from an illegal recourse to armed forces."

The next day a much more detailed statement was presented to the Secretary-General of the League by an Ethiopian representative, Wolde Mariam. It was very forceful, and it placed different and more compelling emphases upon recent events. It is worth quoting at length as an example of the skillful formulations of the Ethiopian message to the world.

> I. The crime is consummated. The Covenant is in shreds. Article 10 has been outrageously violated. Article 16 has not been applied. In this treacherous war with the Ethiopian warriors struggling with obsolete weapons and supplied with inadequate munitions, the government has been unable to furnish its troops with the means of defense because of the refusal of financial assistance, because of the embargo imposed before the attack, and because of hindrances to the import of arms after the war began. Despite crushing inferiority, the Ethiopian troops passionately resisted the aggressor and held him in check until the moment when the Italian command, despairing of victory if he continued to observe the law of war, had recourse to terror and the extermination of the population by the most atrocious methods known to modern civilization.

> II. The Ethiopian troops and people have been struck with hopelessness by the use of poison gas and by numberless airplanes that have sought a tragic glory through the bombing of ambulances,

burning of defenseless villages, massacres of innocent people. As the Italian chiefs declared, it was a hunt without peril for the hunter.

The appeals of distress issued by the Ethiopian government have not availed to rouse against the criminal aggressor the active support of the signatories of the Covenant.

The Ethiopian people, deserted, were reduced to infinite despair when, at the beginning of the month of March, it became clear that they must abandon the hope and faith they had placed in the League of Nations . . .

III. Will Ethiopia now be abandoned to its pitiless assailant which has struck from the list of nations the name of the world's oldest empire?

I am here to address to all the peoples of the world the protest of the Ethiopian people against the triumphant aggressor. The Italian government has hurled an insolent challenge to the more than fifty nations; it expects to make them retreat before its threats. Today, gory with the blood of its victim, it sits proud and scornful on the Council of the League of Nations, offering as a shameful bargain its promise of collaboration in European affairs, hoping to secure thus exculpation, implicit or express, for its crime.

The Empire of Ethiopia, member of the League of Nations, denounces once again this bargain.

IV. The people of Ethiopia are not crushed.

The largest part of their territory, to the west of the capital, remains free and independent. They continue to defend themselves. They refuse to recognize the illegal occupation forced on them by the Italian army.

They keep in their hearts the memory of other peoples which, before them, have known the horrors of invasion and have freed themselves by a long-continued, patient effort.

Will the League of Nations, itself a victim of Italian aggression, submit to the use of violence?[26]

Most of the facts were perfectly accurate. The rhetoric, however, was much more important than the facts. Today it sounds like a collection of clichés of the sort incessantly uttered by all threatened governments. The letter, like so many of the Ethiopians' documents, was a prototype. It had its precedents in the propaganda statements of oppressed peoples in the past, but now the principles were set forth as a passionate cosmology, presaging very accurately the techniques and "lines" and moral assumptions commonplace in World War II and after. The allegation of brutality, the crescendo of pathos, the charge of imperialism, the hint of racism, the plaintive appeal—all these became the common idiom of later public statements about international relations. They were to be much abused and to lose their impact through abuse. But here, when they were being fused into a fresh idiom, they had the force of novelty and the ring of truth, and they were powerful. It was their power that made the themes clichés. From 1936 on nobody who wanted to complain about the international conduct of anybody else could resist invoking just such style and substance. One of the things that the Ethiopian War demonstrated was how fecund and popular such arguments were; and how dead were those the Italians tried to use against them. The impressiveness of power, the rights of the strong, the glory of empires, the superiority of European minds and European culture and European methods, these were dry and depressing themes. Both Ethiopia and Italy were in fact pleading nationalism and the rights of nations; but the rights of great nations to conquest were no longer so attractive as the rights of small and persecuted ones to resist and—in the jargon of much later times—to fight for liberation.

The League could not deny the injured party a hearing. Nor could its members conveniently recognize at once, as some of them may have intended to do, the Italian title to the newly acquired empire. The interment of Ethiopia could not be carried out without a seemly delay. Public opinion, or a powerful section of it, was still demanding that Mussolini be punished and obliged to disgorge his new empire. Prince Otto von Bismarck, the German chargé d'affaires in London, observed on June 26 the trouble the government was having. "The Englishman," he said, "generally reacts slowly to new facts; and the realization that the disappearance of the Empire of Abyssinia from the map . . . is irrevocable has not quickly penetrated here."[27]

And the Emperor Haile Selassie could not be kept forever in the hotel that was named for his ancestor King David. Not without apprehension that Italy might be irritated, Prime Minister Baldwin agreed to grant him asylum in the United Kingdom, on condition that he would not "participate in any way in the furtherance of hostilities."

It was all very awkward. There was anxiety (it is hard to take it seriously, but it may have been sincere) that the Italians might hijack a British ship to abduct the imperial passenger while he was en route to Britain. The party was picked up at Haifa by a warship on its way home from India, H.M.S. *Capetown*, then transferred to a packet ship, S.S. *Orford*, at Gibraltar once the dangerous Mediterranean waters had been safely traversed. On June 3 Haile Selassie and his family and suite reached London. He was greeted, unexpectedly and embarrassingly, by mobs of Londoners who crowded to Waterloo Station and lined the way to the Ethiopian legation. The emperor's car was ordered by the police to go by a different route.[28] It was typical of the awkwardness of giving asylum to a symbol. But a much greater awkwardness took place in Geneva.

The Council of the League had held a meeting to take the decision on ending sanctions. It had not acted, however; it had been outmaneuvered by the Ethiopians. Their representative, Prince Nasibu, a general who had emerged from the disaster with a record for heroism and military skill, argued persuasively. In the *couloirs*, Colson (who was again with the emperor) told reporters that he was going to ask for a safe-conduct for the emperor through Egypt and the Sudan, to re-enter his country from the back door. It was an ingenious idea, since governments could hardly withhold a safe-conduct to his own country from a ruler whom they all still, in law, regarded as the chief of a friendly state. The Council decided to postpone action until the Assembly, where all the member states were represented, should meet.

The atmosphere in Geneva, and in the League, that June was one of crisis. Nobody doubted what would happen in the end, but much could happen before the end. At the very least, the reputation of the governments that were going to inter the corpse of the League of Nations could be further damaged. At most, there was the possibility that Germany or Italy or both might seize the moment to make war. The nerves of the world were frayed, and there was despair in the air. One woman at Geneva announced to the press that she thought all women should refuse to bear children; it would be a crime, she said, to bring more humans into a world so wicked and so dangerous. A young Czech shot and killed himself in the League building as a protest against the betrayal of small nations.

Into this tense and doom-ridden forum, Haile Selassie made his entry. He had come inconspicuously into the hall where the Assembly met and took his place in the fifth row, where he sat quietly while the President of the Assembly called the meeting to order and read a letter from Mussolini. It was conciliatory. The Italian dictator said the war was over and he had no further intention of disturbing the peace. He promised that he would not conscript Ethiopians into the Italian army—a prospect the British were said to be especially worried about, for fear of the effects upon the inhabitants of their own black colonies and the balance of power in Africa. The delegates who were about to vote for the end of sanctions were reassured.

Then Haile Selassie was called to speak. He made his way to the rostrum, a small, frail, tired figure in a white tunic and black cape. He was, the reporters agreed, immensely dignified and very moving. As he started to speak, there was a sudden uproar in the galleries.

It was started, apparently, by Eugenio Monreale, the Italian press attaché at Vienna, who screamed "Murderer!" at the emperor. The cry was immediately taken up by other Italian press men, who stood up, shouting obscenities, crying out "Long live the Duce!" The disruption assumed the proportions of a riot. Nothing like it had ever been known in the League before. The emperor waited impassively for ten minutes. And then the chairman of the session, the Romanian delegate, Nicolae Titulescu, lost his temper. He shouted a millennially portentous order: *"Throw out the savages."*

The savages were thrown out, and the speaker quietly began again, "I, Haile Selassie I, emperor of Ethiopia, am here today to claim that justice which is due to my people." The contrast to the shrieking Italians exemplified for very many people who heard it, and for many more who read about it, the difference between the good and evil forces in the world.

The incident undoubtedly helped his cause. The *New York Times* correspondent observed, "Nobody believes the offenders acted in the way they did without arrangement."[29] The London *Times* wrote, "It was . . . an illumination of the type of mind behind the Italian policy that Rome should have chosen the moment to organize and let loose upon this solitary figure, bearing his manful part in an international meeting without self-pity, a braying claque of Italian journalists. Nothing else was wanting to add the last touch of dignity to one side . . . and remove the last traces of it upon the other."[30] The London *Times*, like Titulescu, spoke for a new age.

Haile Selassie's speech was a masterpiece. He pointed out that he was the first head of state to address the Assembly—logically, since he was the first head of state whose country had been destroyed in violation of the Covenant. He recalled the futile guarantees that had been given Ethiopia; the statement of fifty nations that aggression had been done; the Italian conduct of hostilities, barbaric, inhumane, and illegal; the treachery of governments that had tried to bargain with the criminal, Italy, in defiance of their obligation. And finally he said what was both ingenious and prescient:

> I assert that the problem submitted to the Assembly today is a much wider one than the removal of sanctions. It is not merely a settlement of Italian aggression. It is collective. It is the very existence of the League of Nations. It is the confidence that each State is to place in international treaties, it is the value of promises made to small States that their integrity and independence be respected and ensured. It is the principle of the equality of states on the one hand or, on the other, the inevitability that they will be forced to accept the bonds of vassalship. In a word, it is international morality that is at stake. Apart from the Kingdom of the Lord there is not on this earth any nation which is superior to any other. . . .
> It is us today. It will be you tomorrow.[31]

It may be read either as skillful propaganda or as an almost religious statement of historical truth and universal morality. It was in fact both. No one imagined that it would alter the decision of the League or the Italian occupation; but no one could deny that it induced both guilt and apprehension among its listeners or that it sounded both taps and reveille through the world.

The appearance of the emperor had the most lasting effect of anything he had ever done or would ever do again. His words, with photographs, were widely reported. A climax was reached in the making of world-wide anti-fascist opinion; if Ethiopia did not immediately benefit, the course of world affairs was nonetheless affected. Middle-aged people, in places far from Switzerland or Ethiopia, who have no other recollection of the history of the 1930s often still remember the aspect of Haile Selassie I and his appeal, the small, dignified, moving figure pleading hopelessly for the rights of his people and his country for freedom before what seemed to be the stone wall of the indifference, cynicism, and selfishness of the great powers and their clients.

It was one of the great moments of sentiment, and therefore of germinal history, in recent times.

Everett Colson heard it as a dying man. He had left Ethiopia in March, two weeks after his heart attack at Dessie; he came to Geneva to hear the Ethiopian appeal. (He lived long enough to perform one other and important service for the sovereign. As a member of the board of the Bank of Ethiopia he completed the bare quorum when it met in exile and made legal the vote to turn over control of its foreign assets, which the Italians were claiming as theirs by right of conquest, to the emperor.) It may be that he had a hand in writing the Geneva speech; it has something of his odd, Yankee combination of canny realism, calculation, and soaring idealism. Whether he did or not, his grief at the occasion must have been mixed with bitter satisfaction at the moral triumph of the emperor's appearance. His career had been spent in the service of black and yellow peoples and governments, and he must have understood much better than most of the delegates the iniquities and fragilities of a world ruled by Europeans. He died a few weeks later, and his death must be counted a punctuation mark in the narrative of the rise and fall of empires.

"For the little good it can do him now, Haile Selassie has and will hold a high place in history. His legend may not be without a growing force hereafter." The London *Times* was prophetic (which it rarely was in these years), and it went on to say, "Is there another in history who has deserved more of fortune and his fellows and has received less?"[32] There were similar pronouncements elsewhere. The *New York Times*, disrobed of its cautious impartiality, said, "The Italian victory was a victory over all of us."[33] The Chicago *Tribune*, an influential and strident voice of isolation in the American press, rejoiced in the discrediting of the League and drew the lesson that no nation could put faith in altruistic international organizations. But by doing so the *Tribune* made the emperor a hero and added its voice to the chorus of sympathy for the rights of small nations and its stress on the evils of aggression. It was a revealing twist; readers who shared the *Tribune*'s opinion that "The League of Nations might well be wishing to trade its new 10 million dollar palace for a good answer to Haile Selassie"[34] might agree that the League was a fraud and the Europeans were rascals; they also had to be left with a corresponding conviction that Ethiopia was the embodiment of a noble cause. For isolationists of the *Tribune* stamp, it was the beginning of ambiguity and therefore of uncertainty. And this ambiguity characterized much of the rest of American editorial response among isolationists of the opposite, leftist, coloration and of internationalists as well. The lesson drawn was of the failure of the League and the decadent democracies of Europe to meet the sinister threat of naked and insatiable aggression. *The Nation* was still, sporadically, in the mood of casting a plague on both houses, but it could not avoid this inference. *The New Republic*, now sternly anti-Fascist, was more explicit; it said that the conduct of the Italian journalists at Geneva must seem indescribably shocking to Americans and that Haile Selassie represented the cause of "honor" as opposed to prestige.[35] *Time* magazine summed up the pregnant confusion of American opinion succinctly: "Everyone agreed it was a great speech, one of the noblest, most factual, irrefutable and moving ever made before the League of Nations. Yet it was totally without effect on Geneva's slick, hard, slippery statesmen."[36] Antipathy to the conciliation of dictators was growing. *Time*'s words were as much a text as Roosevelt's, seven months earlier, for an American crusade.

Such implications were not unnoticed by the slick, hard, slippery statesmen. The *Revue des Deux-Mondes*, dedicated to the most old-fashioned kind of diplomacy and to the conciliation of Italy, deplored in strong terms the fact Haile Selassie had been allowed to appear. He had produced, it said, a scandal, "a psychological shock" that made the work of serious statesmen difficult or impossible.[37] It would not have been possible to find a more precise vindication for the indignation of the Chicago *Tribune* and *Time* magazine. The New World was being called into existence, once again, to redress the balance of the Old.

But this aspect of things was just beginning to show itself. More noticeable was the inference that Ethiopia was the first of the dominoes. It did not help Ethiopia; it had indeed the paradoxical consequence of pushing the Ethiopian problem into oblivion. For all attention from now on turned to the places—European places—where the next aggressions of Germany and Italy could be expected. The Spanish Civil War, which was about to begin, would hasten the process the Ethiopian War had inaugurated, of convincing people that the world was divided three ways, into peaceloving democrats (including, for some, Josef Stalin of the Soviet Union), the aggressive autocracies of which Roosevelt had spoken, and the cynical and effete leaders in Western Europe. After June 30, 1936, the British had their way, which was also the way of the French and the Italians, and the Ethiopian Question was buried. But it smoldered, volcanolike. The memory of the emperor's speech at Geneva was very clinging.

The burial of the body, although not entirely dead, was now rapidly carried out in stages. After a decent interval of three weeks, the League Assembly voted formally to end sanctions. The French, British, and Soviet delegates spoke in favor of doing so. Only the delegate of South Africa spoke against it.

The Ethiopians introduced resolutions that members should not recognize the Italian conquest and that a loan should be made available to support resistance to the occupiers. Paul van Zeeland of Belgium, introduced a different one, that sanctions be lifted without delay. The Ethiopian resolutions were defeated twenty-three to one. The other was carried with one opposing vote and four abstentions. On July 15 the Co-ordinating Committee voted to abandon sanctions.

Nothing had been settled, in Ethiopia or anywhere else. Mussolini's position after victory was not less painful than before. By midsummer the generals' coup in Spain had turned into a civil war. It was another costly drain for the Italian government, which had committed itself to a rebel victory. His ideological partner in Germany was taking advantage of his moment of need. Not only had the Rhineland invasion, which Mussolini had never really liked, been forced on him, but Hitler was moving further toward Nazi meddling in Austrian affairs. The Italians were experiencing what everybody else in the world would shortly experience: the relentless tendency of Nazi Germany to take advantage equally of victory and concession to win more victories and demand more concessions. Prince Ernst von Starhemberg, the Austrian vice chancellor, a sort of pocket *duce* who led an Austrian Fascist movement that was patriotic, pro-Italian, anti-German, had been forced to resign on May 12, 1936, at German insistence. The Germans said they were interested only in protecting the civil rights of Austrian Nazis, but everyone knew they wanted much more than that. Indeed, although Mussolini didn't know it, Hitler sometimes hinted to his associates that the new German empire must one day reach into northern Italy. (It would also, he observed to Albert Speer, include Norway.[38])

The situation suggested to the Italians the desirability of playing the two sides against each other. Such a policy led to troublesome deceptions. In May Baron Aloisi had told the suspicious German ambassador in Rome that rumors about Italian readiness to renew cooperation with the British and French were "entirely erroneous" and that "relations with Germany were in every respect satisfactory; without previous agreement we had played into one another's hands."[39] Mussolini remained dependent on Germany. He still needed German imports. And he was anxious to secure German recognition of the annexation of Ethiopia, which the Germans cautiously, even coyly, refused to give. (The German foreign ministry told Hassell in Rome, "We cannot go so far as to allow ourselves to be used as a cat's paw."[40]) But friendship with Britain was needed, too, as a counterweight to Germany. In Berlin, Italians practiced a sort of extortion. Advances for renewed friendship with Britain were delicately alluded to in conversations with the Germans on frequent occasions in an effort to apply pressure. The Germans were not going to yield to the Italians' pressures—Italian leverage was negligible, now that the Rhineland had been reoccupied.

The flush of victory had had other unfortunate effects on the victor, which made the position of Italy still more difficult. Mussolini felt himself, from time to time, a conqueror of more than Ethiopia, and while he might make advances to the British he had no intention of making concessions to them. One symptom of the impulse to further aggression was Spain. Another was his choice of a new foreign minister. On June 9 he appointed to the foreign ministry Count Galeazzo Ciano, his son-in-law, a career Fascist rather than a career diplomat, the man who had been so daring and colorful a pilot in the Ethiopian campaign and so had become a symbolic embodiment of the youth, audacity, and dynamism of Fascism. It was a symptomatic of other aspects of Fascism that Ciano was a morose and skeptical pessimist behind his mien of virile braggart.

In Ethiopia the situation after the emperor's flight belied the trumpeted triumph in Rome. The American minister at Addis Ababa, Cornelius Engert, was informing the State Department of the extremely limited and precarious nature of the Italian occupation. On June 18, 1936, he reported that the war was far from over and that *de facto* Italian authority had not been established. Almost half of Ethiopia was beyond the sphere of even nominal Italian control, and the Italian forces dared not enter it. He said there was even some question as to whether they could continue to hold Addis Ababa against the mounting hostility and daring of the populace. The American chargé d'affaires in Rome, Alexander Kirk, accepted the Italian government's assertions that the country had been subdued and that *de facto* authority was in full control, but Engert's reports properly were given more weight.

There was also in Washington a clear understanding of what were regarded as the nature of the dictatorships and the imperatives of morality. The Americans realized that revoking executive acts designed to inhibit Italy would, like the withdrawal of sanctions, do much more than adjust policy to reality; it would mean approval of buccaneering. As Engert suggested, such a policy would amount to a futile gesture of placating bandits. Washington compromised: revocation of the embargo on arms shipments was unavoidable, but in keeping with the old and peculiar American tradition of not "recognizing" changes brought about by the illegal use of force, the government refused to accept either *de facto* or *de jure* the new Italian empire. For the next five years Haile Selassie remained, for the United States, the only legal representative of the government of Ethiopia. It was true, too, of the Soviet Union and a few other states, including black Haiti. So far as Europe was concerned, Ethiopia was interred in oblivion, and the Italians could continue their effort to make a colony. But there was no comfort for Italy. The obstinacy of the two most powerful nations in the world was an ill omen for the legions that had won so glorious a victory.

11

Invictus

The life of the new Italian empire was poor, brutish, and short. That was not new. Poverty, brutality, and brevity were the hazards of new empires. For hundreds of years European states had been facing colonial uprisings. They had often lost colonies to other European states and, sometimes, to European settlers; they had not previously lost one to its indigenes. Not before had a conquered government returned in triumph to replace the colonizers. The novelty was solemnly sealed when the emperor of Ethiopia, thirty-five years after the Italians took his country, paid a state visit to Rome and was received by Italy with honor, apology, and reparation.

This shift in the world's arrangement of power and morality was secular and ecumenical, but some of the things that caused it were peculiar to Ethiopia. The Italians, in their efforts to govern their new colony, were not merely anachronistic but also needlessly improvident. The Ethiopians had an acute awareness of their heritage as an ancient polity, and they were not accustomed to being abject. In 1936, however, the conventions of the European Age were strong enough to hide the fact that Ethiopia was a special case. Europeans assumed that this conquest was final, as earlier conquests had been, that Badoglio's entry into Addis Ababa transformed Ethiopia from a matter of high international concern into an obscure domestic concern of Italy's. This was partly a consequence of the crazy legalisms from the nineteenth century, which hopefully proclaimed that what went on inside one country was of no proper concern to others. It was partly the result of Italian policy. After the occupation of Addis, foreign legations and consulates were one by one closed, foreign journalists left or were expelled, and an extremely rigid censorship was imposed. News of Italian Ethiopia was scarce and remained so for five years.

The tightness of the controls was something new in colonial administration, and it was a symptom of the streamlined obsolescence of the whole venture. Fascism, translated into colonial conquest, was the final caricature of Mazzini's hopes of making all men brothers by making them all Italians. The Ethiopian resistance was the negation of these hopes. Adowa had been the overture, faintly heard, to the breakup of colonial empires. Now the drama began in earnest.

In this theatrical episode Marshal Graziani was a principal personage. He may be seen as the exemplar of important aspects of Italian Fascism: its wholesale inhumanity, its sporadic conviction that boldness and superior fire power were the determinants of history, its conversion of neurosis into a system of government. But he was more than a symbol. He was decidedly an individual against whose excesses even loyal Fascists revolted. A definition of Fascism was expressed in his conduct, but his conduct contributed to the definition of Fascism. His policies were often the execution of orders from Rome, but the orders owed a good deal to his suggestions, and the execution was his own. So were, literally, the executions: he is said to have enjoyed personally shooting captured rebels in his palace garden.[1]

Badoglio had been appointed viceroy when Victor Emmanuel was proclaimed emperor. Under his rule, the ruins of the capital, palpable and impalpable, were cleaned up. Ten thousand Italian troops maintained order in the city. Citizens who had fled—50,000 of them, the Italians said—returned. Symbols of lost independence were removed, including six lions, survivors of the imperial menagerie, which were shot. Shops reopened. The construction of the new regime began. Its fiat, however, ran only along well-patrolled highways and in the capital and a few provincial towns. Addis Ababa itself was rumored to be practically surrounded by Ethiopian warriors, largely without weapons but sufficiently numerous (the American legation reported) to make it impossible for Italians to leave the city unless escorted by at least a thousand soldiers.

There was, in Badoglio's time, still an Ethiopian government on native soil. If Victor Emmanuel had his viceroy, so did Haile Selassie. Prince Imru had been appointed by the emperor head of government and commander of the armed forces. He had gone to Gore, where earlier Haile Selassie had planned to establish a provisional capital. It was 250 miles west of Addis Ababa in wild regions where the Italians had not even tried to extend their occupation. Imru had set up a skeletal but organized administration. From a legal point of view it might properly have been regarded as the legitimate government. It commanded the allegiance of the public authorities and people in the region. It did not, however, command any considerable fighting force. It had no source of supply for arms, and fruitless efforts to keep communications open reduced the stores still further. It did not exercise effective authority over the rest of the empire. Prince Desta was again in control of his own province of Sidamo in the south. Other leaders, operating independently of one another, were engaged not so much in resisting the Italians—there were, indeed, no Italians to resist in most of the country—as in establishing chieftaincies, roles that combined those of seigneurial lord and brigand leader. The Ethiopia of the days before the strong emperors of the nineteenth century was re-emerging.

When armed Ethiopians *did* come upon Italians, they usually killed them. The Italian air force commander, General Magliocco, whom Badoglio had embraced on the legation steps the day he entered the capital, made a forced landing in the country southwest of Addis and was surrounded by a resistance force. He and all but one of his party were shot to death. This sort of thing made government difficult and shook Italian morale, but the rain made extension of Italian military control impossible. The weather, however, did not prevent efforts to achieve it by other means. Badoglio tried to control the situation by efficient administration coupled with severity and bribes. Under martial law, the death penalty was decreed for a long list of offenses, including looting. About a hundred people were executed in Addis Ababa during the first few days of the occupation. To more important persons, pardon was offered in return for swearing allegiance to Victor Emmanuel, and during the next month many of the surviving dignitaries of the empire swore the oath—the renegade Prince Hailu (who had been taken as a prisoner by the emperor's party on its flight to Jibuti, but released in Diredawa); Prince Seyum, captured in Tigre after an unsuccessful effort to raise the province against the occupiers—made their submissions. They brought with them—temporarily—the control of several regions. Their statements of fealty, florid and magniloquent, were published in the Italian papers.

Badoglio's tenure lasted only a few weeks. He returned to Italy at the end of May. Graziani was appointed in his place, and the policy of pacification by suasion was revised. More systematic methods were adopted. On June 6 it was ordered from Rome that all rebels be immediately executed. Graziani interpreted this instruction in the broadest possible way, to include mass executions of suspects. No consideration at all was given to the proposition that men fighting in organized troops should be treated, when captured, as prisoners of war. The killers of Magliocco and his companions, who were in fact imperial cadets in uniforms, were apprehended. Three hundred of them—not all 300, obviously, were guilty of the murders—were shot. The Italians, still obliged to fight, nevertheless regarded the war as over and Ethiopian soldiers as traitors. The Ethiopians abroad publicly protested this policy, and the minister in London wrote to the press denouncing it as illegal and barbarous. His legal position was strong, for Britain had not recognized the conquest, but his influence was negligible.

Nor was it only armed opponents who suffered. When raiders made two brief sallies into Addis Ababa from the hills on July 28, the bishop of Dessie (several hundred miles away) was shot in the town square on the following day in reprisal—presumably *pour encourager les autres*. It was said that he was a moving spirit of the resistance movement, but his connection with the particular raids was exiguous. Uneasy Italian soldiers, acting sometimes on orders and sometimes merely out of well-founded fear, continued to kill suspect civilians on their own authority. Often there was no apparent ground for suspicion. There were other innovations. The Fascist salute was decreed as obligatory for all greetings and as a deferential salutation to members of the occupation. Italian military courts replaced the Ethiopian courts.

It was observed that whenever the Italians occupied a new area, often with the initial acquiescence of the populace and local authorities, they rapidly made themselves so much disliked that attacks on them, at first rare, became constant. The fact proved important when the clean-up campaign got underway after the rains stopped in September. Mussolini promised that the "pacification" of Ethiopia would be even more rapid than its "conquest"—a statement made in late October. It did proceed fairly fast once the weather permitted. In Gore, Prince Imru was defeated. By the end of 1936 he had only a few left of his force which had once counted 12,000, and those were ridden by disease and wounds and largely without supplies. Imru surrendered. He fared better than most of the resistance leaders. He was taken to Italy and held captive there for seven years—for a time, by a neat irony, on the island of Ponza, where Mussolini was to be imprisoned after his fall in 1943. The other princes who were still fighting fared less well. Three sons of Prince Kassa, all still in the field with small forces, were surrounded, captured, and shot (along with most of their men) in December. Prince Desta, with a larger force on his home territory, succeeded in beating off or eluding the Italians for a little longer. But most of his army was captured in February 1937, and on February 24 he was taken, summarily tried by a court-martial, and sent before a firing squad.

The tangible remnants of the Ethiopian state were now disposed of, but from the villages came imaginative ways of fighting the occupier. Guerrillas, led sometimes by new men, younger, often in close touch with country people, took over the resistance. They were able to call on popular emotion to engage in a kind of combat for which they were singularly well equipped and for which the Italian army was not equipped at all. The liquidation of organized forces increased rather than reduced the tempo and temper of conflict. Then the new native forces, recapitulating the old work of state building, began the long process of coalescing into a united and organized national movement. A leader emerged, a member of a family of princes and officials and himself a former police officer, who in the fall of 1936 commenced the construction of an Ethiopian national movement. Abebe Aragai was to become, much later, the emperor's appointed commander of the Patriots, as they were called. Much earlier he had begun to make himself a genuine, autochthonous, national leader. The revival of Ethiopia began anew at the grass roots.

Some Europeans, too, resisted the Italian effort to civilize Ethiopia. A powerful and exemplary contributor to the frustration of the Italians was a French businessman, Antonin Besse, who represented Royal Dutch Shell. Before the invasion he had known of the rapid increases in purchases of gasoline in Eritrea, had warned the emperor about it, and had assisted the government in increasing its own stocks of fuel. He was expelled as undesirable by the occupying authorities in January 1937 and thereafter devoted himself to building head-quarters for the resistance in Jibuti and Aden. His communications with Ethiopia were excellent, and much of what the world learned about conditions under the occupation was due to M. Besse's activities. He also provided a channel for smuggling currency to the resistance leaders.[2]

The new resistance and its dangers vastly irritated Marshal Graziani. After the capture of Prince Imru and the destruction of the agencies legitimate Ethiopian government, he had announced that "all Ethiopia" was under his control. This turned out to be an embarrassing claim, and its very falseness dictated a furious intensification of his policy. "We must continue," he is said to have remarked in late October 1936, "with the work of total destruction."[3] He ordered bombing and gas attacks on guerrilla forces in areas whose terrain made them inaccessible to the occupying army. Sporadic outbreaks throughout late 1936 were dealt with according to the rule that rebels, and suspected rebels, were to be executed out of hand. The official *Italian* reports on the results of this program are staggering.[4] As they duly noted, the Ethiopian resisters dealt quite as harshly with traitors among their own people as the Italians did with the rebels, but the disorder and the casualties constituted an indictment of Italy. Mass shootings became common occurrences. Pitched battles were fought everywhere. Nor was the occupiers' effort rewarded with any success. A large part of the country remained completely closed to Italians and virtually independent of all external control. The important provinces of Begemder and Gojam, north and northwest of the capital, and most of southwestern Ethiopia remained in the hands of the resistance.[5] Graziani, not the first or last proconsul to find himself on such a treadmill, reacted to frustration in monstrous ways.

On February 19, 1937, in the imperial palace where the viceroy had established his residence and the seat of the government, he arranged a celebration of the birth of an heir to the Italian throne, the prince of Naples, son of Prince Humbert and Princess Marie José. This event was to be greeted by an ancient local practice: when heirs were born to the Ethiopian throne, it was customary for the emperor to distribute largesse to the deserving poor in the palace garden.

Some 3,000 deserving poor were lined up in the garden in front of a large table upon which Maria Theresa dollars were spread. Each deserving poor person was to take one dollar and then proceed to refreshments, in the presence of the primate and the great officers of the viceroyalty. As people were beginning to move forward to pick up their dollars, nine hand grenades were thrown, one after another, into the group of presiding dignitaries. Thirty of them were seriously injured, including the viceroy (presumably their principal target), several generals, and the mayor of the capital. The *carabinieri* acting as guards fired on the deserving poor in the belief that more grenades might be expected unless the crowd were instantly dispersed. The firing continued for three hours while the Ethiopians tried to escape. A very large number of them were killed before order was restored in the palace garden, which at the end, it was officially reported, was "littered with bodies."[6]

The murderous reaction of the *carabinieri* was due to loss of poise. What happened next was an act of policy. On the orders of the wounded viceroy, the Fascist squadrons began that afternoon a three-day program of reprisal. The grenades had, it turned out, been thrown by two adventurous and injudicious young men (interestingly, they were Eritreans, not Ethiopians, and were employees of the Italian government) who had been supplied with them by one of the new commanders of the guerrilla movement. Although their identity was known, all three men escaped with their lives. But many did not. Throughout the Italian-controlled parts of the empire there was a massacre. There were large-scale atrocities, both bizarre and blood-curdling. In one valley in the capital, where hundreds of women and children had come to do their washing in a stream, machine-gunners opened fire. No attempt was made to save the injured or to bury the bodies. The place was at the edge of the European quarter, which shortly became uninhabitable from the stench of rotting corpses. An Armenian merchant bought, at his own expense, enough gasoline (which was difficult to find) to drench the bodies and burn them.[7]

The occupying authorities also used gasoline. It is reported (by an Italian) that they would spray houses, huts, and shops occupied by living persons and then set fire to them. In this fashion, whole quarters were destroyed with their inhabitants. This was reported in the Italian press as "cleaning up" sections of the city "suspected of harboring seditious elements."[8] The Fascists who took part in it were in large part not soldiers but civilian party members, amateur *squadristi*, some of them long-time residents in the country. Del Boca wrote, "Many of these maniacs were known to me personally. They were tradesmen, chauffeurs, officials—people I'd always thought of as law-abiding and respectable, people who'd never fired a shot during the entire war—I'd never even suspected at all this hatred was bottled up in them."[9]

It is said that 30,000 people were killed—this is the figure given by the Ethiopian government. Other estimates run very much lower—as few as 1,400—but people who were there put the number higher than that. In any case it is impossible to compute; records were not kept by the killers.

The slaughter was, in some of its more appalling aspects, the product of a release from civic inhibitions, just as the May 1935 slaughter had been. But that had been the consequence of the collapse of authority. This time slaughter had been initiated and approved *by* authority, in the person of the viceroy. It was also rewarded by him: the more active participants were given medals. Graziani was reported by several people who were in close contact with him to have been very badly affected by the attempt on his life; as General Alessandro Lessona said, "he displayed an excess of cruelty that led to even more widespread rebellion, and finally to his removal."[10] He is said to have written in an official dispatch, "After the attempt on my life on February 19, I learned through departmental channels and police headquarters that the greatest menace to public order came from the soothsayers, traditional story tellers . . . it was essential to root out this unhealthy and dangerous element [so] I gave orders that all the soothsayers, story tellers, and witch doctors . . . were to be rounded up and shot."[11] Apparently this class of persons was shot in large numbers. And even larger numbers were involved in a program aimed at eliminating what might be called the opposite class of persons, the educated and westernized minority who had been trained to form a governing elite.

Graziani and the authorities in Rome thought it expedient to wipe out all educated people in Ethiopia. The program was logical from the point of view from which Fascists tended, spasmodically anyway, to consider problems of state. The building of an empire was like perfecting a new and intricate machine whose inefficient or superfluous parts had to be discarded. The educated class had been created to serve as an administrative corps for the former regime. This class was, from the state-as-machine standpoint, no longer necessary, since its functions would be performed by Italians. More cogently, it was almost by definition loyal to the idea of an independent Ethiopia. Like other elites in what are now called "emerging" nations, it was the probable source of leadership and passion for nationalist ideas of a modern sort. It was certainly, in its opposite way, a more likely source of intractable opposition than witch doctors and soothsayers.

Graziani evidently formally submitted the program for exterminating Ethiopian intelligentsia to Rome for approval. And Rome formally approved it, with the provision that it should be carried out in secrecy with as few witnesses as possible.[12] The viceroy specified the classes of people who were to be killed: holders of university degrees and high school diplomas; members of the Young Ethiopia Party; officers and cadets of the imperial military academy.

This wholesale readjustment of the mechanism of Ethiopian society was begun, but the extent to which it was completed is conjectural. Some think that there were only a few hundred killed, but an American government man who has studied the matter thinks that some 6,000 people in the condemned categories were eliminated. It is said in Ethiopia that when the Italian regime ended, there were only two university graduates and twelve high school graduates alive in the entire empire. It appears to be true that (considering that the intelligentsia was very small in 1936) there was literally a lost generation of educated Ethiopians.

Other categories (as distinct from innumerable individuals) suffered. The most important national institution to survive the Italian conquest was the Church. It was natural that an effort should be made to terrorize and control it. The primate, who had collaborated with Badoglio and was one of those wounded in the attack on Graziani, later opposed Italian control and retired to Egypt, his native land. Archbishop Peter of Addis Ababa, a popular figure, was publicly shot and became a martyr and hero. Most of the episcopacy disappeared; two bishops were executed in July 1936, and others followed them or went into exile.

On the other hand, efforts were made to conciliate some groups.

The Italians had strongly emphasized the role of religious freedom in their mission. The efforts at dividing and ruling, begun as political warfare long before the border was crossed, continued as official policy. Favor was given non-Christian peoples, most of them the Moslems, who were thought to be particularly susceptible to Italian guarantees of protection against oppressors. There were, for example, suggestions for a Greater Somalia, to be erected as a separate entity of Italian East Africa. In 1937 Graziani's photograph, showing him addressing a crowd of Moslems, appeared in a German magazine with the caption, "I will liberate you from the slavery of the Amharas."[13]

This policy was based on realities, and it might have helped to consolidate Italian rule if it had been consistently adopted as a guiding principle. But it was completely overshadowed by one of the strangest of all the anomalies and mistakes in Fascist dealings with the Ethiopians. It was Fascist Italy that invented, before the South Africans had thought of it, the principle of *apartheid*.

This singularly rigid system of racial segregation had no precedents in Italian colonial policy. Somalia and Eritrea had both been run in a largely authoritarian way (although local populations had been associated in the administration), but the authority was paternalistic in form and intention, and there was no separation of races. Racial prejudice and discrimination and theories of the superiority of one ethnic group to another were peculiarly absent from the tradition of the Italian homeland and, in earlier years, from Fascist doctrine. Mussolini, in trying to justify the war to Britain and France, had talked about the threat to white rule in the rest of Africa and about the war as a test of white supremacy. But until 1935 he had been consistently a theorist of cosmopolitanism, as an admirer of Imperial Rome would have to be. He had repeatedly recognized and applauded the fact that Italian civilization had been built by a blending of many peoples. On several occasions he had denounced the racial theories of the Nazis. He had expressed his outrage at the treatment of Jews to the German government when Hitler became chancellor—there were Jews in high position in the Fascist hierarchy. Of all European societies, Italy had always been, and still was, the one least inclined to espouse notions of *genetic*, as distinct from *national*, superiority. A great deal had been written in Italy about the benefits to Ethiopia of equality for all races. One poet exuberantly observed, "When Ethiopia's ours, we'll be one vast united family."[14]

With the conquest of Ethiopia an enormous aberration took place. "Italian policy," a French journalist observed three years later, "rejects the doctrine of assimilation as both false and dangerous."[15] But the regulations governing the relations between Italians and Ethiopians that began to be issued as soon as the vice-regal government was set up went far, far beyond "rejecting the doctrine of assimilation." The Italians eventually produced a remarkably complete blueprint for segregation based quite explicitly on the importance of preventing Italian blood from being tainted by mixture with the blood of Africans. In March 1937, shortly after the attack on Graziani, an Italian newspaper had as a front-page headline THE FASCIST EMPIRE MUST NEVER BECOME AN EMPIRE OF MULATTOS. Paolo Monelli, later to write a sensational exposé of Mussolini's personal life and to take a strong anti-Fascist line, wrote in the accompanying article that all Ethiopian women, of whatever ethnic origin, were "equally filthy, they stink of ancient dirt," and added that thoughts of interbreeding "spring from a kind of mentality we want nothing to do with, a puerile mentality sicklied o'er with false romanticism, a mentality that is diseased.[16] General Lessona, now the minister of colonies, warned against diluting "the blood of the dominant race."[17] And the government pronounced, in an official document, "Italy is the first European nation to uphold the universal principle of the superiority of the white race and take the appropriate steps to ensure that the purity of its blood is not polluted by miscegenation."[18]

Concern for the purity of the white race was translated into extremely strict laws forbidding mixed marriages and the cohabitation of an Italian with an Ethiopian woman (the Italian was liable for five years' imprisonment, although no penalties were imposed on the Ethiopian). But the restrictions were not only eugenic: Ethiopians were forbidden to enter the restaurants, movie houses, parks, and all other places of entertainment reserved for whites. An Italian court adjudged it libel, for which damages could be collected, to call a white man an "Abyssinian."[19]

The segregationist décor of the Italian regime in Ethiopia was perhaps not very important; it did not much affect what would have been logically expectable practices. But it is interesting that the prac-

tices should have been *justified* by principles so remote from the
Italian tradition, so contradictory of the previous propaganda line,
and so unpleasantly prophetic. One explanation could have been the
desire of the government at Rome to impress and to associate itself
with Nazi Germany. This later influenced, probably determined, the
adoption in 1938 of anti-Semitism as an official creed of Italian Fascism. Mussolini's progressive dependence on Germany led him, in
many spheres, to slavish emulation.

The adoption of such principles both in official programs and as
loudly trumpeted by the Italian publicists at home may be taken as
representing the logical extreme of European colonial dominion. It
was the final expression, in a symbolic way anyhow, of the subordina-
tion of the rest of the world to Europeans. Like the annexation of
Ethiopia itself, it came at a time when the *idea* of a world run by
westerners was just on the verge of disintegration. The real bases for
such an idea had been undermined long before; its inherent weakness
was being shown by the extreme difficulty the Italians were having in
subduing their new colony and the even greater difficulty they were
having in providing what had once been the real foundation and
justification for colonies, a flow of capital resources from the colonizing
power into them. Italy was the weakest of the great powers of
Europe from this standpoint, but none of them had, any longer, the
kind of surplus of power and money to assure their supremacy in
the world.

Italian attempts to exploit Ethiopia demonstrate very clearly both
the limitations of tangible power and the ambiguity of the purposes
for which that power was supposed to be exercised. It was an old
problem. As Robert Hess has shown in his careful study of Somalia,
Italians had no coherent idea or intention about exactly what a colony
was or was supposed to *become*; colonialism for Italy was in part
anyway simply a projection of national greatness and glory. The benefits that colonial enthusiasts talked about were all either prophecies or
rationalizations. A similar situation existed in Ethiopia.

The prophecies reflected an idea of civic good that in the nineteenth and early twentieth centuries many Europeans took for granted:
order, stability, commerce, the expansion of wealth based on investment. These were supposed to benefit businessmen and home and
give colonial peoples a taste of prosperity and progress. This notion

of progress required capital equipment, which often meant sacrifices for the population at home, but it achieved wide acceptance, transcending geographical and ideological lines. It informed the whole of the Soviet system, for example, where the creation of capital equipment became and was long to remain an article of faith. It was later to inform the policies of most of the emancipated colonies. And it was the idea that capital equipment must be created—almost for its own sake—that informed the Italian policy in Ethiopia.

Considering the obstacles—the scarcity of surpluses and the budgetary difficulties in Italy, the fact that no return could be expected for years—the capital investment in Ethiopia looks staggering. Haile Selassie, when he returned to his country in 1941, was astounded and impressed by what had been done. Educated Ethiopians since have tempered their memories of Fascist brutalities with admiration for Italian munificence and particularly for Italian technical accomplishments. One may discern a conscious Italian effort to make manifest parallels with the Roman empire; perhaps one may imagine dedication to the kinds of public works that had been that empire's cornerstone. The remarkable skills that had earlier built the Italian railroad system and were later to build its incredible highway system through Alpine and Apennine landscapes not altogether unlike Ethiopia's, were for five years applied, at enormous cost, to the pursuit of undefined aims.

There were some aspects of the program that were reasonable enough, given the assumptions about capital development. Two facts were seen as justifying the outlay. First, any increase in the wealth and productivity of Ethiopia demanded vast improvements in transport, health, education, and hydroelectric power. Secondly, it was hoped to make Ethiopia attractive for Italy's surplus population. This was reasonable in economic if not in human or political terms. Italians who settled as farmers would improve their own standard of living and relieve unemployment and rural poverty at home. But such practical objectives were evidently a small part of the reason for the enormous flow of Italian public investment into the new colony. It was in much larger part a reflex, often romantic and sometimes frivolous, to build an image of Italian civilization in Africa and to equip it with the familiar amenities. It remains today a source of wonder to Ethiopians that so much time, money, and effort were expended on, for example, mineral baths.

The spa—a popular nineteenth-century European institution, densely inhabited by shades of ancient Romans—seems to have been an almost obsessive preoccupation with the Italians. A number of such resorts, equipped with comfortable hotels and medical services, appeared in the unlikely setting of the Shoan mountains. Cultural self-assertion may be inferred: a luxurious thermalism was a symbol of the gulf between ruling foreigners and unwashed natives. But the impression of extravagant romanticism remains.

The roads were no less extravagantly romantic. Their construction could be described, more plausibly than spas could, as a realistic capital investment. But even for military purposes they seem to have been in some cases more of a gesture than the fulfillment of a need. It may certainly be questioned whether they were of any benefit to the members of a society that, when it was not based on pure subsistence agriculture, was at most completely local in its marketing, and where donkeys were usually the only available form of transport. Nonetheless, the road building is for a later generation of Ethiopians the most impressive Italian contribution to their country, and Italians who still live there boast of it. During the short life of the Italian empire, 3,000 miles of roads were built. Some of them, in particular the road from Asmara to Gondar, which traverses the breath-taking gorge of the Tacazze and the even more breath-taking mountains south of it, still seem almost unbelievable achievements. Seen from the air the Tacazze highway composes a picture of man's triumph over hostile nature of almost Miltonian grandeur.

The record of construction of projects more immediately useful than highways was not less startling. Hospitals, power lines, post offices, schools, hotels, telephone system, all burgeoned. It was, of course, a drop in the bucket. A foot traveler might wander forever through the empire without seeing any of them. And, like the spas, and even the roads, some of these amenities were for the convenience of the occupiers and the development of *their* economy. Still, regarded simply as a feat and an investment, their construction was imposing in the highest degree.

The effort to settle immigrants under their own flag was less successful. Some publicists envisaged 10,000,000 Italian settlers in Ethiopia. Prompt attention was given to encouraging them. Credit facilities were provided. According to the ministry of agriculture 3,500 families were settled in newly built villages that reproduced in appearance and amenity the best of their home provinces. The conditions of life, however, were precarious in Ethiopia. There was no flow of pioneers. The will to leave home was lacking.

All told, Italy spent about 10 billion lire on its colonizing effort. In the end all of the tangible Italian achievements were inherited by the Ethiopian state, and some of them proved valuable to the Ethiopian people. But for Italy, the effects were summed up by a British observer: "Naboth's vineyard viewed from within was not what it had seemed to be from a distance. Minerals which could have justified the lavish expenditure on sea bases, public works, roads and bridges, had not been found in quantities that would repay the necessary machinery; the expected discovery of oil had not been made; trade was negligible; public security was nonexistent and revenue from agriculture could not be collected in consequence."[20] The new Italian empire turned out, like so many of Mussolini's accomplishments at home, to be a very expensive and unrewarding form of ostentation.

Everything, in short, went badly. Within a year of Graziani's appointment there was dissatisfaction in the inner circles of Fascism with his administration—not yet, it would appear, because of his severities but because of the slow pace of both pacification and development. There was "nothing to be pleased about" in the living conditions and "progress" in Ethiopia, Augusto Turati, a former secretary-general of the party, told Ciano in October 1937.[21] It was not agreed whose fault this was. The minister for East Africa was blamed by some. He himself blamed the Italian people for their lack of pioneering spirit—the Fascists who regarded their mission as being to redeem Italians from idleness were annoyed by the intractable hedonisms of the immigrants. They were said to display a "certain luxury mentality which is in opposition to the discipline of Fascism."[22] Some of the people sent out to the agricultural settlements refused to stay on them; they preferred the life of shopkeepers in the towns.

Graziani was an obvious target for impatient Fascists worried by failure to achieve an impossible goal. He was known to be in an abnormal state of anxiety. He professed himself harassed by what he called interference from Rome as well as by his ungovernable subjects; he had always been an obsessive complainer. Mussolini decided that

although he was a good general he was a bad governor. (The Duce
was characteristically to change his mind several times on this point
later. Four years later Graziani was officially censured by court-martial
for his catastrophic 1940–41 campaign against the British in Libya,
although he was almost certainly not to blame, and resigned in disgrace. Later still, however, at the end of Fascism, when he would try
to build an army for the Fascist republic, he was one of the last,
small band that was loyal to Mussolini to the finish.)

By the fall of 1937 the occupation of Ethiopia was actually
losing ground. In some northern provinces, rebellion broke out in
September. Isolated Italian posts in the neighborhood of Gondar, the
old capital near Lake Tana, were captured, and a number of Italian
officials and soldiers killed. Some of the lost positions were not
reoccupied. Such outbreaks were spreading through the highlands.
Although no one realized it at the time, an important kind of
warfare—guerilla fighting by non-whites against colonizers—one that
would recur sporadically until it became one of the characteristic forms
of twentieth-century combat—was developing. It was, as it was designed to be, singularly effective in neutralizing the technologically
superior armament that was the chief achievement and defense of
great powers. At the time, however, it looked like another symptom of
primitivism, the old sort of ambuscade that had annoyed but rarely
defeated established authorities in all parts of the world in all ages
past. This was all blamed on Graziani and his brutal methods.

At the end of 1937, after a year and a half as viceroy, Graziani
was recalled and replaced by the king's cousin, the duke of Aosta. By
the standards of the House of Savoy, Aosta was an impressive figure.
He was thirty-nine, soon to be an air force general, a man of exceptional cultivation, intelligence, and humanity. By instruction and
temperament he was opposed to the sort of terrorism that Graziani
had rejoiced in, and his rule was remarkably conciliatory.

He did not succeed. Maybe nothing could have saved Italian rule.
From the standpoint of the Ethiopians, and of the most elementary
precepts of humanity, Aosta's regime was certainly greatly to be preferred to that of his two predecessors, but preference is not acceptance. In achieving pacification—which was what, after all, his princi-
pals were concerned with—humanity was not visibly more efficacious
than bestiality. There were inherent contradictions in Italian policy

and purposes. For one example, the favoring of the non-Amharic peoples and particularly of the Moslems—and indispensable and natural part of Italian policy euphemistically called "freedom of religion"— was bound to lead to the alienation of the Christian populations. For another, the expropriation of good land for Italian settlers, the most coherent of Italian purposes, was bound to alienate the people who were displaced and many other Ethiopians as well.

In any case, Aosta's temperate policies failed. Italian rule was restricted to the major cities, a few other heavily garrisoned places, and some well-patrolled lines of communication. Italian forces were simply unable to patrol the whole of a huge and seething empire. It had been planned to build an Ethiopian army, similar in purpose and structure to the forces from Somalia and Eritrea that had, on the whole, proved loyal and efficient in 1935–36. But such an army never came anywhere near taking shape. The only troops that could be counted on to remain loyal were those of dissident peoples who disliked their fellow nationals more than they disliked the Italians, so the Italians achieved not an efficient army but an institutionalized civil war.

The ubiquity of the Ethiopian Patriots was not more disquieting than their fervor. Their spirit of self-sacrifice, early noted, was singularly difficult for the Italians to deal with. They did not hesitate to undertake any action, however suicidal; and they seemed to take pride in being executed if they were captured. They died, an Italian journalist later said, with the invariable words, "I did what I did for my country."[23]

An ironic gulf between Italian and Ethiopian social ethics lay in this. Even the fiercist Fascists had a strong inherited tradition of the sanctity of life, mixed with the publicized notion of sacrifice. Fascists glorified both; humanistic culture, what in the cant of a later day would be called "life-affirmation," was extolled, but so was martyrdom. The Ethiopian Patriots exhibited single-minded dedication to martyrdom. The ordinary Italian, try as he might to imitate them, did not often succeed. The "softness" that Fascists so deplored was a reality, for it was also what they called civilization. This was the basic confusion of Fascist propaganda and perhaps of Fascist minds: the Fascists justified the need for "hardness" by saying it was necessary if the civilization of Italy, of Europe, of white men, were to prevail. But all of the deepest traditions of that civilization were "soft."

In 1938 and 1939, while Italians could still deal with their intractable booty without outside interference, failure was already inducing something like despair in Rome. Ciano wrote in his diary on March 14, 1939, "The Duke of Aosta spoke with considerable optimism about the condition of the Ethiopian Empire. I must, however, add that among the many people who have come from there he is the only optimist. He urges [us] to avoid a conflict with France which would bring on to the high seas the task of pacifying our empire and would jeopardize the conquest itself." And Ciano then adds an oddly archaic note that suggests the snobbish and obsolescent Fascist notions of what mattered in the world: "I do not quite understand whether he was speaking as the Viceroy of Ethiopia or the son of a French princess."[24]

The web of history in which Italy had entangled itself made arguments about pacification and a millennial empire meaningless. The very act of conquering Ethiopia in itself led to two consequences that seem in retrospect to have been fatal and inseparable. For one thing, the new kind of guerrilla war emerged; for another, conquest led automatically to the enmity of other great powers which, though tardily and reluctantly, found themselves obliged to support the rebels and to undertake the liberation of Ethiopia. The two things worked together as a single force. If Italian rule and morale had not been gravely weakened by the nerve-wracking hostility of the Ethiopians *and* by the distressing events in Europe, the British would not, and could not, have undertaken the campaign that so rapidly put an end to that rule; and if the British had not found it necessary to support the rebels, the latter could not have operated so effectively as they did, and they might in the end have failed.

The Patriot operations were exceedingly efficient. Even when almost without ammunition, Patriots succeeded in drawing Italian fire by feint, leading them into exposed positions, and then attacking them from the rear. In rainy seasons, when airplanes were grounded so that besieged Italian units could not be supplied, they were starved out. The Patriots were fanatically dedicated and supremely elusive. Their leader, Abebe Aragai, was repeatedly ambushed and several times captured, but he always escaped. They were skilled at calling forth the enthusiasm of their compatriots. Their propaganda was as evocative as their tactics; the slogan of the Gojami Patriots was "A white eagle is eating you."[25] People of all sorts, without distinction of class or cultural affiliation,* were associated in the Patriot cause. Their organization and functions were highly local. They early developed a Patriots' Association, through which money and supplies were acquired, although resources remained meager.

Despite a coalescing leadership, localism was strong. There was no common language of command. The local, sometimes tribal, allegiances led to trouble. In both Gondar and Sidamo, the most important localities in Patriot hands, there was combat between two resistance forces, and one party even appealed to the Italians for support. There were strong prejudices among ethnic or clan groups in the same region. There was treachery. Some Patriots had the misfortune to be captured by other, inimical, Patriots who sold them as slaves to still other Patriots. But on the whole, considering the circumstances, the movement was effective and united.

The politics of the resistance is obscure. The monarchy, once restored, did not encourage exploration of dissident political ideas. It is difficult to tell whether any substantial Soviet or other foreign political influence was present, and there was no way to measure the impulse—undoubtedly extant, as later developments showed—to reject the exiled regime and try to build a new and revolutionary society. In any conscious or organized form, such kinds of heterodoxy were probably extremely limited. The crown was still, apparently, generally accepted as the font of honor and authority.

It is said that Patriot leaders hesitated to confer titles, even military rank, on the ground that this was a prerogative of the crown.[26] The Patriots found themselves obliged to perform functions of government, but generally the imperial regime managed to remain in titular control. Abebe Aragai assumed the functions of a viceroy. He was the emperor's agent, and with liberation he became governor of Addis Ababa and later minister of defense. It is a suggestive fact that he was shot to death by the revolutionaries who briefly seized the capital in 1960.

What was happening was precisely analogous to what happened

---

* Roman Catholics, however, were suspect, for obvious reasons, and were not given much confidence.

later in European countries like France and Greece. Dissidence
and possible social revolution were in the end throttled, but drastic
changes took place anyway. Even the loyalists in Ethiopia had, by
1941, constructed a new political tradition. People, with the encouragement of distant, exiled governments, were finding the weapons with
which to fight the twentieth-century state. Against the Patriot operations, the weapons of conquest did not avail. Air bombardment and
poison gas and heavy artillery might injure but could not extirpate
forest warriors. The whole structure of Italian rule was undermined
by the very technology that made it possible. This was a significant
fact of historical timing.

The second co-ordinate of liberation was support from outside. It
was several years before the anti-fascist crusade provided an army of
liberation. Tokens of support, however, appeared early. In Patriot fast-
nesses, foreigners began to appear. Two Italian anti-Fascists, Velio
Spano and Ilio Barontini, went to Gojam. Mussolini's second adventure, the Spanish Civil War, produced small but tangible assistance
to the Ethiopian rebels. Veterans from the service of the Spanish republic, after its extinction in March 1939, looked for new battlefields. Paul Langrols, a distinguished officer, a Frenchman in the
Spanish loyalist forces, was one of them. He went to Ethiopia under
the auspices of the French government. Romantic internationalism—
the converse of romantic imperialism—that had led so many young
men of good will to death in Spain now led a few more to Ethiopia.
Like the Fascists, they represented the identification of self-fulfillment
with a transcendent idea.

This was the meaning of what now began to happen in Ethiopia:
an old-fashioned ideal (which Fascists could easily understand), the
national salvation of Ethiopia, was being blended with a new conception of a battle against international fascism, tyranny, capitalism,
and imperialism. There were some of the same anomalies that fascism
suffered from as a world movement. For the new fighters, national
liberation was conceived of as somehow an international phenomenon,
just as fascists managed to see fascist nationalism as international.
People in the new movement talked about the nationalism of "the
people" or "the masses" instead of reactionary rulers, but this was just
what the Fascists and Nazis talked about too. The Soviet Union was
already proclaiming national liberation as a goal of communism, in

much the same spirit as Hitler proclaimed, when he occupied Czechoslovakia in March 1939, that he was engaged in liberating the Slovaks
from the Czechs. But logic is not frequently a force in political commitment, and committed men were trying to square circles in Ethiopia
and Spain. It might now be said that Mussolini was merely "incorrect" in saying that freedom meant freedom for Italians to conquer; what freedom meant was the freedom of victims of Italy to resist
conquest, in the name of the same ideal. The skill with which Haile
Selassie had called forth the conscience of the world had helped
fashion this phenomenon, and the world had thereby changed.

To the service of conscience was now recruited, incongruously, the
power of the British empire. The British government, under Chamberlain and Churchill, could have no real sympathy with "national liberation" any more than with Fascist aspirations to revive the Roman
empire. But to resist the Fascists it was necessary not merely to co-
operate with the national liberation forces but to proclaim it as a commendable ideal in selected cases. For in the spring of 1939 it had
become necessary for impartial people in Paris and London to contemplate a possible war with Italy and Germany combined—the very
eventuality that British policy, in permitting Ethiopia to be conquered,
had been designed to avoid.

This was a bitter disappointment to the British. After the abandonment of sanctions by the League, the policy of conciliating Italy
was pursued with higher hope and greater determination than ever. To
many it looked as if Anglo-Italian friendship were a lost cause. But
the conflicts between Germany and Italy remained, and the British
hoped to exploit them.

Italian-German relations were, to be sure, now outwardly cordial,
but their inner reality demonstrated the inherent contradiction of international fascism. In September 1936 Hitler had assured Mussolini
that he was prepared to recognize the Italian empire in Ethiopia and
that he regarded the Mediterranean as a "purely Italian sea."[27] In
October Ciano visited Germany, and a written agreement was signed
providing for an amicable alignment of policies on many international
questions from Japan to Spain and for formal German recognition of
Ethiopia as an Italian possession. On November 1, 1936, Mussolini
referred, with considerable éclat, to "an axis" connecting Rome
and Berlin. Ten months later he paid a state visit to Germany in

which he was lavishly entertained and wildly applauded by more than a million people in Berlin—although many of them had been assembled by the authorities for the purpose.

Nevertheless, on both sides there were doubts. The Germans still regarded the Italians as frivolous, unreliable, and militarily incompetent. Ciano, the leading sponsor of the Axis, had written:

> Will the solidarity between two regimes suffice to form a real bond of union between two peoples drawn in opposite directions by race, culture, religion, and tastes? No one can accuse me of being hostile to the pro-German policy. I initiated it myself. But should we, I wonder, regard Germany as a goal, or rather as a field for maneuvre? The incidents of the last few days and above all Mussolini's fidelity to his political allegiance made me incline to the first alternative. But may not events develop in such a way as to separate our two peoples again? We shall see.[28]

Powerful forces in Rome worked against the Axis and for Anglo-Italian understanding. These were led by the king and included many of the military and especially the naval people. Their most effective members were Dino Grandi, the ambassador at London, and the duke of Aosta. Aosta, the viceroy of Ethiopia, had strong British connections (and was hostile to the Germans) and even stronger professional reasons for not alienating the British. Britain's power surrounded him in Egypt, the Sudan, Kenya, and British Somaliland. British naval power controlled the Mediterranean, Suez Canal, and Red Sea. Italian East Africa was an island in the sea of Britain's imperial power. In the end, it was not any deep devotion to the Axis that wrecked the chances of a real reconciliation with Britain. It was Italy's own policies.

The Spanish Civil War contributed. The Italian-backed rebels infringed on neutral shipping rights. The British government might regard with complacency the prospect of a victory for General Francisco Franco and his quasi-fascist supporters; it was not at all complacent when British ships were attacked by Italian submarines in support of Franco's cause. Mussolini's talk of the Mediterranean as *mare nostrum* (our sea) echoed even in Whitehall. Mussolini (like the German emperor three decades before) proclaimed himself the "Protector of Islam," strengthened Italian forces in Libya, and ordered the construction of a coastal highway to the Egyptian frontier leading toward Suez and the British bases in Alexandria. His oratory abounded in defiance of Britain's power in the Mediterranean.

Neville Chamberlain became prime minister in May 1937, and he was determined to overcome such obstacles. He had no regard for Mussolini and thought him insolent. He wrote in his diary that if only a settlement could be reached with Germany "I would not care a rap for Musso."[29] But as things were, friendship with Italy was one of his principal concerns, and he was determined to reach some sort of written pact. One of his agents, characteristically, was his sister-in-law, Lady Chamberlain, the widow of a former foreign secretary, a woman who much admired Mussolini and made approaches to him during a social visit to Rome. It was this sort of unprofessional, private diplomacy that Chamberlain saw as a means for rescuing the world from the toils of his hidebound, war-mongering, foreign policy experts.

One of his first acts as prime minister was to send a friendly note to Mussolini whose text he did not show to his foreign minister, for "he had the feeling" that Eden would "object to it."[30] He rebuked the Foreign Office for its tendency to regard Mussolini as a Machiavellian conspirator and observed, "if we treat him like that, we shall get nowhere."[31] Even Mussolini's trip to Germany, with its exuberant rhetorical flourishes and massive demonstrations of Axis solidarity, had not discouraged him in his resolution to lure "Musso" into being pro-British.

He was encouraged by Léon Blum's resignation as French Premier in June 1937. The French now seemed prepared to follow, although with occasional shows of obstinacy, the British lead. Eden, worn out by trying to palliate policies he disliked, resigned on February 20, 1938. By then Mussolini had recovered from the exuberance of his Berlin visit. He worried again about the British navy; in gloomy moments he even worried that Britain would attack Italy without warning. Moreover, the demands made on him by the Germans were alarming. The Axis in no way slowed—indeed it speeded—the erosion of Austrian independence. In March 1938 the Germans occupied and annexed Austria. The eventuality that the Ethiopian venture had been in part designed to avert—the presence of German troops on the crest of the Alps, overlooking Italy—was being brought about as one of its consequences.

So the Italians took a more friendly line with the British. After a good deal of difficult negotiation of troublesome points, agreement was reached in April 1938. Mussolini agreed to withdraw his "volunteers" from Spain (which he never did) and promised that he sought no privileged position in Spain (which he did). The British agreed not to fortify Cyprus (no limit was placed on the Italians' freedom to fortify anything they chose) and promised to recommend the recognition of the Italian conquest of Ethiopia to the League of Nations. Chamberlain thought the agreement a triumph, and was satisfied that he had outmanuevered the war-mongering bureaucracy of the Foreign Office. In November 1938 His Britannic Majesty's ambassador at Rome was at last accredited to the king of Italy *and* emperor of Ethiopia.

But the agreement had almost no effect on anything except the minds of Chamberlain and his friends, and sensational events a year later led to changes in both British and Italian policy. In March of 1939 the Germans invaded Czechoslovakia without telling the Italians in advance. At first it looked as if this would help the cause of detaching Italy from the Axis. It worked the other way, however, because of Mussolini's wild response to it.

Italians were outraged by Austria and Czechoslovakia. There were anti-German demonstrations from the Italian public of all classes and regions. Mussolini himself shared in private the public indignation. The Italian aspirations to control of the Mediterranean had received no measurable impetus from the Axis connection. The fit of Germanophilia had produced a further degree of diplomatic dependence; it had made Mussolini swallow the loss of Austria; it had led to the introduction of brutal and gratuitous anti-Semitic measures on the Nazi pattern into Italy; it had forced the Italian army to adopt the Prussian goosestep, which the king of Italy and a good many other people thought was carrying flattery by imitation to the point of the grotesque. But it had availed Italy no benefits whatever, and of this Mussolini was acutely and resentfully aware. "Every time he takes another country, he sends me a message," he observed grumpily to Ciano.

Mussolini raged against the obduracy of the Italian people (who showed a notable reluctance to accept the anti-Semitic policy), against the decadent British with their throttling navy, and against the Germans, who were keeping him the junior partner in the Axis. He was frightened by the possibility of war, for practically every informed person in Italy knew that the show of power in Ethiopia had been factitious. He was, in short, a frustrated man in the spring of 1939, and his regime, increasingly onerous and unpopular, was again in long-range jeopardy if not at all in immediate danger. To this frustration he responded by annexing the kingdom of Albania.

The action was a sort of trivial recapitulation of the Ethiopian venture. Although all the circumstances were different, Mussolini's personality imposed upon them a pattern almost uncannily similar.

The conquest of Ethiopia had been partly designed to impress the Germans by showing them that Italy was a great military power. The conquest of Albania was explicitly designed to show that Italy's capacity for annexing foreign states was as great as Germany's. Like Ethiopia, Albania was not a new idea. On April 30, 1938, Ciano noted that Mussolini felt that "so long as we get Albania, he is prepared even to have a war."[32]

Albania, which lies across the Adriatic from the Italian heel and with it forms an entrance strait, had for a long time been an Italian puppet. So far as Italy's power, safety, and real interests went, annexation brought no change. It merely made Italy look bigger on maps and gave Victor Emmanuel the new title of king of Albania. It was a whimsy, tempered by one rational consideration. The Devoli oil fields in Albania produced 65,000 tons of oil a year, which would have relieved Italy of dependence on imports across waters that the British controlled. But the oil could have been bought from the pliant government of King Zog in any case; and it was of such poor quality that enormous expenditures on new refineries in Italy were necessary to make it usable.

The Albanians offered very ineffective resistance, and their king and queen fled their capital long before the Italians reached it. The cautious military operations of De Bono and Badoglio in Ethiopia also characterized those of General Alfredo Guzzoni in Albania. Having landed successfully, Guzzoni refused to advance. Geography was a factor, along with inefficiency. It was Mussolini's unhappy gift to choose cautious generals for conquests in places with vertiginous mountains and poor roads.

The tragedy of Addis Ababa was repeated in the Albanian capital, Tirana. The sovereign having departed and the conqueror having refused to advance, the residents gave themselves over to looting and burning. It was several days before the Italians took over the disheveled town.

To the world it looked like another skillfully master-minded act of Axis aggression, part of the same plan that had led to the extinction of the Czech state. The Axis powers, ferocious and resolute, had, it seemed, a blue-print for knocking down dominoes: Ethiopia, Spain, Austria, Czechoslovakia, Albania. This appearance, like the appearance of redoubtable Italian power, was wholly an illusion.

The reaction in Berlin to the Albanian grab was in fact angry. The Germans' rage was veiled by proprieties; Field Marshal Hermann Goering of Germany attended the ceremonies of Victor Emmanuel's coronation as king of Albania. But they had been taken by surprise (as they had taken Rome by surprise by invading Czechoslovakia), and Hitler was much put out. There were indeed grounds for disapproval. It was clear that each time the Axis aggressed, the rest of the world became more distrustful and hostile. Every country anywhere near Germany or Italy seemed to be in imminent danger. The Germans feared that world suspicions might adversely affect their own projects.[33]

They were correct. The immediate response was dramatic, and it presaged the war that came in September. In Washington, Roosevelt, confirmed in his views, appealed to the Axis powers, in an embarrassingly public way, to give guarantees that they would respect the independence and freedom of their neighbors. Both the Germans and Italians expressed outrage at the impertinence of the president. The British had already begun a program of offering "guarantees" to the eastern European countries; now they pursued it with increased urgency.

Mussolini was frightened by the reactions of both the Germans and their opponents. He knew that the Germans were planning to attack Poland in the fall, at the risk of a European war, and he dreaded the prospect, but fear of total isolation impelled him to secure himself by tightening the Axis into an alliance. In May 1939, the "Pact of Steel" alliance between Italy and Germany was signed. Mussolini's loss of independence was consummated. Chamberlain, still wistfully hopeful, had not quite lost confidence in Italy, and he wrote in his diary that the latter's messages to him "indicate a desire on [Mussolini's] part to allay any fears or suspicions on mine."[34] One can

well believe that they did. But there was little freedom of action left
to Mussolini. He could delay and sulk, but he was at the mercy of the
power of Germany, now vastly superior.

London was not, in 1939, inclined to explore the possibilities of
undermining Italian power in Africa. For the Chamberlain government,
as long as it existed, Ethiopia remained an embarrassment, not an
opportunity, let alone a cause. It was an issue as dead as the government could make it. As an unwelcome guest of Chamberlain, the
emperor of Ethiopia was in a position both uncomfortable and perplexing.

Haile Selassie was consigned to oblivion. Oblivion was intensified
by the distraction of his sympathizers. People who had been preoccupied with Ethiopia became preoccupied first with Spain, then with
Austria, Czechoslovakia, and Albania, and finally with Poland. A few
still gave the exiles encouragement, but they could not do much to
alleviate their dismal circumstances.

The emperor had chosen the city of Bath as his place of exile,
perhaps because his health was indifferent and it was believed that the
legendary waters—in which, by a neat irony, Roman emperors had
sought therapy—would prove beneficial. The British government was
eager to get him out of London, and in 1936 he bought a large
house at the edge of Bath where he lived for almost four years. It
served as a sort of clandestine palace, the seat of an informal government. Until the fall of 1938 the emperor was still recognized by
Britain as a reigning sovereign, and he was, at least sporadically,
treated as one as far as outward shows went. (He was officially invited,
for example, to attend the coronation of George VI in the spring of
1937, to the immense irritation of Mussolini.) But these formalities
were small consolation.

Awkwardness arose from lack of funds. The emperor himself said,
"We have absolutely no income."[35] The considerable fortune which
had been brought from Ethiopia was state property and was used only
for official purposes, mainly to aid refugees and send support to the
Patriots. The deposits of the Bank of Ethiopia in Great Britain, which
Colson had saved from the Italians, were blocked. The emperor's
private means were small. It is reported that his personal silver was

sold to pay for the house in Bath and that at times there was not enough money for coal.

There was unpleasant prejudice among the townspeople of Bath against "all those black people." The empress, for example, was rumored to have been seen "squatting on the floor of the greenhouse, shredding cabbage leaves"—an interesting example of projection, since the shredding of cabbage was an occupation presumably more common among the people of Bath than in court circles in Addis Ababa. Such conduct was reprobated as bizarre and unbecoming. (In point of fact, the greenhouse had been converted into a chapel, and the empress was praying, not shredding cabbage.[36]) The English climate was a hardship for those accustomed to the exhilarating atmosphere of the Ethiopian highlands. All the circumstances of life in Bath intensified a melancholy which would in any case have been severe, with the terrible reports from Ethiopia and the British attempts at conciliation of Mussolini.

But changes were in the making. One of them was the work of a powerful British voice being raised by a remarkable and dedicated Englishwoman, Sylvia Pankhurst. She embodied, in an extreme form, what Ethiopia had meant to the development of anti-fascist opinion everywhere, and her case is worth attention.

Her interest in Ethiopian affairs, like that of almost everyone else outside the empire, had developed suddenly, not from personal acquaintance but from abstract principle. She had long been a worker for causes. She had achieved international fame, when she was in her twenties, as one of the formidable family of militant suffragists who had convulsed Britain in the years before 1914. She proceeded from feminism through a logical ideological evolution that led to revolt, in violent rhetoric, against the whole existing order of society. She had helped organize an anti-Soviet international communist movement, and she had denounced fascism long before it was fashionable to do so. Her early, trenchant warnings about its nature were singularly accurate and prophetic.

Sylvia Pankhurst was a person of strongly independent spirit, strong resolution, and strong intelligence. When the Ethiopian crisis developed it struck her—as it struck many others—as a public testing of the Fascist regime, of the efficacy of the League, and of the "sincerity of the high-minded liberalism of Britain's intelligentsia."[37] Unlike most others similarly struck, however, she stayed with the cause and became its leading spokesman in Britain.

During the Ethiopian War she fought a valiant battle of words in favor of a strong stand against Italian aggression, showing herself a good deal more accurate in her appraisal of Fascist Italy as a paper eagle than most of the experts she so disliked. She wrote private letters to statesmen and public letters to the press, insisting, as Roosevelt and Haile Selassie were simultaneously insisting, that one successful aggression would lead to others. She contrived to disseminate anti-Fascist propaganda in Italy itself. And when Addis Ababa was oc- cupied and other sympathizers began to lose interest, she produced the first issue of a new magazine, *New Times and Ethiopian News*. It continued to appear through the years of occupation and long after- ward, and at times it reached the considerable circulation of 40,000 copies. It was well edited and attracted writers of stature, including a number of future cabinet ministers. Some issues were published in Amharic and distributed in Ethiopia among the Patriots. It conveyed by far the most copious and widely distributed information about affairs in Ethiopia of any news source in the world.

Sylvia Pankhurst's percipience continued to inform it. In 1940, when the British were preparing their campaign to throw the Italians out of East Africa, she clearly saw the possibility that liberation might mean the replacement of Italian overlordship by British, and she pressed in the *New Times* for categorical promises that full independence would be restored. When Churchill showed signs of repeating ominous formulas about the primitive stage of Ethiopian development and a need for guidance by Europeans, she wrote, "How dare he speak so slightingly of a people who even as he spoke were helping to pin down Italian troops that might otherwise have turned the scale against the Allies . . . ?"[38]

The *New Times* was a significant publication, and in one respect its policy illustrated the process of blending the ideals of national liberation with a program acceptable to the wartime leaders of the Allies. It was editorially devoted to the cause of the emperor and helped to identify him in British minds with the cause of Ethiopian liberation. For Britain, Sylvia Pankhurst was a republican; for Ethi- opia, a determined monarchist. She became a friend and helpful men- tor of the court at Bath, and she kept its presence before her readers while she was keeping the horrors of the Italian occupation before them. The reports, emotional, sensational, and sometimes unreliable, were a sharp spur to Britain's awareness of what happened to people who had fallen victim to fascist aggression. They were also powerful pleas for returning Haile Selassie to power in a liberated empire.

Similar conclusions were being reached, for quite different reasons, by French and British officers in the Middle East. The French had decided much earlier that something might be gained by exploiting the Ethiopian resistance as a means of embarrassing Italy. In June 1939 a Frenchman, Colonel Monnice, had actually entered Ethiopia from Khartum, the capital of what was then the Anglo-Egyptian Sudan and a British garrison town, to make contact with the Patriots. He died of malaria almost immediately, but the British commander at Khartum had been interested by his venture and views. Major General Sir William Platt was an officer with flexible ideas. Intelligence reaching him from inside Ethiopia, mainly through the European volunteers who were fighting with the Patriots, convinced him that the rebellion was indeed powerful, widespread, and important. He concluded that the Patriots regarded Haile Selassie as their proper leader and his restoration as their chief aim. Such reports led to several inferences. First, if there were war with Italy, the situation in Ethiopia would offer an inviting opportunity for harassing Italy and distracting important Italian forces at minimum outlay. Second, while outright intervention could not be considered while Britain and Italy were still officially at peace, the opportunity might be discreetly exploited from Khartum. Third, that the exile at Bath should be treated by the British government not as an embarrassment but as a trump. Platt had no interest in Ethiopia for its own sake, let alone in the future of the emperor. Rather, he was a perceptive strategist who saw opportunities that could be exploited in case of conflict with Italy. He saw corresponding dangers in neglecting those opportunities. If the Italians were *not* undermined, the British position in the Sudan, in Egypt, and in the whole Middle East might be threatened.

Platt convinced Lieutenant General Sir Archibald Wavell, the commander in chief of British forces in the Middle East, of the utility of these notions. Wavell sent to Britain for experts in Ethiopian affairs. One was Major R. E. Cheesman, who had served as consul in western Ethiopia and knew the country that bordered on the Sudan. Another was Lieutenant Colonel D. A. Sandford, who left his post as treasurer of Guildford cathedral for less tranquil occupation as a member of Wavell's staff. He was a man of remarkable ability and discrimination who had lived long in Ethiopia, having been consul at Addis Ababa as early as 1914 and having later settled as a farmer in the country. By the autumn of 1939 Sandford was already drawing up plans for the destruction of Italian rule, which were later to be successfully followed.

At first there was opposition from London to these activities. In 1939 and early 1940, before Italy entered the war, the War Office was reluctant to undertake any policy, however hypothetical, that might annoy Mussolini. But the necessary condition for a drastic change of attitudes toward Ethiopia was fulfilled when Churchill replaced Chamberlain as prime minister in May 1940. Churchill had been in the past. and conceivably still was when he took office, an admirer of Mussolini, a much more genuine one than Chamberlain had ever been. But he was not at all given to self-deception or to faith in tenuous negotiations with the dictators, and his view of imperial and strategic problems was the reverse of defensive. A month after he took office, Britain and Italy were at war, and there was prompt and dramatic victory for the point of view of Platt and Sandford. A proclamation, written by Cheesman and signed by Platt, was addressed to the Patriots. "We have decided," it said, "to help you in every way possible."[39] It went on to promise arms, ammunition, food, and clothing. The numerous Ethiopian refugees in Khartum were organized into a "frontier battalion."

At Bath a sudden and sensational event took place. The emperor was informed that he was to leave Britain at once for Khartum to take command of the Ethiopian forces that were being formed there, and on June 12, 1940, two days after the Italians declared war on France and Britain, he arrived in Egypt. It was a startling testimony to the vigor of Churchill's methods.

The emperor was accompanied by his son, a small staff, and—interestingly—the newspaperman George Steer, whose writings had served his cause so well. A rather strange band of supporters began to assemble at the transplanted court, supplementing the Ethiopian refugees. A French count, who had served as a pilot for the emperor years before;

an English history professor; a Dutch water diviner; a selection of old Ethiopia hands anxious to assist in the liberation. An imperial head-quarters was set up in the Sudan, and there was an encouraging in-crease in the tempo of preparations and of communication with the interior.

There were also delays and disappointments. Some of the cold atmosphere of Bath persisted in the heat of the desert. The British com-mand, while it wished to use the emperor and the Ethiopians, seemed to have no great interest in them or regard for them. This was under-standable enough; a reigning sovereign in Khartum was almost as much of an embarrassment, although in a different way, as a reigning sover-eign in Bath. There were some who regarded him as a necessary but inconvenient public-relations gimmick. Others had serious doubts about the wisdom of sending him to Khartum at all or of allowing him to re-enter Ethiopia. One of Wavell's staff, Lieutenant Colonel H. C. Brocklehurst, was strenuously arguing that plans should be made to partition Ethiopia (with large portions being assigned by implication as British colonies) and sponsoring the aspirations of the non-Amharic peoples.[40]

Wavell himself, although he found the emperor personally attrac-tive, also found him difficult to deal with. There were misunderstand-ings. Someone in the Foreign Office in London ("a moron," Wavell called him) had given Haile Selassie the impression that large forces were to engage immediately in a war of liberation under the sovereign's command. No such forces were available. Relations were not eased by the emperor's insistence (Wavell wrote) in refusing to speak any-thing but Amharic, while the only person available to interpret Amharic could do so only into Arabic. The emperor, during their conversations, had a tendency to stare at the ceiling in dignified and recalcitrant silence, and this annoyed the general. The situation was tense, uncertain, and disturbing for everybody.[41]

Churchill was the emperor's most important and determined sup-porter and in a certain sense Ethiopia's best friend. He intractably and loudly espoused the cause of restoration. He urgently prodded the mili-tary for a faster build-up of invasion forces, and he backed the emper-or's proposals for using them. He defied the lethargy of bureaucracy in London, Cairo, and Khartum.[42] But the prime minister's policy did not mean acquiescence in the world vision that animated people like Sylvia Pankhurst and mobilized so many minds in a crusade against fascism and aggression and for a better world of true democracy and the internationalism of national liberations. The war was a crusade for Churchill, but a conservative one. He had a marked disposition to favor monarchies—it was logical that, having saved the throne of Haile Selassie, he should later try, almost single-handedly, to save the throne of the kings of Italy. He was a convinced and consistent imperialist. Wise in the ways of a world that was ceasing to exist, he was glad to use the forces dedicated to a brave new world to accomplish his own purposes. But his purposes included saving the British empire and the old order everywhere. He was, pre-eminently, a legitimist.

The policy was to have, in the short run anyway, a singular success. The restoration of stability *was* achieved, during and after World War II, everywhere outside the zones of occupation of the Soviet army. It was so successful, indeed, that it appears in retrospect to have been natural, inevitable, imperative. In fact, it was for the legitimists an astounding and difficult achievement, in which Haile Selassie played a vital role. Contemporary opinion, even some of the more progressive elements of it, welcomed the return of Haile Selassie as natural, inevitable, imperative, and just. They had been conditioned by his role of conscience of the world. That role helped powerfully to prevent a rift between Churchill's restorationism and the liberal idealists.

The adventure in legitimacy was in fact precarious and speculative. Four years after Haile Selassie returned to Ethiopia, the governments of western and northern Europe returned from exile to their liberated capitals (a vast recapitulation of the Ethiopian experience), but in many cases the return was accomplished with difficulty. In Greece, for example, the restoration of King George II was achieved barely and only after prolonged fighting. Nevertheless, legitimism was carried through wherever there were western armies to support it, and it proved remarkably durable. Ethiopia was the precedent in a situation where there were no others. As a model it helped to implant the principle of restoration as a war aim of the western allies.

Haile Selassie was the most prominent and admired of the exiled rulers, and he was the first to go back. He became a prototype for the sovereigns of the Netherlands, Norway, and Greece, and even for Italy. The astonishingly orderly history of western Europe since the summer of 1945 owes something to Haile Selassie's skill in identifying legitimacy with righteousness.

In late 1940 the course and objectives of the policy of restoration were still inchoate and unclear. The only thing that was clear, indeed, was that offensives and victories were at last in fashion in London. Ironic echoes are faintly audible: there was a startling, if superficial, resemblance between the sort of message Churchill was now sending to Wavell, with impetuous and sometimes conflicting demands for action, and those that Mussolini had sent five years earlier to De Bono and Badoglio.[43] It was not decided whether the primary purpose of action was to relieve pressure on Egypt, to forestall an invasion of Kenya, or to liberate Ethiopia, an uncertainty that corresponded in a way to the uncertain aims of the Italians in 1935. And there was another resemblance. Great Britain was in urgent need of victories. With France and the other continental allies defeated and occupied, with Britain beleaguered, with threats to Egypt and the Mediterranean and control of the seas appearing everywhere, morale at home and abroad, political imperatives of every sort, demanded offensive action—and success. Like De Bono and Badoglio, Platt was careful and thorough. There was much emphasis, no doubt entirely justified, on the difficulties of the project and the inadequacy of available resources for coping with them.

One thing lacking in Khartum was enthusiasm. It appeared suddenly, along with a pyrotechnic display of energy, in the person of the eccentric and gifted Orde Wingate. Major Wingate was regarded by some of his superiors as a genius. He was in the tradition of earlier geniuses, such as T. E. Lawrence and "Chinese" Gordon, soldiers fascinated by the mysterious East and moved by powerful personal drives. Sent from England to take command of the operations inside Ethiopia, he at once established good relations with the discontented Ethiopians and with Sandford; together they urgently demanded, and got, support and money from Wavell. A million pounds sterling credit for support of the Ethiopian Patriots was produced. Wingate was the first officer of first-rate talents who was principally concerned with Ethiopia rather than with the large and indefinite strategic problems of East Africa and the Middle East as a whole. He wanted to make the restoration of Haile Selassie an official and major goal of British policy. A complicated and difficult campaign had to be waged to secure this goal against the ideas of men like Brocklehurst, a political campaign almost as difficult as the coming military campaign. But eventually Eden announced in the House of Commons that "His Majesty's Government would welcome the reappearance of an independent Ethiopian State and recognize the claim of the Emperor Haile Selassie to the throne" and that the British "affirm that they have themselves no territorial ambitions in Abyssinia."[44]

The Italians in Ethiopia were in serious trouble by the fall of 1940. Morale was low. They did not know of their enormous numerical superiority (like so many other generals in so many other situations, the leaders greatly exaggerated the size of the British forces and were cowed by their own misinformation). When Italy first went to war against Britain, they had captured a few frontier posts in the Sudan, but these token offensives had been hard fought and the Italians had been shaken by the cost. From other fronts, notably from Libya where once hopes had flourished for a rapid advance into Egypt and the Suez, news of disaster came to Rome in late 1940 and 1941. Most depressing, Italian East Africa was shut off from home supplies. The Suez Canal was closed now to Italian shipping. The greatest handicap of the Italian authorities in East Africa was that so large a part of their quarter of a million men were occupied in trying to hold the country against domestic foes. Knowledge that the British were now at war and organizing to advance stirred the Patriots to new action. The duke of Aosta, in spite of the immense nominal superiority of the Italian forces in all branches, was besieged in a flimsy fort.[45]

The liberation of Ethiopia began in November 1940. There was an attack on a fort near the border. With a single brigade and almost no air support but with a very able and distinguished commander, Brigadier W. J. Slim, the British force of mixed local soldiers, Indian, and U.K. units recaptured the occupied Sudanese town of Gallabat.

The Italians were concerned about a British attack on Eritrea, "Italy's oldest colony." The British had been able to transfer some armored units from Libya, where their offensive had gone well, to the border of northwestern Eritrea, which was very vulnerable. Aosta had no choice but to make some withdrawals somewhere, and withdrawal in Ethiopia was strategically and politically less damaging than in Eritrea. About the same time that the British crossed the Eritrean frontier, on January 20, 1941, the emperor of Ethiopia, with Major Wingate in command of a force of Ethiopians and Sudanese and a large supply train of camels, re-entered his country.

It was a solemn but not a very majestic moment. The Ethiopian frontier was undefended and the emperor arrived at a nearby landing strip in an old British transport plane. He disembarked and walked to the dry river bed that marked the border. A flagpole had been erected at the line, and he personally raised the Ethiopian colors. In the absence of champagne, a toast was drunk in beer. The event was given full propaganda treatment by the British. Militarily insignificant, it did exactly what Churchill intended it to do: it signaled the new spirit in Britain, a British victory in a worldwide campaign of liberation against fascist aggressors and fidelity to a cruel used ally.

The territory east of the point of entry was held by Patriots. The imperial party, preceded by the British commander, moved by truck 300 miles across desert to an oasis called the Elephant's Water Hole. The emperor went fishing with a net and caught enough to make supper. After that, the trip was more difficult. The trucks had to be abandoned and the last stages, to the highlands, were covered by horse. (The camels all died on the way.) The party proceeded slowly to Debra Marcos, the capital of Gojam, which the emperor entered on April 6, 1941, and received the surrender of the Italian-appointed governor, Prince Hailu. The same day, word was received that South African troops, advancing from Kenya in the south against no Italian resistance, had entered Addis Ababa. They hauled down the Italian tricolor from the imperial palace and hoisted in its place the British, not the Ethiopian, flag. And Major General Sir Alan Cunningham, the South African commander, was extremely reluctant to permit the emperor to come to the capital. It was feared that his return might be a signal for an outbreak against the 25,000 white men, mostly Italians, still in Addis Ababa. Only a month later did Haile Selassie ride in, in an old Alfa Romeo abandoned by the occupiers in Debra Marcos.

Cunningham had been appointed head of British military government in Ethiopia, and he seems to have regarded himself as a competitor of the emperor, charged particularly with safeguarding European interests (including Italian). He was the most determined of those who envisaged the reduction of the empire to the status of Egypt, permanently occupied and dominated by British troops and advisers. It was only after intervention by the London government that the Ethiopian authorities were able to take over the administration of the country. Apparently he imagined a vast British African sphere of influence from Capetown north, including Kenya.[46]

The old-fashioned attitude of men like Cunningham was similar to that of the Fascists: that Africans were not only incompetent and insufficiently civilized to rule themselves, but that it was immoral to let them try. It was not very dissimilar to the attitude of Churchill. It was indeed a deep European reflex. It was a serious mistake, however (from the standpoint of those who thought in these terms), that the rationalization adopted to justify it in Ethiopia was the theory that British overlordship was necessary to prevent the massacre of all white men by vindictive and barbarous Ethiopians. It became immediately clear that this was not a danger at all. The conduct of the Ethiopians to white men, including the Italians, was so magnanimous as to be incredible.

It arose, perhaps, from what is widely asserted to be an oddity of Ethiopian culture, noticed by Europeans centuries earlier: the Amharic ethos (in contrast to the Islamic or the European) does not approve revenge or even vindictiveness. The feud is notably absent from Ethiopian social history and so, even, it is said, is personal resentment at wrongs. For all the tempestuous violence of Ethiopian life, grudges are not held. If this is indeed the case, the professional Europeans like Cunningham (or Graziani) not only were rationalizing their own impulses but also projecting their own hostilities. But whether it is true or not,* what is certain is that Haile Selassie, from the moment of his return, pursued a policy which was exactly a continuation of that which he had followed earlier. He was determined to demonstrate that western proprieties not merely were observed but observed more faithfully than by westerners themselves: he carried out a policy so perfectly Christian, in the popular sense, as to appear to be practically without precedent in the history of nations. It was made clear the day he arrived in Addis Ababa. His speech to the screaming crowds must

---

* Strong anti-Italian feelings lingered. The commander of the Ethiopian force in the Korean war, ten years later, threatened to withdraw from the U.N. armies if an Italian unit were admitted.

have reassured (and conceivably irritated) even Cunningham and his South African troops. He said:

> On this day which men on earth and angels of heaven could neither have foreseen nor known, I owe thanks unutterable by the mouth of man to the loving God who has enabled me to be present among you. Today is the beginning of a new era in the history of Ethiopia . . . Since this is so, do not reward evil for evil. Do not commit any act of cruelty like those which the enemy committed against us up to this present time. Do not allow the enemy any occasion to foul the good name of Ethiopia. We shall take his weapons and make him return by the way he came.[47]

This was the most famous document in recent Ethiopian history, the Golden Proclamation.

The Italians were specifically forgiven. They were also invited to remain as residents of Ethiopia. Some 14,000 of them are said to have done so. Many of those who stayed were soldiers who, it may be presumed, had no strong wish either to become prisoners of war or to be repatriated to Italy, where they would be called upon to serve in the European battles of Fascism's losing war. The remark most often heard among Italians in East Africa, it is said, was "It was Mussolini's war, not ours."[48]

From the purely practical point of view, the results were advantageous to Ethiopia. Almost no one capable of managing things like telephone systems, dams, or roads remained except Italians. Most of the country's commerce was in their hands. Some of its agriculture was. Moreover, practically everybody involved attests to the fact that most ordinary Italians (as distinct from their officials and their policies) had been congenial and had gotten on remarkably well with the Ethiopian citizens. The Ethiopians accepted the precepts of the Golden Proclamation without question. (The only opposition to it came from the British authorities.) The news of it in the rest of the world was drowned in the larger events of 1941. It had much less impact than the Geneva speech, for example. But it deserved more attention, for it was the crown and triumph of Haile Selassie's role as prophet and as the voice of the world's conscience.

The Italian defense in Ethiopia did not immediately collapse, although nothing more was heard of it after the loss of Addis Ababa. It was to the interests of both London and Rome to conceal the long, painful, futile fighting that followed. But resistance, frequently gallant and fierce, continued for more than six months after the liberation of the capital. It was a lost cause. The vice-regal government had ended. On May 19, the duke of Aosta had surrendered unconditionally (with full military honors) along with most of his staff and his generals. They had taken up strong positions on Mount Alaghi, the great plateau south of Aradam where the decisive battle had been fought in 1936. Aosta was made a prisoner of war and died of tuberculosis in captivity in Kenya the following year. Ciano failed to note the surrender in his diary; the Italians were too busy in Rome organizing the dismemberment of Yugoslavia, which the Germans had procured for them by the Balkan campaign that spring. Censorship assured that the loss of empire would pass almost unnoticed in Italy; Mussolini called it "a vendetta on the part of the English which was completely personal and can have no effect on the outcome of the war [in Europe]."[49]

Later both Mussolini and Ciano were to blame their East African disaster, in the bitterest terms, on the inadequate fighting qualities of the Italian generals, but in fact the generals and their men had fought hard and continued to do so. Not until November 1941 was Eritrea cleared, Italian Somaliland conquered, British Somaliland (earlier taken over by the Italians) retaken, and the whole of Ethiopia freed of Italian forces. Nothing was heard in Italy of their hopeless struggle. East Africa simply disappeared from the news. They were heroes without honor in their own country, victims of the supremely capricious dictator and ideology which they had tried to serve.

Ethiopia had been the last independent state of Africa to go down before the power of Europe. It was the first to recover its independence. Its conquest in 1936 had been the last, grotesque expression of Europe's will and capacity to rule the world, appropriately embodied in a political movement that was itself an anachronism and whose inventor was a psychopath. Liberation in 1941 was an incident in the suicidal destruction of European power by its own most dedicated apostles, the men who, however little else they shared, shared the conviction that the greatness of their nations was the ultimate purpose of existence: Mussolini, Hitler, Churchill, and De Gaulle. But its real meaning was far different from the purposes of either the conquerors or the liberators. During the war of 1936, the Fascism and aggression had become inextricably blended in many minds with moral imperatives for international politics. The ghost of Woodrow Wilson and the spirit of Ho Chi Minh attended the event. It was the Ethiopian War that helped to shake the frigid isolationism of the United States; it was the Ethiopian War that forged the Rome-Berlin Axis that American and Soviet power would soon destroy, along with the remnants of Europe's world power. And it was the Ethiopian War that saw the beginning of the age when the word "imperialism" would become an obscenity instead of a noble aspiration and even American power would not suffice to control the forces that Haile Selassie had unleashed.

NOTES

---

1 THE SONS OF SOLOMON

1. Quoted in Leonard Mosley, *Haile Selassie*. London, 1964. P. 36.
2. Jerome Lobo; quoted in R. Pankhurst, *Travellers in Ethiopia*. London, 1965. P. 47.
3. Quoted in George Martelli, *Italy Against the World*. New York, 1938.
4. W. L. Langer, *The Diplomacy of Imperialism*. New York, 1935. Vol. I, p. 281.
5. Quoted in Richard Greenfield, *Ethiopia*. London, 1965. P. 109.
6. Quoted in Princess Asfa Yilma, *Haile Selassie*. London, 1936. P. 101.

2 THE LION OF JUDAH

1. Asfa Yilma, p. 112.
2. Mosley, pp. 39–40.
3. Quoted in *The Literary Digest*, May 24, 1930.
4. Quoted in *The Literary Digest*, July 13, 1935.
5. Quoted in *Living Age*, March 1935.
6. Quoted in Greenfield, p. 155.
7. Mosley, p. 72.
8. Ivone Kirkpatrick, *Mussolini: A Study in Power*. London, 1964. P. 293.
9. Quoted in Martelli, p. 23.
10. G. W. Baer, *The Coming of the Ethiopian War*. Cambridge, Mass., 1967. Pp. 9–10.
11. Quoted in Baer, p. 20.
12. Mosley, p. 168.
13. Ellen N. La Motte, "A Coronation in Abyssinia," *Harper's*, April 1931.
14. The fate of Joshua is uncertain, as will be discovered later.
15. Blata Sirak Hirouy, in an interview with L. Lafore.
16. *John Melly of Ethiopia*, eds. Kathleen Nelson and Alan Sullivan. London, 1937. Pp. 114–15, 137.

3 THE SON OF ROMULUS

1. B. Mussolini, *I Discorsi*. Milan, 1927. P. 107.
2. Laura Fermi, *Mussolini*. Chicago, 1962. P. 349.
3. Quoted in G. A. Borghese, *Goliath*. New York, 1938. P. 100.
4. Quoted in Christopher Seton-Watson, *Italy from Liberalism to Fascism*. London, 1967. P. 350.
5. Quoted in Seton-Watson, p. 366.
6. A. Balabanoff, *My Life as a Rebel*, p. 57–61; quoted in Kirkpatrick, p. 40.
7. Quoted in Kirkpatrick, p. 53.
8. Quoted in Kirkpatrick, p. 55.
9. Quoted in Seton-Watson, p. 393.
10. Seton-Watson, p. 421.
11. Quoted in Seton-Watson, p. 423.
12. Kirkpatrick, pp. 64ff.; he examined the evidence carefully and interviewed some of the surviving participants and concludes that the story is true.
13. In *Fabian Essays*. London, 1948.
14. Luigi Barzini, *The Italians*. New York, 1964. P. 136.
15. In Charles Petrie, *Life and Letters of the Rt. Hon. Sir Austen Chamberlain*. London, 1939. Pp. 290, 295–96.
16. A detailed study of these and other startling American reactions is to be found in an unpublished M.A. thesis by Steven Bianco, *Richard Washburn Child*, prepared in May 1970 for the History Department of the University of Iowa.
17. Quoted in Seton-Watson, p. 670.
18. *New York Times*, March 15, 1934.
19. Carlos Baker, *Ernest Hemingway*. New York, 1969. Pp. 92, 103.
20. Quoted in Fermi, p. 238.
21. A. L. Rowse, *Appeasement*. New York, 1961. P. 25.
22. W. Starkie, *The Waveless Plain*. New York, 1938. Pp. 391–92.
23. Alan Cassels, *Mussolini's Early Diplomacy*. Princeton, 1970.
24. Gaetano Salvemini, *Under the Axe of Fascism*. New York, 1936. P. 239.
25. All these quoted in Salvemini.
26. Salvemini, p. 346.
27. Quoted in Salvemini, p. 347.
28. Quoted in H. W. Schneider, *Making the Fascist State*. New York, 1968. P. 35.
29. Roland Sarti, *Fascism and the Industrial Leadership in Italy, 1919–1940*. Berkeley, 1971. Pp. 110ff.
30. Sarti, p. 115.

4 INCIDENT

1. From the personal papers of A. T. Curle, made available to James Dugan.
2. Pietro Badoglio, *The War in Abyssinia*, p. 7.
3. By the British ambassador; quoted in Kirkpatrick, p. 306.
4. Raffaele Guariglia, *Ricordi*; quoted in Baer, p. 6.
5. Borghese, p. 384.
6. Speech in the Chamber, May 25, 1935; quoted in Kirkpatrick, p. 294.
7. Quoted in R. Collier, *Duce*. London, 1971. P. 120.
8. Franco Bandini, *Facetta Nera*, in *Domenica del Corriere* (12 issues on Ethiopian War, January–March 1966), No. 13.
9. Massimo Magistrati, "La Germania e l'impresa italiana de Etiopia," *Rivista di studi politici internazionali* 17:569.
10. Ladislas Sara, "Ethiopia Under Mussolini's Rule," *New Times*, V, 221, p. 2.
11. Emilio de Bono, *Anno XIIII*, with an Introduction by Benito Mussolini. London, 1937. P. 12ff.
12. De Bono, p. 12; italics De Bono's.
13. Schuschnigg, *Austrian Requiem*. New York, 1946. P. 115.
14. *Foreign Relations of the United States, 1934*. Washington, 1951. Vol. II, p. 754.
15. Cordell Hull, *Memoirs*. New York, 1948. P. 418.
16. U. S. Department of State, *Peace and War*. Washington, 1943. Pp. 29, 234–36.
17. E. Caviglia, *Diario*, pp. 126–28; quoted in Baer, p. 43.
18. Greenfield, p. 192.
19. *United States Diplomatic Papers, 1934*. Washington, 1934. Vol. II, p. 773.
20. Quoted in Asfa Yilma, p. 274.
21. In A. Lagardelle, *Mission à Rome*. Paris, 1955. P. 279–83.
22. Viscount Simon, *Retrospect*. London, 1952. P. 127.
23. Trevor Wilson, *The Downfall of the Liberal Party*. London, 1966. P. 363.
24. Quoted in Collier, p. 124.

5 THE POLITICS OF EVASION

1. G. L. Steer, *Caesar in Abyssinia*. London, 1936. P. 30.
2. Ethiopian note of March 29, quoted in Baer, p. 115.
3. Quoted in Baer, p. 273.
4. Evelyn Waugh, *Waugh in Abyssinia*. London, 1936. P. 49.
5. *Melly*, p. 137.
6. *Melly*, p. 129.
7. Waugh, p. 49.
8. W. D. Hubbard, *Fiasco in Ethiopia*. New York, 1936.

9. Quoted in *Melly*, p. 151.

10. *Petit Journal*, September 29, 1935.

11. From a paper by G. W. Baer delivered before the American Historical Association in December 1971.

12. Arthur Marder, "The Royal Navy and the Ethiopian Crisis of 1935–36," *American Historical Review*, LXXV, No. 5 (June 1970), p. 1327. This article, by an authoritative historian of the Royal Navy, is an admirable and quite staggering revelation based on unpublished records.

13. Quoted in Marder, p. 1329.

14. Quoted in Tom Jones, *A Diary with Letters*, 1931–1950. London, 1954. Pp. 159–60.

15. Quoted in Baer, p. 237.

16. Atherton to Hall, September 16, 1935, *Foreign Relations of the U.S.*, 1935. Washington, 1951. Vol. I, p. 649.

17. *Chips: The Diaries of Sir Henry Channon*, ed. R. R. James. London, 1967. P. 40. Channon was an expatriate Chicagoan who had made it in London society. He seems almost deliberately to have chosen to typify all that was worst about that society.

18. Quoted in Baer, p. 327ff.

19. One was G. F. T. Colby, a British colonial servant in Nairobi, who was in touch with Franklin Roosevelt. See *Franklin D. Roosevelt and Foreign Affairs*, ed. Edgar B. Nixon. Cambridge, Mass., 1969. Vol. II, p. 531.

20. Quoted in Baer, p. 329.

21. Quoted in Gaetano Salvemini, *Prelude to World War II*. New York, 1954. P. 227.

22. Quoted in Baer, p. 335.

6 CRISIS

1. Quoted in *Franklin D. Roosevelt and Foreign Affairs*, Vol. II, p. 611.

2. J. P. Diggins, *Mussolini and Fascism: The View From America*. Princeton, 1972.

3. Quoted in Diggins, p. 308.

4. *Chistian Century*, September 4, 1935, p. 1099.

5. Avro Manhattan, *The Vatican in World Politics*. New York, 1949. P. 123.

6. A careful study of Italian-American attitudes is available in Diggins.

7. Brice Harris, *The United States and the Italo-Ethiopian Crisis*. Stanford, 1964. P. 42.

8. Quoted in Harris, p. 44.

9. *Business Week*, October 5, 1935.

10. *The New Republic*, August 14, 1935, p. 1.

11. *The New Republic*, September 25, 1935.

12. *Franklin D. Roosevelt and Foreign Affairs*, Vol. II, p. 614.
13. Arnold A. Offner, *American Appeasement*. Cambridge, Mass., 1969. P. 126ff.
14. Harris, Chapter III.
15. Quoted in Harris, p. 31.
16. Quoted in Harris, p. 34.
17. *Franklin D. Roosevelt and Foreign Affairs*, Vol. II, p. 428.
18. Long to Hull, September 17, 1935, *For. Rel. U.S.*, *1935*, I, p. 652.
19. Long to Hull, September 12 and 17, 1935, *For. Rel. U.S.*, *1935*, I, pp. 749, 752.
20. *Business Week*, September 21, 1935, p. 27.
21. Quoted in Baer, p. 315.
22. Long to Hull, September 17, 1935, *For. Rel. U.S.*, *1935*, I, p. 652.

7 APPOINTMENT IN ASMARA

1. Most of the information about Ethiopian defenses is drawn from Steer, who provides the most detailed and objective account.
2. Anthony Eden, *Facing the Dictators*. Boston, 1962. P. 321.
3. Steer, p. 65.
4. Quoted in Baer, pp. 369–70.
5. Aldo Castellani, *Microbes, Men and Monarchs*. London, 1963. P. 141.
6. E. W. Polson Newman, *Italy's Conquest of Abyssinia*. London, 1937. P. 97.
7. Quoted in De Bono, p. 218.
8. Quoted in Polson Newman, p. 967.
9. Collier, p. 129.
10. Angelo del Boca, *The Ethiopian War 1935–1941*, tr. P. D. Cummins. Chicago, 1969. P. 6.
11. Herbert L. Matthews, *The Education of a Correspondent*, New York, 1964. P. 32.
12. Carlo Scarfoglio, *England and the Continent*. London, 1939. P. 320.
13. W. L. Shirer, *The Rise and Fall of the Third Reich*. New York, 1960. P. 290.
14. Eden, p. 328.
15. Alan Bullock, *Hitler*. New York, 1953. P. 311.
16. Harris, pp. 72–73.
17. *Franklin D. Roosevelt, Press Conferences*, VI, October 30, 1955, p. 226.
18. *New York Times*, October 13, 1955.
19. *Araldo di Washington*, April–May 1935, p. 5.
20. Quoted in Harris, p. 124.
21. Steer, p. 153.
22. Waugh, pp. 155–56.

23. Waugh, pp. 200–1.
24. Quoted in Alan Barker, *The Civilizing Mission.* New York, 1968. P. 181.
25. Salvemini, *Prelude,* p. 367.
26. De Bono, *La Conquista,* p. 13; quoted in Salvemini, *Prelude,* p. 367.
27. Quoted in Polson Newman, p. 105.
28. Matthews, p. 41.
29. Matthews, p. 39.

8 INTERMISSION WITH THUNDER STORMS

1. P. Monelli, *Mussolini.* New York, 1954. P. 187.
2. Monelli, p. 139.
3. *Melly,* p. 169.
4. Department of State, *Press Releases,* XIII, November 16, 1935, p. 382.
5. "*Fortune* Quarterly Survey: III," *Fortune,* January 1936, pp. 46–47; quoted in Harris, p. 92.
6. London *Times,* November 25, 1935.
7. W. Churchill, *While England Slept.* New York, 1938. P. 231.
8. London *Times,* September 9, 1935.
9. Paul Schmidt, *Hitler's Interpreter.* London, 1951. P. 60.
10. Eden, p. 329.
11. Eden, p. 338.
12. Eden, p. 342.
13. Salvemini, *Prelude,* p. 396.
14. Barker, p. 218.
15. Quoted in Eden, p. 348.
16. G. M. Young, *Stanley Baldwin.* London, 1952. P. 217.
17. London *Times,* December 19, 1935.
18. J. Colton, *Léon Blum.* New York, 1966. P. 122.
19. D. W. Brogan, *The Development of Modern France.* London, 1940. P. 695.
20. Quoted in Barker, p. 227.
21. Guariglia, p. 67; quoted in Kirkpatrick, p. 318.
22. Adolf Hitler, *Hitler's Secret Conversations.* New York, 1953. P. 498.
23. E. Wiskemann, *The Rome-Berlin Axis.* New York, 1949. P. 52.
24. *The New Republic,* October 2, 1935, p. 202.
25. *The New Republic,* November 20, 1935, p. 41.
26. *The New Republic,* February 12, 1936, p. 20.
27. *New York Times Book Review,* December 15, 1935, p. 3.
28. James J. Martin, *American Liberalism and World Politics,* New York, 1964. Vol. 1, chapter heading for Ch. 14. Martin's book was a bigoted, latter-day statement of Roosevelt-baiting by reactionaries of a sort that had been common in the 1930s.

29. Manfred Jonas, *Isolationism in America 1935–1941*. Ithaca, 1966. P. 184.
30. For these two evocative recollections L. Lafore is indebted, respectively, to Dr. James Murray of Iowa City and Miss Isabelle Palmer of New York.
31. *New York Times*, January 4, 1936, p. 1.

9 THE MACHINE IN THE MOUNTAINS

1. Quoted in Harris, p. 115.
2. Polson Newman, p. 215ff.
3. Polson Newman, pp. 307–8.
4. Badoglio, p. 7.
5. Del Boca, p. 113.
6. Del Boca, p. 113.
7. Steer, p. 244.
8. Del Boca, p. 109.
9. The report appears in its most graphic form in an article by Paolo Monelli in *Storia Illustrata*, May 1963, p. 651. Monelli, the author of a scathing and somewhat scandalous biography of Mussolini, is a journalist who worked for the *Gazetta del Popolo* and *Corriere della Sera*. His writings are vivid but mostly undocumented.
10. Badoglio, p. 56.
11. Quoted in Del Boca, p. 110.
12. Greenfield, p. 193.
13. Steer, p. 252.
14. Greenfield, p. 182.
15. Steer, p. 257.
16. The name of the surrounding area, which the Italians gave to the battle, is Enderta; but the name of the eminence, used by the Ethiopians, is more familiar in accounts in English.
17. Luigi Barzini, *Con l'esercito in Africa orientale*. Milan, 1936. Vol. II, p. 692.
18. Badoglio, p. 85.
19. Steer, p. 262.
20. Steer, p. 265.
21. Eden, p. 365.
22. Vittorio Mussolini, *Voli sulle Ambe*, p. 28; quoted in Del Boca, p. 60.
23. Barker, p. 255.
24. Alessandro Paolini, in the *Corriere della Sera*, March 3, 1936; quoted in Del Boca, p. 141.
25. D'Annunzio's message to Mussolini, in *Gazetta de Popolo*, March 1, 1936; quoted in Del Boca, p. 144.
26. Quoted in Badoglio, pp. 143–44. Badoglio gave the date of the letter as March 23, but this is an error. It must have been written some weeks earlier.

27. An interview with Del Boca, quoted in Del Boca, p. 152.
28. According to Steer, p. 275.
29. Prince Imru, in an interview with Del Boca, quoted in Del Boca, p. 156.
30. Badoglio, pp. 140–41.
31. Badoglio, p. 142. The authenticity of the text may be open to doubt. There is no reason to assume the reliability of anything Badoglio wrote, but since the text must convey to any moderately impartial reader a touching and appealing fatalism, which Badoglio must have overlooked, it may be accurate—another example of misfiring propaganda.
32. Mosley, p. 220. Mosley's account of the battle preparations was based in part on Colonel Konovaloff's memoirs.
33. Badoglio, p. 145.
34. Badoglio, p. 146.
35. Quoted in Badoglio, p. 147.
36. Quoted in Mosley, p. 225.
37. Quoted in Mosley, p. 225.
38. Badoglio, p. 147.
39. Badoglio, p. 148.
40. Quoted in Badoglio, p. 148.
41. Quoted in Mosley, p. 227.
42. Eden, p. 356.
43. *Documents on German Foreign Policy, 1918–1945.* Washington, 1949–. Series C, Vol. IV, Document #352, p. 728.
44. Hassell to Neurath, January 31, 1936, *German Foreign Policy*, Series C, Vol. IV, Document #352, p. 1072.
45. Memo by Hassell, January 20, 1936, *German Foreign Policy*, Series C, Vol. IV, Document #506, pp. 1013ff.
46. *Ibid.*

10   END OF A BEGINNING

1. Mosley, p. 228.
2. Quoted in Steer, p. 336.
3. *Melly*, pp. 245 *et seq.*
4. Badoglio, p. 160.
5. Badoglio, pp. 161–62.
6. Quoted in Steer, p. 342.
7. Quoted in Del Boca, p. 187.
8. Telegram of March 29. *League of Nations Series*, XVIIth Year No. 4 (Part II), April 1935, Annex 1592, pp. 457–58. The report is not necessarily accurate; the Ethiopians bombarded Geneva with details of Italian outrages which were sometimes exaggerated. But other witnesses attest that the damage in Harar was as extensive as it was gratuitous.

9. The poet Adriano Grande, who was present, wrote this effusion in his memoirs; quoted in Del Boca, pp. 196–97.
10. Steer, p. 356.
11. Engert to Hull, May 2, 1935; quoted in Harris, p. 139.
12. Steer, p. 358.
13. Steer, p. 367.
14. Steer, p. 385.
15. *Melly*, pp. 260–61.
16. Steer, p. 401.
17. Quoted in Del Boca, p. 205.
18. Eden, p. 428.
19. Marie José, Princess of Piedmont, *Infermiera in Africa Orientale*. Milan, 1937. P. 124.
20. Robert L. Hess, *Italian Colonialism in Somalia*. Chicago, 1966. P. 162.
21. Pompeo Aloisi, *Journal*. Paris, 1957. P. 377.
22. Eden, p. 430.
23. Quoted in Eden, p. 433.
24. Eden, p. 435.
25. Quoted in Del Boca, p. 209.
26. *De l'Invasion à la Libération de l'Ethiopie*, ed. A. Gingold Duprey. A collection of documents printed in France in 1955. Annex S. 126, letter of May 11, 1936, from the Ethiopian delegate to the Secretary-General, p. 665. The translation from the French is L. Lafore's.
27. Bismarck to the Foreign Ministry, June 26, 1936, *German Foreign Policy*, Series C, Vol. V, Document #315, p. 519.
28. Barker, p. 294.
29. *New York Times*, July 1, 1936, p. 1.
30. London *Times*, July 2, 1936, p. 15.
31. Quoted in Mosley, p. 241.
32. London *Times*, July 2, 1936, p. 15.
33. *New York Times* editorial, July 7, 1936, p. 20.
34. Chicago *Tribune*, July 2, 1936, p. 14.
35. *The New Republic*, July 15, 1936, p. 7.
36. *Time*, July 13, 1936, p. 13.
37. *Revue des Deux-Mondes*, July-August, 1936, p. 471.
38. Albert Speer, *Inside the Third Reich*. New York, 1970. P. 70.
39. Hassell to the German Foreign Ministry, May 8, 1936, *German Foreign Policy*, Series C, Vol. V, Document #315, p. 519.
40. Foreign Ministry to Hassell, May 19, 1936, *German Foreign Policy*, Series C, Vol. V, Document #335, p. 562.

11 INVICTUS

1. According to a German diplomatic agent in Addis Ababa who is said to have told it to Ladislas Sara. *New Times*, V, 222, p. 2.
2. Unpublished manuscript by Maurice L. Weerts, *The Late Mr. Antonin*

Besse and the Ethiopian Resistance, made available by Dr. Richard Pankhurst, director, Institute of Ethiopian Studies, Haile Selassie I University, Addis Ababa.

3. In a telegram to General Gallina, quoted in *La civilisation de l'Italie Fasciste en Éthiopie*, p. 39. The authenticity of this collection is not clear. It consists of documents, taken from abandoned Italian archives, published after the liberation of the empire, by the Information Department of the Imperial Government in Addis Ababa. Quoted in Del Boca, p. 213.

4. In *La Guerra italo-etiopica*, published by the government general of Italian East Africa, doc. no. 222, dated July 29, 1936; quoted in Del Boca, p. 215.

5. Salomé Gabré-Egziabher, "The Ethiopian Patriots, 1936–1941," *Ethiopian Observer*, Vol. XII, No. 2, p. 63.

6. *La Guerra italo-etiopica*, quoted in Del Boca, p. 221.

7. Reported to L. Lafore by an Armenian businessman in Addis Ababa.

8. *Gazetta del Popolo*, February 22, 1937; quoted in Del Boca, p. 223.

9. Del Boca, p. 22.

10. Alessandro Lessona, *Memorie*, p. 305; quoted in Del Boca, p. 224.

11. *La civilisation de l'Italie Fasciste en Éthiopie*, pp. 61–62.

12. See *Documents on Italian War Crimes Submitted to the United Nations War Crimes Commission*, Vol. I, Italian telegrams and circulars, *passim*.

13. Mentioned in Sara, "Ethiopia Under Mussolini's Rule," in *New Times*, V, 222 (August 3, 1940), p. 1. The magazine was the Berlin *Illustrierte Zeitung*.

14. Quoted in Del Boca, p. 228.

15. Paul Gentizon, in *Le Temps*, August 18, 1939; quoted in Del Boca, p. 229.

16. Quoted in Del Boca, p. 230.

17. Quoted in Del Boca, p. 230.

18. *Gli Annali dell Africa Italiana*, I, No. 2, Milan, 1938; quoted in Del Boca, p. 231.

19. Sara, in *New York Times*, August 31, 1940, p. 1.

20. A report by R. E. Cheesman, quoted in Christopher Sykes, *Orde Wingate*. Cleveland, 1959.

21. G. Ciano, *Hidden Diary, 1937–38*, tr. Andreas Mayor. New York, 1953. P. 19.

22. Barker, p. 308.

23. Luigi Lino, in an interview with Del Boca, p. 248.

24. Ciano, *Diaries, 1939–1943*. New York, 1946. P. 42.

25. Gabré-Egziabher, p. 64.

26. Gabré-Egziabher, p. 68.

27. From *Ciano's Diplomatic Papers*, quoted in Bullock, p. 320.

28. Ciano, *Hidden Diary*, p. 16.
29. Quoted in Keith Feiling, *Life of Neville Chamberlain*. London, 1946. P. 329.
30. Feiling, p. 330.
31. Quoted in Feiling, p. 331.
32. Ciano, *Hidden Diary*, p. 107.
33. Quoted in Ernst von Weizsacker, *Memoirs*. Chicago, 1951. Pp. 179, 184.
34. Quoted in Feiling, p. 404.
35. Quoted in Mosley, p. 243.
36. These and other details reported by Mosley, p. 243.
37. David Mitchell, *The Fighting Pankhursts*. New York, 1967. P. 250. Mitchell's book is neither very thorough nor very sympathetic, but it offers a brief and readable account of Miss Pankhurst's work in connection with Ethiopia.
38. Quoted in Mitchell, p. 25.
39. Quoted in Mosley, p. 249.
40. Sykes, p. 253.
41. John Connell, *Wavell*. New York, 1964. Pp. 427, 304.
42. Winston Churchill, *Their Finest Hour*. Boston, 1949. P. 622.
43. See the admirable account in A. J. Barker, *Eritrea 1941*. London 1956. P. 74 *et seq.*
44. Quoted in Mosley, p. 274.
45. For a definitive and very detailed description of developments in Ethiopia from the summer of 1941 through the liberation, including texts of the various imperial proclamations and announcements, see the superb article of Richard Pankhurst, "The Ethiopian Patriots and the Collapse of Italian Rule," in *Ethiopian Observer*, Vol. XII, no. 2, p. 92.
46. Mosley, pp. 274ff.
47. Quoted in Mosley, pp. 268–69.
48. Quoted in Barker, *Eritrea*, p. 181.
49. Monelli, *Mussolini*, p. 189.

A NOTE ON USAGES
AND LITERATURE

The first problem for an English-speaking writer who tries to deal with Ethiopia is to discover what the name of the country is. Until very recently most westerners knew it as Abyssinia. Ethiopia, a name used by the Greeks and Romans, may—but may not—have been applied to a territory approximating that of the modern empire. An Englishman, Walter Plowden, who, in the nineteenth century, knew the country well, believed that classical Ethiopia was quite a different place, located somewhere to the west near what is now the republic of the Sudan. He was probably wrong. The Amharic people, the dominant group in the modern empire, have always called their land Ethiopia and that is its official name, on which all Ethiopians insist.

The confusion about the name of the country is only the first and largest of a general perplexity in nomenclature. There is no Ethiopian proper name—not even that of the emperor's—that is not spelled by foreigners in at least two ways, and sometimes in as many as ten. The town where the fateful treaty with the Italians was signed over eighty years ago is generally called Uciali or Uccialli, which, pronounced by an Italian, resembles the Amharic sound. But in English it is more nearly correct if written Wuchalé or Wichali. The variations and uncertainties can never be satisfactorily settled, and with place names it has seemed best to use the form that appears on the World Aeronautical Charts (WAC), which comes as near to constituting a universal language for geography as can be found. In a few cases, though, familiarity seems to outweigh other considerations, and a more common English spelling is used. For example, Makale, and Adowa, which is also often spelled Adua, appears on the WAC as Auda. This may be a misprint and would in any case be baffling to most readers.

Personal names and titles are even more confusing. It seems mannered, even foolish to call the late Empress Zawditu or Zaudito when her name can be translated as Judith. It seems pointless to call the king of Italy Vittorio Emanuele instead of Victor Emmanuel. Titles present more of a problem, since most of the Ethiopian ones refer to positions and functions that have no foreign equivalents. Here, an approximately corresponding English term has mostly been used. The most famous of Ethiopian titles is *ras* (head). The word has entered several western languages in the sense of grandee or, sometimes, boss. A *ras* is a provincial governor or war lord, but the word is also used as a title of honor. *Ras* implies great dignity and power. It is a personal, not a hereditary title. But it seems more natural, and less likely to interrupt the narrative with an exotic punctuation mark, to substitute the English word "prince." The title and status of princes have had so many meanings in European history, it is so vague a rank, that it commits the writer and the reader to nothing.

The available literature on the Ethiopian War and its background and effects presents unusual problems for both the historian and the general reader, problems that reflect the fact that this was a conflict between two cultures with very different notions of the value of records, of the meaning of truth. There is no dearth of records; several careers could be devoted to exploring the materials concerning the Italian background, the diplomacy of the period, the reactions of public opinion, the economic forces at work. For anthropologists equipped with the necessary languages, other careers could be (and are being) devoted to the history and civilization of Ethiopia. Most of the relevant European archives, including the Italian, are at least partly accessible. But they reflect the values and emphases of Europeans, and Ethiopia was a little-known country, infinitely remote in time, space, and anthropological character. The people in the rest of the world who wrote and worried about Ethiopia lacked information, imagination, and a sense of immediacy. More subtly, there is a huge difference in understanding of what matters. Western officialdom tends to *like* keeping records, and it thinks of records as statistical and factual, in which passion, local color, and morality have no place. Modern government documents almost always flush out feelings with an oceanic douche of data. But for the Ethiopian of the 1930s, data had less reality. Feelings and morals were what mattered. Such records as are available reflect a society that placed little value on narrow, factual accuracy and none at all on filing cabinets.

Things have changed, as they have everywhere in the world. There are filing cabinets aplenty now in Addis Ababa. In the climactic clash of the 1930s between the record keepers and the believers, the former were discredited and the latter finally avenged. But in the end, record keeping won, and it is likely to prove a much more durable sovereignty than were the lost colonial empires.

Still, the Ethiopian War was the first between a European and a non-European people in modern times that became a major world crisis and was closely followed in the west. It marked the beginning of the end of the certainty that white Europeans and Americans knew what civilization was and had a monopoly on it. The correspondents who informed the world were in some ways the most important people involved in the war, and their writings are the most interesting. Of these, *Caesar in Abyssinia,* by G. L. Steer, is a superb story and is rich with prophetic meaning. Evelyn Waugh, in *Waugh in Abyssinia,* is, as the title suggests, a subjective and self-important companion piece. It is also beautifully written, and as a record of a highly educated and rather arrogant Englishman's reaction it is illuminating. Herbert Matthews, who covered the Italian campaign, wrote among others a competent and compelling book called *The Fruits of Fascism.* The soldiers are less interesting, but Badoglio's *War in Abyssinia* and De Bono's *Anno XIIII,* often dull and unreliable, give a great deal of indispensable military information. They also give some understanding of the way the European military mind worked. So does Major E. W. Polson Newman's *Italy's Conquest of Ethiopia,* which is full of rich material blurred by a British soldier's myopia.

There was a flood of contemporary periodical writing in the west. Most of it seems, today, oddly sterile and badly informed. Innumerable articles in high-brow magazines professed sober erudition in western Europe and the United States. Magazines like *Foreign Affairs* published pieces (with titles such as "The Testing of the League") which now have the characteristic quality of out-dated respectability—decorum, insensate impartiality, and a tendency to legalism that not only induced bloodlessness, but also missed the point. Editorials and features in magazines and newspapers aimed at the general public were worse. If they had correspondents abroad, editors tended to cut and distort their reports. What was written at home was often badly informed and often very prejudiced. The liberal and leftist press in both America and western Europe—magazines like *The New Republic* in particular—displayed a gullibility and bias which suggests that right-mindedness can be as misled as the massive wrong-headedness of a Polson Newman. And most of the news and commentary were so concerned with diplomacy and the legend of "collective security" that they overlooked all but the most picturesque and sensational aspects of what was happening in Ethiopia. As mentioned in the text, an important exception was Sylvia Pankhurst's *New Times and Ethiopia News,* but while it was influential in Britain, it reached a relatively small audience. What is interesting and significant is that despite the initial ignorance and misunderstanding of western editors, they learned fast. For whatever reason, perhaps only because the Ethiopian cause was sentimentally and romantically appealing, an about-face in attitudes, a genuine and intense interest in Ethiopia itself, began to be evident before the war had gone on very long.

The documentary materials, rich and indispensable, are mostly not easily accessible to ordinary readers, and not very intelligible either. It takes a good deal of specialized knowledge to read documents, and even when diplomatic dispatches are in English they are written in a language foreign to most citizens.

In the reminiscences of western statesmen of the period, the Ethiopian War plays its usual part as an aspect, and extension, of European international relations. But these reminiscences are necessary to understanding the situation, and the very obscurity of Ethiopia (in Lord Simon's memoirs it is not mentioned at all) is illuminating. One can find out what 'was on the authors' minds. The most interesting, in general and for the light they cast on the Ethiopia crisis, are Anthony Eden's *Facing the Dictators* and Count Ciano's *Diaries*.

Later writing has also been, in many cases, tangential. For a long while, the Ethiopian War attracted little attention from scholars. It was lost in the larger events that followed it. What has, however, been amply covered are the broader aspects of French, German, and British relations and, in particular, the history of Fascist Italy and its dictator. The literature in European languages is huge. But to a surprising extent, except in learned journals, Ethiopia figures merely as an important incident in the story of Mussolini and his regime and is briefly dealt with. There have been some important books on the war, however. The most interesting and devastating of the Italian works to appear in translation is Angelo del Boca's *The Ethiopian War*. Probably the best biography of Mussolini in English is Ivone Kirkpatrick's *Mussolini: A Study in Power*. It is very thorough and extremely readable, though its balance and its originality may both be criticized. Among American works of scholarship there are several of value and importance. *Mussolini and Fascism: The View From America*, by John P. Diggins, is extraordinary in both its accumulation of arcane information and the conclusions that emerge. Another, Roland Sarti's *Fascism and the Industrial Leadership in Italy, 1919–1940*, is indispensable for its subject. Robert L. Hess, *Italian Colonialism in Somalia*, while not strictly pertinent to Ethiopia, is important in showing the curious aimlessness of Italian colonial policy. Brice Harris, *The United States and the Italo-Ethiopian Crisis*, is a significant book of impressive scholarship. And the best and most important of all is an entirely admirable and intensely interesting study by G. W. Baer, *The Coming of the Ethiopian War*. Professor Baer deals mainly with diplomatic history, and his book stops with the outbreak of war (although a sequel is in preparation), but it is a monument of good historical writing.

There are some important biographies. Leonard Mosley's *Haile Selassie* is full of information and well written, if perhaps somewhat worshipful. Christopher Sykes's *Orde Wingate* is a fascinating study of a fascinating man.

The most recent general study of the war is Alan Barker, *The Civilizing Mission*. It is admirably written, well balanced, sound, and extremely good reading. It does not deal largely with the backgrounds or deeper implications, such as the long story of Italian aspirations or the impact of the war on the United States.

Books on Ethiopia, its history, customs, and dynasty, are numerous. Of those designed for the general public, few deal in detail with the events of the late thirties, however. For background, Richard Greenfield, *Ethiopia,* is probably the most useful. It can hardly be said, however, to hold the reader spellbound, and its catalogue of names and details is untouched by any awareness of sociological, economic, or anthropological learning. *Wax and Gold,* by Donald N. Levine, is a marvelous, first-hand, sociological study. The most eminent contemporary scholar who deals in Ethiopian history in the English language is Richard Pankhurst, director of the Institute of Ethiopian Studies at the Haile Selassie I University in Addis Ababa. He edits the *Ethiopian Observer* and contributes fine articles to it, as well as being the author of several specialized works on Ethiopian history. But all in all the literature on Ethiopia is not very satisfactory for the layman. It is a discouraging country to write about. There are enormous language barriers. There is little in the way of written records compared to European, American, or Asian countries. There is a high barrier of official discretion. There is the strange, unnerving combination of a modern state superimposed upon a society whose understanding requires peculiar skills and qualities of imagination—those of an anthropologist who is also a political scientist, a theologian, and a poet.

Index

PICTURE CREDITS

1. U.P.I.
2. NEW YORK LIBRARY PICTURE COLLECTION
3. THE BETTMANN ARCHIVE
4. THE BETTMANN ARCHIVE
5. U.P.I.
6. U.P.I.
7. U.P.I.
8. WIDE WORLD
9. U.P.I.
10. WIDE WORLD
11. U.P.I.
12. THE BETTMANN ARCHIVE
13. U.P.I.
14. U.P.I.
15. U.P.I.
16. U.P.I.
17. U.P.I.
18. U.P.I.
19. U.P.I.
20. U.P.I.
21. U.P.I.
22. U.P.I.
23. WIDE WORLD
24. COURTESY OF TIME MAGAZINE
25. U.P.I.
26. U.P.I.
27. U.P.I.
28. U.P.I.
29. U.P.I.
30. U.P.I.
31. U.P.I.
32. COURTESY OF GEORGIANA REMER

Other Books in the Crossroads of World History Series